Children's Literature Remembered

Children's Literature Remembered

Issues, Trends, and Favorite Books

Edited by
Linda M. Pavonetti

LIBRARIES
U N L I M I T E D
A Member of the Greenwood Publishing Group

Westport, Connecticut • London

Library of Congress Cataloging-in-Publication Data

British Library Cataloguing in Publication Data is available.

Copyright © 2004 by Libraries Unlimited

ISBN: 0–313–32077–2

First published in 2004

Libraries Unlimited, Inc., 88 Post Road West, Westport, CT 06881
A Member of the Greenwood Publishing Group, Inc.
www.lu.com

Printed in the United States of America

The paper used in this book complies with the
Permanent Paper Standard issued by the National
Information Standards Organization (Z39.48–1984).

10 9 8 7 6 5 4 3 2 1

Copyright Acknowledgments

Excerpts from "black is brown is tan" by Arnold Adoff, copyright © 1975 by Arnold Adoff, used by permission of HarperCollins Publishers.

Excerpts from "All the Colors of the Race" by Arnold Adoff, copyright © 1982 by Arnold Adoff, used by permission of HarperCollins Publishers.

Aldis, D. "Everybody Says," "Ironing Day" (illustration) by Margaret Freeman, from ALL TOGETHER by Dorothy Aldis, © 1925–1928, 1934, 1939, 1952, renewed 1953, © 1954–1956, 1962 by Dorothy Aldis, © 1967 by Roy E. Porter, renewed. Used with permission of G. P. Putnam's Sons, an imprint of Penguin Putnam Books for Young Readers, a division of Penguin Putnam Inc.

Hopkins, Lee Bennett. "Good Books, Good Times." Copyright © 1985, 1995 by Lee Bennett Hopkins. Now appears in GOOD RHYMES, GOOD TIMES, published by HarperCollins Children's Publishers. Reprinted by permission of Curtis Brown, Ltd.

Hopkins, Lee Bennett. "Since." Copyright © 1995 by Lee Bennett Hopkins. Appears in *Been to Yesterdays,* published by Wordsong/Boyd Mills. Reprinted by permission of Curtis Brown, Ltd. Illustrations copyright © by Boyds Mills Press from *Been to Yesterdays: Poems of a Life* by Lee Bennett Hopkins. Reprinted by permission.

Hughes, Langston. "Dreams." Used with permission of Alfred A. Knopf, and Harold Ober Associates. © 2003.

Livingston, Myra Cohn. "In the Middle." From THERE WAS A PLACE AND OTHER POEMS by Myra Cohn Livingston. © 1998 Myra Cohn Livingston. Used by permission of Marian Reiner.

"Liz Meyer who has just put her brothers in the dryer" (illustration) by James Watts, © James Watts. From the book BRATS by X. J. Kennedy, 1986, published by Atheneum Publishers. Used by permission of James Watts.

"Mother and Daughter Washing Their Hair" (Illustration) by Gerald Nailor, Toh Yah, from *I Am a Pueblo Indian Girl* by Louise Abeita, E-Yeh-Shure (Blue Corn), published 1939 by E. M. Hale & Co. by arrangement with William Morrow & Co., Inc. Every effort was made to find the rights holder.

Illustration from NICODEMUS AND THE NEWBORN BABY by Inez Hogan, published in 1940 by E. P. Dutton & Company, Inc. Used with the permission of Mr. Frank H. Hogan.

Illustration from SOMETHING BEAUTIFUL by Sharon Dennis Wyeth and illustrated by Chris K. Soentpiet, copyright © 1998 by Chris K. Soentpiet. Used by permission of Random House Children's Books, a division of Random House, Inc.

Yolen, Jane. "Marchen." Used with permission of the author and Wayne State Press. © 2003.

To all the authors and illustrators who have dedicated themselves—their art and craft— to instilling the love of books in people, young and old.

To Jim—an outstanding teacher, colleague, friend, and book lover. Thank you.

Contents

Acknowledgments

This book's existence is a credit to the dedicated members of the Children's Literature Assembly (CLA), who believed in me and in the twenty-first century. It is because of the CLA programs such as the annual postconference workshop, which was the impetus for this book, and the masters class in teaching children's literature that I am doing what I love to do each day. Thank you.

Thanks also to Michael O. Tunnell, professor of children's literature at Brigham Young University, for rerecording Uri Shulevitz's speech when technology got the best of me. Whew! Thanks.

Finally, my deepest thanks to all of the publishers and their school and marketing representatives who underwrote the authors' and illustrators' speeches at the 1999 National Council of Teachers of English (NCTE) Convention: Marjorie Naughton of Clarion; Jeanne McDermott of Farrar, Straus and Giroux; Lori Benton, Victoria Tisch of Harcourt Brace Children's Books, and Jane Washburn, formerly of Harcourt; William Morris and Catherine Balkin of HarperCollins; Terry Borzumato of Random House; and John Mason of Scholastic. Thank you for your support of kids, teachers, librarians, and, especially—good books.

Introduction

At the end of the first decade of the twentieth century, Rosalie Vrylina Halsey ([1911] 1969) suggested that a society's view of children, or its moral values, were reflected in the children's books published by that culture. Writing in a book titled *Forgotten Books of the American Nursery: A History of the Development of the American Story-Book*, she notes:

> If we consider that there is nothing more rare in the fiction of any nation than the popular child's story that endures; nothing more unusual than the successful well-written juvenile tale, we can perhaps find a value not to be reckoned by the survival or literary character of these old-fashioned books, but in their silent testimony to the influence of the progress of social forces at work even upon so small a thing as a child's toy-book. (227)

Halsey asserts that "the successful well-written child's book has been rare" (227) for two principal reasons: the method or author's craft, that is, the writer was more concerned with the child than producing quality writing; and the subject matter was blatantly and explicitly moral or instructional, that is, the purpose was didactic. As examples Halsey notes that the renowned early-eighteenth-century American minister Cotton Mather penned " 'Good Lessons' for his infant son to learn at school" (227). Subsequently, beginning around 1819 and continuing for more than twenty-five years, numerous editors utilized a common stock of engravings, poems, aphorisms, and lessons. This annual gift book appeared under various titles, all of which included *Affection's Gift*. Its stated purpose was "imparting moral precepts and elevated sentiments, of uniting instruction and amusement, through the fascinating mediums of interesting narrative and harmony of numbers" (as cited in Halsey [1911] 1969, 228). Unfortunately for the child, amusement was often overlooked, except in the title.

"The result of both intentions has been a collection . . . of impressions of what each generation thought good, religiously, morally, and educationally, for little folk" (Halsey [1911] 1969, 228). These early books written expressly for children provide little insight into children and their nature, but they do illuminate "the change and progress in American ideals and thought concerning the welfare of children" (228). Halsey concludes her book by stating that "after all has been said by way of criticism of methods and subjects, these chap-books, magazines, gift and story books form our best if blurred pictures of the amusements and daily life of the old-time American child" (228).

Note that Halsey mentions the didacticism of earlier eras, and although she does not condemn it, she does seem to be saying that this is changing. It is up to the future to decide whether children are the better for it. I wonder how she would view what has happened this past century and what our "blurred picture of the amusements and daily life" of the twentieth-century American child would be?

The authors, illustrators, and educators who contributed to *Children's Literature Remembered: Issues, Trends, and Favorite Books* have much to say about the social influences on children's literature and, incidentally, on the American view of children. *What topics are suitable for children's books?* may be the most heated and frequently debated issue in a discipline replete with philosophical disagreements. The twentieth century did not escape these controversies; in fact, they exploded as the number of adults engaged in writing, reviewing, producing, marketing, teaching, using, and reading children's books expanded.

This volume is an attempt to look back over the century and explore children's books—the social conditions and the people who shaped them. The genesis of *Children's Literature Remembered* was the Children's Literature Assembly's workshop following the National Council of Teachers of English (NCTE) 1999 fall conference in Denver. In keeping with NCTE's conference theme, the workshop's title was *(Re)Imagining Twentieth Century Children's Literature: Connecting the Past to the Future*. Eight of this book's chapters were first presented as speeches at this workshop—those by Michael Cart, James Cross Giblin, Lee Bennett Hopkins, Julius Lester, Lois Lowry, Leonard Marcus, Uri Shulevitz, and Jane Yolen. By the end of that day, this book had taken wings as the audience begged for copies of the authors' and illustrators' speeches.

Children's Literature Remembered serves several purposes, first and foremost to reconnect readers—or even introduce a younger generation of children's literature aficionados—to their love of literature. Literature must sustain an emotional connection with its readers or it will ultimately fail. This may be the overarching lesson of the twentieth century, as children's books matured into the delight that Lewis Carroll conceived of as he penned Alice's outrageous adventures with white rabbits, tea parties, and a bloodthirsty Queen of Hearts.

Additionally, this book purports to remind readers and students of children's literature of the history of the discipline. It is only through remembering what preceded us that we can avoid the pitfalls of the past. During the twentieth century, children's literature became a recognized, if not uniformly respected, area of research in education, library science, and English departments. I hope that this book will further the scholarship on children and the books that motivate them to become lifelong readers.

Children's Literature Remembered begins with a digression: the results of a survey of Children's Literature Assembly (CLA) members. Approximately 10 percent of those surveyed responded to these three open-ended questions:

1. What twentieth-century American children's book do you consider most important, influential, or as having the most lasting impact on children's literature? Why?

2. Who is the most important twentieth-century author of American children's books? Why?

3. Who is the most important twentieth-century illustrator of American children's books? Why?

Chapter 1 contextualizes the book in several ways: first, it provides the names of books, authors, and illustrators who made an impression on people whose job it is to know and understand the history of children's books. Second, respondents submitted rationales for their choices, which subsequently provide areas for reflection and discussion. Third, surveys that cover a century of history remind us of how short, and selective, our memories are.

Chapter 2, "From Mother Goose to Multiculturalism: Toward a History of Children's Book Publishing in the United States," takes us on a time journey. Leonard Marcus, editor and author, has researched and written about some of the great figures in twentieth-century children's literature. His chapter outlines how children's books have dominated the industry even though publishing houses traditionally disdained "juveniles," their editors, writers, and illustrators. As he recalls the century's greats, he also details the conception of Children's Book Week, the Newbery and Caldecott Awards, and the creation of the *Horn Book Magazine*. Hand-in-hand with publishing giants, Marcus explains the rise of the children's library movement, a phenomenon restricted to the United States. Marcus chronicles the social and economic effects of the century and their effects on children's books. Decade by decade, he makes a case that "in every generation, children's books mirror the values and aspirations of the people who make them."

Uri Shulevitz's speech presented a problem when it came to including it in this book. We recorded all of the speeches, but for some reason, whether human error or gremlins in the system, his was the only one that was not captured on tape. Furthermore, since he spoke from notes and not from a prepared speech, we did not have a permanent record of his comments. After much hand-wringing and brainstorming, Dr. Michael Tunnell offered to record Shulevitz as he spoke from the same notes at Brigham Young University in July 2000. Consequently, we have an approximation of Uri Shulevitz's humorous and highly personal reflections on the making of an artist. His reflections begin with his childhood favorite, *The Wonderful Wizard of Oz,* which he had to leave—unfinished—when his family emigrated from Russia. In Paris, Shulevitz discovered comics and movies, and in Israel he apprenticed as a rubber stamp maker and a house painter. All the while he continued drawing. He came to the United States to study art, and the rest is, as they say, history—in this case, Caldecott history. Shulevitz concludes that art is better today than at the beginning of the twentieth century, even though "it's become a market driven field." Because this chapter took place in a slightly different venue, there was a question-and-answer session after Shulevitz's speech that we have included in the chapter.

Barbara Elleman wrote her chapter, "The Picture-Book Story in Twentieth-Century America," to supplement Leonard Marcus's and Uri Shulevitz's presentations. She notes important illustrators, books, and trends for each decade. One of her major contentions is that "no decade saw the widespread changes in the picture-book arena as did the 1960s." The space race subtly altered publishing companies' focus from libraries to an educational market. As civil and women's rights challenged traditional thinking, societal mores shifted, the world shrank because of technological advances, and children's authors took on previously taboo topics. Elleman provides an entrée into the multitude of people and books—the twentieth-century stars—of the picture-book story.

Chapter 5 is Jane Yolen, par excellence. Yolen—picture storybook author, novelist, folklorist, dreamer, and spinner of tales—assumes a scholar's perspective for this speech. She addresses four approaches to children's folklore: anthologies or collections of folktales, single-tale picture storybooks, original fairy tales, and novelizations of folktales. Yolen asks three questions to elicit critical response for each of these approaches:

1. Is it a good book for children?

2. Is it good folklore?

3. Is its teller mired in society?

Again, as in other speeches and chapters, Yolen immediately faces the cultural value of examining children's books: "[Lang] refers to children in the way that right-thinking adults of that period did, as 'little innocents' (Lang 1968, viii)." Yolen warns readers to be aware that many of the children's tales from the late nineteenth through much of the twentieth century include implicit and explicit racism, symptomatic of the author's or reteller's era. Another precaution is that not all folktales are appropriate for young children. As an example, she suggests that *The Juniper Tree and Other Tales from Grimm* (Segal and Jarrell 1973), a beautifully executed gift set illustrated by Maurice Sendak, is better suited to adult or young adult audiences than children. In like vein, Yolen lauds—with a cautionary finger wag—the glorious illustrations that sometimes mask sterile or racist folktales. Yolen concludes, after discussing original folklore and novels carved from folktales and fairy tales, that the future of traditional literature is assured. "Because in the end, it is the good story that calls to us."

In his companion chapter to Yolen's speech, "What Tales Do We Tell of the Twentieth Century? Folktales and Fairy Tales Prosper," Jim Cipielewski discusses the aspects of fantasy that are congruent with folk literature: What are the differences? Does it matter? A second theme Cipielewski addresses is the origins of tales; that is, the theories of monogenesis or polygenesis. Subsumed within this discussion is folk literature's fluidity in both format and language—how an oral tale becomes a written tale then reverts to an oral tale, all the while meandering across national, cultural, racial, and social borders. Additionally, the place of folk literature within educational curricula, especially as it is utilized for multicultural purposes, is a major facet of Cipielewski's interest in twentieth-century changes in folk literature for children. Finally, he discusses the development of parodies and tall tales into major forces within the genre. In conjunction with Jane Yolen's speech, this chapter represents folk literature's continuation and expansion as a major emphasis within children's books.

Chapters 7 and 8, Lee Bennett Hopkins's speech and Amy McClure's supplementary chapter, focus on a genre in which change has been enormous—and enthusiastically embraced: poetry. Once known as the stepchild of juvenile literature, poetry has claimed its well-deserved place in children's hearts and classroom libraries. No longer are children's anthologies stuffed with adult poems—topics such as love, death, and nature's wonders. Now they are the product of poets writing specifically *for* children and *about* topics that are within a child's purview. Hopkins comments that Langston Hughes's volume, *The Dream Keeper* (Hughes [1932] 1994), stood as a lone representative of poetry by African American men until Ashley Bryan published *Sing to the Sun* (1992). He also discloses that more poets were published during the decade of the 1990s than any other during the twentieth century. Hopkins also emphasizes how changes in children's poetry underscore social changes—topics such as divorce, loneliness, or interracial families became relevant during the later half of the century.

Research and awards are additional facets of poetry that Hopkins and McClure address. The majority of the poetry studies undertaken during the twentieth century investigate children's preferences. From her discussion of these landmark studies, McClure leads us through selection issues, teaching methodology, and response to poetry. Both Hopkins and McClure agree that poetry's future is bright. However, McClure cautions that in order to appreciate poetry, children "must be immersed in reading and writing it." Her fear is that state- and nationally mandated tests will elbow poetry out of the classroom, along with imagination, creativity, and a love of reading.

James Cross Giblin spoke about informational books during the workshop. He titled his retrospective "From *The Story of Mankind* to Studies of AIDS: A Hundred Years of Informational Books for Children." His survey begins with Louise Seaman, head of Macmillan's children's book department, the first juvenile publishing department in the world. Because of her teaching background, Seaman recognized the value of child-friendly informational books. Other publishers followed. Giblin proceeds to describe the first Newbery Award, *The Story of Mankind* (Van Loon 1921). Both Giblin and Evelyn Freeman, who contributes Chapter 10, "Nonfiction: A Genre Comes of Age," decry the subsequent lack of awards for nonfiction. Since Van Loon's book, there have been five Newbery Awards presented to informational books, and all of those were biographies: *Lincoln: A Photobiography* (Freedman 1987); "*Carry On, Mr. Bowditch*" (Latham 1955); *Amos Fortune, Free Man* (Yates 1950); *Daniel Boone* (Daugherty 1939); *Invincible Louisa: The Story of the Author of "Little Women"* (Meigs 1933). Granted, there were Newbery Honors awarded to informational books, but that is little consolation to authors and admirers of the genre. "*Carry On, Mr. Bowditch,*" which, given today's standards, would likely be classified as historical fiction, typifies Giblin's old-style biography in which authors fictionalized conversations and other details. All that changed during the last two decades of the twentieth century. Other trends, notably the quality and quantity of illustrations, the emphasis school districts place on its inclusion in the curriculum, the proliferation of journal articles and professional books for educators, new awards from organizations other than the American Library Association, and the sales figures for these types of books, all indicate that high-quality informational books will be a mainstay of the twenty-first century. Freeman predicts that technology will have an impact on children's nonfiction text in ways we can't even imagine.

Chapter 11 is Julius Lester's "Reflections," the speech he presented during the workshop. He reflects on the lack of books during his childhood and the days during the 1940s and 1950s when his "life was in danger if [he] raised his eyes and they accidentally met those of a white girl or woman." Lester contends that "the major transformative event of the twentieth century" in life and in literature was the Civil Rights movement of the 1960s. But even in light of that, his authorial road has not been smooth. There are two points that seem to encapsulate much of this chapter's gist and illustrate Lester's predictions of future trends: first, multiculturalism cannot be put on like a cloak. Other cultures cannot be forced into an Anglo-European mold. Second, multiculturalism requires an openness rather than combativeness about voice and ownership of tales. "Multiculturalists cannot have it both ways, that is, demand that their viewpoints be included while simultaneously seeking to squelch the viewpoints of anyone who disagrees with them."

Vivian Johnson and Jonella Mongo continue Julius Lester's discussion of twentieth-century children's literature, with a focus on books written and illustrated by African

Americans. Whereas Lester's speech is peppered with personal anecdotes, Johnson and Mongo begin with a historical perspective and track the trends in publishing from W. E. B. Du Bois, *The Brownies' Book* (1920), and early biographies of famous black Americans through the generally dismal publishing opportunities for black persons during the twentieth century.

A recurring theme throughout the final decades of the twentieth century was that people of color were underrepresented in the body of children's literature. Even though world cultures were a matter of curiosity during the late nineteenth and early twentieth centuries—just leaf through the table of contents of any *St. Nicholas* magazine to observe the preponderance of these types of articles—*American* children of color were simply caricatures. Johnson and Mongo stress literature's critical role in allowing all children to see themselves in good literature and celebrate the progress that has been achieved—even if it is too little and was delayed much too long.

In Chapter 13, Debbie Reese continues Johnson and Mongo's discussion but shifts the focus to Native Americans in children's literature. She points out that most twentieth-century social studies textbooks portrayed Native peoples as "primitive, bloodthirsty savages who attacked innocent settlers." To combat these negative images, Native authors adopted the Euro-American writing model so that their books would have a better chance of publication, which meant they had to forsake their traditional oral narrative format. One of the most amazing issues that Reese confronts is the labeling of "good" and "bad" Native books. Using author Zitkala Sa as an example, Reese explains that if Sa conformed to mainstream perceptions, her books were acclaimed as "good"; if she criticized the government's Indian policies, her books were denounced as "bad." Similar to African American children's books, Native children were stereotyped in most publications. Biases and inaccuracies were widespread, and still continue. Two of the more common, according to Reese, are the generic—in which authors and illustrators portray tribal markers indiscriminately—and the sentimental portrayals of Native Americans as ecoconscious remnants of a past era.

The good news is that Native authors have found a voice, and publishers are more aware of the need for books that feature all races and cultures in a positive light. Reese concludes her chapter with an optimistic outlook. "Native people have endured and persisted through hundreds of years of oppression and injustice, and they are bringing that same endurance and persistence to improving the literature that tells their stories."

Chapter 14 characterizes, analyzes, and critiques another genre that, although a major presence in twentieth-century children's literature, was not featured during the CLA workshop. The popularity of historical fiction from the authors' and publishers' points of view never waned during the past hundred years: it was profusely represented at the beginning of the century and remained so throughout. However, its popularity with readers—the children who selected historical fiction for their recreational reading, and the librarians who awarded prizes for literary quality—had as many valleys as peaks.

Linda Pavonetti contends that part of the genre's appeal has traditionally been its fast-paced, electrifying plots and its exotic settings. She notes, however, that plot and setting can also be blamed when historical fiction goes bad. Chapter 14 traces the transition from *Otto of the Silver Hand* (Pyle 1888) and *Ivanhoe* (Scott 1820) to *Johnny Tremain* (Forbes 1943), which won a Newbery Medal for author Esther Forbes and set a new standard for historical fiction writing.

Pavonetti further describes how thoughtful critics and authors, such as Newbery medalist Christopher Collier, challenged the assumptions of American historical fiction for children. Chapter 14 explores researchers' and critics' mounting awareness that historical fiction cannot be neutral because authors write from a particular perspective, utilize language that provokes or justifies, and selectively decide on incidents that support the author's stance. Overall, the major change in historical fiction for young readers over the past hundred years is an expansion of the genre and an improving accuracy and honesty that encourages readers to investigate perspectives other than the author's.

Chapters 15 and 16 continue the discussion of children's fiction. However, Lois Lowry and Sylvia Vardell move the conversation from the past into the present with their examination of contemporary realistic family stories. Lowry, who has received two Newbery Medals—one for historical fiction and one for fantasy—has written more than twenty realistic fiction books, most of which revolve around families. Even her historical and fantasy books center on families. Lowry's chapter, "A Long Way from Pleasantville," which is based on her reflections at the CLA workshop, spotlights her own memory of realistic fiction. She notes the commonalities between life and fiction but concludes that realistic fiction today is more honest and less patronizing than it had been during much of the twentieth century.

Vardell evaluates the role of family in Lois Lowry's books. Thoughtfully, she explains that even though other authors dispense with adults, especially in young adult novels, Lowry's books are populated by well-rounded characters of all ages. Single-parent families struggle side by side with extended families; homeless people coexist alongside Anastasia and her professor father. Family is at the heart of Lois Lowry's books, and, as Vardell concludes, they are "all interacting in ways that are authentic and true."

Michael Cart and Teri Lesesne delve into the relatively recent phenomenon of young adult literature in Chapters 17 and 18. Cart explains in his speech that there *was* no adolescence, and consequently no young adult literature, at the beginning of the twentieth century. He traces its evolution from Louisa May Alcott's *Little Women* (1868) to G. Stanley Hall's (1904) early treatises on the psychological foundations of adolescence, and on through some of the early indicators that adolescence was here to stay. Rose Wilder and other 1930s novelists may not have known that their audience would be teenagers, but by the end of World War II, adolescence was as well established as childhood—even in the world of books. Cart continues his history of young adult literature through the problem novels of the 1970s and 1980s and the difficulties that almost destroyed the genre during the 1990s. Cart ends on a hopeful note: he indicates that, at the end of the century, young adult literature will survive because it "speak[s] with integrity about the real lives of real young adults."

Lesesne provides an interesting comparison between the development of a separate body of children's literature and books for young adults. Briefly, she sketches the genesis of children's books: books adults shared with children, didactic volumes meant to enlighten and indoctrinate, and, finally, with the arrival of Lewis Carroll's *Alice's Adventures in Wonderland* (1865), books that provided the reader with a deep and abiding sense of pleasure. Lesesne's three phases for the development of children's books—preach, teach, and reach—also exist in young adult literature:

- Preach: Moral lessons that upheld normative, socially agreed upon, middle-class behaviors, were the backbone of books such as *Mr. and Mrs. Bo Jo Jones* (Head 1967).

- Teach: Career paths, such as Cherry Ames and her nursing adventures, always led to a husband and family.

- Reach: Realism in character and plot began with *The Outsiders* (Hinton 1967), followed rapidly by *The Pigman* (Zindel 1968), but reached a zenith with Robert Cormier's *The Chocolate War* (1974).

The end of the twentieth century witnessed a young adult literature that was stronger and healthier than at any other point in the past. Multiple awards, established by the American Library Association and other groups, pointed to an increasing awareness—and acceptance—of the quality and diversity within the field. Of all the types of literature for young people, it is possible that young adult literature may have advanced furthest during the past century. It is certainly the most daring area of nonadult literature—in format, content, and style—as the new century commences.

The final two chapters depart from the pattern established both at the conference and in the first eighteen chapters: they are not genre-based. Marjorie Hancock explores the place of children's literature in the classroom in Chapter 19, "Children's Books in the Classroom: Milestones and Memories of the Literature-Based Revolution." She traces the shifting role of literature in the reading and language arts program from the perspective of an elementary student in the 1950s, a preservice and novice teacher during the tumultuous 1960s, and finally as an experienced teacher, then researcher and university professor, through the waning decades of the century. Hancock explains the genesis of teachers' interest and involvement in whole language, reader response, and literature discussion groups through a personal lens.

The final chapter brings this book full circle: Peggy Oxley is a master teacher whose second-grade classroom exudes her love of literature. Peggy assumes a very personal stance when she invites us to share her literate life—as a child reader, a parent, and a teacher. Hers is the type of stroll down memory lane that generated the Children's Literature Assembly's workshop and this book. I hope that her memories—the books she mentions and the love of teaching she epitomizes—spark some personal recollections for you, just as they did for me.

As I envisioned the book's table of contents, I imagined including several sections I could not integrate into the workshop because of time constraints. Though these chapters enlarge the purview, by no means do they cover all the areas of children's literature that are important. For example, the area of science fiction is largely ignored, although the twentieth century produced some great books and intense interest from a dedicated group of readers. Biography does not receive its own chapter, although there were great changes in this genre, especially regarding accuracy. Several chapters do discuss biography, especially those by Giblin and Freeman. In like manner, fantasy, especially high fantasy, is not specifically noted. However, the chapters by Yolen and Cipielewski do explore the area of art tales and novels derived from fairy tales. Likewise, there are chapters representing the century's changes in literature for African American and Native American children, but, unfortunately, no other racial groups. I sincerely hope that whoever writes the next century's retrospective will be able to show major gains for those groups also.

What I hope you find is an insightful reflection on where we have been and where we are headed in American children's literature. Each chapter can stand alone—as an introduction to an author or genre study in the classroom; as a scholarly research article that chronicles the progress of twentieth-century children's literature in the United States. The book can be read for pleasure—the variety of voices and informal presentation by the conference participants are a pleasant change of pace from research documents. And for students of children's literature, this book provides the kind of historical documentation that may prompt further reading and discussion. The twentieth century certainly provided ample material.

References

Alcott, L. M. 1868. *Little women*. New York: Little, Brown.

Bryan, A. 1992. *Sing to the sun: Poems and pictures*. New York: HarperCollins.

Carroll, L. 1865. *Alice's adventures in Wonderland*. Illus. J. Tenniel. London: Macmillan.

Cormier, R. 1974. *The chocolate war*. New York: Pantheon.

Daugherty, J. H. 1939. *Daniel Boone*. New York: Viking.

Du Bois, W. E. B., ed. 1920. *The Brownies' book*. New York: Du Bois & Dill.

Forbes, E. 1943. *Johnny Tremain*. Boston: Houghton Mifflin.

Freedman, R. 1987. *Lincoln: A photobiography*. New York: Clarion.

Hall, G. S. 1904. *Adolescence: Its psychology and its relations to physiology, anthropology, sociology, sex, crime, religion and education*. New York: Appleton.

Halsey, R. V. [1911] 1969. *Forgotten books of the American nursery: A history of the development of the American story-book*. Detroit: Singing Tree/Gale Research.

Head, A. 1967. *Mr. and Mrs. Bo Jo Jones*. New York: G. P. Putnam's Sons.

Hinton, S. E. 1967. *The outsiders*. New York: Viking.

Hughes, L. [1932] 1994. *The dream keeper and other poems*. Illus. B. Pinkney. New York: Knopf.

Lang, A., ed. 1968. *The olive fairy book*. New York: Dover.

Latham, J. L. 1955. *"Carry on, Mr. Bowditch."* Boston: Houghton Mifflin.

Meigs, C. 1933. *Invincible Louisa: The story of the author of "Little Women."* Boston: Little, Brown.

Pyle, H. 1888. *Otto of the silver hand*. New York: Scribner's.

Scott, W. 1820. *Ivanhoe: A romance*. Philadelphia: M. Carey & Son.

Segal, L. G., and R. Jarrell, eds. and trans. 1973. *The juniper tree, and other tales from Grimm*. Illus. M. Sendak. New York: Farrar, Straus and Giroux.

Van Loon, H. W. 1921. *The story of mankind*. New York: Boni & Liveright.

Yates, E. 1950. *Amos Fortune, free man*. Illus. N. S. Unwin. New York: E. P. Dutton.

Zindel, P. 1968. *The pigman*. New York: Harper & Row.

1

Twentieth-Century Movers and Shakers in American Children's Books

A Survey of Children's Literature Assembly Members

Linda M. Pavonetti and
James F. Cipielewski

A great way to begin arguments among lovers of children's literature is to ask who is the best author or what book was the best of the year. Look at all the discussions resulting from the Newbery and Caldecott Awards each year about who *really* deserved to win or "why did *that* book even get considered?" Well, not being ones to shrink from controversy, we decided to add fuel to the fire by asking the members of the Children's Literature Assembly of the National Council of Teachers of English to respond to a survey asking these tough questions:

1. What twentieth-century American children's book do you consider most important, influential, or as having the most lasting impact on children's literature? Why?

2. Who is the most important twentieth-century author of American children's books? Why?

3. Who is the most important twentieth-century illustrator of American children's books? Why?

These seemingly easy questions were sent to the 644 members who were asked to respond by e-mail. There were sixty-five responses, although not everyone gave an answer for each question. Although this is not a great response rate (about 10 percent), the results are still interesting and show surprising agreement in the area of the most important book of the twentieth century and the most important illustrator.

1

In the area of the most important book, two books garnered the lion's share of the responses: *Where the Wild Things Are* by Maurice Sendak and *Charlotte's Web* by E. B. White. These books received twelve and eleven votes, respectively, as well as a great deal of praise. Some of the comments about the books included the following:

> [*Where the Wild Things Are*] has become a touchstone picture storybook against which all others are judged. Just as Robert Cormier dared to disturb the universe of young adult literature when he penned *The Chocolate War*, Sendak also disturbed the sometimes saccharine world of children's books by reminding us all that children, like adults, have a need to "let the wild rumpus begin." His editor, the great Ursula Nordstrom, said it best, "I think *Wild Things* is the first complete work of art in the picture book field, conceived, written, illustrated, executed in entirety by one person of authentic genius."

Another correspondent wrote: "I think it signaled to the field that a single creator could create a powerful book in which the art and text work so closely to make an impact." Which is echoed by: "The brevity of text, the bond between text and illustrations, the uniqueness of the pictures work together to create the quintessential picture book."

And there were comments about the greatness of E. B. White's classic.

> Written by a master literary stylist, it nevertheless reaches young readers in a poignant and unforgettable way. Not only does *Charlotte's Web* tell a good tale, have intriguing and believable characters, and a smooth mix of realism and fantasy, but it has brought the rural scene (diminishing in today's world), an awareness of animal life, and the essence of courage and bravery to the attention of children.

And a comment that really seems to capture much of what makes a book great: "*Charlotte's Web* is the book that makes such indelible footprints on our hearts that we never forget it."

Certainly, these seem to be good choices, but there were others. Books that were chosen by one or more respondents as being the most important book of the twentieth century are listed in Table 1.1.

The question of best author of the twentieth century elicited more responses than the other categories. The top two authors couldn't be more dissimilar, Katherine Paterson and Dr. Seuss, Theodore Geisel. They received ten and eight votes, respectively. They were followed by E. B. White, Lois Lowry, Margaret Wise Brown, and more than a score of others. As before, people's comments captured why they thought so highly of these authors.

Children's Literature Assembly (CLA) members really stressed the quality and character of Katherine Paterson's writing. "Paterson has set the standard for quality writing in the world of books for children and young adults. . . . Each of Paterson's novels and beautiful speeches belie the disciplined work of rewriting that creates her polished art." In the same vein: "Her books are filled with lasting images and thoughtful themes that young readers ponder and remember." And "Katherine Paterson shows the many ways we can give more than we receive and be more than we think we are."

Table 1.1
Books Chosen by One or More Respondents as the Most Important Book of the Twentieth Century in Rank Order

Where the Wild Things Are
Charlotte's Web
Bridge to Terabithia

Two votes for each of the following:

Goodnight Moon
Harry Potter series
Lincoln: A Photobiography
Miss Rumphius
The Cat in the Hat
The Giver
The Wonderful Wizard of Oz
A Wrinkle in Time

One vote for each of the following:

Catcher in the Rye
The Chocolate War
Harriet the Spy
Henry Huggins
Owl Moon
Pink and Say
The Lion, the Witch, and the Wardrobe
The Little House series
The Magical Adventures of Pretty Pearl
The Outsiders
Where the Red Fern Grows

The praise for Dr. Seuss stressed both his influence on early readers and the lessons he imparted. "[Dr. Seuss] has been a cultural director of almost all children. His early books are just plain fun. His later books are wonderful lessons." And again, "Not only did he create easy readers that early readers latch on to and read over and over again with success and building confidence, he also has written books with timeless lessons about the environment, self-esteem, friendship and war."

As we saw earlier, praise for E. B. White's *Charlotte's Web* was quite profuse and deservedly so. Another correspondent commented further: "Charlotte as a writer and friend does not fail to move each generation of young hearts exposed to her beauty."

Lois Lowry was recognized with the following:

[Lois Lowry's] range, from Newbery winning *Number the Stars,* to Newbery winning *The Giver,* to the humorous Anastasia and Sam books, is amazing. Again, quality of writing, depth of emotion expressed, complex characters and relationships, all epitomize the twentieth century standard for excellence in literature for children.

And, finally, Margaret Wise Brown was recognized, along with Maurice Sendak, for her understanding of children.

———

The works of these artists in words and pictures, made powerful through metaphor, endure because they deal with universal themes forever of crucial importance to young children; among these are relationships with parents and siblings, such seemingly mundane issues as going to bed, the need to belong, and the yearning at once for both freedom and security. Brown and Sendak created psychologically powerful books that reach children at their core. This is especially true of *Goodnight Moon* and *In the Night Kitchen*.

Table 1.2 is a list of authors who were named in this survey.

Table 1.2
Authors Named the Best of the Twentieth Century in Rank Order

1. Katherine Paterson	12. Laura Ingalls Wilder	23. Eloise Greenfield
2. Theodore Geisel (Dr. Seuss)	13. Alma Flor Ada	24. S. E. Hinton
3. E. B. White	14. Aliki	25. Langston Hughes
4. Lois Lowry	15. Jim Aylesworth	26. Patricia MacLachlan
5. Margaret Wise Brown	16. Natalie Babbitt	27. James Marshall
6. Beverly Cleary	17. L. Frank Baum	28. Gary Paulsen
7. Virginia Hamilton	18. Clyde Robert Bulla	29. Bill Peet
8. Bill Martin Jr.	19. Barbara Cooney	30. J. K. Rowling
9. Patricia Polacco	20. Sharon Draper	31. Robert San Souci
10. Cynthia Rylant	21. Robert Frost	32. Shel Silverstein
11. Maurice Sendak	22. Jean Craighead George	

Finally, we come to the illustrators that the survey respondents felt were the most important in the past century. The person who received 35 percent of the votes was Maurice Sendak. Chris Van Allsburg, Tomie dePaola, Ezra Jack Keats, and Patricia Polacco followed. Fourteen others were named as well. Although we heard praise earlier for Sendak, there was much more. For example: "His art breaks through conventional boundaries to present an unadulterated version of real children's landscape in an unique style that is both humorous and serious, realistic and symbolic, down-to-earth and ethereal." That is consistent with the comment: "Sendak's innovative book designs have stretched the field of illustration, and his books have become a benchmark for artists of today." And, finally, a quote that Mr. Sendak would surely appreciate: "Maurice Sendak . . . combine[s] the knack for illustrating other people's stories and then creating his own thought-provoking, entertaining, and universal stories that preserve the influence of Randolph Caldecott."

Chris Van Allsburg also receives high praise for his creative expression. "His creativity is unbounded. His constant bending of illustrator's rules, history and his fresh approaches are wonderful." And, "Chris Van Allsburg . . . pushed the boundaries of illustration in many ways. . . . He is constantly pushing his readers to see the world anew through his wonderful illustrations." Which might be summed up with "his work has set a new standard for variety and style."

Tomie dePaola's work was nominated "because his art work is so widely enjoyed by American children and adults. . . . It is . . . admired greatly and [is] memorable to many American readers/viewers of many ages. [It has] become beloved in America." And, "His illustrations and stories are unique and special."

Ezra Jack Keats received praise for leading the way into new communities. Keats's collage illustrations deliberately set out to portray the lives of inner-city children at a time when no one else was doing so. Though today his work is questioned for its authenticity and perspective, forty years ago he brought the lives of a black urban family into mainstream publishing with his innovative torn paper, wallpaper, and mixed-media collage. His books have won numerous awards for style, technique, media, and subject matter. They have had a lasting effect on the assumptions we have about race, culture, and ethnicity.

Finally, who could quarrel with the comment that all illustrators would like to hear: "[Patricia] Polacco's illustrations give the text of her books life!" Table 1.3 is a list of illustrators who were named in our survey.

Table 1.3
Illustrators Named the Best of the Twentieth Century in Rank Order

1. Maurice Sendak	8. Leo and Diane Dillon	15. Thomas Locker
2. Chris Van Allsburg	9. Steven Kellogg	16. Peter Sis
3. Tomie dePaola	10. Jerry Pinkney	17. Garth Williams
4. Ezra Jack Keats	11. Marcia Brown	18. Ed Young
5. Patricia Polacco	12. Theodore Geisel (Dr. Seuss)	19. Paul O. Zelinsky
6. Eric Carle	13. Trina Schart Hyman	
7. Barbara Cooney	14. Robert Lawson	

So, there you have it: a new list to argue about. Who hasn't been included? Who's here that you would not have included? Our hope is that we've given you new ideas to consider and, yes, to discuss and perhaps to argue.

2

From Mother Goose to Multiculturalism

Toward a History of Children's
Book Publishing in the United States

Leonard S. Marcus

"The publishing of books for children has always been a very prominent part of American publishing" (Seaman and Lowrie 1920, 555). So reported *Publishers Weekly* in 1920, just one year after Macmillan established the first juveniles department in the United States.

According to Frank Luther Mott's *Golden Multitudes* (1960), children's titles ranked among the nation's best-selling books from the first decades of the republic, and in the thirty-five years between the end of the Civil War and the turn of the century, they dominated the lists. During the latter period, some of America's leading literary critics, including William Dean Howells and the *Atlantic Monthly*'s Horace Scudder, wrote regularly on children's books, and such respected magazines as the *Nation* and *Harper's Magazine* gave regular review space to the genre throughout the year.

Another clue to the scope and makeup of the field prior to 1920 lies in the key role played by children's magazines in supplying nineteenth-century American youngsters with their reading matter. Not only were there scores of these periodicals in circulation both before and after the Civil War, but most of the larger ones—*Our Young Folks* (published by Ticknor and Fields), *St. Nicholas* (published by Scribner's), and *Harper's Young People* (published by Harper)—worked in tandem with their book publisher owners to ferret out new talent and to advertise and promote their established authors. Several of the most enterprising nineteenth-century American writers for children, including Samuel Griswold Goodrich (who wrote under the pseudonym Peter Parley), Louisa May Alcott, Mary Mapes Dodge, and Frank R. Stockton, doubled as editors of the periodicals. Alcott, who by 1875 had left the editorship of *Merry's Museum* and was riding high on her considerable fame as the author of *Little Women* (1868), even used the pages of *St. Nicholas* to attack as sensational the work of one of her arch rivals, William T. Adams—the man known to legions of young readers as Oliver Optic. Adams responded in his own *Oliver Optic's Magazine* by dismissing the charge and turning it back on his competitor. The interest of the episode lies in the fact that both authors saw an advantage in distinguishing their own writings from the unashamedly coarse—and exceedingly popular—dime novels of the day. Just a few years later, members of the newly formed American Library Association would contrive to keep these very sorts of pulp literature out of young people's hands.

By the turn of the century, most general interest children's magazines had failed, to be replaced by others designed for more specialized readerships (and advertising markets). In that period of increased specialization societywide, library service to children became an established profession. And at a time when *censorship* had yet to acquire any of its present-day pejorative connotations, librarians created the first children's reading rooms as much with a view to excluding unsavory types of books as to fostering a taste for what they considered "good." As children's library work became a national phenomenon, publishers realized the value of having specialists of their own to address the particular needs of this well-organized group of book buyers.

The moment came when, just after the end of the First World War, Macmillan appointed Louise Seaman editor of its precedent-setting Books for Boys and Girls. With the help of one assistant, Seaman (later Bechtel) assumed responsibility not only for the editing of all her fledging department's books but also for many aspects of their design, production, promotion, and sale. In doing so she set the pattern for her future colleagues, who, like her, came to enjoy a large measure of autonomy in return for their considerable labors.

During her fifteen-year-long tenure, Louise Seaman Bechtel published a long list of distinguished books by Dorothy P. Lathrop, Rachel Field, Elizabeth Coatsworth, Padraic Colum, and others. Determined to make children's books available to the widest possible audience, she created the Little Library series of classics as a sort of children's book counterpart to the Boni and Liveright (later Random House) Modern Library; began the Happy Hour series of fifty-cent picture books; and, in the early years of radio, was among the first to take to the air waves with a children's story hour. Known also for her high standards in design and production, she published one of the decade's best-loved gift books, *The Adventures of Pinocchio* (1925) with Attilio Mussino's illustrations. Even the Macmillan catalogues were admired, and reviewed, as works of art.

During the 1920s, the outlines of a powerful new structure for children's book publishing came into view as the successor to the less centralized nineteenth-century scheme that had depended so heavily on the fate of often-ephemeral magazines. The establishment of National Children's Book Week and of Macmillan's department, both in 1919; of the Newbery Medal in 1922; of the *Horn Book Magazine* in 1924; and of juveniles departments at Doubleday, Page (1923), E. P. Dutton (1925), Harper & Brothers (1926), Little, Brown (1927), Harcourt Brace, Coward-McCann, and Oxford (1928) all represented important links in the new structure, which secured an independent status for itself at the expense of a certain isolation from the publishing mainstream. Because women were assumed to know more about children than men, the owners of the houses envisioned the new departments as an all but exclusively female domain. For the next fifty years, juveniles publishing would remain the only specialty within book publishing and one of the very few professions in which American women routinely rose to positions of authority.

Riding the wave of 1920s prosperity, children's-only bookshops opened in several of the nation's larger cities. More important in the long run, however, than these often short-lived ventures would be the growing recognition of children's librarians, and in particular of leading figures within the group such as the New York Public Library's Anne Carroll Moore, as the ultimate gatekeepers standing between children's book publishers and children. Thereafter, few literary critics outside the field deigned—or saw the need—to write about children's literature. One of the few who did, the *New Yorker*'s Katharine S. White, would wonder whether children's books, having fallen into the hands of experts, had not become culturally "sacrosanct" and thus subject to a peculiarly modern kind of sentimentality that was "far more insidious than the simple-minded sentimentality of the Victorians."

Moore in any case made a seminal contribution to her field. She set an important precedent by significantly lowering the age requirement for library admittance, opening the New York Public Library's resources to any child able to sign his or her name and present a clean pair of hands. She became a reviewer of national prominence, a valued advisor to publishers, a list maker and prize giver, and a mentor to the entire generation of librarians who followed in her considerable wake. Like Katharine S. White and the other legendary "strong women" who debated the standards and goals for children's books, Moore expressed her opinions in no uncertain terms. After persuading E. B. White, the *New Yorker* essayist and husband of Katharine, to try his hand at writing for children, Moore urged that *Stuart Little* (1945) not be published, warning that White's quirky tale about a mouse-child born into an American family was sure to damage his reputation.

Not long after the concept of library work with children won widespread acceptance, the progressive nursery school movement produced a new set of experts ready to challenge the standard library view of books for the youngest ages. Lucy Sprague Mitchell, the visionary founder of New York's Bureau of Educational Experiments (later the Bank Street College of Education), proposed, on scientific grounds, to replace traditional fairy tales and Mother Goose rhymes with a new "here-and-now" literature rooted in children's sensory experiences. With E. P. Dutton's publication of Mitchell's *Here and Now Story Book* (1921), the battle was joined. Despite the initial contempt expressed by Moore and her colleagues for a social scientist's attempts at conjuring up literature in a laboratory, the here-and-now idea established itself, finding lasting expression in books as varied as *The First Picture Book* (1930) by Mary Steichen Calderone, photographed by Edward Steichen; *Men at Work* (1932) by Lewis W. Hine; *Pat the Bunny* (Kunhardt 1940); in picture books by students of Mitchell's including Margaret Wise Brown, Edith Thacher Hurd, and Ruth Krauss. Less directly, Mitchell's impact can be seen in the great stacks of board books and other "very young" books published for children today. On retiring from Macmillan in 1934, Bechtel would work as a critic and serve as a bridge between the mutually suspicious worlds of the librarians and progressive educators.

If Mitchell's literary adventures represented one assault on the romantic storytelling tradition favored by the librarians, a critique of another, perhaps more disturbing kind came to light in the form of a survey of children's reading preferences commissioned in 1926 by the American Library Association. When researchers asked 36,000 children in thirty-four cities to name their favorite books, fully 98 percent responded by listing titles written by Edward Stratemeyer, the fabulously prolific—and to the librarians, reviled—author of the Rover Boys and Dave Porter series and publisher of, among others, the Hardy Boys, Bobbsey Twins, Tom Swift, and, starting in 1930, the Nancy Drew series.

The librarians' disapproval of series, in which they saw the application of Henry Ford–style mass-production techniques to the writing of books of Theodore Dreiser–ish vulgarity, spilled over to taint, to some extent, the critical reception of multivolume works of literary merit, including those by Laura Ingalls Wilder, the first of whose novels, *Little House in the Big Woods,* appeared in 1932. Wilder's books were repeatedly named Newbery runners-up (the old term for Honor book) and refused the medal itself; it was with the sense of righting a past injustice that in 1954 the American Library Association created a lifetime achievement award in Wilder's name and chose Wilder as its first recipient.

The coming of the Great Depression brought retrenchment at some publishing houses and a period of rigorous economizing for all who remained active in the field. Doubleday's dismissal of May Massee in 1932 took the prize as the period's most spectacular act of managerial shortsightedness. The following year, Massee joined the eight-year-old Viking Press, where she soon confirmed her reputation as the preeminent editor of her pioneering generation, a publisher of lists consistently notable, in friendly rival Louise Seaman Bechtel's estimate, for their "originality, balance of interest, humor, good taste, daring in production and book patterns." Among the authors and artists who signed on with Massee during her first decade at Viking were Marjorie Flack, Kurt Wiese, Robert Lawson, Munro Leaf, William Pène du Bois, Ludwig Bemelmans, Marie Hall Ets, Robert McCloskey, Ruth Sawyer, and Kate Seredy. Under Massee, Viking books epitomized the librarians' twin ideals of the aesthetically uplifting "book beautiful" and of the emotionally safe and nurturing well-told tale.

The burden of the Depression eased for the publishers of trade books somewhat earlier than it did for the economy as a whole. In 1935, the number of new children's titles rose for the first time in four years. The previous year, Charles Scribner's Sons—longtime publisher of the N. C. Wyeth and Howard Pyle classics and of *The Wind in the Willows* (Grahame 1909)—appointed Alice Dalgliesh as its first full-time juveniles editor. (Once Dalgliesh made it clear that she did not wish to do her work at home, she was given a desk in the corner of another editor's office.)

In 1935, one privately financed new firm, Holiday House, opened for business. A second small house devoted exclusively to children's books, William R. Scott, followed suit three years later. The idealistic founders of Holiday House and Scott shared a commitment to progressive tendencies in fine press design and printing. William R. Scott also wholeheartedly embraced Lucy Sprague Mitchell's here-and-now philosophy; and, with Margaret Wise Brown as his editor and star author, he and the small group of enthusiasts he gathered around him set out to make modern books for modern children. Some librarians found much to object to in their unconventional approach to bookmaking; nonetheless, Scott-style books soon achieved a sort of backdoor respectability. Critics who dismissed Margaret Wise Brown's *The Noisy Book* (1939) as subliterary, praised *Red Light, Green Light,* written in a similar vein by Brown under the pseudonym Golden MacDonald and published in 1944 by the mainstream house of Doubleday.

By the mid-1930s, American publishers could take justifiable pride in having brought out a wide array of picture books rivaling anything being done in Europe. (Several of the leading illustrators—Ingri and Edgar Parin d'Aulaire, Feodor Rojankovsky, Boris Artzybasheff, Miska Petersham—were recent European émigrés.) To recognize, and further encourage, the trend, Frederic G. Melcher, the president of R. R. Bowker and a longtime advocate for children's books, established the Caldecott Medal for illustration as a companion prize to the Newbery Medal, which he was also responsible for having created. Dorothy P. Lathrop received the first Caldecott in 1938 for *Animals of the Bible* (1937), with biblical texts selected by publisher Frederick A. Stokes's highly regarded children's book editor Helen Dean Fish. (Stokes, as the publisher of Frances Hodgson Burnett's *The Secret Garden* [1911], the majority of L. M. Montgomery's books, and Helen Bannerman's [1900] *Little Black Sambo,* was among the nation's leading juveniles publishers around the turn of the century. In 1941, it was sold to Lippincott.)

General interest in children's books appeared to be on the rise. Returning from England in 1941 to head Houghton Mifflin's juveniles department, Grace Hogarth was astonished by the volume of submissions that piled up on her desk—the same desk, as it happened, at which Thomas Bailey Aldrich had written his classic *The Story of a Bad Boy* (1869) seventy years earlier. One evening, after casually remarking to the janitor that most of the manuscripts in her office were trash, she found to her horror that the janitor had taken her words literally and had thrown them out. Not long after her arrival at Houghton, Hogarth heard from Margret and H. A. Rey, refugees from German-occupied France, whom the editor had first communicated with while at Chatto and Windus in London. Among the manuscripts the Reys sold to Hogarth, in a then highly unusual four-book deal as demanded by Margret, was *Curious George* (Rey 1941).

During the war, paper and printing quality declined; books for older children had reduced trim sizes, narrower margins, and fewer illustrations. Fewer titles appeared overall, but those that were published enjoyed a robust sale as wartime rationing of rubber and metal left many types of toys in short supply.

Books on patriotic themes moved to the fore: Walter Edmonds's *The Matchlock Gun* (1941) took the 1942 Newbery Medal; Esther Forbes's *Johnny Tremain* (1943) won in 1944. Books about the war were also widely available. In those frightening times, scary stories about ghosts and goblins achieved an unprecedented popularity, and Robert McCloskey, winner of the Caldecott Medal for 1942 for *Make Way for Ducklings* (1941), joined Frank Capra and Norman Rockwell as one of the nation's most reassuring articulators of the American dream. In *Homer Price* (1943), McCloskey also poked gentle fun at the new mass-market comic books that children's librarians vigorously condemned as an aesthetically inferior and intellectually dishonest form of escapism.

The most spectacular development of the war years was unquestionably the launch in 1942 of the Little Golden Books series of twenty-five-cent, full-color picture books. Coming at a time when the typical trade picture book sold for $1.50, the new series vastly increased the retail market for and presumably the readership of books for the younger ages and precipitated an unladylike competition for the services of the period's best artists. An early advertising slogan—"Books and Bread!"—played up the populist aspect of the mass-market enterprise, which was a joint venture, in its first years, of Simon and Schuster and the Artists and Writers Guild. (The Guild was the New York City–based arm of the Western Printing Company of Racine, Wisconsin. It was Simon and Schuster's business partner in the publication of Golden Books from the imprint's founding in 1942.)

When Golden Books went on sale in five-and-dime stores, drugstores, and supermarkets nationwide—the same nontraditional outlets opened up by Pocket Books a few years earlier—librarian critics discovered to their dismay that it did not much matter what they thought of the cheery little volumes with their tinsel trim and endorsement by "Mary Reed, Assistant Professor of Education, Teachers College." Parents would buy them anyway. They did so by the hundreds of thousands. For large numbers of book-buying parents then and in the immediate postwar years, the Golden name became synonymous with books for preschoolers.

The postwar baby boom prompted heightened interest on the part of the older trade houses in books for the nursery ages. *Goodnight Moon* (1947) by Margaret Wise Brown and illustrated by Clement Hurd would be the era's quintessential contribution to the genre. At the same time, as millions of Americans hoped for "perfect" babies of their own, *Stuart Little* (1945), E. B. White's off-center tale of a mouse-child born to red-blooded Americans, offered comic relief for older siblings and new parents alike.

Houses not previously known for picture books looked for chances to tap into the expanding market; thus, Whittlesey House, the juvenile trade division of the scientific and technical publisher McGraw-Hill, brought out *The Happy Lion* (1954) by Louise Fatio, with illustrations by her husband Roger Duvoisin. Distinguished artists with young children at home—designer Paul Rand, printmaker Antonio Frasconi, and others—turned to picture-book-making for the first time.

The postwar period saw a general expansion in the field. In 1945, representatives of thirty publishing houses and other organizations formed the Children's Book Council to discuss common concerns. Chastened by the experience of the war, editors wondered what they might do to promote peace and a spirit of international exchange for the future. As Japan dispatched young women to the United States to be trained in children's library service and began in earnest to import American children's books for its home market, Margaret K. McElderry, of Harcourt Brace, contributed to the healing process by bravely publishing one of the first works of the postwar era by a Japanese American, Yoshiko Uchida's *The Dancing Kettle* (1949). McElderry also brought out the first postwar novel by a German writer for children, Margot Benary-Isbert's *The Ark* (1953). Thereafter, Harcourt's editor led the way for American publishers as importers of books from abroad. Velma Varner (at G. P. Putnam's Sons and later at both World and Viking) and Ann K. Beneduce (at World and afterward at Philomel) later joined McElderry in fostering a new internationalism.

Publishers also turned their attention to another baby boom phenomenon, the rapidly expanding school library market. Morrow Junior Books, a new imprint in 1946, opened for business with a former school library supervisor, Elisabeth Hamilton, as its founding editor. Hamilton, who had come from Harcourt Brace, championed the work of science writers Herbert Zim, Millicent Selsam, and others whose books met the educational needs of school-age children. On the fiction side, it was Hamilton who discovered the preeminent comic novelist of modern-day American home and school life, Beverly Cleary.

In 1950, the success of Random House's Landmark Books on history and biography set other publishers scurrying to create rival series. As was noted with envy at the time, Landmark books did not simply end up on library shelves. In cities and towns lacking a single bookshop, stationery and drugstores often stocked the Landmark books as well, along with precious little else for young readers. Volumes in the series became gifts of choice for an entire generation of book-buying parents.

Elizabeth Riley made T. Y. Crowell a formidable contender across the nonfiction field, from science to poetry. In 1957, when the launch of the Soviet *Sputnik I* satellite sent tremors through America's scientific and education communities, Crowell already had an impressive backlist of the very kinds of science books that the public then clamored for. The house profited handsomely from Riley's foresight. That same year of 1957, Harper's I Can Read Books and Random House's Beginner Books addressed another widespread concern of the parents of the outwardly placid, but short-fused 1950s: the fear that large numbers of the nation's children were not learning to read as well as they should.

If by the 1950s children's book publishing had become a more institutionally secure and substantial enterprise than it had been thirty years earlier, its distinctive pattern as a publishing subculture remained largely intact. It continued to be a sisterhood of well-educated professional women who enjoyed editorial autonomy, a well-bred spirit of competition among themselves, and a highly profitable relationship with their librarian sisters, whose business accounted for as much as 80 percent of their departments' sales. Even during the rapid expansion of the 1950s, when the number of children's books published increased from 907 in 1950 to 1,540 books in 1959, hats, white gloves, and an overarching self-confidence about the nature and success of their mission remained the rule. Holt, Rinehart and Winston's Ann Durell recalled the period in a 1982 *Horn Book* article featuring an imaginary editor named Bunky Bannister:

Over Bunky's desk hung the same invisible list of taboos that had charted the course of children's books since 1900 and before. No lying or stealing or any other crime or felony unless it is suitably punished. No drinking or smoking. No description of bodily functions more sexually suggestive and/or scatological than sneezing. (Durell 1982, 25)

The white gloves came off during the 1960s. Editors who had taken for granted their role as protectors of childhood realized that they held too sheltered a view of American society. Among her colleagues, Harper's editorial director Ursula Nordstrom had the surest grasp of the changes at work within American society that were rapidly turning so many of the literature's time-honored conventions into shopworn clichés. In a succession of groundbreaking Harper books by Maurice Sendak, Louise Fitzhugh, Ezra Jack Keats, Russell Hoban, John Steptoe, and others, Nordstrom turned up the temperature on emotional candor and championed a new spirit of impertinence in children's books that perfectly suited the post-Freudian, post-Hiroshima, post–*Father Knows Best* decade of the sixties. It was sheer coincidence, of course, but a telling juxtaposition nonetheless that *Where the Wild Things Are* (1963) was published within weeks of the assassination of President John F. Kennedy. Sendak's triumph was a turbulent book for turbulent times.

From Harper the following year came Louise Fitzhugh's *Harriet the Spy* (1964), a seriocomic first novel that showed, among other things, that parents sometimes drank and put their children in therapy. At Viking, Velma Varner published S. E. Hinton's *The Outsiders* (1967), another first novel that shocked some readers with its frank depiction of class conflict and gang warfare in an apparently typical American town. Adding to the drama surrounding the book was the fact that the author was still in her teens.

Just as the "new realism" was becoming the dominant trend in children's fiction, a new note of realism was sounded in the marketplace. In 1962, the Dell Laurel Leaf Library of books for upper elementary school children and teens became the first modern trade paperback imprint for young readers. Dell Yearling, with books for younger grade school children, followed in 1967. Dell Yearling became one of the first modern children's trade paperback imprints. Under George Nicholson's direction, Yearling published, in a format rejected (at first) as cheap by tradition-minded librarians, a wide range of fiction "by distinguished authors" in editions that children could afford to purchase. Over the next decade, the standard-setting Yearling list won widespread acceptance in both trade and mass-market outlets, with Judy Blume and Beverly Cleary as the imprint's best-selling authors. With that acceptance, librarians began to purchase paperbacks in large quantities.

The race question became a tensely debated topic as the Civil Rights movement prompted a reexamination of publishers' assumptions both about the audience they served and the racial makeup of the world as depicted in the books they published. The issue had previously been broached in the mid-1940s, during and after a war that had seen the nation's armed forces belatedly integrated. During the 1960s, it resurfaced with greater urgency in the work of Ezra Jack Keats, Virginia Hamilton, Julius Lester, Tom Feelings, Walter Dean Myers, and others. Nancy Larrick's 1965 *Saturday Review* essay, "The All-White World of Children's Books," became the most-talked-about article of the decade. At the Dial Press, Phyllis Fogelman led her generation of editors in championing what later would become known as the new "multiculturalism" in children's literature.

As part of the Johnson administration's Great Society, Congress in 1965 enacted the Elementary and Secondary Education Act, providing funds to public schools for the purchase of nontextbooks. Publishers expanded (and in some cases seriously over-expanded) their lists to take advantage of the government's "golden largesse"; when the pressures of a wartime economy and a change of administrations brought an end to the funds a few years later, imprudent publishers were reminded once more that theirs was a fundamentally cyclical business.

At Macmillan, Susan Hirschman, who like Phyllis Fogelman had trained under Ursula Nordstrom, took charge of a languishing department, revived the venerable backlist, and, presciently, made a specialty of publishing a younger type of picture book than was then considered the norm. Not everyone appreciated the need for these very "simple" books at first, but as the day-care and preschool movements took hold, the timeliness of the books soon became apparent. At World, Ann K. Beneduce was experimenting along similar lines with a versatile commercial artist-turned-picture-bookmaker named Eric Carle.

New houses opened for business, including Atheneum, whose department, headed by Jean Karl, won both the Caldecott and Newbery Medals for 1965 for *May I Bring a Friend?* (1964), written by Beatrice Schenk de Regniers, illustrated by Beni Montresor, and *Shadow of a Bull* (1964) by Maia Wojciechowska, illustrated by Alvin Smith, respectively. The Atheneum list, which also featured the work of Judith Viorst, E. L. Konigsburg, Ellen Raskin, and Ron and Judi Barrett, among others, became identified with an irreverent, sophisticated style of wit that represented, among other things, a continuation of Harper's iconoclasm under Ursula Nordstrom. (Nordstrom, having got caught up in the new market-driven corporate politics of the late 1960s, took early retirement in 1973.)

More men—Michael di Capua and Richard Jackson at Macmillan, Ferd Monjo at Harper, James Cross Giblin at Seabury, and Walter Lorraine at Houghton Mifflin—were rising to prominence as editors. After a stint at Prentice Hall, Jackson and colleague Bob Verrone decided to strike out on their own. Among the upstart Bradbury Press's first discoveries would be Judy Blume.

Emily Arnold McCully's 1969 Book Week Poster featuring an androgynous child at the head of a protest rally for "Book Power" aptly summed up the tumultuous decade for many in the field, even as it—just as aptly—offended others.

As the potential for profitability in children's book publishing became a more widely recognized fact, successful houses became attractive merger and acquisition candidates. The consolidation of ownership that was already under way by the late 1960s continued at an ever-accelerating rate for decades to come.

During the 1970s, the withdrawal of federal funds for library books combined with high inflation to put publishers in a more cautious mood than they had been a few years earlier. Not every house suffered equally, of course. Some large companies, such as Macmillan, got caught short in the changed economic environment. In the fall of 1974, in a move that was at least partly attributable to the need to cut its costs, Macmillan fired approximately two hundred of its employees, including most of its children's book department; Susan Hirschman was among those to resign in protest immediately thereafter. Other houses, however, were in a position to expand; soon after leaving Macmillan, Hirschman formed a new imprint, Greenwillow Books, at Morrow.

Dell Yearling and the pack of imitators it inspired benefited dramatically from the new budget consciousness. In a move that widely was seen as a narrowing of the traditional gap between trade and mass-market publishing, Dell and its hardback counterpart Delacorte began offering hard/soft contracts to authors. And in an arrangement reminiscent of the closely entwined relationship between the great nineteenth-century children's magazines and their book-publisher owners, publication by Dell sometimes served as a tryout for would-be authors on the more prestigious Delacorte list. It was also at this time that international copublishing arrangements increased markedly in importance as publishers sought economies of scale in the production of costly full-color picture books.

Hardly noticed during the 1970s was the founding of a wide variety of small or alternative presses specializing in children's books. A great many of these quixotic ventures were destined to fail; but those that survived—among them San Francisco's Children's Book Press and the Annick and Kids Can presses of Toronto—went on not only to fill important gaps in the literature but to see their once far-out ideas accepted into the mainstream.

As the well-educated grown children of the baby boom generation started families of their own, the largest and most receptive retail market for children's books in history emerged. General interest booksellers who had shunned stocking juveniles in the past saw an overriding advantage in doing so, even if it meant having to cope with unruly children, demanding parents, and their own ignorance of the genre. Even more remarkably, the rise of independent children's-only bookstores in communities throughout the nation made it easy—for the first time—for parents living outside the nation's largest cities to shop for many of the types of children's books previously available only at the library. The number of such stores, many of which were founded by former children's librarians who had lost their jobs during the massive library cutbacks of the 1970s, reached well into the hundreds during the 1980s before fierce competition from the rapidly expanding bookstore chains thinned their ranks. In many communities, knowledgeable independent booksellers augmented or even took over the children's librarians' traditional role as tastemakers and guides to good reading for the young. Meanwhile, as the superstores with their combined power to order (and return) vast quantities of a given title multiplied, publishers were compelled to consider ever more closely the chains' specific book-buying needs and to tailor their efforts accordingly.

Not surprisingly, the power of editors at many houses gradually but steadily declined relative to the power of marketing directors. One heard more about focus and decision making by committee, less about editorial vision. In the picture-book realm, advances in printing technology for the first time made full-color art the cost-effective option of choice even in the case of a young illustrator's fledging efforts. And as trim sizes grew conspicuously larger, illustration came increasingly to overshadow text; in the feverishly expanding retail market of the 1980s, it was, after all, the pictures that sold the book, except in the rare case of a "brand-name" author. Future historians will look back on the 1980s in puzzlement as a golden age of book illustration but not of the illustrated book.

Memorable children's books of many kinds nonetheless continued to be published. Board books and early picture books received more serious attention than ever before, and they even found their way into the public libraries. Books depicting the experiences of racial and ethnic minorities were more plentiful. Photography was more widely accepted as an illustration medium.

The 1980s saw the resurgence of illustrated nonfiction as exemplified by the photographic picture books on science by Seymour Simon (Morrow), the pen-and-ink illustrated books on architecture and engineering by David Macaulay (Houghton Mifflin), and the photo biographies and histories by Russell Freedman (Holiday House and Clarion). Breaking with the old pattern of institutional-looking nonfiction, these visually striking, well-written volumes were equally appropriate for school and library use and as gifts; they made a strong implicit case for the continued relevance of books in the television era. And in one of several indications that both the age classifications within children's literature and the boundary line between books for children and those for grown-ups were becoming blurred, the new nonfiction also crossed over to attract an adult readership. Books in other categories—the archly sophisticated picture books of Chris Van Allsburg, Jon Scieszka and Lane Smith, Maira Kalman, and others; the "older" young adult fiction by such novelists as Kyoko Mori—confirmed the trend.

During the 1980s, retail sales of children's books doubled twice, reaching $1 billion by the end of the decade. Yet even with this phenomenal growth, the field remained relatively small compared with the toy and movie industries. With growing competition from these as well as a whole range of new media ventures, publishers scrambled either to expand their own activities or to forge alliances with companies in related media in the hope of maintaining their competitiveness. In this respect, as in many others by the start of the 1990s, Scholastic, with its market-driven approach to publishing and its skill at developing its books for television, film, and other formats, seemed to set the new industry paradigm.

By the mid-1990s, the once separate world of children's book publishing had come more and more to resemble that of adult publishing with its overheated emphasis on front-list sales and perennial quest for blockbuster titles, star authors, and media tie-ins. Of course, most children's books did not qualify in any of these categories, but those that did received an increasingly disproportionate share of marketing attention. Emblematic of the changes was the decision on the part of many publishers to close their doors for the first time to unsolicited manuscript submissions.

The industry mood at mid-decade was watchful and subdued as everyone, having come down a notch from the heady boom days of the 1980s, struggled to grasp the impact of seemingly daily changes in corporate ownership, industry personnel, and communications technology.

Yet children's book publishing remained a strong and growing concern; if it had entered a period of uncertainty, the 1990s were nonetheless a far cry from the days when New York's Oxford University Press debated whether or not to open a children's book department at all. The decision to do so had come in 1928. Recalling the firm's reluctance, Oxford's first editor, Winifred Howard (1930), observed: "Some thought it beneath the dignity of the Oxford University Press to deal with anything so trivial as children's books! Also they said it would spoil the sale of our other books" (44). Seventy years later, no one was likely to make that argument again. The children's book departments at several houses had in fact propped up if not actually carried the general trade throughout the postwar decades.

How was it, though—with so much talent, activity, and sheer success to the publishers' credit—that large numbers of the nation's children reportedly still had not learned to read? Why were the books being published for children not reaching the children who needed them most? Publishers could hardly be expected to solve a society-wide problem of this magnitude on their own, a problem that until recently the nation's leaders had shown little interest even in acknowledging. Yet as the century and millennium drew to a close, all publishers—not those of children's books alone—would have to ask what future there could possibly be for themselves in a nation of nonreaders.

If CD-ROMs and other new media merchandise aimed at children were cutting noticeably into book sales in the 1990s, it was nonetheless also true that high-tech alternatives had failed to render the traditional book obsolete, as some had predicted. And these technologies were not likely to do so any time soon. For large numbers of parents, teachers, librarians, and children, books (increasingly paperbacks) still held the advantage in overall variety, portability, and price.

For publishers, competition from the new media clearly pointed to the need to re-think the book as a unique medium within the increasingly large and varied constellation of media alternatives. Yet it was far from clear whether the larger houses' non-publisher-owners were prepared to support the kind of experimentation that could, ideally, flow from such a thoroughgoing reexamination. On the contrary, corporate caution had all too obviously become the rule. Meanwhile, small new houses continued to appear, and sometimes to take hold, as had happened continually since early in the previous century; perhaps the future would belong to them.

Although illiteracy among America's schoolchildren remained a deeply distressing problem, it was also the case that larger-than-ever numbers of the current generation of the nation's young were discovering reading, meeting authors, and seeing how books were made—and would doubtless want their children to do so, too. In the larger scheme, the question of who would fill that future demand hardly mattered. As for how well it would be filled, there was but one certainty: in every generation, children's books mirror the values and aspirations of the people who make them; children always get the books that their parents deserve.

References

Alcott, L. M. 1868. *Little women; or, Meg, Jo, Beth and Amy.* Boston: Little, Brown.

Aldrich, T. B. 1869. *The story of a bad boy.* Boston: Houghton Mifflin.

Bannerman, H. 1900. *The story of little black Sambo.* New York: F. A. Stokes.

Benary-Isbert, M. 1953. *The ark.* New York: Harcourt Brace.

Brown, M. W. 1939. *The noisy book.* Illus. L. Weisgard. New York: William R. Scott.

———. 1947. *Goodnight moon.* Illus. C. Hurd. New York: Harper.

Burnett, F. H. 1911. *The secret garden.* 2d ed. New York: F. A. Stokes.

Calderone, M. S. 1930. *The first picture book; Everyday things for babies.* Photographer E. Steichen. New York: Harcourt Brace.

Collodi, C. 1925. *The adventures of Pinocchio.* 3d ed. Trans. C. Della Chiesa and illus. A. Mussino. New York: Macmillan.

De Regniers, B. S. 1964. *May I bring a friend?* Illus. B. Montresor. New York: Atheneum.

Durell, A. 1982. If there is no happy ending: Children's book publishing—Past, present, and future. Part I. *Horn Book Magazine* 58 (1): 23–30.

Edmonds, W. D. 1941. *The matchlock gun.* Illus. P. Lantz. New York: Dodd Mead.

Fatio, L. 1954. *The happy lion.* Illus. R. Duvoisin. New York: Whittlesey House.

Fish, H. D. 1937. *Animals of the Bible.* Illus. D. P. Lathrop. New York: F. A. Stokes.

Fitzhugh, L. 1964. *Harriet the spy.* New York: Harper & Row.

Forbes, E. 1943. *Johnny Tremain, a novel for old & young.* Illus. L. Ward. Boston: Houghton Mifflin.

Grahame, K. 1909. *The wind in the willows.* New York: Scribner's.

Hine, L. W. 1932. *Men at work; Photographic studies of modern men and machines.* New York: Macmillan.

Hinton, S. E. 1967. *The outsiders.* New York: Viking.

Howard, W. 1930. Preparing to make children's books. *Horn Book Magazine* 6 (February): 43–48.

Kennedy, X. J. 1986. *Brats.* Illus. J. Watts. New York: McElderry Books.

Kunhardt, D. M. 1940. *Pat the bunny.* New York: Simon & Schuster.

Larrick, N. 1965. The all white world of children's books. *Saturday Review of Literature* 48: 63–65, 84–85.

McCloskey, R. 1941. *Make way for ducklings.* New York: Viking.

———. 1943. *Homer Price.* New York: Viking.

Mitchell, L. S. 1921. *Here and now story book: Two- to seven-year-olds: Experimental stories written for the children of the City and Country School (formerly the Play School) and the Nursery School of the Bureau of Educational Experiments.* Illus. H. W. Van Loon. New York: E. P. Dutton.

Mott, F. L. 1960. *Golden multitudes: The story of best sellers in the United States.* New York: Bowker.

Rey, H. A. 1941. *Curious George.* Boston: Houghton Mifflin.

Seaman, L. H., and R. L. Lowrie. 1920. Introduction to "Notes on children's books." *Publishers' Weekly*, September 11, 555–558.

Sendak, M. 1963. *Where the wild things are.* New York: Harper & Row.

Uchida, Y. 1949. *The dancing kettle, and other Japanese folk tales.* Illus. R. C. Jones. New York: Harcourt Brace.

White, E. B. 1945. *Stuart Little.* Illus. G. Williams. New York: Harper & Row.

Wilder, L. I. 1932. *Little house in the big woods.* Illus. H. Sewell. New York: Harper & Brothers.

Wojciechowska, M. 1964. *Shadow of a bull.* Illus. A. Smith. New York: Atheneum.

3

Children's Books

Personal Observations and Memories of How Things Were and How They Are Now

Uri Shulevitz

My topic is the personal observations and memories of how things were and how they are now in children's books. My personal recollections about publishing and my book career are very personal and don't pretend to be a scientific assessment. Therefore, since these are personal observations and memories, I will begin with some personal recollections as well.

It is well known that art began on walls. Prehistoric humans drew on walls in the caves. The ancient Egyptians drew on temple walls and tomb walls. Well, I, too, began drawing on a wall—when I was in my cradle. You see, I was a precocious kid. My cradle period was possibly one of my more revolutionary periods. I'm saying this because before I was one year old, I made abstract expressionist drawings on the wall way before there was such a movement in art. When war erupted, I was four years old. Now, don't be fooled by appearances. I'm talking of World War II, not World War I. But although I was only four years old, I remember quite well the blitz over Warsaw where I was born, of streets caving in, of no electricity, people carrying water from the river, of charred buildings or burning buildings that were all around us. The world was falling apart. There was only one place where I felt safe and to which I escaped by means of drawing. But after the Nazis invaded Poland, escape into drawings was no longer possible. So, we went to Russia.

We spent the war years in the state of Kazakhstan, in the city of Turkestan. It's in central Asia. It was a totally different world from the one I knew. It was a city of clay houses; there were no books, no newspapers. There were no paper or pens. There was also no running water. We were the only ones who ran. But I continued to draw on any kind of paper I could find, scraps, old letters. Because of the lack of pencils, I used charcoal that was made of sticks of burned wood. For color, I used flower petals. But that wasn't the worst of it. The worst was a lack of food. For five years, I went to bed hungry and my favorite fairy tale that I used to ask my mother to tell me again and again was how, after the war, I could eat as many rolls and butter as I wished. I never tired of asking her to tell me that fairy tale again and again. In those days, it was easier for me to believe in the story of Cinderella than in my mother's tale.

When I was ten years old, my mother gave me my first book. It was *Till Ulenspiegel* by Charles de Coster (1916, 1978). When she was a patient in a hospital, she saved the sugar cubes instead of using them for her tea. She traded the sugar with a hospital maid for the book. That's how she was able to give me the book. My other memorable reading experience in those days was reading *The Wonderful Wizard of Oz* (Baum 1900) with a friend who had a copy of it; I had no books in Russia. In the meantime, while he was reading the book to me, the war had ended, but not our reading of the book. I didn't want to leave Russia before knowing the end of the story. But I had no choice. We had to leave, so, at that time, I never heard the end of the story.

After the war, we went to Paris, France. As you know, Paris is a city for lovers, so at twelve I fell in love with movies and comics. I also developed a passion for books—cloak and dagger and musketeers as portrayed by Alexandre Dumas, the author of *The Three Musketeers* (originally published in 1844), *The Count of Monte Cristo* (originally published in 1845), and many, many more books. Dumas, as a matter of fact, wrote enough books to keep me quite busy. I also began drawing my own comics with a classmate who wrote the words. Considering the movies, comics, and musketeers, it was no less than a small miracle that I found time for school. As you can see, I was a very busy young man.

From France we went to Israel. After elementary school, I worked as an apprentice rubber stamp maker, as an assistant house painter, as a dog license clerk. I worked in an orange grove and at a laundry factory. All these I did during the day. In the evening, I divided my time between high school and art school. Later on, I worked in an agricultural kibbutz. I was the baker for a couple of days, and I also was a self-taught carpenter. But I also kept drawing.

Then I came to study art in the United States. In art school, in order to pay for art supplies, I had a part-time job as art assistant for a small publisher. Arnold Lobel, the author of the Frog and Toad series, worked there before me. I was twenty-six years old when I sold my first picture book. It was a revelation. Here was a genre into which I could channel my love of story and drawing. Knowing nothing about the field, I decided to try my luck with Harper. At that time they were considered the best publisher and were located in a small building on East 33rd Street. The children's department was headed by the great Ursula Nordstrom. I had no trouble making an appointment, although Ursula was away in Europe. I met with her assistant, Susan Carr, better known as Susan Hirschman these days, who is an outstanding editor in her own right. I owe my entry into children's books—and ultimately my first six books with Harper— to Susan Carr Hirschman.

Ursula Nordstrom was a visionary who saw book potential everywhere. She instructed her staff to view everyone who called or just walked off the elevator as a potential genius. That is how she discovered Else Minarik who walked in without an appointment, straight off the elevator. Minarik is the author of *Little Bear* (1957), which Maurice Sendak illustrated. Ursula also discovered Sendak, among many others, all of whom she brought into children's books.

In those days, the children's book industry was a quiet, semiforgotten small province on the side roads of publishing. I liked it and I hoped it would stay that way, but nothing ever does. Money advances were very small, and I had trouble making ends meet. Ursula Nordstrom was concerned, wrote me a nice note, and said, "Uri, some day you'll make money."

Ursula, I hope you can hear me. I'm still waiting.

I hung her note on my bulletin board next to a check for $1 million that a friend gave me on the strict condition that I don't ever try to cash it. And next to it, I hung a royalty check for $0.73.

In those days, there were dedicated editors who worked very hard. They didn't get paid proportionate to their merits or amount of work, which is still true today. Books weren't always beautiful. They were technically limited. They were color preseparated, which meant that in order to save costs, the artist painted a book's twenty-five color illustrations four times each because each picture was made up of numerous overlays. But the books had feeling in those days. Today, books are generally well illustrated. They're very attractive. They're in full color, beautifully printed. Although there are always exceptions, frequently they lack feeling as well. There are many slick books now, which the buying public loves.

In those days, children's books were primarily sold to libraries. President Lyndon Johnson was particularly generous in supporting libraries. More money to libraries meant more sales; more sales led to more children's book departments. In the meantime, art schools began turning out more and more technically skilled art students who chose children's books as a career. Artists were also discovering children's books because magazines and adult books seldom used illustrations. Printing techniques were improving, and more and more books were done in full color.

Children's book departments were also growing in size. Harper, my first publisher, moved to a large building on East 53rd Street. Now it looks just like another large corporation. Even the small publishers, like my current publisher, Farrar, Straus and Giroux, that used to be on a single floor have expanded onto three floors. Eventually, federal funds for libraries began diminishing and in order to survive, children's book publishers had to find new outlets, new markets. So, they became more and more dependent on bookstores. Michael Lynton of Penguin Books summed it up this way, "A big change in distribution occurred." This was a profound change in book publishing.

Librarians are trained in literature, and independent bookstores are sometimes run by former librarians who know and love books. But the chain bookstores are pushing them out of business. For children's bookstore employees, selling books is frequently a job for which they receive little compensation and they don't necessarily know books. Unlike librarians, the buying public has little knowledge of children's books and depends on reviewers and the media to tell them what to buy, what to think, and how to feel. Reviewers are generally more familiar with words than with pictures and since art is half of a picture book, they lack stereo vision, so to speak. It's as if they see only half a book. The library buyer knows books, the general population doesn't always.

Now, in this brave new world, publishers have to catch the buying public's attention at all costs. Children's books are thrown into the wilds of the marketplace. Now children's books have to become catchy, often at the cost of quality. Others depend on name recognition, which, of course, is no guarantee of quality or knowledge of what a picture book is. Ursula Nordstrom would nurture authors and illustrators because they had the potential to create a good children's book. Now publishers may select authors because of name recognition or something else that might attract attention. Whereas once, many only *thought* they could write a children's book, now many *do* it. Well-known actors, actresses, and singers—it's become very fashionable. Children's books are no longer below the dignity of *even* British royals: a prince has written a children's book and so has a duchess. In the United States, an ex-state governor and also an ex-president have contributed their own children's books. Never mind that their children's books aren't really appropriate for kids. Being an ex-president is no guarantee that one can write a good children's book.

Children's books are also facing competition from movies, TV, and electronic games. More and more books are chasing fewer and fewer readers. Large companies and corporations are swallowing publishing houses to form corporate giants and marketing groups. The bottom line becomes increasingly more and more important. Words like "children's books best-sellers," "books as merchandise," "blockbusters," and "products" resound throughout the country. Children's books are joining mass culture.

The days when books used to be intimate vehicles seem part of a very distant past. Books were intimate vehicles—they were coming, it seems to me, more directly from the heart of the author. And in today's atmosphere—one that is more commercial and mercenary—it is much harder for an author to envision books as intimate vehicles. It has become harder to create them, but not impossible. Writing and illustrating children's books is more grueling than when money wasn't so much of an issue—there wasn't as much at stake.

In the olden days, there was less pressure on children's book departments and less pressure from corporate bottom line. Editors could nurture young talent who were allowed to develop, do six or seven books, without being arbitrarily terminated. The emphasis then was on the love of books. Now, authors or artists must be fully developed, immediately produce a profitable bottom line. Creating books is viewed as a job and a way to make money, so I hear. It's become a market-driven field like other kinds of entertainment.

Well, you may ask, "Was everything better then?" No. "Is everything worse now?" No. The art is better today in many instances, and, paradoxically, large corporations are giving rise to small, independent publishers. If you ask me, "Am I pessimistic about children's books?" No, I'm not. After all, the mighty dinosaurs are extinct but the humble pencil is still alive and well.

[The following are informal comments in response to audience inquiries. Although they are not integral to Mr. Shulevitz's formal presentation, they are interesting nonetheless.]

There are artists who have inspired me, but since I don't want to offend anybody, I will only mention some who are not exclusively children's illustrators or, in some cases, no longer alive. The list is rather very long. You see, my background wasn't in illustration. My background is as a painter, and I still do painting and sculpture. I've also done printmaking. My illustration is an outgrowth of that. And so the people (or the periods in art) who are important to me are really the painters. Of course, I greatly admire some illustrators and I can mention their names because they are safely dead. Among them is the French illustrator, Gustave Doré. I like particularly his early books rather than the late ones. The late ones that are well known, such as his Bible illustrations, are beautiful drawings. There's no question they are very impressive, but I like the ones that are a little more awkward. And the ones he did when he was starting out. He was a very precocious illustrator; unfortunately he died in his forties.

I like the work of George Cruikshank, the English illustrator, and, of course, Sir John Tenniel, who illustrated *Alice in Wonderland* (1865). *Alice in Wonderland* has been illustrated by many other people, some of whom have done beautiful work, but I don't think anybody has done better than the original illustrator.

Of course there is Grandville, another great French illustrator. And painters: I love the ancient Egyptians, the archaic Greeks, some artists from the very early Renaissance, Sienese art, medieval art, Chinese and Japanese art. The list is long.

There are also individual artists, modern artists—Matisse, Picasso—but it also very much depends on the paintings. Some late paintings by Braque and Giacometti, the Italian painter—there are so many wonderful painters—Ambrogio Lorenzetti and his brother, and the brothers Van Eyck, the Flemish painters, not to mention the ones I can't remember at the moment. So, as you can see, it's a long list.

When I write a book, I consider a very specific audience, an audience of one—myself. I have to love the book I'm doing. If it sounds selfish or egocentric, it isn't really. I think it is difficult or impossible to second-guess anybody else. But it is important to do something that you truly love. And if you love doing it, then you'll do your best. And if you love it, then at least there's one person in the world who loves it. And if there is one person, then chances are there might be two or three. If there are three, there might be many. Whereas if you try to second-guess, you may not like the story and the audience may not like it either. Then you're left with nothing.

Notes

This is a re-creation of the speech that Mr. Shulevitz presented at the 1999 Children's Literature Assembly's Post-Conference Workshop, "(Re)Imagining 20th-Century American Children's Literature: Connecting the Past to the Future" (NCTE Fall Convention in Denver, November 22, 1999). We are indebted to Dr. Michael O. Tunnell for allowing us to record and use Mr. Shulevitz's speech at Brigham Young University on July 14, 2000.

References

Baum, L. F. 1900. *The wonderful wizard of Oz.* Illus. W. W. Denslow. Chicago: G. M. Hill.

Carroll, L. 1865. *Alice's adventures in Wonderland.* Illus. J. Tenniel. London: Macmillan.

de Coster, C. 1916. *Till Ulenspiegel.* Illus. R. Grossmann. Berlin: Bruno Cassirer.

———. 1978. *The legend of the glorious adventures of Tyl Ulenspiegel in the land of Flanders and elsewhere.* Illus. A. Delstanche. Westport, CT: Hyperion.

Dumas, A., and A. Marquet. 1844. *Les trois mousquetaires.* Paris: Baudry.

———. 1845. *Le Comte de Monte-Cristo.* Paris: Pétion.

Lobel, A. 1970. *Frog and Toad are friends.* New York: Harper.

Minarik, E. H. 1957. *Little bear.* Illus. M. Sendak. New York: HarperCollins.

4

The Picture-Book Story in Twentieth-Century America

Barbara Elleman

The last years of the nineteenth and the beginning of the twentieth century saw the germination of the first seeds of what we now call American children's literature. Books for children had had a secure foothold in England for some time, but there were few American picture storybooks at all. While Kate Greenaway, Walter Crane, and Lewis Carroll provided British children with reading pleasures, children in the United States were fed mostly moralistic stories meant to instruct rather than entertain. Some titles, published for adults, garnered a child audience because of their appealing story lines. Mark Twain's *Adventures of Tom Sawyer* (1876), Louisa May Alcott's *Little Women* (1868), Frances Burnett's *Little Lord Fauntleroy* (1886), Margaret Sidney's *Five Little Peppers and How They Grew* (1881), and Anna Sewell's *Black Beauty* (1877) offered adventure and romance to young readers, but small children had little in printed form to entertain them.

As the twentieth century marched forward, however, a breath of fresh air swept along with it. Librarian Anne Carroll Moore developed a children's department at the New York Public Library in 1906, exerting her considerable influence over books published and selected; Mary Mapes Dodge's *St. Nicholas* magazine continued to offer children a wide variety of fantastical and adventure stories; Helen Bannerman published her now highly controversial *The Story of Little Black Sambo* (1900) to public and critical acclaim; Andrew Lang introduced the age-old fairy tales to American children through his "color" collections; and Beatrix Potter penned *The Tale of Peter Rabbit* (1902). According to critic Marjorie Allen (1996), author of *100 Years of Children's Books in America,* Potter's books became the "prototypes for the picture storybook format in children's book publishing, a format that was uncommon in Great Britain at the turn of the century and practically nonexistent in America until the 1930s" (31).

Slowly, the seeds were sprouting and growing: Bertha Mahony Miller opened the Bookshop for Boys and Girls in Boston in 1916; Frederick G. Melcher, editor of *Publishers Weekly* and an advocate of children's books, established Children's Book Week in 1919. That same year, Macmillan appointed Louise Seaman to head what became the first children's book department; the Newbery Award was established in 1922 (the Caldecott, in 1938); and both the *New York Herald* (1924) and the *New York Times* (1930) began reviewing books for children.

Although these people and events certainly helped set the world of children's fiction in motion, the picture-book format continued to lag behind, with a couple of notable exceptions. Beatrix Potter was a continuing influence, delighting children on both sides of the Atlantic, as were A. A. Milne and Ernest Shepard. In 1924, the latter two produced *When We Were Very Young,* heralding the beginning of the Pooh phenomenon. But it wasn't until Johnny Gruelle introduced Raggedy Ann and Andy in 1918 and Marjorie Williams Bianco wrote *The Velveteen Rabbit* (1926), illustrated by William Nicholson, that American children found picture storybooks that appealed directly to them. Finally, American writers and illustrators were beginning to make an impact on the picture-book scene.

Certainly, one of the bell ringers of the time was Wanda Gág's *Millions of Cats* (1928). Although Watty Piper's *The Little Engine That Could* (1930), with its message of victory over adversity, was far more popular, *Millions of Cats* is a landmark book in terms of creativity—a fresh, original story presented in a vigorous form. The black-and-white block-print drawings, with hand-lettered text, are well paced and bring a pleasing harmony to the page. Many people, in fact, believe that Gág's effort incorporates all of the qualities needed in an exemplary picture book—text and illustrations in equal balance, a developing story line, simple language, and strong characterizations. Published in 1928, the book has never been out of print. Gág went on to write numerous other books, receiving two Newbery Honor citations, *The ABC Bunny* (1933) and *Millions of Cats* (1928), and two Caldecott Honor citations *Nothing at All* (1941) and *Snow White and the Seven Dwarfs* (1938)—a tribute to both her writing and illustration abilities.

Gág, an artist born of eastern European immigrants, represented a growing trend of illustrators who found their way to the United States in the 1920s and 1930s, leaving their indelible mark on the pages of children's books. For example, Austrian Ludwig Bemelmans captured American hearts with his Madeline books, Hungarian Miska Petersham (with his American wife Maud) demonstrated in *The Story Book of Clothes* (1933) that attractive visual interpretation could make facts more interesting, and Russian-born Esphyr Slobodkina's art of cutout collage in *Caps for Sale* (1940) brought an avant-garde look to the world of children's illustration.

When the stock market crashed, ending the euphoric 1920s, the American public, interestingly, shielded its children from the hard times that followed. Children's books perpetuated the American dream, carrying a theme of hope and belief in the future. Despite the depressed economy, children's books continued to be a fast-growing publishing venture. Helped along by the development of photo-offset technology, the production of picture books quickly increased. In tandem with this technical development, interest arose in books for the youngest child.

Two picture-book authors who had major impact in that area were Margaret Wise Brown and Ruth Krauss. Each had a subtle way of expressing children's inner thoughts and needs that created a natural link to the prereading child.

Brown's auspicious beginning was *The Noisy Book* (1939). A student of Lucy Sprague Mitchell at Mitchell's Bank Street School, Brown believed in providing settings in which young children would feel comfortable, and illustrator Leonard Weisgard aptly provided matching visual arenas. The book signaled the first of their many collaborations. Brown's partnership with Clement Hurd for the still-popular *The Runaway Bunny* (1942) and the now-classic *Goodnight Moon* (1947) brought the same kind of evocative expression.

Krauss, whose work teems with pattern and rhyme, demonstrated an abiding commitment to language and to the intellectual and emotional life of children. This is apparent in *The Carrot Seed* (1945), illustrated by her husband Crockett Johnson, and the eight books, including *A Hole Is to Dig* (1952), that she collaborated on with Maurice Sendak, who was then a budding illustrator. These books, simple and appealing to children, are now staples for the preschool set, but at the time they were considered to be highly innovative.

A book that set a new course for the picture-book format was Dr. Seuss's (Theodore Geisel's) *And to Think That I Saw It on Mulberry Street* (1937). Although popular authors today such as Marc Brown and Jan Brett sell upward of 200,000 copies per book, Seuss's reported sales of 30,000 copies in the book's first years of publication set new records. *Mulberry Street*'s tongue-in-cheek humor, jangly verse, and robust artistic style were repeated in *The 500 Hats of Bartholomew Cubbins* (1938), as they were in later titles by this prolific creator.

On the far side of Seuss, realistic undertones rarely seen before in children's picture books were developing. In contrast to the early 1930s, world events began to be reflected in books for children. The rise of technology, for instance, brought Lois Lenski's *The Little Auto* (1934) on the scene, with Mr. Small's popularity spawning other adventures such as *The Little Airplane* (1938) and *The Little Train* (1940). Other author-illustrators who brought a realistic edge to their stories were Hardie Gramatky in *Little Toot* (1939) and Virginia Lee Burton in *Mike Mulligan and His Steam Shovel* (1939). The machines supplied the realism, the anthropomorphizing of the vehicles provided a touch of fantasy—a combination that readers loved.

Although children of the late 1930s devoured these adventures (as do youngsters today), librarians choosing the first Caldecott recipient in 1938 awarded the medal to a much different kind of book. Helen Dean Fish's *Animals of the Bible* (1937a), illustrated by Dorothy Lathrop, was deftly rendered in stunning black-and-white lithographs, but has never been a favorite with children. And neither have the two honor books for that year: *Seven Simeons, a Russian Tale* (1937) retold and illustrated by Boris Artzybasheff, a folktale involving a king, a princess, and seven talented brothers; and *Four and Twenty Blackbirds* (Fish 1937b), a collection of nursery rhymes compiled by Helen Dean Fish and illustrated by Robert Lawson. None of these three titles contains even a whiff of the realism that children found and loved in *Little Toot* and *Mike Mulligan*. As has often been the case, awards given by adults don't match the choices of children.

As the writings of Ruth Krauss and Margaret Wise Brown began to be recognized, the role of the illustrator became more important, and with it came the increasing success of the picture book in general. Many reviewers, for instance, cited the combined efforts of Munro Leaf and Robert Lawson when evaluating *Wee Gillis* (1936b) and *The Story of Ferdinand* (1936a).

Interest in the realistic aspects of life brought new attention to biographies. James Daugherty, Ingri and Edgar D'Aulaire, and Robert Lawson set the stage for the Jean Fritzs, David Adlers, and Russell Freedmans of the future with their insightful pictorial presentations. Although today's biographies are often accompanied by photographs, the earlier author-artists visually profiled their subjects with sensitive well-drafted drawings. Daugherty's were often larger than life and full of action, the D'Aulaires' were quietly compelling, and Lawson's lively renditions were often touched with humor.

When Pearl Harbor drew the United States into war in the 1940s, bringing shortages to almost every aspect of life on the home front, surprisingly, children's books did not suffer accordingly. Instead, books, considered important to education, became big business.

Simon and Schuster and Western Printing released a new line called Golden Books and made these colorful titles easily accessible to the general public through supermarkets and department stores. Jeanette Lowrey's *Poky Little Puppy* (1942), priced at $0.25, was the first of twelve Little Golden Books released; ten years later it had sold more than three million copies. Another significant title published was Dorothy Kunhardt's *Pat the Bunny* (1940), as it became the model for future tactile books.

The success of Golden Books generated Bank Street Books, which focused on children's real-life experiences. It was here, under Lucy Sprague Mitchell's support, that Margaret Wise Brown, Leonard Weisgard, Edith and Clement Hurd, and Garth Williams were able to concentrate on the kinds of books they had long thought to be important. Brown (writing under the name Golden MacDonald) and Weisgard's joint efforts peaked in their 1947 Caldecott Medal book *The Little Island* (1946). Based on a real island off the coast of Maine, which Brown often visited, it reflected her reaction to the destruction caused by the atomic bomb at the end of World War II—a subtle reflection, as the story focuses on the seasonal life cycle of the island.

This ingrained subtlety also can be found in Virginia Lee Burton's Caldecott-winning *The Little House* (1942) and in her *Katy and the Big Snow* (1943) and *Maybelle the Cable Car* (1952). All three quietly evince Burton's reaction to the growing impact of technology and to societal changes happening around her.

Possibly as a backlash to the hardships and tragedies of war, several books, filled with humor, carried an underlying theme of hope for the simplicity and pleasures in life. Books such as Robert McCloskey's *Make Way for Ducklings* (1941), H. A. Rey's *Curious George* (1941), James Thurber and Louis Slobodkin's *Many Moons* (1943), and Ruth Stiles Gannett's *My Father's Dragon* (1948) elicited laughs but also gave a sense of safety, comfort, and joy.

A message of appreciating nature and its awe-inspiring forces also became a significant theme—at least if Caldecott-winning books are a criterion. In the 1940s, medal winners included Alvin Tresselt and Roger Duvoisin's *White Snow, Bright Snow* (1947), Berta and Elmer Hader's *The Big Snow* (1948), Robert McCloskey's *Blueberries for Sal* (1948), Marie Hall Ets's *In the Forest* (1944), and Alvin Tresselt and Leonard Weisgard's *Rain Drop Splash* (1946).

With the war over, America settled into years of complacency until the launching of Russia's *Sputnik* capsule in 1957. Then schools were forced to reevaluate their teaching methods—especially in regard to science and technology—as the public demands for improvement of education grew. Following a *Life* magazine article by John Hersey suggesting that perhaps America's ailing educational system be handed over to

Dr. Seuss, William Spaulding of Houghton Mifflin challenged Seuss to create a book from a list of 300 words. The result, the innovative *Cat in the Hat* (1957), created a new format called "easy readers." Seuss subsequently became the editor of Beginner Books at Random House, Coward McCann developed Break-of-Day Books soon after, and Harper introduced its I Can Read series, which featured Else Holmelund Minarik's Little Bear books. Illustrated by Maurice Sendak, these books smoothly fuse images with text and are especially significant in their depictions of mischievous children that show a mix of cultures.

The 1950s era became a brilliant showcase for the varied artistic talents, styles, and media of new illustrators arriving on the scene. A small representation includes Katherine Milhous's Pennsylvania Dutch folk art in *The Egg Tree* (1950); Don Freeman's lively, cheerful chalk drawings for his wife Lydia's amusing *Pet of the Met* (1953); Marcia Brown's ethereal rendering of *Cinderella, or the Little Glass Slipper* (Perrault 1954); Crockett Johnson's spare simplicity in *Harold and the Purple Crayon* (1955); Feodor Rojankovsky's lively, colorful images in *Frog Went A-Courtin'* (1955), retold by John Langstaff; Barbara Cooney's richly colored *Chanticleer and the Fox* (1958); Leo Lionni's unique collage shapes in *Little Blue and Little Yellow* (1959). But no decade saw the widespread changes in the picture-book arena as did the 1960s. Beginning in the early part of that decade, the economic backbone of children's publishing was significantly altered as publishing departments expanded to meet a new demand for children's books and the sociopolitical climate of the country underwent dramatic upheaval. The effects are still being felt today. When the early children's books departments were formed, the editors came from library backgrounds, published titles were distinctly child oriented, and stories contained pristine characters and uplifting themes. In the aftermath of *Sputnik,* millions of dollars were pumped into schools and publishers were quick to step in to meet the new demands of teachers and librarians. To fulfill this need, publishers began an active recruitment of new authors and illustrators who were encouraged to experiment and explore new styles. This kind of license resulted in beautifully illustrated books with provocative themes and stretched the field to new boundaries.

Although the upheavals in lifestyles, traditions, mores, and language as well as protests against sexism and racism were felt most profoundly in novels of the sixties, picture books were also affected. One of the books to fit this bill mostly profoundly was Maurice Sendak's *Where the Wild Things Are* (1963). Combining realism with fantasy, Sendak took children on a magical journey. Although the book still evokes some controversy today, it has been beloved by children for four decades. But *Wild Things* was not the only standout book of that time. Russell Hoban's *Bedtime for Frances* (1960) features a spunky character not unlike Max. Other unforgettable characters emerged and have stayed with us. Well-rounded, multisided protagonists were no longer just relegated to novels. Evidence abounds: Peter in Ezra Jack Keats's *The Snowy Day* (1962); Samantha in Evaline Ness's *Sam, Bangs & Moonshine* (1966); Stevie in John Steptoe's book *Stevie* (1969); and *Corduroy* (1968) by Don Freeman, who demonstrated that even a teddy bear can have a distinct personality.

Another major contribution to the picture storybook market in the 1960s was the illustrated fairy tale. Marcia Brown received her second Caldecott Medal for her woodcut renderings in the East Indian fable *Once a Mouse* (Brown 1961); Ed Emberley also used woodcuts for his wife Barbara's *Drummer Hoff* (1967) adapted from a folk verse; and Blair Lent used pen-and-wash drawings in illustrating Arlene

Mosel's retelling of the Chinese folktale *Tikki Tikki Tembo* (1968). And while Uri Shulevitz received a Caldecott Medal for Arthur Ransome's retelling of a Russian tale, *The Fool of the World and the Flying Ship* (1968), it was Shulevitz's *One Monday Morning* (1967) that depicts his deft ability to expand story through pictures and where his talent for understatement is most visible.

Despite a widespread penchant for folktales, original stories—many with a humorous bent, perhaps attributable to quirky story lines—found a welcome audience. William Steig penned and illustrated *Sylvester and the Magic Pebble* (1969); Bernard Waber created *Lyle, Lyle Crocodile* (1965); Ellen Raskin brought out *Nothing Ever Happens on My Block* (1966); and Chris Van Allsburg invented the exotic *The Garden of Abdul Gasazi* (1979). More and more, books were being written and illustrated by the same person: illustrator-author became a noticeable trend.

The 1970s are often characterized as a decade that offered stories by and about other cultures. Again, folktales played a major role. Leo and Diane Dillon received back-to-back Caldecott Medals for their renditions of *Why Mosquitoes Buzz in People's Ears* (1975), an adaptation of an African folktale by Verna Aardema, and for *Ashanti to Zulu: African Traditions* (1976) by Margaret Musgrove. Gerald McDermott provided *Arrow to the Sun* (1974), a traditional Pueblo Indian story executed with abstract bright paintings; Paul Goble's *The Girl Who Loved Wild Horses* (1978) features a Plains Indian girl; and Margot Zemach's *It Could Always Be Worse* (1977) is a jocular retelling of an old Jewish story.

The sober realism that proliferated the 1970s, reflecting the turbulence of the country, is reflected in books such as Miska Miles and Peter Parnell's *Annie and the Old One* (1971), Judith Viorst and Erik Blegvad's *The Tenth Good Thing about Barney* (1971), and Sharon Bell Mathis and Leo and Diane Dillon's *The Hundred Penny Box* (1975). Humor, however, also filtered through, bringing balance. Most notable are the first in a number of individual and outstanding series: Harry Allard and James Marshall's *Miss Nelson Is Missing!* (1985), Marshall's own *George and Martha* (1972), and Arnold Lobel's *Frog and Toad Are Friends* (1970). Also adding wit to the time was Tomie dePaola's *Strega Nona* (1975), Marc Brown's *Arthur's Eyes* (1983), and Florence Parry Heide and Edward Gorey's *The Shrinking of Treehorn* (1971).

Illustration made its mark in another genre. Although poetry purists often prefer decorative or simple background images in books of verse, integrated and sometimes elaborate illustrations became more common. Shel Silverstein's bold and somewhat wacky drawings in *Where the Sidewalk Ends* (1974) and Arnold Lobel's haunting images for Jack Prelutsky's *Nightmares: Poems to Trouble Your Sleep* (1976) signaled a shift in the look of children's poetry books. The change in children's publishing was bringing many a new face to the field as well as a variety of styles, themes, and story lines—and children were the beneficiaries.

The 1980s brought another major transformation to the children's picture-book field: the introduction of the whole language movement in schools and the integration of literature into the curriculum increased the demand for trade books. It was here that picture-book publication truly bloomed, enhanced by the availability of full-color reproduction, high-speed presses, scanners, and other high-tech devices.

The proliferation of folk- and fairy tales continued into the 1980s. Tales of the Grimm brothers and Hans Christian Andersen were still regular staples, masterfully interpreted by artists such as Trina Schart Hyman, Susan Jeffers, and Paul Zelinksky, but other sources were also being explored. Steven Kellogg delighted fans with *Paul

Bunyan (1984) and *Pecos Bill* (1986); Jerry Pinkney drew from his African American roots, most notably in *Mirandy and Brother Wind* (1989) by Patricia McKissack and in Julius Lester's *The Tales of Uncle Remus* (1987). Other artists were finding opportunities in Asian, Hispanic, African, Eastern European, Scandinavian, and Middle Eastern stories. In too many cases, however, the artwork overpowered the story and in the rush to find unusual tales, choices often contained abstract concepts and sophisticated themes difficult for young children to comprehend.

The overuse of these traditional tales gave rise, inevitably perhaps, to the fractured tale. Jon Scieszka and Lane Smith led the pack with *The True Story of the 3 Little Pigs! By A. Wolf* (1989), and no end of variations of other stories followed.

These parodies, however, were just another part of an emerging trend: picture books for the older child. While some of this phenomenon rode in with the whole language movement, middle school and junior high teachers began using picture books in teaching language arts, social studies, and science. The establishment of children's-only bookstores also helped the movement along. Knowledgeable salespeople with a passion for quality literature were reaching parents and teachers and selling thousands of children's books—not all to child readers. Sophisticated books such as Chris Van Allsburg's *The Mysteries of Harris Burdick* (1984), Mordecai Gerstein's *Mountains of Tibet* (1987), and David Macaulay's *Black and White* (1990) were purchased by adults for adults. Children's books had found a whole new market.

Another development to evolve from the literature-based curriculum was the rise of the informational picture book. Heavily illustrated, these topic-specific books found their way into the market and gained easy acceptance. Joanna Cole and Bruce Degen's The Magic School Bus series; Gail Gibbons's illustrated explorations of wide-ranging subjects such as pumpkins, tunnels, cats, and puffins; George Ancona's photo essays featuring Hispanic and Native American lifestyles; and Stuart Murphy's inventive MathStart books are only a few examples. These titles, in turn, affected informational books for older children, which began to evince an increase in photos, maps, drawings, and other kinds of visual materials.

At the youngest end of the publishing spectrum, concept books were also finding a ready audience. Titles such as Eric Hill's *Where's Spot?* (1980), Lois Ehlert's *Color Zoo* (1989), Eric Carle's *The Very Busy Spider* (1984), and Rosemary Wells's Max and Ruby board books (e.g., Wells 2000) were purchased for home use but also for the growing number of nursery school and day-care centers that opened to accommodate working parents.

The needs of the changing school population brought multicultural books into the limelight in the 1990s, and publishers actively sought writers and illustrators from the African American, Native American, Asian, and Hispanic communities. They, too, relied heavily on folktales for their artistic efforts. But not all did, as evidenced by Alan Say's thoughtful and artistically beautiful *Grandfather's Journey* (1993), Faith Ringgold's *Tar Beach* (1991), and Sherley Ann Williams and Carole Byard's *Working Cotton* (1992). These books emanated from the backgrounds and lives of their artistic creators.

Concern for the environment also stood out as a 1990s topic that children took to heart. Books such as Jane Yolen and John Schoenherr's *Owl Moon* (1987) provided a quiet expression of respect, while Chris Van Allsburg's *Just a Dream* (1990) pushed a more upfront message.

Blunt realism also surfaced. The most startling, to many, was the awarding of the Caldecott Medal to David Diaz for a story, written by Eve Bunting, set during the riots in Los Angeles called *Smoky Nights* (1994). Bunting, a prolific writer, was one of many who wrote numerous message-driven books in the early 1990s. In collaboration with illustrator Ron Himler, she created *The Wall* (1990), about the Vietnam Veterans Memorial in Washington, D.C., and *Fly Away Home* (1991), about a homeless father and son who live in an airport. Michael Willhoite's *Daddy's Roommate* (1990) and Leslea Newman's *Heather Has Two Mommies* (1989), about gay and lesbian parents, also signified the way children's books had changed. Of course, factions continue to exist—just as they did in the 1930s when Lucy Sprague Mitchell advocated realism in books for young children, while Ann Carroll Moore worked to shield children from such scenes.

Children, however, are not concerned with trends. They gravitate naturally toward good stories such as David Wiesner's wordless *Tuesday* (1991), Kevin Henkes's tragicomic *Lilly's Purple Plastic Purse* (1996), and Tomie dePaola's poignant *The Art Lesson* (1989) in which action, plot, and character meld smoothly to a satisfying conclusion.

As the last decade of the twentieth century opened, children and adult advocates of children's books found a wide array of picture-book stories available. Nearly every topic imaginable from fantasy to realism was being produced in a wide range of styles, media, and design. From the etchings of Arthur Geisert, to the realistic paintings of Wendell Minor, the impressionistic interpretations of David Christiana, the romantic realism of Trina Schart Hyman, the expressionistic images of Chris Raschka, and the cartoon sketches of Susan Meddaugh, readers continue to have voluminous choices. To provide greater understanding of the book process, many illustrators are providing notes on the media and technique used as well as comments on why and how the book was created. It is certainly a nod to the growing recognition of illustration as an important art form.

Some illustrators are turning to the computer—working directly on screen or using software as an assist to their pens and brushes. Younger illustrators, who are growing up with the microchip, will undoubtedly make the computer a strategic tool in the picture-book world.

As publishing companies continue to merge and the corporate eye becomes ever more cognizant of profitability, quality is on the line. Merchandizing in the twenty-first century will surely be a more dominant feature, and books likely to succeed will often have a toy, a game, a movie, or television tie-in to encourage sales. Publishers, hoping for a wide market, look to past successes such as Laura Ingalls Wilder's Little House books or Marc Brown's Arthur (Aardvark) titles for heavy sales, and with the emphasis on retail markets, where people shop for the familiar, promotions like this will undoubtedly continue.

Story is what children most love, yet when surveying the current offerings, story making often seems an endangered species. Still and all, there are many authors and illustrators with the passion and ability to provide good storytelling in both written and visual form. During her 1943 Caldecott acceptance speech for *The Little House*, Virginia Lee Burton stated: "The basic things are always the most important, and good art, certainly a basic thing, impressed on young minds through the medium of children's books is without doubt one of the best possible ways of giving children a true conception of the world they live in" (Miller and Field 1957, 92). As twenty-first-century children grow up in our technologically oriented world, it will be increasingly necessary to have top-quality literature—books that will reach their hearts, their minds, and their imaginations.

References

Aardema, V. 1975. *Why mosquitoes buzz in people's ears.* Illus. L. Dillon and D. Dillon. New York: Dial.

Alcott, L. M. 1868. *Little women.* New York: Little, Brown.

Allard, H. 1985. *Miss Nelson is missing!* Illus. J. Marshall. Boston: Houghton Mifflin.

Allen, M. N. 1996. *One hundred years of children's books in America: Decade by decade.* New York: Facts On File.

Artzybasheff, B. 1937. *Seven Simeons, a Russian tale.* New York: Viking.

Bannerman, H. 1900. *The story of little black Sambo.* London: Grant Richards.

Bianco, M. W. 1926. *The velveteen rabbit.* Illus. W. Nicholson. New York: Doubleday.

Brown, M. 1961. *Once a mouse.* New York: Scribner's.

———. 1983. *Arthur's eyes.* Boston: Little, Brown.

Brown, M. W. 1939. *The noisy book.* Illus. L. Weisgard. New York: William R. Scott.

———. 1942. *The runaway bunny.* Illus. C. Hurd. New York: Harper.

———. 1947. *Goodnight moon.* Illus. C. Hurd. New York: Harper.

Bunting, E. 1990. *The wall.* Illus. R. Himler. New York: Clarion.

———. 1991. *Fly away home.* Illus. R. Himler. New York: Clarion.

———. 1994. *Smoky nights.* Illus. D. Diaz. San Diego: Harcourt.

Burnett, F. H. 1886. *Little Lord Fauntleroy.* New York: Scribner's.

Burton, V. L. 1939. *Mike Mulligan and his steam shovel.* Boston: Houghton Mifflin.

———. 1942. *The little house.* Boston: Houghton Mifflin.

———. 1943. *Katy and the big snow.* Boston: Houghton Mifflin.

———. 1952. *Maybelle the cable car.* Boston: Houghton Mifflin.

Carle, E. 1984. *The very busy spider.* New York: Crowell.

Cooney, B. 1958. *Chanticleer and the fox.* New York: Crowell.

dePaola, T. 1975. *Strega Nona.* New York: Prentice Hall.

dePaola, T. 1989. *The art lesson.* New York: G. P. Putnam's Sons.

Ehlert, L. 1989. *Color zoo.* New York: Harper.

Emberley, B. 1967. *Drummer Hoff.* Illus. E. Emberley. New York: Prentice Hall.

Ets, M. H. 1944. *In the forest.* New York: Viking.

Fish, H. D. 1937a. *Animals of the Bible.* Illus. D. Lathrop. Philadelphia: Lippincott.

———. 1937b. *Four and twenty blackbirds.* Illus. R. Lawson. New York: Stokes.

Freeman, D. 1968. *Corduroy.* New York: Viking.

Freeman, L. 1953. *The pet of the Met.* Illus. D. Freeman. New York: Viking.

Gág, W. 1928. *Millions of cats.* New York: Coward.

———. 1933. *The ABC bunny.* New York: Coward.

———. 1938. *Snow White and the seven dwarfs.* New York: Coward.

———. 1941. *Nothing at all.* New York: Coward.

Gannett, R. S. 1948. *My father's dragon.* Illus. R. C. Gannett. New York: Viking.

Gerstein, M. 1987. *Mountains of Tibet.* New York: Harper.

Goble, P. 1978. *The girl who loved wild horses.* New York: Bradbury.

Gramatky, H. 1939. *Little toot.* New York: G. P. Putnam's Sons.

Gruelle, J. 1918. *Raggedy Ann stories.* Chicago: P. F. Volland.

Hader, B., and E. Hader. 1948. *The big snow.* New York: Macmillan.

Heide, F. P. 1971. *The shrinking of Treehorn.* Illus. E. Gorey. New York: Holiday House.

Henkes, K. 1996. *Lilly's purple plastic purse.* New York: Greenwillow.

Hill, E. 1980. *Where's Spot?* New York: G. P. Putnam's Sons.

Hoban, R. 1960. *Bedtime for Frances.* Illus. G. Williams. New York: Harper.

Johnson, C. 1955. *Harold and the purple crayon.* New York: Harper.

Keats, E. J. 1962. *The snowy day.* New York: Viking.

Kellogg, S. 1984. *Paul Bunyan.* New York: Morrow.

———. 1986. *Pecos Bill.* New York: Morrow.

Krauss, R. 1945. *The carrot seed.* Illus. C. Johnson. New York: Harper.

———. 1952. *A hole is to dig: A first book of first definitions.* Illus. M. Sendak. New York: Harper.

Kunhardt, D. 1940. *Pat the bunny.* New York: Golden Books.

Lang, A. 1889. *The blue fairy book.* Illus. H. J. Ford and G. P. Jacomb Hood. London: Longmans Green.

———. 1910. *The lilac fairy book.* Illus. H. J. Ford. New York: Longmans Green.

Langstaff, J. E. 1955. *Frog went a-courtin'.* Illus. F. Rojankovsky. New York: Harcourt.

Leaf, M. 1936a. *The story of Ferdinand.* Illus. R. Lawson. New York: Viking.

———. 1936b. *Wee Gillis.* Illus. R. Lawson. New York: Viking.

Lenski, L. 1934. *The little auto.* New York: H. Z. Walck.

———. 1938. *The little airplane.* New York: H. Z. Walck.

———. 1940. *The little train.* New York: H. Z. Walck.

Lester, J. 1987. *Tales of Uncle Remus: The adventures of Brer Rabbit.* Illus. J. Pinkney. New York: Dial.

Lionni, L. 1959. *Little blue and little yellow.* New York: Ivan Obolensky.

Lobel, A. 1970. *Frog and Toad are friends.* New York: Harper.

Lowrey, J. S. 1942. *The poky little puppy.* New York: Simon & Schuster/Golden Books.

Macaulay, D. 1990. *Black and white.* Boston: Houghton Mifflin.

MacDonald, G. 1946. *The little island.* Illus. L. Weisgard. New York: Doubleday.

Marshall, J. 1972. *George and Martha.* Boston: Houghton Mifflin.

Mathis, S. B. 1975. *The hundred penny box.* Illus. L. Dillon and D. Dillon. New York: Viking.

McCloskey, R. 1941. *Make way for ducklings.* New York: Viking.

———. 1948. *Blueberries for Sal.* New York: Viking.

McDermott, G. 1974. *Arrow to the sun: A Pueblo Indian tale.* New York: Viking.

McKissack, P. 1989. *Mirandy and brother wind.* Illus. J. Pinkney. New York: Knopf.

Miles, M. 1971. *Annie and the old one.* Illus. P. Parnell. Boston: Little, Brown.

Milhous, K. 1950. *The egg tree.* New York: Scribner's.

Miller, B. E. M., and E. W. Field, eds. 1957. *Caldecott Medal books, 1938–1957.* Vol. 2. Boston: Horn Book.

Milne, A. A. 1924. *When we were very young.* Illus. E. Shepard. New York: E. P. Dutton.

Minarik, E. H. 1957. *Little bear.* Illus. M. Sendak. New York: HarperCollins.

Mosel, A. 1968. *Tikki Tikki Tembo.* Illus. B. Lent. New York: Henry Holt.

Musgrove, M. 1976. *Ashanti to Zulu: African traditions.* Illus. L. Dillon and D. Dillon. New York: Dial.

Ness, E. 1966. *Sam, Bangs & moonshine.* New York: Holt, Rinehart and Winston.

Newman, L. 1989. *Heather has two mommies.* Illus. D. Souza. Boston: Alyson Publications.

Perrault, C. 1954. *Cinderella.* Trans. and illus. Marcia Brown. New York: Scribner's.

Petersham, M. F., and M. Petersham. 1933. *The story book of clothes.* Philadelphia: John C. Winston.

Piper, W. 1930. *The little engine that could.* New York: Platt & Munk.

Potter, B. 1902. *The tale of Peter Rabbit.* London: Frederick Warne.

Prelutsky, J. 1976. *Nightmares: Poems to trouble your sleep.* Illus. A. Lobel. New York: Greenwillow.

Ransome, A. 1968. *The fool of the world and the flying ship.* Illus. U. Shulevitz. New York: Farrar, Straus & Giroux.

Raskin, E. 1966. *Nothing ever happens on my block.* New York: Atheneum.

Rey, H. A. 1941. *Curious George.* Boston: Houghton Mifflin.

Ringgold, F. 1991. *Tar beach.* New York: Crown.

Say, A. 1993. *Grandfather's journey.* Boston: Houghton Mifflin.

Scieszka, J. 1989. *The true story of the 3 little pigs! by A. Wolf.* Illus. L. Smith. New York: Viking.

Sendak, M. 1963. *Where the wild things are*. New York: Harper.

Seuss [Theodore Geisel]. 1937. *And to think that I saw it on Mulberry Street*. New York: Vanguard.

———. 1938. *The 500 hats of Bartholomew Cubbins*. New York: Vanguard.

———. 1957. *The cat in the hat*. New York: Random House.

Sewell, A. 1877. *Black Beauty: His grooms and companions*. London: Jarrold & Sons.

Shulevitz, U. 1967. *One Monday morning*. New York: Scribner's.

Sidney, M. 1881. *The five little Peppers and how they grew*. New York: Lothrop.

Silverstein, S. 1974. *Where the sidewalk ends*. New York: Harper.

Slobodkina, E. 1940. *Caps for sale*. New York: W. R. Scott.

Steig, W. 1969. *Sylvester and the magic pebble*. New York: Simon & Schuster.

Steptoe, J. 1969. *Stevie*. New York: Harper.

Thurber, J. 1943. *Many moons*. Illus. L. Slobodkin. New York: Harcourt.

Tresselt, A. 1946. *Rain drop splash*. Illus. L. Weisgard. New York: Lothrop.

———. 1947. *White snow, bright snow*. Illus. R. Duvoisin. New York: Lothrop.

Twain, M. 1876. *Adventures of Tom Sawyer*. New York: Harper.

Van Allsburg, C. 1979. *The garden of Abdul Gasazi*. Boston: Houghton Mifflin.

———. 1984. *The mysteries of Harris Burdick*. Boston: Houghton Mifflin.

———. 1990. *Just a dream*. Boston: Houghton Mifflin.

Viorst, J. 1971. *The tenth good thing about Barney*. Illus. E. Blegvad. New York: Atheneum.

Waber, B. 1965. *Lyle, Lyle crocodile*. Boston: Houghton Mifflin.

Wells, R. 2000. *Goodnight Max*. New York: Viking.

Wiesner, D. 1991. *Tuesday*. New York: Clarion.

Willhoite, M. 1990. *Daddy's roommate*. Boston: Alyson Publications.

Williams, S. A. 1992. *Working cotton*. Illus. C. Byard. San Diego, CA: Harcourt.

Yolen, J. 1987. *Owl moon*. Illus. J. Schoenherr. New York: Philomel.

Zemach, M. 1977. *It could always be worse*. New York: Farrar.

5

Once upon a While Ago

Folktales in the Course of Literature

Jane Yolen

Humans are storytelling animals. It is what distinguishes us from the other beasts. We are dreamers, too, always looking for that bit of luck, that bit of magic, that bit of courage that guarantees us the prize. Our stories reflect the human condition, and none more so than the folktales that have been an inheritance from our great-great-ever-so-many great-grandparents back to the beginning of time. We polish those stories and send them on. Stories about transformations and transportations, about miracles and mayhem, about fairy wives and demon lovers, about the gods walking about as humans and humans walking on the streets of heaven.

Now children, those great eavesdroppers, have overheard these stories for years. They remembered the ones they wanted to remember, forgot the rest. Somewhere in the nineteenth century, many of the tales began to be set down specifically in books for children. Oh, there had been chapbooks before and school books and religious books and "courtesy" books. But the great movement of children's publishing did not get its kick start in a major way until the mid-1900s.

Still, children had been coveting and keeping some of the great folk romances and legends such as King Arthur and Robin Hood and Saint George, resurrecting for their own use the sly fabliaux of Aesop and the stories of Reynard the Fox. Children had been hearing bits of the *Arabian Nights* and the *Ocean Stream of Stories* and the jokes and jests out of the mouth and from the page of the medieval storehouse of such tales.

We could call this—as John Rowe Townsend (1983) does in *Written for Children,* the "prehistory" of children's interest in folklore (18). But I believe the real interest in folktales in books for children can be dated to Andrew Lang's Colour Fairy Books, a series that began appearing in 1889 and was brought into America soon after. (I certainly date my own interest in fairy tales to the Lang Colour Fairy Books, wearing out any number of volumes with my rereading.)

Yes, before that there had been Perrault for French fairy tales, Jacob and Wilhelm Grimm for German, Asbjørnsen and Moe for Scandinavian stories, and Andersen for his own art tales. Joel Chandler Harris's Remus stories had come out in the early 1880s. There had been other collections from around the world before the Lang books. But with the *Blue Fairy Book*'s publication (Lang 1889), world folklore became an ever-expanding franchise in children's literature. I use the word *franchise* with care. It means to authorize the selling of a company's goods in a certain area. We humans are the company, folklore the goods, and the certain area, of course, is children. From Lang's time on, the bowdlerization, the tarting up, the cleaning up, the culture appropriations (some would say misappropriations) of the folktale became big business for children's books.

I thought that I would look at four different approaches to the folktale in children's literature from the last hundred years. Remember that this is a very personal critique. I come to each volume with three critical responses in mind:

1. Is it a good book for children?

2. Is it good folklore?

3. Is its teller mired in society?

The four approaches I will look at are these:

1. Collections of folktales

2. Picture books retelling a single tale

3. The art or original fairy tale

4. The novelization of a folktale

Since children's books are most often illustrated, a discussion of the illustrations will also be part of my evaluations. Pictures—good or bad—can change the way we read a book. The books I have chosen are not necessarily the best books available. But each is identifiably folklore, and each one is particular to an approach.

Folktale Collections

The *Olive Fairy Book,* edited by Andrew Lang, was first published in 1907 (thus keeping it within the hundred years we are talking about), though the only easily obtained edition these days is a Dover reprint which—alas—has seriously muddied the eight brilliantly colored H. J. Ford romantic illustrations (Lang 1968). This compendium, like all the colored fairy books before it, is chock full of folktales retold by Lang (though more often his wife is the translator and reteller) and made *suitable* for young listeners. *Suitable* means, of course, leaving in all those cultural attributes that his era valued, or changing them to something better suited. He called this "adapt[ing] to the conditions of young readers" (Lang 1968, ix). Lang's political stand on these stories is to modern sensibilities a bit to the right of Louis XIV. He speaks in the introduction of "savage and peasant fairy tales" (Lang 1968, vii), for example. And he refers to children in the way that right-thinking adults of that period did, as "little innocents" (Lang 1968, viii). Lang's approach—and one that was to be used over and over again by editors of children's folklore collections for the rest of the century—was eclectic, to say the least. The stories come from India, Armenia, Germany, France, Sudan, Denmark, Turkey. There is even a retelling of an Anatole France story.

As often happens with a collection in which all are retold by the same person, the tales have a sameness to them, whether they originated on the Indian subcontinent or Europe. They are very identifiably told by a Victorian/Edwardian British gentleman or gentlewoman. The locutions, the emphases, the pronouncements are all terribly British and colonialistic. For example, in one Punjabi story, "The Billy Goat and the King," Lang writes: "This king, I must tell you, was a Hindu; and when a Hindu eats his food, he has a nice little place on the ground freshly plastered with mud, and he sits in the middle of it with very few clothes on—which is quite a different way from ours" (Lang, 211).

The stories found in the various color fairy books often are difficult to find anywhere else. They are translated from collections no longer easily available to us: Perrault's work as found in *Le Cabinet de Fees,* Major Campbell's *Feroshepore,* Monteil's *Contes Sudanais.* The stories are certainly engagingly told. As a child I could not get enough of the Lang fairy books.

But—is this good folklore? I would call this a starting place for beginning folk story lovers. The books should all come with the following warning, however: Be ever aware of the implicit racism in many of the tales, a cultural knee jerk that comes directly from the teller of the tales.

Half a century later, Ingri and Edgar Parin D'Aulaire wrote and illustrated a volume of folklore, *Norse Gods and Giants* (1967), that set a different kind of standard for folk storytelling. Ingri was Norwegian, and the retellings in the book—according to Anita Silvey (1995), were "authenticated in the stories and experiences of Ingri's childhood in Norway" (189). In this collection, the folklore is treated as part of a larger and integrated culture, not just small cultured pearls on a strand. If the storytelling is straightforward and unadorned, it is the kind of book that a nonfiction reader might enjoy as well as a story lover. This is a book to treasure, but not to fall in love with. It is useful the way an information book is useful. It pares down the stories to their essences. After the D'Aulaires came books such as Georgess McHargue's brilliant *The Impossible People,* and the deliciously compelling Eerie series, and of course all of the wonderful Alvin Schwartz folklore books.

In 1973, one of the events of the season was the publication of *The Juniper Tree, and Other Tales from Grimm,* translated by Lore Segal with four tales translated by Randall Jarrell and stunning black-and-white pictures by Maurice Sendak (Grimm and Grimm 1973). Sendak was the darling of the New York literary scene at the time, and the two-volume boxed edition was seen as the height of smart and elegant publishing. At the time, no one questioned the appropriateness of the particular stories selected by Segal and Jarrell. It was enough that these were tales from the Grimms. I would like to suggest that the book, published in the children's book department, is really a book for adults. Or at least for young adults. In any event, teachers and parents must be reminded that simply because a tale is from folklore does not make it acceptable fare for children. In fact, a lot that comes out of the folk tradition is bawdy, anal, dirty-mouthed, extremely violent, and/or culture-specific.

The eponymous story in *The Juniper Tree* is one of those Grimm grimoire tales in which not only does a stepmother cruelly abuse her stepson, but she beheads him, blames her own daughter, then "hacked him in pieces and put the pieces in the pot and stewed him in the sour broth" (319). True, in the end the cruel stepmother gets her own, the boy magically returns, but this scarcely mitigates the horror and it is one of those stories hard to find a good reason for inflicting on a young fairy tale lover. In fact, the entire collection has an emphasis on the more difficult stories. To be fair, the collection also includes in its twenty-seven stories such popular ones as "Rapunzel," "Hansel and Gretel," and "Snow White."

In *The Juniper Tree,* the romanticism of the Lang, and the gorgeous pre-Raphaelite paintings of Ford have given way to a celebration of a quasi-troll style in both story and illustration. This is a very masculine book. Sendak's women as well as his men have a lumpen look to them. Indeed, even with breasts, the girls could be boys.

Seven years later, Alison Lurie (1980) produced a heavy shot across the bloody boy's bow with *Clever Gretchen and Other Forgotten Folktales,* the first of the feminist folktale revisionist collections. Clever herself, Lurie decided that the time was right for a book of girl heroes because, as she puts it, "the heroes seem to have all the interesting adventures. . . . As for the heroines, things just happened to them" (xi). Her fifteen stories are followed by condensed source notes, something the Segal book did not have, nor did the Lang except in a few instances. After Lurie came similar collections by Ethel Johnston Phelps, Angela Carter, and others. I must admit I have one myself called *Not One Damsel in Distress* (Yolen 2000).

Single-Tale Picture Books

Today we have a positive glut of single picture-book folktales. It's the publisher's major response to the call for multicultural literature. This is not the place to debate whether that is the best way to introduce multiculturalism in the classroom. I simply am stating the glut as fact. Once upon a time, earlier in the century, we had similar gluts. Only almost all the picture books at that time were retellings of single Grimm, Andersen, or European folktales.

Typical of the earlier books is *The Three Little Pigs, also, The Foolish Pig* (1941), part of a series of hand-sized board-covered books that Rand McNally put out in the World War II years. The author is not credited, and we have to therefore assume it was written in-house, but the creator of the cartoony illustrations, Tony Brice, is named. The bare-boned story is plainly told, and the book clearly owes much to Disney.

One of the positive changes in retold folktales has been the proliferation of cultures from which we now draw tales. At least we have broadened our horizons a bit. In 1978, Tomie dePaola took an old French saint's legend, about the juggler of Notre Dame, and retold it as *The Clown of God.* So complete is the transformation, both in the simplified yet musical text and the brilliant illustrations, that this has become the story, replacing all other tellings. DePaola has done in this storybook what Disney has done for "Snow White" and "Cinderella" and "Sleeping Beauty"—simply changed the text for all time. Yet unlike the Disneyfications, dePaola has stayed true to the core of the tale, though he has shifted much—Notre Dame in Paris to the monastery church of the Little Brothers in Sorrento, Italy, being the least of those shifts. The tale is artfully told in both words and pictures.

Gerald McDermott's 1975 Caldecott Medal for *Arrow to the Sun,* an adaptation of a Pueblo Indian legend, with its bold graphics and simplified text, certainly signaled a change in library acquisitions, at that time still the most important part of any book's sales. McDermott's use of traditional folk design was what made his book stand out. The pictures are in the flat, brilliant colors of Pueblo design. The text is more bare-boned than any tribal telling of the story, and its spareness is underlined by the san serif type McDermott employs. But all the passion in the story has been boiled away. The listener has to become involved in the story by way of the pictures, else it does not happen at all.

The same might have been said of Paul Zelinsky's sumptuous Caldecott Honor book, *Rumplestiltskin* (1986) except that he stuck close enough to the variants of the tale, shifting dialogue from one to the other when needed. Still, his artwork is so rich, with its late medieval details, that a careless reader—or a new reader—might be excused from really understanding the basic immorality of this popular old tale. Think of it: a duplicitous miller, his daughter silently complicitous in his lie, the king openly greedy for gold. Who is the central moral figure in the tale? A small, ugly man with an unpronounceable name who is a kind of moneylender—straw into gold. A little man who wants the young woman's as-yet unconceived child for some unnamed blood rites. It sounds vaguely like an anti-Semitic tale to me. Small stature, strange name, moneylender, blood rites. If you think Zelinsky hasn't guessed this, look at the big nose on his little man, look at the path that forms a cross between the castle and the dark forest where the little man lives. (Interesting enough, the English version of the story is called "Tom Tit Tot" and the devilish little creature who helps the girl is coal black!) Zelinsky tells a secondary story with his art, while he quotes a primary story with his words. He also produces full notes at the back of his book, which has now become the norm for picture-book retellings of folk material. In fact, critics now regularly mention the inclusion or exclusion of notes as part of their reviews.

Inspired by a story in a nineteenth-century book of Kaffir folktales, John Steptoe created his Caldecott Honor book, *Mufaro's Beautiful Daughters,* in 1987. Setting the story in a kind of mythological Africa—though the actual paintings used some ruins and flora and fauna from Zimbabwe—Steptoe's lush retelling actually sounds very much like a variant of the "Good Girl/Bad Girl" stories that are found throughout Europe. Still, *Mufaro* was an important book within the folk story movement because it showed a proud African family within an African setting, yet was told in a way that made it immediately accessible to American children. The book has become an African American icon, partially because of—I believe—its parallels in European folklore.

Many of the picture-book retellings of folktales are more about the art than about the story. Look at the list of Caldecott winners that are folkloric—Marcia Brown's *Cinderella* (Perrault 1954), John Langstaff and Feodor Rojankovsky's *Frog Went A-Courtin'* (1955), Nonny Hogrogian's *One Fine Day* (1971), Barbara Cooney's *Chanticleer and the Fox* (1958), Ruth Robbins and Nicholas Sidjakov's *Baboushka and the Three Kings* (1960), Marcia Brown's *Once a Mouse* (1961), Uri Shulevitz's *The Fool of the World and the Flying Ship* (Ransome 1968), Gail Haley's *A Story, a Story* (1970), Arlene Mosel and Blair Lent's *The Funny Little Woman* (1972), Paul Goble's *The Girl Who Loved Wild Horses* (1978), Verna Aardema and the Dillons' *Why Mosquitoes Buzz in People's Ears* (1975), Margot Zemach's *Duffy and the Devil* (1973), Margaret Hodges and Trina Schart Hyman's *Saint George and the Dragon* (1984), Ed Young's *Lon Po Po* (1989), Paul Zelinsky's *Rapunzel* (1997), and David Wisniewski's *Golem* (1996). The best of the books are actually less about cultural differences and more about the stories that bind us one to another. But I'm tempted to add that if an illustrator wants to win the Caldecott, he or she has a better chance by using folklore.

Art Folktales

This is a category that Professor Alan Dundes, the grand master of folklore, calls "fakelore": stories that look and smell and feel like folklore but come from an author's fertile imagination. The earliest master of this was clearly Hans Christian Andersen. Not a publishing season goes by without a story of his being newly released with pictures by the most popular illustrators of the day. Though I must mention that a few years ago a Marianne Mayer retelling of *The Ugly Duckling* (1987) was brought out without Andersen's name on either the jacket or the title page. How quickly art becomes folk.

Other early art fairy story creators include George Macdonald's "The Light Princess" and "The Golden Key," Oscar Wilde's "The Happy Prince" and "The Selfish Giant," Carl Sandberg's *Rootabaga Stories,* Frank Stockton's "The Bee Man of Orn" and "The Lady, or the Tiger?" and Howard Pyle's *King Stork.*

At the end of the nineteenth century and well into the beginning of the twentieth there was a great vogue for chinoiserie. Some of what passed for Orientalia was real. Much was—like the "Mikado"—as fakelore as all get-out.

Jay Williams's *Everyone Knows What a Dragon Looks Like* (1976) is a puzzle to me. When I first read it back in the seventies, I enjoyed its sassy humor, its moral center. I liked the fact that it is the child who bests the great men of the kingdom with his humble courtesy to the fat old man. But now I read the book with a thorn in my critical shoe. Is this Orientalia? Is it true to the culture even though it is not *of* the culture? Are the illustrations by Mercer Mayer comically satirical, or are they offensive? I remember when I wrote *The Emperor and the Kite* (1967), how the illustrator, Ed Young, who is Chinese, vetted the story for me. He helped me name the characters when the Maoist printer down the block couldn't give me the proper answers.

As we enter the twenty-first century, a new question emerges for folktale readers: do we use the same critical checklist for stories from the imagination as we now seem to do for retold folktales? Even as I ask myself these questions, I wonder if I am overinflating the critical response, bending to the will of cultural knee-jerkism. It is one of the problems with being a liberal.

Aesopian fables are always being reillustrated and retold. But there hadn't been a new fabler in some time. We count among the great fablers Phadrus of first-century Greece, Pilpay in India in the fourth century, the *Gesta Romanorum* in fourteenth century, ninth-century Sanskrit fables from the Hitopadesha, Jean La Fontaine in the seventeenth century, Jonathan Swift in the eighteenth century, Leo Tolstoy in the early nineteenth century, and others such as Ambrose Bierce and Oscar Wilde. In the twentieth century, James Thurber certainly turned his hand at fables, but for adults, really.

Then along came Arnold Lobel in 1980 with his witty *Fables* (1980) that won the Caldecott and—if rumor is correct—almost won the Newbery as well. Like Aesop and La Fontaine and the others, Lobel uses animal characters to tell his pithy stories and point to the moral at the end. But these are tales particularly created for young readers. And one can't help believing that Lobel was talking about his own creative vision in the story "The Camel Dances" in which a camel is not discouraged by the critics in the audience who call her "lumpy, humpy . . . baggy and bumpy" (22), but continues to dance just for herself.

Folktale Novels

Another use of folk material especially notable in the twentieth century has been the folktale novel. Yes, back at the beginning of the century, we started with L. Frank Baum's *The Wonderful Wizard of Oz* (1900). But even though it often has been called an American fairy tale, it is really a fantasy novel and wholly original, though it has since spawned its own group of fairy-story novel spin-offs, including Gregory Maguire's brilliant *Wicked: The Life and Times of the Wicked Witch of the West* (1995).

But I mean books like Eleanor Farjeon's classic 1955 Cinderella novel *The Glass Slipper* and Robin McKinley's 1978 besotting *Beauty,* Diana Wynne Jones's brilliant 1985 Tam Lin transformation *Fire and Hemlock,* Shirley Rousseau Murphy's engaging 1977 *Silver Woven in My Hair* redaction of Cinderella, and Elizabeth Marie Pope's astonishing *The Perilous Gard* (1974) retelling of Tam Lin. In these books fairy tale and narrative are woven seamlessly together, but instead of the normal fairy-tale character with one or two recognizable traits and no growth potential, we get well-rounded characters living through the magic and learning from it. Like all good fiction for young readers, these books are about the getting of wisdom, and the authors have discovered in the simple tales at their novels' cores even more than we normally find there.

Future of Folktales

Where will the folk traditions go in the twenty-first century? Onto the Internet, certainly. They are already there, on many Web sites devoted to such stories from all around the world.[1] There will continue to be many more individual picture books and thematic collections of stories, whether those themes are by country or by category. I am part of the expected spate, with thematic collections coming out featuring cat stories, mother-and-daughter stories, as well as retellings or transformations of *Baba Yaga, Firebird,* and others.

The fractured fairy tale, which James Thurber may have originated but which Jon Scieszka with *The Stinky Cheese Man and Other Fairly Stupid Tales* (1992) certainly helped speed on its way, will continue to be produced.

Look for fairy-tale poems, fairy-tale movie scripts, and more wrangling over the parallel cultures debate, with such phrases as "cultural misappropriation" and "exclusive memories" thrown in for good measure.

As for me, I will continue to read and write without and within the folktale culture. Because, in the end, it is the good story that calls to us, mouth to ear; it is the good story that demands our attention, page to eye; it is the good story that competes successfully for our dollars and our hearts. It will be in the future, what it was: Once upon a time . . .

I want to end with a poem of mine, which first appeared in the magazine *Marvels and Tales: Journal of Fairy-Tale Studies.*

Marchen
Wilhelm Grimm loved words,
not stories,
they waterfalled from his pen.
He was deaf to the telling,
only the told.
Words like *camphor,*
goblet, *ruby*, *anvil*
waxed and waned in him.
He was tidal
with words.
I, on the other hand,
drink in tales,
giving them out again
in mouth-to-ear
resuscitation.
It does not matter
if the matter of the stories
is the coast of Eire
or the Inland Sea,
I swim—ah—ever deeper in them.

"Marchen" © 1994 by Jane Yolen. Used with permission of the author.
First published in *Marvel & Tales* (1994, v. 8).

Note

1.   Some sources of interest on the Internet are as follows:

teacher.scholastic.com/fieldtrp/childlit/folk.htm
www.langlab.wayne.edu/MarvelsHome/links.html
www.surlalunefairytales.com/

References

Aardema, V. 1975. *Why mosquitoes buzz in people's ears.* Illus. L. Dillon and D. Dillon. New York: Dial.

Baum, L. F. 1900. *The wonderful wizard of Oz.* Illus. W. W. Denslow. Chicago: G. M. Hill.

Brice, T. Illust. 1941. *Three little pigs.* Also *The foolish pig.* Chicago: Rand McNally.

Brown, M. 1961. *Once a mouse.* New York: Scribner's.

Cooney, B. 1958. *Chanticleer and the fox.* New York: Crowell.

D'Aulaire, I., and E. P. D'Aulaire. 1967. *Norse gods and giants.* Garden City, NY: Doubleday.

dePaola, T. 1978. *The clown of God: An old story.* New York: Harcourt Brace Jovanovich.

Farjeon, E. 1955. *The glass slipper.* Illus. E. H. Shepard. New York: Viking.

Goble, P. 1978. *The girl who loved wild horses.* New York: Bradbury.

Grimm, J., and W. Grimm. 1973. *The juniper tree, and other tales from Grimm.* Trans. L. G. Segal and R. Jarrell and illus. M. Sendak. New York: Farrar, Straus and Giroux.

Haley, G. E. 1970. *A story, a story; An African tale.* New York: Atheneum.

Hodges, M. 1984. *Saint George and the dragon: A golden legend.* Illus. T. S. Hyman. Boston: Little, Brown.

Hogrogian, N. 1971. *One fine day.* New York: Macmillan.

———, ed. 1889. *The blue fairy book.* Illus. H. J. Ford and G. P. Jacomb Hood. London: Longmans, Green.

Lang, A., ed. 1907. *The olive fairy book.* Illus. H. J. Ford. New York: Longmans, Green.

———, ed. 1968. *The olive fairy book.* Illus. H. J. Ford. New York: Dover.

Langstaff, J. E. 1955. *Frog went a-courtin'.* Illus. F. Rojankovsky. New York: Harcourt.

Lobel, A. 1980. *Fables.* New York: Harper & Row.

Lurie, A. 1980. *Clever Gretchen and other forgotten folktales.* Illus. M. Tomes. New York: Crowell.

Maguire, G. 1995. *Wicked: The life and times of the wicked witch of the west.* New York: Regan Books.

Mayer, M. 1987. *The ugly duckling.* Illus. T. Locker. New York: Macmillan.

McDermott, G. 1974. *Arrow to the sun: A Pueblo Indian tale.* New York: Viking.

McKinley, R. 1978. *Beauty: A retelling of the story of Beauty & the beast.* New York: Harper & Row.

Mosel, A. 1972. *The funny little woman.* Illus. B. Lent. New York: E. P. Dutton.

Murphy, S. R. 1977. *Silver woven in my hair.* Illus. A. Tiegreen. New York: Atheneum.

Perrault, C. 1954. *Cinderella, or the little glass slipper.* Illus. M. Brown. New York: Scribner's.

Pope, E. M. 1974. *The perilous gard.* Illus. R. Cuffari. Boston: Houghton Mifflin.

Ransome, A. 1968. *The fool of the world and the flying ship: A Russian tale.* Illus. U. Shulevitz. New York: Farrar, Straus and Giroux.

Robbins, R. 1960. *Baboushka and the three kings.* Illus. N. Sidjakov. Berkeley, CA: Parnassus Press.

Scieszka, J. 1992. *The Stinky Cheese Man and other fairly stupid tales.* Illus. L. Smith. New York: Viking.

Silvey, A., ed. 1995. *Children's books and their creators.* Boston: Houghton Mifflin.

Steptoe, J. 1987. *Mufaro's beautiful daughters: An African tale.* New York: Lothrop, Lee & Shepard.

The Three little pigs, also, The foolish pig. 1941. Illus. T. Brice. Chicago: Rand McNally.

Townsend, J. R. 1983. *Written for children: An outline of English-language children's literature.* New York: Lippincott.

Williams, J. 1976. *Everyone knows what a dragon looks like.* Illus. M. Mayer. New York: Four Winds Press.

Wisniewski, D. 1996. *Golem.* New York: Clarion.

Wynne Jones, D. 1985. *Fire and hemlock.* New York: Greenwillow.

Yolen, J. 1967. *The emperor and the kite.* Illus. E. Young. New York: World.

————. 1994. Marchen. In *Marvels and Tales: Journal of Fairy Studies.* Detroit: Wayne State Press.

————. 2000. *Not one damsel in distress: World folktales for strong girls.* Illus. S. Guevara. San Diego: Silver Whistle/Harcourt Brace.

Young, E. 1989. *Lon Po Po: A Red-Riding Hood story from China.* New York: Philomel.

Zelinsky, P. O. 1986. *Rumplestiltskin.* New York: E. P. Dutton.

————. 1997. *Rapunzel.* New York: Dutton Children's Books.

Zemach, H. 1973. *Duffy and the devil: A Cornish tale retold.* Illus. M. Zemach. New York: Farrar, Straus and Giroux.

6

What Tales Do We Tell of the Twentieth Century?

Folktales and Fairy Tales Prosper

James F. Cipielewski

The world of folktales and fairy tales for children flourishes at the beginning of the twenty-first century in the United States, although its form has continued to evolve over the course of the past century. It has grown from the roots and seeds of the wonderful collections of Andrew Lang, Joseph Jacobs, and Howard Pyle, among others, into inventive single-tale picture books illustrated by award-winning artists such as Marcia Brown, Jerry Pinkney, and Ed Young. Anthologies of tales continue to be retold for children as well as for literary collections written for academic purposes. And, over the course of the past century, scholars such as Carl Jung, Bruno Bettelheim, J. R. R. Tolkien, and Jane Yolen have written a multitude of books and essays aimed at helping those working with children understand the importance and impact of folk and fairy.

Several themes emerge as we look back over the twentieth century. One issue that is of interest more to students of folklore rather than teachers and readers is what differentiates a folktale from a literary fairy tale. How can we recognize which is which? More important, how does it matter for the student of children's literature? Another point to be explored is how folktales and fairy tales have continued to flourish around the world, how they have spread beyond their own borders and crossed back and forth from speech to print and back again. Third, collections of tales based on cultural roots have flourished with the growing educational emphasis on authentic literature and studies of other cultures. Fourth, the production of parodies of folktales and fairy tales begun in the nineteenth century has continued and accelerated. Fifth, there has been a proliferation of tall tales that represents the American spirit. These humorous exaggerations have assumed a firm place in our libraries and schools. Finally, wonderfully illustrated retellings of individual tales, nearly nonexistent at the onset of the twentieth century, are now ubiquitous.

Folktale? Fairy Tale? What's the Difference?

Most people do not spend much time or energy trying to integrate and differentiate the similarities and differences between literary works, traditional folktales, fairy tales, and literary fairy tales. To most readers, all of them are literary works and the differences that scholars point to mean little or nothing. Yet there are many people who study folk literature and fairy tales to whom these differences matter a great deal. It is necessary to realize that many people are interested in folktales from varying viewpoints. Anthropologists, linguists, folklorists, among others, collect and compare folklore and folktales to determine cultural beliefs and histories and possible relationships with other cultures. They are most interested in determining whether a tale or a practice is indigenous to a particular culture and what it might tell us about that culture. In most cases, these practices and narratives would be transmitted from one generation to the next orally. As a result, most traditional literature has come to be defined as that which has originated and been handed down in the oral domain—one teller to another. Many of these tales are recognizable. There are "noodlehead" tales such as "Lazy Jack"; trickster tales such as "Sheer Crops"; patterned stories such as "The Gingerbread Man"; realistic tales such as "Dick Whittington and His Cat"; *pourquoi* tales such as "Why the Sea Is Salt"; and the fairy tale or *Märchen* such as "The Frog King." These stories may be theoretically traced back to oral retellings that were then collected by nineteenth-century folklorists such as the Brothers Grimm, Joseph Jacobs, and others.

On the other hand, scholars generally define literary fairy tales as those having a form similar to those of the wonder tales or *Märchen,* but attributed to a recognizable author. The most famous of the literary fairy tales are those of Hans Christian Andersen such as "The Little Mermaid" and "The Princess and the Pea." An important modern author in this genre, and also a contributor to this book—Jane Yolen—has made this form her forte. Now this seems quite simple—if it has a recognizable author, it is a literary fairy tale; if it does not and has been handed down orally, it's a traditional fairy tale. Oh, if only life and literature were that simple. What happens to those tales that seem to have originated in the oral tradition but then were written down? Storytellers read them and later told new listeners their own versions, again taking them back into the oral tradition. Are they now literary fairy tales or folktales? This may seem a rare occurrence, but some suggest that many of our best-loved tales have followed this path.

Jack Zipes (2000) suggests that the *contes de fées* written in France by such notables as Charles Perrault and Madame d'Aulnoy (who "wrote" stories such as "Cinderella" and "The Beauty and the Beast") were quickly taken over by the *Bibliothèque Bleue* and chapbooks and widely distributed across France and then into other countries.

These tales were often read aloud and made their way into or back into the oral tradition. Interestingly, the tales were retold innumerable times and circulated throughout diverse regions of Europe, often leading to some other literary appropriation and publication. In addition, there were numerous translations into English, German, Spanish and Italian. (Zipes 2000, xxiii)

Does this mean that tales later collected by such people as the Grimms or Peter Christen Asbjørnsen and Jørgen Moe were really remnants of those earlier written tales? Or were they authentic to the time and place they were discovered and written? These are controversies that are best left to the folklorists. Most critics understand and the Grimms were clear that they used written as well as oral sources. "The Grimms never made a secret of their data-compiling methods, which exploited both literary and oral sources" (Dégh 1991, 69; see also Kamenetsky 1992).

Perhaps for the scholars of children's literature it is sufficient to understand the background by which the tales originated and to be able to distinguish the major groupings within the tales such as cumulative tales, trickster tales, *pourquoi* tales, and so on. As for fairy tales, we may be best served by adopting Jane Yolen's (1986) classification.

Francis James Child, collector of the Child ballads (and himself not above aiding the process), once suggested that the tradition is abetted by one of three different kinds of tellers: The blind singer, the nurserymaid, and the clerk. The blind beggar sings for his supper and so is constrained to change his story to suit the listening audience, the better to be paid for his tales. The nurserymaid changes stories to suit what she assumes are the appetites and moral needs of her young charges. And the clerk is the literary teller, writing down stories that suit the needs of an audience of one, the self. (5–6)

As Yolen says, the "blind singer" and the "nurserymaid" are the sources that most of us acknowledge in collecting folktales and fairy tales. However, it is often the "clerk" who has made an impact on the fairy tales we most often share with children. The stories that have been popular with adults and children come from the "clerkish" pens of Mme. Le Prince de Beaumont, Hans Christian Andersen, and Isaac Bashevis Singer. "Such stories owe their settings, their archetypal characters, even bits of their magic to the past, but thematically they draw upon the century and the place in which they are written" (Yolen 1986). As true artists of the pen, these clerks bring their literary talents to these stories, taking the stuff of fairy and using their craft to create compelling tales.

So, it is up to us as scholars in children's literature to understand the roots of folktales and fairy tales and to understand that traditional literature contains many forms, not just the fairy tale. We should also understand the rise of the literary fairy tale, the art tale, from the bones of the traditional tale. Importantly, we should be aware of and perhaps celebrate the continuing movement back and forth between the oral and the written, which has been the path for many of our best-loved fairy tales.

Folktales and Fairy Tales: Citizens of the World

Although the purpose of this book is to look at what has happened to children's literature in the twentieth century, it is difficult to look at folktales and fairy tales from such a limited perspective. Folktales and fairy tales published and read in the United States have their origins around the world. This is certainly not a new phenomenon, having been true of the nineteenth century as well. In fact, many American books originated in Great Britain prior to the development of a resident community of children's authors and illustrators as well as high-quality printing processes. However, as the twentieth century progressed, the United States produced its own great authors and illustrators, a well-developed publishing industry, and a system of libraries and schools eager to purchase and use high-quality books. Now the United States could choose the best of all the books written in English, both from home and abroad. The century began with L. Frank Baum and W. W. Denslow's *The Wonderful Wizard of Oz* (1900), an all-American fairy tale. But it has not been an all-American century when it comes to folktales and fairy tales.

Fairy tales had been somewhat suspect as suitable reading for children. As Bottigheimer (1996) puts it: "Fairy books remained conspicuously absent [prior to the twentieth century] from children's reading, because American intellectuals, and especially the teachers among them, rejected their magic as contradictory to the enlightened rationalism that underlay and guided American political thought" (160). Kamenetsky (1992) suggests that during the second half of the nineteenth century: "Parents and educators preferred that their children read informational and didactic books while shunning folktales, fantasies, and tales of adventure, which they considered not only a distraction from what was useful and practical but also a source of moral corruption" (231–232). While this sentiment lingered on (see Wheeler 1929, "The Psychological Case against the Fairy Tale"), how did folktales and fairy tales go from being such a small, disreputable part of literature for children to becoming part of every child's life both at home and school?

I think that the advent of professional children's librarians and, with them, the children's story hour contributed immensely to the acceptance of folktales and fairy tales. Betsy Hearne (2000) in her recent essay on Ruth Sawyer points out that Sawyer represents a strong link between the oral tradition and the world of literacy. Ruth Sawyer was educated as both a teacher and as a folklorist. She was working as a professional storyteller for the New York Public Lecture Bureau in 1908 after having spent time at the Garland Kindergarten Training School, collecting and telling stories in Cuba, attending Columbia University, and graduating from Teachers College in 1904 (Helbig 1988). Those first storytelling sessions were often for adult audiences as well as children. In *Way of the Storyteller,* Sawyer (1976) recounts telling stories at the Five Points Mission in one of the worst sections of New York City. "The hall was crowded with sailors, longshoremen, draymen and bums. Some of them slept, many were drunk; more were in that heavy stupor which overtakes human beings exhausted by hard work, over-full of food and drink, coming to rest in a hot room" (88).

But there, Sawyer found her voice and found a confidence in story, too, as one of the men responded: "[He] shook his sleeping neighbor and shouted for the whole hall to hear: 'Wake up, man! You're missing the night of your blasted life' " (89). At around that time, 1908, Ann Carol Moore was initiating the first story hour at the New York Public Library, and Sawyer was intimately involved in its infancy (Hearne 2000; Helbig 1988). And this was certainly a great beginning with similar happenings across many libraries. Moore was one of many women who championed the cause of folklore and children's literature. As Hearne (2000) points out, many of them are now forgotten:

Marie Shedlock, Sara Cone Bryant, Güdrun Thorne-Thompsen, Anna Cogswell Tyler, Mary Gould Davis, Eileen Colwell, Ruth Toose, Augusta Baker and others. . . . These women linked folklore and children's literature both literally and figuratively. They told folktales, myths, and legends in library settings while other women waited in the wings with books that would allow children to read the same stories in print. (281)

The librarians never seemed to relent in their love of folktales and fairy tales. They may have not liked them all, or even most famously, *The Wonderful Wizard of Oz,* but they definitely preserved and made them available to their charges, the youth of America. The *Children's Catalog* is a compilation of suggested titles for children's libraries, updated every five years from lists of books suggested by librarians. A quick survey of the *Children's Catalog* (Andrews 1936; Bacon 1918; Dill 1976; Giles, Cook, and West 1946; McConnell and West 1956; Potter 1909; Shor and Fidell 1966) over the first seventy-five years of its publication demonstrates the staying power of traditional literature and fairy tales, at least in the eyes of the people most responsible for evaluating and acquiring books for children, children's and school librarians. (See Table 6.1.) The fact that the proportion of traditional and literary fairy tales remained so constant throughout the century speaks to the important role these tales had in children's literature.

Table 6.1
Proportion of Traditional and Literary Fair Tales in the *Children's Catalog*

Type of Book	1909	1918	1936	1946	1956	1966	1976
Fable	15	19	15	10	10	20	31
Fairy tale	152	121	386	189	218	243	236
Folklore	94	107	2	224	148	217	330
Legend	25	34	28	65	29	28	53
Myth (mythology)	53	82	79	43	25	32	41
Total titles included per year	~3,000	~3,500	~4,000	~4,200	~3,204	~4,274	~5,415
Percentage of total titles	11.3	10.4	12.7	12.6	13.4	12.6	12.7

Finding Our Cultural Roots

As the twentieth century progressed, folktales and fairy tales became a staple of children's books both in school and at home. However, there was little or no emphasis placed on where the stories originated or what source material had been used for the retelling. There were collections of Native American or Chinese stories, but there was little explanation of the original sources or how faithfully the tales had been retold. At the same time, these stories were providing a view for American children that there was a world outside their own. (The problems with some of these views are discussed elsewhere in this book.) Just as Ruth Sawyer and her counterparts had provided stories familiar to the immigrant children in the cities, there were books making stories from other countries available to those same immigrants. But it was not just immigrant children listening and reading those stories, but all the children assembled.

Just as Andrew Lang's stories from around the world in his colored fairy books were loved by all children, so, too, these new stories and collections reached a new audience. As we move through the century we see great collections for the adult reader with the Pantheon editions, formatted by country or culture. We also find a multitude of collections for children that come from every continent. The series Favorite Fairy Tales Told In . . . (Haviland 1959a, 1959b, 1961a, 1961b, 1963a, 1963b, 1963c, 1965, 1966a, 1966b, 1967, 1970, 1971, 1973; Haviland and Asbjørnsen 1961) included retellings of folktales from sixteen countries. We also have books such as *Tisza Tales* (Schwimmer 1928) that are Hungarian tales, *Tales of a Finnish Tupa* (Bowman and Bianco 1936), and *Czechoslovak Tales* (Fillmore 1919).

Jack Zipes (1988) suggests that there is now a "canon of 'classical' fairy tales for children: *Cinderella, Little Red Riding Hood, The Frog Prince, Jack and the Beanstalk, The Ugly Duckling, Beauty and the Beast, Rumpelstiltskin, Sleeping Beauty, Bluebeard, Hansel and Gretel, Rapunzel, etc.*" (24). This is a result of the tales being a "staple of education." If Zipes is correct, is it possible to predict that more Asian, African, Latin American, and Native American tales will become part of that canon as schools continue to stress multicultural education using folktales as a the primary vehicle?

When we look across the shelves of folktales and fairy tales in our libraries, schools, and homes, what we should see is a collection that displays the wonders of diversity and sameness across cultures. Certainly, this is the one area in a book about twentieth-century children's literature in America that should celebrate diversity and the fact that we are not limited or restricted to those tales that are "home grown." Here is where we want to celebrate the world, and, in the twentieth century, America's children were able to do that. Though there have been inroads, the literature remains primarily dominated by European tales. We need to have a better representation of all cultures presented in authentic ways.

Fairy-Tale Parodies and Revisions

Certainly, the nineteenth century produced one of the greatest parodies of a fairy tale, *Alice's Adventures in Wonderland* by Lewis Carroll (1865). The twentieth century opened with Baum's attempt to write a fairy tale for American boys and girls that moved away from the European tales of earlier years. Hearn (Baum and Hearn, 2000) states the following in his introduction:

The old-time fairy tale, having served for generations, may now be classed as "historical" in the children's library; for the time has come for a series of newer "wonder tales" in which the stereotyped genie, dwarf and fairy are eliminated, together with all the horrible and blood curdling incidents devised by their authors to point a fearsome moral to each tale. Modern education includes morality; therefore the modern child seeks only entertainment in its wonder-tales and gladly dispenses with all disagreeable incident.

Having this thought in mind, the story of *The Wonderful Wizard of Oz* was written solely to pleasure children of today. It aspires to begin a modernized fairy tale, in which the wonderment and joy are retained and the heart-aches and nightmares are left out (4).

Hearn (2001) declares that

Baum's introduction was a manifesto for the new century, demanding the liberation of American children's books from the domination of European juvenile literature. Just as the Brothers Grimm a century before called for the overthrow of the French influence on German literature, Baum suggested replacing Grimm and Andersen. (16–17)

Regardless of Baum's intentions, the Oz books and their ilk did not replace the European fairy tale nor those of any other country. The Oz books and their companions did, however, maintain a tradition of using fairy-tale elements in new ways to create new and exciting tales. As Leland Jacobs (personal communication 1984) tells it, all authors and storytellers draw from the same well of story. Each dips his or her bucket down and draws up a bit of the water. The new story that emerges contains elements that are the same but still different from all the other tales. The stories are intimately linked and yet still all individual. Certainly, the best authors of literary fairy tales have accomplished this. We can see the traditional roots, similar motifs, and yet unique stories.

The twentieth century brought us great stories based on familiar (and sometimes not-so-familiar) tales, but stories that stand on their own merits. Gail Carson Levine's Newbery Honor book, *Ella Enchanted* (1997), is a wonderful retelling of "Cinderella." It explains in novel format how Ella is under a spell to obey every command, including those of her enemies. The novel-length retellings of "The Frog Prince," "Hansel and Gretel," and "Rapunzel" by Donna Jo Napoli use a common device of changing the point of view. The *Prince of the Pond* (Napoli 1992) is narrated by a female frog who becomes the enchanted prince's mate rather than acting as the traditional detached third-person voice; she is in awe of the unfroglike things the prince wants to do, such as protect his mate and children. In *The Magic Circle* (1993), Napoli explains how a healer who uses white magic is trapped and forced to turn to the powers of evil. As a witch, she hides in the middle of the forest where she has gone to keep herself from harming children, but she waits in a cottage clearly designed to attract children. And, finally, in *Zel* (Napoli 1996) we learn how Rapunzel has been hidden away in a tower by her adopted witch/mother supposedly to protect her from evil. In fact, the witch/mother is trying to keep Rapunzel from finding out about the world and men so that mother and daughter will never be separated. These wonderful retellings allow us to explore the ideas of the tales, to look beneath the surface and try on differing explanations for why things are the way they are, and to investigate why people act as they do.

Moving toward the young adult and even the adult audience, Robin McKinley first retold "The Beauty and the Beast" for a teen audience (McKinley 1978) and then almost twenty years later explored the sisters' motives in *Rose Daughter* (McKinley 1997). Jane Yolen (1992) has used the art tale as an extended metaphor for a grandmother's Holocaust experience in *Briar Rose*. Ellen Datlow and Terri Windling have edited anthologies of short stories such as *A Wolf at the Door* (2000) and *Snow White, Blood Red* (1993). These stories capitalize on alternative viewpoints and character motives.

The twentieth century witnessed more than just novel points of view. Authors also created new literary fantasies that incorporated younger children's favorite characters in novel ways. For example, *The Jolly Postman* (Ahlberg and Ahlberg 1986) and *Ten in a Bed* (Ahlberg 1990) depict familiar characters from tales such as "The Three Bears," "Jack and the Beanstalk," "Sleeping Beauty," and so on. *The Jolly Postman,* intended for a younger audience, allows readers to follow a postman who delivers invitations to favorite fairy-tale characters. The book includes envelopes on each page that contain letters to each of the fairy-tale characters. *Ten in a Bed* is a bit more sophisticated. The main character Dinah Price discovers a fairy-tale character in her bed each time she tries to go to sleep, so she must find ways to outwit them and get them out of her bed. Other books have followed the format of using familiar characters in unfamiliar settings.

Certainly, one of the most popular categories of fairy-tale variants is the parody—stories that take a familiar plot and change it radically through point-of-view or character role reversal. *The True Story of the 3 Little Pigs* by Jon Scieszka (1989) led the way. Scieszka's version is quite similar to the emphasized alternate point of view mentioned earlier (such as Donna Jo Napoli's), but his tale variant is written to emphasize the exaggerated humor and surprise. Michael Emberley's (1990) "Little Red Riding Hood" variant *Ruby* features a smart-mouthed rat-girl named Ruby as the protagonist and a suave cat-stranger stalking her, and a mastiff replaces the woodsman. Fiona French (1986) in *Snow White in New York* brings us a great retelling of the traditional Snow White tale. Instead of the generic woods and castle, French's version is set in the Roaring Twenties. The evil stepmother becomes the "Queen of the Underworld." Similarly, there are many tales moved to new settings; for example, *The Three Javelinas* (Lowell 1992), set in the Southwest, and *Little Red Riding Hood: A Newfangled Prairie Tale* (Ernst 1995). Of course, Andersen's tales have not been spared with parodies such as *The Cowboy and the Black-Eyed Pea* (Johnston 1992) and *The Principal's New Clothes* (Calmenson 1989).

Last but not least, we have new tales that present an author's concept of how things should have been. This is best epitomized by Diane Stanley's *Rumpelstiltskin's Daughter* (1997). In this sequel to "Rumpelstiltskin," the miller's daughter, Meredith, decides to marry Rumpelstiltskin instead of the king who was willing to kill her if she didn't perform as expected. Then, true to the comedic rebirth so typical of good fairy tales, Meredith manages to transform the kingdom by manipulating the king into becoming a beneficent monarch in deed if not disposition. Another original fantasy dependent on a familiar tale is Raymond Briggs's *Jim and the Beanstalk* (1989). Jim visits the original giant's son and rejuvenates him by procuring glasses so that he can read his poetry books, a wig so he looks and feels years younger, and new teeth. In fact, the giant feels so good, he warns Jim that he might like "three fried boys on a slice of toast" just like the old days.

Tall Tales—An American Form?

A controversial form of folk literature that seems to epitomize the American character during the twentieth century is the tall tale. The tall-tale form existed earlier, especially in Davy Crockett's writings and later in the almanacs published using his name. But the twentieth century witnessed a flowering of this type of literature, first directed at adults and then at children. There is some question as to whether tall tales are truly folklore or rather "fakelore" as designated by Richard Dorson (1973). Regardless of their categorization, these tales seem to celebrate the American spirit and the American worker. As Dorson (1973) puts it,

> Folklore, now for the first time deliberately collected from taletellers and ballad singers, depicts Economic Man in a series of occupations connected with outdoor industries of the period: cattle raising, coal mining, white-pine lumbering, oil drilling, railroading. In the early days of these industries, before the streamlining of modern technology, the strength, skill and courage of the individual worker counted for more than machine tools, and cycles of folk narratives and folksongs recall homely and heroic incidents of men at work in the forests, on the prairies and underground. The legendary type to emerge from these occupational lores is the master workman, an updated version of Davy Crockett, still a commoner and a mighty fellow but not the eccentric nor the braggart, rather a laconic, no-nonsense figure dedicated to his work, a proud and independent wage earner. He is the cowboy, the lumberjack, the miner, the driller, the engineer. (5)

Or, as Amy Cohn (1993) says by way of introduction to her section on tall tales, "Building America was a colossal undertaking, and it took some larger-than-life characters to do the job" (271). Both authors emphasize the size and the character of the subjects of their tales. These tales were about men and women, uncommon in size, but common to the ideals of America. Richard Dorson (1952) makes a case that tall tales were not uniquely American: "The 'tall tales' usually ascribed to the American genius turn up on the lips of many European storytellers. Peasant folk heroes, like Jussi the Finnish crofter or Janosek the Hungarian outlaw, perform rogueries and escapades very much like Davy Crockett and Jesse James" (10). Others make the case that, if not unique, tall tales may be typical. Carolyn Brown (1987) reports on the types and motifs collected in the United States and England with the following results:

> In the United States the tall tale has flourished in both folklore and folklore collecting. By 1966, when Ernest Baughman compiled his *Type and Motif-Index of the Folktales of England and North America*, more than half of the types and motifs collected in America were humorous, and most of these (3,710 out of a total of 3,871) were tall tales. Among the 3,966 tales collected in England and Lowland Scotland, only twenty-nine were tall tales. (12)

This would seem an overwhelming indication that tall tales are a much larger part of American folklore than in other English-speaking countries.

The issue of whether these tales really belong to folklore is perhaps beyond the scope of a chapter on children's folktales and fairy tales. For the most part, tales of Paul Bunyan, Pecos Bill, Sally Ann Thunder Ann Whirlwind Crockett have been adopted as children's fare and are included in most textbooks under traditional literature. I would go so far as to suggest that just as the work of the early French authors of the *contes de fées* saw their work appropriated by the folk and heard the tales being told rather than read, much the same has happened to the "common" tall tales. They've taken on a life of their own as various tellers have retold, altered, added bits from earlier tales, and made these new works that have entered into the folklore of the country.

Aside from the dispute about authenticity, we are blessed with a wonderful array of tall tales, whether traditional or literary. There is a terrific body of American tall tales in children's literature, most of which were sanitized and popularized during the twentieth century. Many of us were introduced to Paul Bunyan by Glen Rounds in *Ol' Paul, the Mighty Logger* (1936), or perhaps by Louis Untermeyer's *The Wonderful Adventures of Paul Bunyan* (1945). Others may have found James Cloyd Bowman's (1937) *Pecos Bill, the Greatest Cowboy of All Time*. One of my favorite anthologies was Adrien Stoutenburg's *American Tall Tales* (1966), which contains familiar as well as unfamiliar tales, such as the one about Joe Mararac, the Hungarian steelworker. Another that I discovered from folk song before I read the book was *John Henry, an American Legend* by Ezra Jack Keats (1965). Today we have a magnificent retelling of *John Henry* by Julius Lester (1994). All of these stories had common elements—giants with the touch of the common man, outwitting, out-battling the forces of nature and industry to build America. At the same time, the characters were imbued with humor, a humor that was told as matter-of-factly as I might tell you about my day at the office.

Currently, we have a veritable explosion of tall tales, some rooted in folklore and some whose roots are in authors' imaginations. We've had series of tall-tale books by Ariane Dewey; for instance, *Gib Morgan, Oilman* (1987), *Febold Feboldson* (1984), *Pecos Bill* (1983), and her illustrations for Caron Lee Cohen's *Sally Ann Thunder Ann Whirlwind Crockett* (1985). Steven Kellogg has certainly left his mark on the tall tales he has retold and illustrated: *Paul Bunyan* (1984), *Pecos Bill* (1986), *Johnny Appleseed* (1988), *Mike Fink* (1992), *Sally Ann Thunder Ann Whirlwind Crockett* (1995), and *I Was Born about 10,000 Years Ago* (1996). Retellers continue to produce great collections of tall tales, such as those collected by Mary Pope Osborne, Amy Cohn, and Diane Goode, among others. I, for one, continue to look forward to the work of Robert San Souci, who has been able to find the new and unusual, always staying a step ahead. Of particular commendation is his *Cut from the Same Cloth: American Women of Myth, Legend, and Tall Tale* (1993), in which he accentuates the roles played by larger-than-life women. He has not been alone in this effort. Although not necessarily tall tales, Jane Yolen's (2000) *Not One Damsel in Distress* also fills this role. As noted earlier, the parodies of folktales often make the female characters much more dynamic than the more commonly male-dominated tales of the past. Finally, in the realm of an art tale in the tall-tale tradition, we cannot overlook *Swamp Angel* (Isaacs 1994), which certainly celebrates the independence of women.

Just as twentieth-century authors created literary tales based on traditional folktales and fairy tales, so, too, have authors done the same with tall tales. Sid Fleischman's creation of the McBroom family and their many adventures certainly illustrates this well. Going back a bit further, we also can celebrate the work of Carl Sandburg with his Huckabuck family, recently released in a picture-book format illustrated by David Small, *The Huckabuck Family and How They Raised Popcorn in Nebraska and Quit and Came Back* (Sandburg 1999). This is a trend I expect will continue well into the future.

The Picture-Book Explosion

Certainly, the twentieth century has been characterized by the rise of the picture book. From *Clever Bill* (Nicholson 1927) and *Millions of Cats* (Gág 1928), the picture storybook has been a favorite form. This has been true as well for the single folktale or fairy tale. Many, if not most, of the early folktales were collected in anthologies such as Andrew Lang's Colour Fairy Books or the collections of the Brothers Grimm or Joseph Jacobs. In the twentieth century, it became popular to turn one tale or folk rhyme into a single illustrated book. Some illustrators built their reputations by illustrating folktales. Marcia Brown won six of her nine Caldecott Medals and Honor awards for folktales she translated, retold, and illustrated. A perusal of the Caldecott Awards over the years suggests that the best way to become a contender is to illustrate folktales and fairy tales. In a quick count of awards (gold and honors) from 1961 to 1990, 38 of 110 awards were for traditional literature or fairy tales, which equals almost 35 percent.

This seeming advantage to traditional tales may not be accidental. Perhaps it is the common elements of humanity in these that lend themselves to such insightful and individual interpretation by other authors and illustrators. Maybe it is as Dorson (1973) says, "Increasingly, folklorists are recognizing that they should consider traditional ideas and values which may be expressed within tale and song and other genres or in ordinary conversation. These codes of values reveal the drives and goals of a given culture" (xv). As new authors and illustrators look at the motifs and tales from earlier years, they interpret them according to their time and experiences, their hopes and desires. Today's readers have the opportunity to experience "Snow White" as interpreted by Nancy Ekholm Burkert (Jarrell 1972) and compare that to the illustrations created by Trina Schart Hyman (Heins 1974). We have the best artists illustrating books, and they often choose the same or similar stories to reinterpret, allowing readers to explore that miraculous interaction between text and illustration that forms a work of art. When stories are similar, we decide what makes each work unique in its own right and which we prefer, as we begin to develop our own criteria for evaluating literature and art. It is surprising how we can find much to like in Suekichi Akaba's illustrations in *The Crane Wife* (Yagawa 1981) even when comparing them to the sumptuous illustrations by Gennady Spirin in a later version of the same title (Bodkin 1998). We can compare the wonderful connections between *Rumpelstiltskin* (Zelinsky and Grimm 1986), *Tom Tit Tot* (Ness 1965), and *Duffy and the Devil* (Zemach 1973), looking at all the similarities among these imps who perform wondrous deeds but who are ultimately outwitted. Still, each book has a completely different look and feel as to how the devilish antagonists are portrayed by the illustrator, not to mention the setting, the style, the mood. It is exciting to explore the effect all this has on how the reader feels about the tale. Certainly, if readers want to explore versions of the same tale, there is no competing against "Cinderella" in all its variations. I have more than sixty versions of this common tale in my personal collection—more than enough to give each of my students her or his own copy to compare with classmates. And Cinderella is not alone. Multiple variants are available for many common and not-so-common tales. The blossoming of the illustrated single tale has helped this to come about.

Still, the biggest advance during the twentieth century is that individual illustrated fairy tales represent so many different cultures and countries. Shelves can be filled with books representing African, African American, South and Central American, and Native American cultures. But here, too, we must be careful to ensure that these are representative of the best we can offer our children. The term *authenticity* conjures up many different and contradictory feelings, but the minimum we must strive for is cultural accuracy. Though it is not necessary that an author or illustrator be from a particular culture to represent it accurately, it is certainly the responsibility of the author, illustrator, and publisher to make certain that the work represents cultures accurately. There are ways to accomplish this. We must not cut corners with our children's books or with our children's futures.

Summary

Folktales and fairy tales are alive and well in children's literature. Their forms have spanned centuries and continents. We will continue to see many more tales appear from diverse lands and cultures. We must carefully preserve the quality of these stories, take care in translating them and making them authentic and accessible to our children and teachers. Too many poorly translated and illustrated folktales from other countries (not to mention our own) already exist. We must be vigilant in our use of these books, continually advocating for the best for our children and not settling for anything second rate.

References

Ahlberg, A. 1990. *Ten in a bed.* Illus. A. Amstutz. New York: Puffin Books.

Ahlberg, J., and A. Ahlberg. 1986. *The jolly postman, or, Other people's letters.* Boston: Little, Brown.

Andrews, S., ed. 1936. *Children's catalog: A dictionary catalog of 4000 books with analytical entries for 1020 books and a classified list indicating subject headings.* 5th ed. New York: H. W. Wilson.

Bacon, C., ed. 1918. *Children's catalog: Supplement to the second edition, 1916.* New York: H. W. Wilson.

Baum, L. F. 1900. *The wonderful wizard of Oz.* Illus. W. W. Denslow. Chicago: G. M. Hill.

Baum, L. F., and M. P. Hearn. 2000. *The annotated wizard of Oz: The wonderful wizard of Oz.* Illus. W. W. Denslow. New York: Norton.

Bodkin, O. 1998. *The crane wife.* Illus. G. Spirin. San Diego: Harcourt Brace.

Bottigheimer, R. B. 1996. Fairy tales and folk-tales. In *International companion encyclopedia of children's literature,* ed. P. Hunt and S. G. B. Ray, 152–165. New York: Routledge.

Bowman, J. C. 1937. *Pecos Bill, the greatest cowboy of all time.* Illus. L. Bannon. Chicago: A. Whitman.

Bowman, J. C., and M. W. Bianco. 1936. *Tales from a Finnish tupa.* Illus. L. Bannon. Chicago: A. Whitman.

Briggs, R. 1989. *Jim and the beanstalk.* New York: Coward-McCann.

Brown, C. S. 1987. *The tall tale in American folklore and literature.* Knoxville: University of Tennessee Press.

Calmenson, S. 1989. *The principal's new clothes.* Illus. D. Brunkus. New York: Scholastic.

Cohen, C. L. 1985. *Sally Ann Thunder Ann Whirlwind Crockett.* Illus. A. Dewey. New York: Greenwillow.

Cohn, A. L., ed. 1993. *From sea to shining sea: A treasury of American folklore and folk songs.* New York: Scholastic.

Datlow, E., and T. Windling, eds. 1993. *Snow white, blood red.* New York: Avon.

———. 2000. *A wolf at the door: And other retold fairy tales.* New York: Simon & Schuster Books for Young Readers.

Dégh, L. 1991. What did the Grimm Brothers give to and take from the Folk? In *The Brothers Grimm and folktale,* ed. J. M. McGlathery, 66–90. Urbana: University of Illinois Press.

Dewey, A. 1983. *Pecos Bill.* New York: Greenwillow.

———. 1984. *Febold Feboldson.* New York: Greenwillow.

———. 1987. *Gib Morgan, oilman.* New York: Greenwillow.

Dill, B. E., ed. 1976. *Children's catalog.* 13th ed. New York: H. W. Wilson.

Dorson, R. M. 1952. *Bloodstoppers and bearwalkers: Folk traditions of the Upper Peninsula.* Cambridge, MA: Harvard University Press.

———. 1973. *America in legend: Folklore from the colonial period to the present.* New York: Pantheon.

Emberley, M. 1990. *Ruby.* Boston: Little, Brown.

Ernst, L. C. 1995. *Little Red Riding Hood: A newfangled prairie tale.* New York: Simon & Schuster Books for Young Readers.

Fillmore, P. H. 1919. *Czechoslovak fairy tales, retold by Parker Fillmore.* Illus. J. Matulka. London: W. Collins Sons.

French, F. 1986. *Snow White in New York.* Oxford: Oxford University Press.

Gág, W. 1928. *Millions of cats.* New York: Coward-McCann.

Giles, R., D. E. Cook, and D. H. West, eds. 1946. *Children's catalog: A dictionary catalog of 4200 books with analytical entries for 637 books and a classified list indicating subject headings.* 7th ed. New York: H. W. Wilson.

Haviland, V. 1959a. *Favorite fairy tales told in England: Retold from Joseph Jacobs.* Illus. Bettina. Boston: Little, Brown.

———. 1959b. *Favorite fairy tales told in France.* Illus. R. Duvoisin. Boston: Little, Brown.

———. 1961a. *Favorite fairy tales told in Ireland.* Illus. A. Marokvia. Boston: Little, Brown.

———. 1961b. *Favorite fairy tales told in Russia.* Illus. H. Danska. Boston: Little, Brown.

————. 1963a. *Favorite fairy tales told in Poland.* Illus. F. Hoffmann. Boston: Little, Brown.

————. *Favorite fairy tales told in Scotland.* Illus. A. Adams. Boston: Little, Brown.

————. 1963c. *Favorite fairy tales told in Spain.* Illus. B. Cooney. Boston: Little, Brown.

————. 1965. *Favorite fairy tales told in Italy.* Illus. E. Ness. Boston: Little, Brown.

————. 1966a. *Favorite fairy tales told in Czechoslovakia.* Illus. T. S. Hyman. Boston: Little, Brown.

————. 1966b. *Favorite fairy tales told in Sweden.* Illus. R. Solbert. Boston: Little, Brown.

————. 1967. *Favorite fairy tales told in Japan.* Illus. G. Suyeoka. Boston: Little, Brown.

————. 1970. *Favorite fairy tales told in Greece.* Illus. N. Hogrogian. Boston: Little, Brown.

————. 1971. *Favorite fairy tales told in Denmark.* Illus. M. Zemach. Boston: Little, Brown.

————. 1973. *Favorite fairy tales told in India.* Illus. B. Lent. Boston: Little, Brown.

Haviland, V., and P. C. Asbjørnsen. 1961. *Favorite fairy tales told in Norway.* Illus. L. Weisgard. Boston: Little, Brown.

Hearn, M. P. 2001. "Toto, I've a feeling we're not in Kansas City anymore . . . or Detroit . . . or Washington, D.C." *Horn Book Magazine* 77: 16–34.

Hearne, B. 2000. Ruth Sawyer: A woman's journey from folklore to children's literature. *Lion and the Unicorn* 24: 279–307.

Heins, P. 1974. *Snow White.* Illus. T. S. Hyman. Boston: Little, Brown.

Helbig, A. K. 1988. Ruth Sawyer. In *Writers for children: Critical studies of major authors since the seventeenth century,* ed. J. M. Bingham, 511–517. New York: Scribner's.

Isaacs, A. 1994. *Swamp Angel.* Illus. P. O. Zelinsky. New York: Dutton Children's Books.

Jarrell, R. 1972. *Snow White and the seven dwarfs: A tale from the brothers Grimm.* Illus. N. E. Burkert. New York: Farrar, Straus and Giroux.

Johnston, T. 1992. *The cowboy and the black-eyed pea.* Illus. W. Ludwig. New York: G. P. Putnam's Sons.

Kamenetsky, C. 1992. *The Brothers Grimm and their critics: Folktales and the quest for meaning.* Athens: Ohio University Press.

Keats, E. J. 1965. *John Henry, an American legend.* New York: Pantheon.

Kellogg, S. 1984. *Paul Bunyan: A tall tale.* New York: William Morrow.

Kellogg, S. 1986. *Pecos Bill: A tall tale.* New York: William Morrow.

————. 1988. *Johnny Appleseed: A tall tale.* New York: Morrow Junior Books.

————. 1992. *Mike Fink: A tall tale.* New York: Morrow Junior Books.

———. 1995. *Sally Ann Thunder Ann Whirlwind Crockett: A tall tale.* New York: Morrow Junior Books.

———. 1996. *I was born about 10,000 years ago: A tall tale.* New York: Morrow Junior Books.

Lester, J. 1994. *John Henry.* Illus. J. Pinkney. New York: Dial.

Levine, G. C. 1997. *Ella enchanted.* New York: Scholastic.

Lowell, S. 1992. *The three little javelinas.* Illus. J. Harris. New York: Scholastic.

McConnell, M. L., and D. H. West, eds. 1956. *Children's catalog: A classified catalog of 3,204 children's books recommended for public and school libraries with an author, title and subject index.* 9th ed. New York: H. W. Wilson.

McKinley, R. 1978. *Beauty: A retelling of the story of Beauty and the beast.* New York: Harper & Row.

———. 1997. *Rose daughter.* New York: Greenwillow.

Napoli, D. J. 1992. *The prince of the pond: Otherwise known as De Fawg Pin.* Illus. J. Schachner. New York: Dutton Children's Books.

———. 1993. *The magic circle.* New York: Dutton Children's Books.

———. 1996. *Zel.* New York: Dutton Children's Books.

Ness, E. 1965. *Tom Tit Tot: An English folk tale.* New York: Scribner's.

Nicholson, W. 1927. *Clever Bill.* Garden City, NY: Doubleday Doran.

Potter, M. E., ed. 1909. *Children's catalog: A guide to the best reading for young people based on twenty-four selected library lists.* Minneapolis: H. W. Wilson.

Rounds, G. 1936. *Ol' Paul, the mighty logger: Being a true account of the seemingly incredible exploits and inventions of the great Paul Bunyan.* Eau Claire, WI: E. M. Hale.

San Souci, R. D. 1993. *Cut from the same cloth: American women of myth, legend, and tall tale.* Illus. J. B. Pinkney. New York: Philomel.

Sandburg, C. 1999. *The Huckabuck family and how they raised popcorn in Nebraska and quit and came back.* Illus. D. Small. New York: Farrar, Strauss and Giroux.

Sawyer, R. 1976. *The way of the storyteller.* New York: Penguin.

Schwimmer, R. 1928. *Tisza tales.* Illus. W. Pogány. Garden City, NY: Doubleday Doran and Company.

Scieszka, J. 1989. *The true story of the 3 little pigs.* Illus. L. Smith. New York: Scholastic.

Shor, R., and E. A. Fidell, eds. 1966. *Children's catalog.* 11th ed. New York: H. W. Wilson.

Stanley, D. 1997. *Rumpelstiltskin's daughter.* New York: Morrow Junior Books.

Stoutenburg, A. 1966. *American tall tales.* Illus. R. M. Powers. New York: Viking.

Untermeyer, L. 1945. *The wonderful adventures of Paul Bunyan.* Illus. E. G. Jackson. New York: Heritage.

Wheeler, H. E. 1929. The psychological case against the fairy tale. *Elementary School Journal* 29: 754–756.

Yagawa, S. 1981. *The crane wife.* Illus. S. Akaba. New York: William Morrow.

Yolen, J. 1992. *Briar Rose.* New York: Tom Doherty Associates.

———. 2000. *Not one damsel in distress: World folktales for strong girls.* Illus. S. Guevara. San Diego: Silver Whistle Books.

———, ed. 1986. *Favorite folktales from around the world.* New York: Pantheon.

Zelinsky, P. O., and J. Grimm. 1986. *Rumpelstiltskin.* E. P. Dutton.

Zemach, H. 1973. *Duffy and the devil.* Illus. M. Zemach. New York: Farrar, Straus and Giroux.

Zipes, J. D. 1988. The changing function of the fairy tale. *The Lion and the Unicorn,* 12(3): 7–31.

———, ed. 2000. *The Oxford companion to fairy tales.* New York: Oxford University Press.

7

Looking at Poetry for Children in Twentieth-Century America

Lee Bennett Hopkins

In the United States, poetry by American writers became recognized in the 1920s when Hilda Conkling, a ten-year-old prodigy, published *Poems by a Little Girl* (1920). Four other poets came onto the scene during the 1920s, including Dorothy Aldis, whose work is still widely anthologized. Aldis tapped into a range of emotions of the young childhood years with timeless works such as "Everybody Says" (Aldis 1925, 101):

> Everybody says
> I look just like my mother.
> Everybody says
> I'm the image of Aunt Bee.
> Everybody says
> My nose is like my father's.
> But I want to look like ME!

A curious thing about the 1930s was that, with the exception of two poets, Laura E. Richards and Aileen Fisher, who created verse specifically for children, poems for young people were written by prominent adult poets: Carl Sandburg, Rosemary and Stephen Vincent Benet, T. S. Eliot, and Langston Hughes. Aileen Fisher, who became known in the 1930s, continued to write for more than seven decades. Another mind-boggling fact of this decade is that Langston Hughes, who published *The Dream Keeper and Other Poems* in 1932—a book still cherished today—is the only major male African American poet whose work has endured, work that will last forever and ever. *The Dream Keeper* has never been out of print since it was first published. A new edition, recently brought out by Knopf, is also available in paperback with illustrations by Brian Pinkney. I am proud to have contributed the introduction. Me, a white kid from a Newark, New Jersey, project, whose own life could be found through Hughes's passionate words. In a brilliant use of just eight lines in his verse "Dreams" (Hughes [1932] 1994, 4), Hughes gave us, gives us, the power to go on as long as we can "hold fast to dreams":

> Hold fast to dreams
> For if dreams die
> Life is a broken-winged bird
> That cannot fly.
> Hold fast to dreams
> For when dreams go
> Life is a barren field
> Frozen with snow.

Sixty-one years passed—*61*—before we heard a second African American male voice—that of Ashley Bryan in *Sing to the Sun,* published in 1993, which is the first book to receive the Lee Bennett Hopkins Poetry Award.

More curious is the decade of the 1940s—only two poets emerged during an entire ten-year span: Elizabeth Coatsworth and Harry Behn. Their work didn't come about until the end of the decade; there is a nine-year lapse between T. S. Eliot's *Old Possum's Book of Practical Cats,* published in 1939, and Coatsworth's *Summer Green,* in 1949.

Between the 1950s and 1970s, poetry flourished with at least thirty major poets making debuts. A roster of incredible names from Gwendolyn Brooks to Shel Silverstein, Arnold Adoff to Charlotte Zolotow emerged.

During the 1980s, there was another lull. Although only three voices rose, those of Jane Yolen, Nancy Willard, and Paul Fleischman, each of these writers went on to set new records in the world of publishing. In addition to their works of poetry, each has created a wide variety of books, from picture books to novels to beyond. Willard and Fleischman are the only two authors to win the Newbery Medal during the twentieth century for books of poetry. Willard received the 1982 Newbery Award (and a Caldecott Honor) for *A Visit to William Blake's Inn: Poems for Innocent and Experienced Travelers* (Harcourt 1981), and Fleischman received the 1989 award for *Joyful Noise: Poems for Two Voices* (Harper 1988). Yolen has published more than twenty-three volumes of poetry and a host of anthologies in children's verse. Her oeuvre numbers close to three hundred published works: adult, young adult, and children's books, not only poetry and folktales, but also fantasy, science fiction, contemporary realistic fiction, and nonfiction.

Finally, the 1990s! A wondrous overwhelming disclosure: more poets were published then than in any other decade of the twentieth century. May this trend continue with a *hurrah!*

During the eight decades highlighted, poets introduced children to a wide variety of poetic forms and have dealt with an infinite number of subjects, from caterpillars to computers, pine trees to pimples, pinafores to pizza. Times change. Children change. And so did their poetry.

For example, on page fourteen of *All Together* by Dorothy Aldis, published in 1925, an illustration for her poem "Ironing Day" depicts a woman clad in a long dress and apron standing behind an ironing board, proudly displaying a starched and stiff dress to a little girl who delights in how the wrinkles are smoothed away—how the dress looks "very well behaved and good!"

"Ironing Day." From *All Together,* by Dorothy Aldis and illustrated by Margaret Freeman.

**"Liz Meyer, who has just put her brothers in the drier." From *Brats*,
by X. J. Kennedy and illustrated by James Watts.**

In contrast, on page ten of X. J. Kennedy's *Brats,* published in 1986, artwork shows a modern child, Liz Meyer, dressed in an oversized sweatshirt, baggy pants, and sneakers, maliciously grinning after having flung her brothers in the drier at the Laundromat.

In "The Little Hat," Dorothy Aldis (1925, 25) describes a concern of children living in the early and mid-twentieth century: losing a favorite hat with ribbons tied around it. Being a bit leery that a school of fish might nip one's toes appeared in "Wading" by James S. Tippett (1973, 42).

The types of issues that poets broach have changed dramatically. Many contemporary poets address life situations children deal with today. A breakthrough book, *black is brown is tan* (Adoff 1973), was the first book of poetry to depict an interracial family. In it, Arnold Adoff writes in rhythmical free verse. "this is the way it is for us / this is the way we are" (7). Racial consciousness was also the theme in his *All the Colors of the Race,* wherein mama is chocolate, daddy is vanilla, and "all the colors of the race / are / in my face" (Adoff 1982, 5). Various lifestyle issues such as divorce, separation, new parents, or children caught in the middle appear in Myra Cohn Livingston's *There Was a Place and Other Poems* (1988), as in the following terse, haunting verse:

> In the Middle
> Mom
> says
> she wants me
> more than Dad.
> How do I ever choose?
> Dad
> says
> he wants me
> more than Mom.
> Somebody has to lose. (18)

My own *Been to Yesterdays: Poems of a Life* (Hopkins 1995) also deals with events of a parents' divorce, an unstable home life, and a hand-to-mouth existence—a journey of my own life between the ages of twelve and thirteen.

> "SINCE
>
> your
> sister's asleep
> and your brother
> is, too,
> there are
> some things
> I must say to you
> 'cause
> you're the oldest,
> strongest,
> my number one son.

"Someday
you will understand
that life can't flow
as you always planned.

"Your daddy and I
don't see eye to eye,
can't get along
anymore—
I don't even
know why.

"But he's still
your Daddy.
He always will be.
He's still a good man.
Still part of me.

"It's important to know
that he'll always
love you,
your sister
your brother,
and grandma, too.

"Although we're
going to be apart
he'll always love you
with all his heart.

"That's all I have
to tell you now.

"I know daddy's leaving
is hard to bear.

"The four of us
will have to fare—

"no matter
what
no matter
where." (27–29)

Homophobia is expressed in Ralph Fletcher's verse "Justin and Frank" in his fine young adult collection, *I Am Wings* (1994). On the first day of school, a boy named Luke screams, "fags, stinking fags," and beats up Justin, who goes home all covered with blood. But a true friend of Justin and Frank idles to a beach that following Saturday, where he finds the boys sitting together, all by themselves; Justin's lip is still puffy (22–23). During the week of Matthew Shepard's savage murder in Laramie, Wyoming, I used this poem in a sophomore class in New York City. When I finished, girls and boys sat and cried together and perhaps learned tolerance through poetry.

Of course, there are still poems, thank goodness, being written for children that depict daffodils, daffiness, geese, goofiness, Queen Ann's lace, quilts. But poems dealing with contemporary lifestyles are available more than ever before.

Awards honoring children's literature were established very early in the twentieth century—the Newbery Award in 1922, the Caldecott Award in 1938—but it was not until 1977 that the first major award for children's poetry, the National Council of Teachers of English (NCTE) Award for Excellence in Poetry for Children, was established. Presented every three years, the honor goes to a living American poet for his or her aggregate body of work. To date, thirteen poets have received this prestigious award. (Information on the award can be found on NCTE's Web site, www.ncte.org/elem/poetry/.)

New directions for children's poetry were recorded in the 1980s. For example, in 1982, for the first time in its sixty-year history, the Newbery Medal was presented to an original collection of verse, *A Visit to William Blake's Inn,* by Nancy Willard (1981). Another first for verse came in 1981 when *A Light in the Attic* by Shel Silverstein reached number one on the *New York Times* adult best-sellers list and remained there for over three years. In 1982, T. S. Eliot's *Old Possum's Book of Practical Cats,* upon which the London and Broadway musical productions of the hit show *Cats* were based, reached more readers than it had since it was first published in 1939. In 1989, a second Newbery for poetry was given to Paul Fleischman for *Joyful Noise* (1988).

Concerned with the fact that only one major award for poetry existed in the country, in 1993, I founded the Lee Bennett Hopkins Poetry Award, an annual award administered by Pennsylvania State University that is given to the author or editor of a distinguished volume of poetry, either an original collection or anthology. Then, in 1995, I founded the Lee Bennett Hopkins/International Reading Association Promising New Poet Award, which is presented every three years to a poet who has published no more than two books. Other awards have since been established, including the Claudia Lewis Poetry Award, given annually by Bank Street College in New York City where Lewis taught; the Myra Cohn Livingston Poetry Award, given annually to a California poet by the Children's Literature Council of Southern California.

In 1994, Young People's Poetry Week was initiated. It is held each April and, since its inception, has sparked a tremendous amount of interest in the entire realm of children's poetry. For information on ways to highlight and celebrate next year's event, go to the Children's Book Council Web site, www.CBCbooks.org/.

It is my hope that we can continue to keep poetry flowing, flourishing in the lives *of children* everywhere. How exciting to see what the next decades hold for us.

In 1985, I had the honor of being the National Children's Book Week Poet. The theme that year was "Good Books, Good Times!" I am honored to have penned a verse for this wondrous annual event, for it shares my love of children, my love of books, my love of educators, dedicated educators—us—who bring "Good Books, Good Times" (Hopkins 1990, 17) into the lives, hearts, minds, beings of all boys and girls.

Good books.
Good times.
Good stories.
Good rhymes.
Good beginnings.
Good ends.
Good people.
Good friends.
Good fiction.
Good facts.
Good adventures.
Good acts.
Good stories.
Good rhymes.
Good books.
Good times.

References

Adoff, A. 1973. *black is brown is tan*. Illus. E. A. McCully. New York: HarperCollins.

————. 1982. *All the colors of the race*. Illus. J. Steptoe. New York: Lothrop, Lee & Shepard.

Aldis, D. 1925. *All together: A child's treasury of verse*. Illus. H. D. Jameson, M. Flack, and M. Freeman. New York: G. P. Putnam's Sons.

Bryan, A. 1992. *Sing to the sun*. New York: HarperCollins.

Coatsworth, E. 1948. *Summer green*. New York: Macmillan.

Conkling, H. 1920. *Poems by a little girl*. New York: F. A. Stokes.

Eliot, T. S. 1939. *Old Possum's book of practical cats*. San Diego: Harcourt.

Fleischman, P. 1988. *Joyful noise: Poems for two voices*. New York: HarperCollins.

Fletcher, R. 1994. *I am wings: Poems about love*. New York: Simon & Schuster.

Hopkins, L. B. 1995. *Been to yesterdays: Poems of a life*. Honesdale, PA: Boyd Mills Press.

————, ed. 1990. *Good books, good times!* Illus. H. Stevenson. New York: HarperCollins.

Hughes, L. [1932] 1994. *The dream keeper and other poems*. Illus. B. Pinkney. New York: Knopf.

Kennedy, X. J. 1986. *Brats*. Illus. J. Watts. New York: McElderry.

Livingston, M. C. 1988. *There was a place and other poems*. New York: McElderry.

Silverstein, S. 1981. *A light in the attic*. New York: HarperCollins.

Tippett, J. S. 1973. *Crickety cricket! The best-loved poems of James S. Tippett*. New York: Harper & Row.

Willard, N. 1981. *A visit to William Blake's inn*. Illus. A. Provensen and M. Provensen. New York: Harcourt Children's Books.

8

Children Responding to Poetry

A Century of Research and Commentary

Amy A. McClure

Poetry is a unique genre. It appeals to both thought and feeling, conjuring up rich sensory images, tapping into our natural propensity for rhythm, and evoking deep emotional responses. Good poems make us sigh and say, "Yes, that's just the way it is. . . . I never thought of it quite that way." That's the power of poetry—to use words that tickle the tongue and tantalize the ear; to make us see ordinary, everyday images in new ways. This close attention to language and emotion, wrapped up in a condensed package, is what gives poetry a unique voice that differs from other genres.

Young children are naturally drawn to poetry. They love the rhythm and rhyme of jump-rope chants, advertising jingles, and popular music. Throughout most of the twentieth century, however, children lost their interest in this genre as they progressed through school. They ranked it at or near the bottom of preference surveys. They often responded to teacher attempts to introduce poetry with indifference and even dislike.

But were these negative responses inevitable? Couldn't teachers find ways to help children recapture that natural affinity for poetry? This chapter examines the evolution of research on children's responses to poetry through the past century. Documentation of poetry preferences, issues related to selecting poetry, debates about teaching methods, and the growing conviction that context and experience influenced response to poetry are examined.

Children's Poetry Preferences

Much of the research on children's response to poetry throughout the twentieth century focused on analyzing children's poetry preferences. These studies revealed strikingly similar patterns when viewed across age, gender, demographic data, and time. It wasn't until innovations developed in research methodology and new theoretical perspectives evolved that results changed. This section describes children's preferences for various poetic elements, topics, and forms throughout the century.

Preferences for the Genre of Poetry

Studies that focused on measuring children's preferences for specific literary genres consistently found that children had little interest in poetry. When asked to rank their preferences for reading various literary genres, children consistently listed poetry at or near the bottom of their lists (Jordan 1921; Kutiper 1985; Matanzo and Madison 1979; Norvell 1958; Schulte 1967). Although interest sometimes increased with age of the respondents and in some surveys girls indicated a stronger preference for poetry than boys, children's preference for prose over poetry remained consistent for most of the century.

The results of the first National Assessment of Educational Progress (NAEP; Johnson 1973) provided some basis for optimism that this negative perception was changing. Results from this study revealed a rise in preference for poetry among nine-year-olds, although its popularity remained low with older children. When asked how often they read eight types of literature, over 33 percent of the nine-year-olds reported that they "often" read poetry. This figure was second only to biographies and nonfiction. Unfortunately, later NAEP survey results show a downward trend in the popularity of poetry in all ages.

Studies in the latter part of the century extended the preference studies by integrating preference with context and instructional method. Researchers now began to ask: "Are these low preferences for poetry inevitable?" What if children were in an environment where they were exposed to many examples of excellent poetry by teachers who were genuinely enthusiastic about the genre? They discovered that when offered a steady diet of good poetry, along with activities that appealed to the interests of children, quite positive preferences for poetry often were discerned. In studies by Shapiro and Shapiro (1972), Matanzo and Madison (1979), McCall (1979), and McClure (1985) and through the informal observations of poets-in-residence such as Heard (1989), Cariello (1990), and others, children who regularly heard poetry read aloud, then participated in extension activities such as discussions, writing poetry, dramatization, and illustration showed significantly more positive preferences for poetry. Although the preferences for particular activities varied from study to study, the relationship between regular exposure to good poetry and positive attitudes toward the genre was consistent.

Specific Poetry Preferences

Additional research explored the preferences for particular types and elements of poetry. Most of these asked students to indicate their preferred poems from a range of choices and to give reasons for their selections. Researchers then inferred that behavior would mirror these choices. Two of the earliest studies were conducted by Helen MacKintosh (1924, 1931). In the first investigation involving fifth graders, a hundred poems were grouped into sets of ten, based on such characteristics as rhythm, rhyme, level of excitement, and humor. She then developed a six-point rating scale on which children indicated their response to each poem along with reasons for their answers. This methodology, with some variation, was used widely in subsequent poetry preference studies. MacKintosh found that certain qualities characterized the children's favorite poems, including rhyme and rhythm, ability to tell a good story, excitement, an element of adventure, creation of dramatic interest, and humor. The most unpopular poems were those characterized by calmness and thoughtful, meditative topics.

MacKintosh's second study (1931) used responses from third- to sixth-grade children and confirmed the findings from her previous studies.

Research conducted from the thirties to the seventies echoed these findings (Avegno 1956; Bradshaw 1937; Bridge 1966; Kangley 1938; Kyte 1942; Nelson 1966; Norvell 1958). Content analyses consistently revealed strong preferences for humorous poems, those related to student interests and experiences, narrative form, and poems with strong rhythm and rhyme. Poems deemed sentimental, reflective, full of figurative language, or those listed by teachers as having "high literary quality," along with free-verse formats, ranked low in the children's preferences.

The most comprehensive study of intermediate children's poetry preferences was conducted by Ann Terry (1972). She selected 113 poems that were divided into 10 listening sessions, then recorded on cassette tapes. This helped keep presentation of the poems constant, a methodological innovation that was used frequently in later studies. A representative national sampling of students listened to the tapes, then scored each poem on a five-point scale for each of three questions: "How much do you like this poem?" "Would you like to hear this poem again?" and "Could this be one of your favorite poems?" Terry found that children preferred narrative and limerick forms, while free verse and haiku were the most disliked forms. Specific reasons cited for preferring a particular poem were the elements of rhythm, rhyme, and sound. In contrast, poems using complex visual imagery or figurative language were not enjoyed. Poetry that was humorous and focused on familiar experiences and animals was the most popular. Contemporary poems were preferred over traditional ones.

Additional studies confirmed and updated Terry's findings (Fisher and Natarella 1982; Ingham 1980; Kutiper and Wilson 1993; Simmons 1980). Fisher and Natarella (1982) found similar preferences among primary children, while Kutiper and Wilson (1993) studied middle-schoolers. The younger children preferred poems about imaginative events and people, while the older students preferred more realistic content. Younger children liked traditional poems more than the older children did. Since methodology of most studies followed Terry's model, comparisons could be made to suggest these findings were consistent across grade levels and demographics. However, even when the methodology was altered, results were consistent. For example, Kutiper and Wilson (1993) examined library circulation records to see whether those reflected students' poetry preferences as suggested by past preference studies. Kutiper found that the rhymed, rhythmic, humorous poetry of Jack Prelutsky and Shel Silverstein dominated the list of circulated volumes. Judith Viorst's (1981) *If I Were in Charge of the World* was the next most popular, but trailed well behind the others. Poetry books with holiday themes were the next most popular. Again, however, the selected holiday books reflected children's preferences for rhyme, rhythm, and narration.

Such consistency across decades of research seemed conclusive, although discouraging. Yet teachers and researchers questioned these results. Were these conclusions inevitable? Were children only capable of appreciating light, humorous poetry? What would happen to student preference for particular types of poetry if they were introduced to a steady diet of increasingly complex poetry by teachers who were knowledgeable about the genre and enjoyed it themselves? McClure (1985) examined children's poetry preferences in two intermediate classrooms where the group was continually exposed to high-quality poetry through read alouds, discussions, choral readings, and other activities. These children were allowed to read poetry extensively on their own and were encouraged to write their own poetry. She found the children not only expressed strong preferences for the genre of poetry, they also preferred reading more complex, sophisticated poems. They were familiar with a wider variety of poetry and also seemed more appreciative of such elements as figurative language and abstract forms such as haiku. Although they did not completely abandon the light, humorous material, their preference for poetry that featured unusual imagery, carefully selected words, and complex meanings was significant. Additionally, they could associate many well-known poets with the poets' works as well as their common themes, style, and use of poetic elements. It seemed these preferences were strongly influenced by contextual factors. Children who regularly participated in the discussion sessions following read alouds, frequently shared poetry with peers, and regularly had their own poems critiqued by peers were invariably the ones expressing preferences for more complex poetry. Teachers also strongly influenced these preferences by modeling the reading of more challenging poetry, providing suggestions, and making assignments. A follow-up study (McClure 1990) extended the investigation to third and fourth graders. Again, McClure investigated children's poetry preferences in poetry-rich contexts in which children were given repeated opportunities to discuss and savor high-quality poetry, then experiment with their growing sense of the genre through writing their own pieces. Children at all grade levels still enjoyed light, humorous pieces but also often expressed preferences for more complex poetry.

Subsequent studies reflected this change in focus from preference to response. Emphasis in these later studies was on analyzing children's responses to poetry in relation to various classroom contexts. Such teachers as Mary Krogness (1995), Lisa Siemans (1996), Kathy Perfect (1999), Lisa Lenz (1992), and others described classrooms where children were exposed to a wide variety of poetry and encouraged to "work side by side as [they] climbed inside their words and felt the rhythms and textures of language" (Krogness 1998, 17). Poetry in these classrooms was considered an integral part of the curriculum, and activities with both reading and writing poetry occurred throughout the year rather than in a short-term "poetry unit." As a result, children in these classrooms were much more likely to name poetry as a favorite genre, and they typically enjoyed a wide range of poems, including those with more abstract imagery and diverse formats.

Selecting Poetry for Children

Despite the research that consistently revealed clear trends in children's poetry preferences, it seems that throughout the twentieth century teachers and other professionals often selected poetry for children that differed in form and content from that which the children enjoyed. Rather than selecting poetry with consistent rhymes and rhythms that spoke directly to children and mirrored their concerns, teachers and other professionals tended to present traditional formal poetry; the kind they thought children ought to like or ones they thought should be part of the canon. This section explores the evolving trends in poetry selection.

Until the 1980s, research results consistently revealed that teachers selected traditional poems about esoteric topics such as nature, fairies, and historic/patriotic events for use with their classes, despite research that suggested children disliked this kind of poetry (Bradshaw 1937; Craven 1980; Eckert 1928; Kyte 1942; MacKintosh 1931; Nelson 1966; Purves and Beach 1972; Thom 1979). One study by Thom (1979) was particularly comprehensive. In a national survey to determine what teachers read to intermediate-grade children, she found that all but four of the forty-one most commonly read poems were written before 1928. These included Frost's "Stopping By the Woods on a Snowy Evening" (1923), Thayer's "Casey at the Bat"[1] (University of Toronto 1997a), Riley's "Little Orphant Annie"[2] (1916), Sandburg's "Fog" (1916), Stevenson's "My Shadow" (1895), and "Hiawatha" (1855) and "Paul Revere's Ride" (1863), both by Longfellow.

Basal readers, district curriculum guides, and other textbook sources were the most commonly used selection tools, further widening the chasm between children's preferences and teacher choices (Craven 1980; Eckert 1928; Hecht 1978; Nelson 1966; Terry 1972). For most of the century, teachers used some sort of basal for reading instruction. Thus, teachers most likely used the poems included in, or recommended by, the basal because they were so readily accessible. Additionally, teachers tended to view poetry as a "filler" or as something to be used on special occasions such as holidays, or, even more disturbing, they used copying a poem as punishment. Most teachers also simply lacked knowledge of poetry and effective practices for presenting it to children. And they admitted disliking the genre themselves. It's no wonder that they relied on textbook sources rather than perusing anthologies or the *Poetry Index* on their own.

The publication of Shel Silverstein's irreverent *Where the Sidewalk Ends* (1974) and *A Light in the Attic* (1981) transformed these practices. Here were poems with definite rhythms, consistent rhymes, and topics that spoke honestly and directly to children's fears and concerns. And they were mischievously humorous. Both children and teachers loved them, and soon these books were widely used across the country. Even at the close of the twentieth century, these collections were immensely popular. See Table 8.1 for a listing of teachers' favorite twentieth-century poetry anthologies.

The advent of the whole language movement with its emphasis on using literature rather than basals in reading instruction brought increased attention to poetry as an important genre for children. Silverstein's work paved the way for other poets such as Jack Prelutsky, X. J. Kennedy, and John Ciardi who also wrote poetry featuring humor and word play. Once children started getting hooked on poetry, some teachers began introducing them to more diverse selections in form and content written by such poets as Myra Cohn Livingston, Karla Kuskin, David McCord, Valerie Worth, Eve Merriam, Mary Ann Hoberman, Aileen Fisher, and Barbara Esbenson. Although anthologies then became the most commonly used selection tool, some teachers began using collections written by a single poet to deepen their children's appreciation of poetry and help them enjoy increasingly more complex imagery, form, and content.

Poets writing for children also began exploring the boundaries of taste, form, and content, experimenting with such topics as divorce, poverty, racism, and pollution that spoke directly to children's needs and life perspectives, in addition to the simple concerns of childhood such as sibling rivalry and friendship. Rather than being condescending and didactic, poetry in the seventies, eighties, and nineties was more honest and straightforward, admitting to children that the world was less than perfect. More minority and international voices were published as well, helping children from diverse cultures see that their life experiences were valued.

Table 8.1

Favorite Poetry Anthologies Used by Teachers in the Twentieth Century

Arbuthnot, M. H. 1952. *Time for poetry: A representative collection of poetry for children.* Illus. A. Paul. Chicago: Scott Foresman.

Clinton, C. 1998. *I, too, sing America: Three centuries of African-American poetry.* Illus. S. Alcorn. Boston: Houghton Mifflin.

Cole, J. 1984. *A new treasury of children's poetry: Old favorites and new discoveries.* Illus. J. G. Brown. Garden City, NY: Doubleday.

De Regniers, B. S., E. Moore, and M. M. White. 1969. *Poems children will sit still for: A selection for the primary grades.* New York: Citation Press. Reissued in 1988 as *Sing a song of popcorn.*

Dunning, S., E. G. Lueders, and H. L. Smith, eds. 1966. *Reflections on a gift of watermelon pickle . . . and other modern verse.* New York: Lothrop, Lee & Shepard.

Ferris, H. J. 1957. *Favorite poems old and new: Selected for boys and girls.* Illus. L. Weisgard. New York: Doubleday.

Frost, R. 1959. *You come too: Favorite poems for young readers.* Illus. T. W. Nason. New York: Henry Holt.

Janeczko, P. B. 1990. *The place my words are looking for: What poets say about and through their work.* New York: Bradbury Press.

Kennedy, X. J., and D. M. Kennedy. 1982. *Knock at a star: A child's introduction to poetry.* Illus. K. A. Weinhaus. Boston: Little, Brown.

Larrick, N. 1968. *Piping down the valleys wild: Poetry for the young of all ages.* Illus. E. Raskin. New York: Delacorte Press.

Livingston, M. C. 1972. *Listen, children, listen: An anthology of poems for the very young.* Illus. T. S. Hyman. New York: Harcourt Brace Jovanovich.

McGovern, A. 1965. *Arrow book of poetry.* New York: Scholastic.

Prelutsky, J. 1983. *The Random House book of poetry for children.* Illus. A. Lobel. New York: Random House.

Sandburg, C. 1930. *Early moon.* Illus. J. H. Daugherty. New York: Harcourt Brace.

Untermeyer, L. 1959. *The Golden treasury of poetry.* Illus. J. W. Anglund. New York: Golden Books.

As a result, many teachers began expanding their poetry selections, moving beyond what they thought children *should* like, to choosing poetry they thought children *would* like. The distinction was an important one. Children's interests and experiential background were an important consideration in the selection process. This did not mean that teachers only chose poems with immediate, visceral appeal—the kind that generated laughter or easy identification. Rather, the offerings widened to include poetry from diverse voices, a span of topics, more free verse, and more sophisticated poetic devices such as metaphor. These were not universal trends. Many teachers rarely used poetry with their children, shared just the collections of Silverstein and Prelutsky, or used poetry only on special occasions. However, those who regularly shared poetry widened their selections to include a varied diet of poems that respected children's preferences, but also helped them stretch beyond those initial preferences to an appreciation of the more sophisticated pieces in this genre.

Supporting Children's Response to Poetry

As the emphasis in research moved from analyzing preferences to how children responded to literature in various contexts, ideas on the nature of poetry and how it should be presented to children also changed. Emphasis shifted from a focus on text and its supposed meaning ("literary-analysis" approach) to an awareness of response as a reciprocal interaction among the elements of text, reader, and social context ("reader-response" approach).

For most of the twentieth century, teachers used a literary-analysis approach when sharing poetry with children. The premise of this approach was that the reader needed knowledge of literary conventions and language to discern the structure as well as the meaning of a literary work. Poetry was viewed as a cryptic word puzzle in which poets hid their meaning or put it into a code that could be deciphered only through an orderly process of deductive analysis. Thus, children were first taught to recognize significant poetic elements, forms, and common poetic devices. Only after receiving extensive drill on these elements were children considered "ready" to study poetry. Children were then shown a course they must follow in order to uncover the "true" meaning inherent in a particular poem. They analyzed words and lines as well as searched for the poetic devices they had been taught to recognize. The teacher acted as arbitrator of what constituted a correct interpretation, controlling both the procedures followed and the response. Children came to believe that the teachers' expected answers were the only ones possible.

This approach was based on a second premise, which assumed that everything worthy of consideration was contained in the words of the poem and the form in which the poem was arranged. It was the individual parts rather than the whole that were deemed important. The reader need not bring self or context to the analytic process.

Although teachers advocated the literary-analysis approach for decades, research results consistently indicated that requiring children to analyze poetry made them dislike it—intensely. For example, Painter (1970) discovered that the main reason her preservice teacher education students hated poetry was the insistence on "correct" interpretation. They described the embarrassment of never getting the same interpretation as the teacher or classmates even after reading the poem several times. Verble (1973) found that elementary children held similar attitudes. When asked why they didn't like poetry, the majority stated "because I can't understand it" and "because my interpretation is never right." Respondents in surveys by Matanzo and Madison (1979), Craven (1980), and Baskin, Harris, and Salley (1984) offered similar opinions. These attitudes prevailed to the end of the century. For example, Dias (1992) found that junior high and high school students disliked poetry because "they could not make sense of and appreciate a poem unless a teacher mediated that process" (11). Additionally, he found that reading poetry was essentially a teacher-controlled activity, meaning that children were given little trust or respect to construct their own meanings.

Many teachers realized, however, that the literary-analysis approach wasn't working. Additionally, the work of Louise Rosenblatt (1968, 1978), which emphasized response as a reciprocal transaction between reader and text, led theorists to question the value of a totally objective analysis of literature, particularly poetry. Because poetry is created as the result of an emotional response to experience or what X. J. Kennedy (1981) termed a "passionate feeling persuaded into form" (279), the reader should come to poetry as a human being who must first experience an effective, emotional response before analyzing why that response occurred. However, teachers didn't know how to change their practice. Few research studies provided answers. Most examined the effectiveness of certain materials or activities rather than providing theoretical or conceptual conclusions about how to help children develop informed, positive, discriminating taste in their responses to poetry. Attention focused mainly on written responses, although oral responses were analyzed in some studies, particularly in relation to writing poetry.

Formulaic or fill-in-the-blank exercises, most frequently found in language arts textbooks, were one way teachers in the 1960s tried to move away from the confining literary-analysis approach. This activity required children to create similes, for example, by providing their own comparisons as in "the pillow is as soft as _____." Children were also taught formulae for writing various poetic forms such as haiku, limericks, or diamante.

Advocates of the fill-in-the-blank approach contended that this structure provided support for teachers who had little experience with poetry and needed some direction. Children could also use their imagination to some degree with this approach. Critics (Larrick 1971; Livingston 1976) thought the possibilities for imaginative response were limited, although some creativity could result if the teacher understood poetry and was skilled at eliciting divergent responses from children.

The work of Kenneth Koch, as set forth in his books *Wishes, Lies and Dreams* (1970) and *Rose, Where Did You Get That Red* (1973), revolutionized thinking about using poetry with children. Koch was a published, award-winning poet who taught poetry writing to young children in the New York City public schools. His experiences are among the most well known examples of the "poet-in-the-schools movement" in which a professional poet went into schools for intense teaching sessions with poetry, usually focused on writing poetry. Koch believed that children had an affinity for poetry and a natural talent for writing it; thus, poetry should be presented as simply as possible without reference to formal literary terms such as *metaphor, alliteration,* or *iambic pentameter.* He thought it was important to surround children with fine poetry so they could intuitively "find and re-create for themselves" the intense feelings inherent in that poetry: "I help them do this by removing obstacles, such as the need to rhyme, and by encouraging them in various ways to get tuned to their own strong feelings, to their spontaneity, their sensitivity, and their carefree inventiveness" (Koch 1970, 25). So, for example, when using Robert Blake's "The Tyger"[3] (University of Toronto 1997b), Koch read the poem aloud, then led a discussion that focused on explaining unfamiliar words, examining the attitude the poet takes toward his subject, and associating the students' personal experiences with the poet's thesis. Frequently, aspects of the poem were dramatized. For example, after reading Blake's lines about the creation of a tiger's heart, Koch would ask the children to close their eyes and listen to the beating of their own heart. With other poems, children might sing various lines, act out some parts, or read alternate lines through choral reading.

He also developed an approach to writing poetry that encouraged divergent, free association that led to creating poems on various themes such as comparisons, wishes, lies, or colors. Children were asked to write what they felt without concern for conventional poetic form or structure. Rather, they were encouraged to tune into their own feelings, spontaneity, unique sensitivities, and personal inventiveness. Sometimes they used the classic poet's basic structure (such as repeated questions as in Robert Blake's "Tyger, Tyger") as a model for their own poetry. However, each child was encouraged to follow personal inclinations without concern for rhyme, meter, and form.

Koch and his supporters argued that his methods did not disregard poetic craft but rather focused on it deliberately and imaginatively. Particularly, the practice of writing in response to a classic poem provided children with unusual images, extended awareness of the possibilities for organizing a poem, and gave them new ideas to consider. They also became familiar with well-crafted poetry that was characterized by intense emotion and complex imagery. Koch then helped them link their personal experiences with the poems, helping them become more sensitive to what poets do. The idea was not necessarily to turn children into poets, but rather to make them poetry lovers.

Koch's later book, *Making Your Own Days: The Pleasures of Reading and Writing Poetry* (1998), furthered the idea that poetry is different; written in a language that differs from prose. He argued that poetry is a separate language that readers and writers must master, a language in which music and sound are as important as syntax and meaning (Sloan 1999). The book included an anthology of poems he considered "good," with reasons why each met his criteria of good poetry.

Critics of his work (Kennedy 1981; Livingston 1976, 1978) argued that although Koch advocated a viable alternative for facilitating poetic response, his ideas were limited. Since children were not required to conform to standards, these critics believed that Koch's students received the false idea that poetry is totally a personal product, unbounded by convention. They contended his methods could discourage children from rigorously pursuing excellence and precise expression. Koch also was criticized for failing to use with his students the wide variety of excellent children's poetry that was then available. Because poetry written specifically for children focused on everyday childhood experiences, argued his critics, using it would facilitate the task of linking children's own experiences with those described in the poetry.

Sloan (1975) advocated a method similar to Koch's, but suggested teachers provide more structure and guidance. Children first listened to many examples of a particular type of poetry such as haiku, limericks, couplets, quatrains, or ballads. Next, a few sample lines exemplifying that type were collaboratively written. Students were then encouraged to write their own poems in the pattern of the particular form under study. Thus, although she encouraged children to follow predetermined patterns, these patterns were more conventional than those advocated by Koch.

Myra Cohn Livingston (1973, 1975, 1976) took our knowledge of how to best help children appreciate poetry in a different direction. She believed that children should be encouraged to write freely, yet they also must be expected to conform to certain poetic conventions and forms. In this way children learned about the craft of poetry while discovering how it related to their lives. Personal response was encouraged. However, if response was in the form of a poem, it had to adhere to convention.

Specifically, Livingston began by sharing aloud poems that were well crafted and stimulated her students' imaginations. She often selected poems that exemplified a particular form such as free verse, or several that used a poetic device in intriguing ways. Children went outside, observed several objects, and recorded their observations. They then returned to the classroom and wrote a poem about their observations.

Livingston worked individually with the children to help them revise their poetry. She first would identify good features of their work. Then she began questioning children about various aspects; pointing out parts that didn't quite work—a rhyme used poorly, an unclear meaning, or a mediocre word choice, for example. In addition to critiquing their writing, she had them share favorite poetry with each other. This provided additional opportunities to discuss how poets use rhyme, meter, form, and word choice to craft their pieces.

The objective of this approach was to achieve a balance between the discipline required to use poetic elements in writing and the child's own voice. Writing poetry was viewed as a complex, challenging task, one that required intellectual discipline. Revision was essential to the process, enhancing rather than destroying creativity. Reading poetry written by professional poets was viewed as an activity that could show children how poets use language and personal vision to craft a poem that was pleasing to the ear while also causing the listener to marvel at the unusual imagery.

Critics of Livingston's ideas contended that her work was done with private school children in suburban southern California, thus the applicability of her ideas to other contexts was questionable. Additionally, her program required teachers who had strong backgrounds in poetry as well as excellent critiquing skills.

McClure (1985) expanded on Livingston's work by examining rural fifth- and sixth-grade children's responses to reading and writing poetry in a program very similar to that advocated by Livingston. She found that after a year of being immersed in the reading and writing of poetry, the children in the study began acquiring a sophisticated understanding of poetry and poetic elements. Initial understandings, which evolved through repeated read-aloud sessions with published poetry, influenced their experimentation with these elements in their own poetry writing. The experimentation in their own writing, in turn, deepened their understanding and appreciation of the crafting required to write published poetry. It was this interdependent cycle of reading and writing poetry, along with opportunities to experiment in their writing, critique each other's work, discuss favorite poems, and work daily with poetry, that made the difference.

Poet Georgia Heard, who worked with children as a poet-in-residence, advocated a similar program (1989, 1999). She describes reading and writing poetry with children as "making joy." First, regularly reading poetry aloud was important because it would "open the doors to their feelings, their imaginations and their voices" (3). Thus, she read many examples of excellent poetry to the children with whom she worked. She also encouraged them to create anthologies of their favorites, study favorite poets, and find poetry that related to their daily lives. This exposure to many examples of good poetry, in turn, helped them become familiar with the voice of the poetic genre, which was crucial for successfully writing their own poems. Writing poetry complemented the reading. Heard encouraged her students to find the strong feelings, unforgettable images, wonderings, and wanderings that could form the nucleus of a poem. Then she helped them "re-vision" their ideas through individual conferences. In addition to helping children clarify and focus their meanings, she also taught them elements of poetic crafting such as line breaks, word selection, form, use of rhyme, and repetition. The poetry her students enjoyed and the pieces they wrote reflected a complex understanding of the genre.

Several other teachers, poets-in-residence, and researchers who wrote about classroom poetry practices also advocated a curriculum that helped children first respond aesthetically to poetry, then look more closely at how it was crafted (Barnes 1976; Cariello 1990; Duthie and Zimet 1992; Krogness 1995, 1998; Lenz 1992; Perfect 1999; Rosen and Rosen 1973; Siemans 1996). Generally, they reported that they read poetry aloud, encouraged children to read poetry individually (with self or peers), allowed time for discussing poetry, and provided students with opportunities to write poetry. Talk revolved around first one's emotional, personal response or what "captured the ear, imagination and soul of the listeners" (Lenz 1992, 598). Then children were frequently asked to take a second look and respond to what made that poem so pleasing. A classroom environment that was safe, supportive, and open to exploration and experimentation undergirded the curriculum.

An additional method recommended throughout the century involved the integration of art, music, dance, and drama with poetry. The performance aspect, in which students deliberately planned and executed choral readings or dramatic presentations, was considered particularly beneficial to children's appreciation of and positive attitudes toward poetry. It seemed that the planning involved in organizing how to arrange words, lines, and stanzas, deciding what to emphasize and what to delete, creating movements and props helped children explore meaning, structure, and how these poetic elements support each other (Fisher 1994). Performing was seen as a way to "get inside a poem" to discover its essence.

However, support for this approach was based more on ideology and conviction than conclusions drawn from carefully designed research studies. Most researchers found insignificant or no differences in attitudes or understanding of poetry between children in control and experimental groups (Bishop 1932; Bowes, Painter, and Vesta 1942; Comeaux 1980; Folta 1979; Glenn 1969; Huettenmueller 1973; Redmond 1978; Snedaker 1925; Squire and Beckerman 1950). It may have been the design of the studies or the lack of sophisticated statistical procedures (not yet developed when these studies were conducted) that caused these results. Or possibly response in the arts was too elusive to measure with traditional research methodology. Nevertheless, educators continued advocating the use of the arts to respond to poetry based on anecdotal and observational evidence that this was effective practice (Apol and Harris 1999; Fisher 1994; Hopkins 1987; McClure 1990). Table 8.2 for a listing of books teachers used to integrate poetry into their instruction.

By the end of the century, recommended practice seemed to take a middle ground between literary analysis and completely free, personal response. Children were encouraged to examine a poem and its workings, but only after they had experienced it personally and aesthetically. Thus, it was suggested that children should first take delight in a poem, then discuss what the poet did to create an intriguing sound or compelling image. This talk could occur in large and small groups, with or without direct teacher guidance. Sometimes the poem would be acted out, read together chorally, or illustrated. Then teachers could informally, yet deliberately introduce more complex imagery or sophisticated language. Heightened enjoyment and awareness of structure, form, and poetic elements would evolve naturally out of these repeated satisfactory experiences with poetry. Teachers could scaffold initial responses and help children link what they already knew about poetry to new ideas and concepts.

Future Trends

If children are to love poetry, they must be immersed in reading and writing it. Neither a short-term poetry unit nor an occasional read-aloud session on a rainy Friday afternoon is sufficient to nourish this love. Continuous, sustained exposure to many

Table 8.2

Significant Books on Teaching Poetry in the Twentieth Century

Booth, D., and B. Moore. 1988. *Poems please! Sharing poetry with children*. Markham, Ontario: Pembroke.

Chatton, B. 1993. *Using poetry across the curriculum: A whole language approach*. Phoenix, AZ: Oryx Press.

Cullinan, B. E. 1995. *Three voices: An invitation to poetry across the curriculum*. York, ME: Pembroke.

Denman, G. A. 1988. *When you've made it your own: Teaching poetry to young people*. Portsmouth, NH: Heinemann.

Esbensen, B. J. 1975. *A celebration of bees: Helping children write poetry*. Minneapolis, MN: Winston Press.

Graves, D. H. 1992. *Explore poetry*. Portsmouth, NH: Heinemann.

Heard, G. 1989. *For the good of the earth and sun: Teaching poetry*. Portsmouth, NH: Heinemann.

Heard, G. 1999. *Awakening the heart: Exploring poetry in the elementary and middle school*. Portsmouth, NH: Heinemann.

Hopkins, L. B. 1987. *Pass the poetry please*. New York: HarperCollins.

Koch, K. 1970. *Wishes, lies and dreams: Teaching children to write poetry*. New York: Chelsea House.

Koch, K. 1973. *Rose, where did you get that red? Teaching great poetry to children*. New York: Random House.

Larrick, N. 1991. *Let's do a poem! Introducing poetry to children*. New York: Delacorte Press.

Livingston, M. C. 1984. *The child as poet—myth or reality?* Boston: Horn Book.

Livingston, M. C. 1991. *Poem-making: Ways to begin writing poetry*. New York: HarperCollins.

McClure, A. A. with P. Harrison and S. Reed. 1990. *Sunrises and songs: Reading and writing poetry in an elementary classroom*. Portsmouth, NH: Heinemann.

kinds of poems and regular opportunities to write poetry seem to be critical variables. So does a teacher who loves poetry and is knowledgeable about the wide array of available choices in children's poetry. These activities provide children with models for how poetry looks, how other poets have described a particular phenomenon, and how various poetic elements complement and extend meaning.

Will this become common practice in the twenty-first century? Will teachers come to value poetry and see it as an essential aspect of the literature curriculum? I hope so. I am heartened by the increased number of poetry books being published at the beginning of the twenty-first century. Publishers would not be supporting so much poetry if it wasn't selling. Many more new poets, increasingly of diverse voice, are also getting published. (See Table 8.3 for a listing of NCTE Award for Excellence in Poetry for Children recipients.) Poetry slams, community poetry festivals, and conferences are springing up all over the country. I find this heartening.

Table 8.3
The NCTE Award for Excellence in Poetry for Children

2000 Recipient: X. J. Kennedy	1982 Recipient: John Ciardi
1997 Recipient: Eloise Greenfield	1981 Recipient: Eve Merriam
1994 Recipient: Barbara Juster Esbensen	1980 Recipient: Myra Cohn Livingston
1991 Recipient: Valerie Worth	1979 Recipient: Karla Kuskin
1988 Recipient: Arnold Adoff	1978 Recipient: Aileen Fisher
1985 Recipient: Lilian Moore	1977 Recipient: David McCord

Note: The National Council of Teachers of English (NCTE) wishes to recognize and foster excellence in children's poetry by encouraging its publication and by exploring ways to acquaint teachers and children with poetry through such means as publications, programs, and displays. As one means of accomplishing this goal, NCTE established its Award for Excellence in Poetry for Children in 1977 to honor a living American poet for his or her aggregate work. The award was given annually until 1982, at which time it was decided that the award would be given every three years. The collection of poetry books of all winners of the NCTE Award for Excellence in Poetry for Children, past and future, will be sustained and preserved in the Boston Public Library's Rare Books and Research Division. For more information, see www.ncte.org/elem/poetry/.

Still, I fear for poetry. With the advent of required state proficiency tests, accountability, "skills," budget constraints, and an emphasis on computers and other technology, I'm afraid that poetry, with its emphasis on enjoyment, feeling, and content, will be deemed irrelevant. Our late-twentieth-century society values rational thought, structure, and measurable objectives. Poetry does not prepare future citizens for these sorts of competencies.

Yet something causes poetry to endure. Maybe it's the appeal to deep emotions and sensitivities not commonly found anywhere else in our lives. Maybe it's the opportunity to experience pleasure in the power of poetic language to help us think symbolically, challenging our usual ways of thinking. Despite our attempts to define, control, analyze, and ignore poetry, it is still available to children at the end of the twentieth century. I think it will continue to be part of their lives into the twenty-first.

Notes

1. First published in the *San Francisco Examiner,* June 3, 1888, p. 4, col. 4.

2. "Little Orphant Annie," first published as "The Elf Child" in the *Indianapolis Journal,* November 15, 1885.

3. First published in 1794.

References

Apol, L., and J. Harris. 1999. Joyful noises: Creating poems for voices and ears. *Language Arts* 76: 314–322.

Avegno, S. 1956. Intermediate-grade children's choices in poetry. *Elementary English* 33: 428–432.

Barnes, D. 1976. *From communication to curriculum.* New York: Penguin.

Baskin, B. H., K. H. Harris, and C. C. Salley. 1984. Making the poetry connection. In *Jump over the moon: Selected professional readings,* ed. P. P. Barron and J. Q. Burley, 77–87. New York: Holt, Rinehart and Winston.

Bishop, M. 1932. Appreciation classes in sixth and seventh grades. *Elementary English Review* 9: 151–152.

Bowes, F., F. Painter, and L. Vesta. 1942. Use of recorded music to introduce literature to children. *Elementary English* 19: 178–180.

Bradshaw, R. 1937. Children's choices in the first grade. *Elementary English Review* 14: 168–176.

Bridge, E. B. 1966. *Using children's choices of and reactions to poetry as determinants in enriching literary experience in the middle grades.* Unpublished Ph.D. diss., Temple University, Philadelphia, PA.

Cariello, M. 1990. "The path to a good poem, that lasts forever": Children writing poetry. *Language Arts* 67: 832–838.

Comeaux, P. A. 1980. *Children performing poetry: A way of learning.* Unpublished Ph.D. diss., Southern Illinois University at Carbondale.

Craven, M. 1980. *A survey of teacher attitudes and practices regarding the teaching of poetry in the elementary.* Unpublished Ph.D. diss., Lamar University, Beaumont, Texas.

Dias, P. 1992. Cultural literacy, national curriculum: What and how does every Canadian student really need to know? *English Quarterly* 24: 10–19.

Duthie, C., and E. K. Zimet. 1992. "Poetry is like directions for your imagination!" *Reading Teacher* 46: 14–24.

Eckert, M. 1928. Children's choices of poems. *Elementary English Review* 5: 145–147.

Fisher, C. 1994. Sharing poetry in the classroom: Building a concept of poetry. In *Children's literature in the classroom: Extending Charlotte's Web,* ed. J. Hickman, B. Cullinan, and S. Hepler, 53–65. Norwood, MA: Christopher Gordon.

Fisher, C. J., and M. A. Natarella. 1982. Young children's preferences in poetry: A national survey of first, second and third graders. *Research in the Teaching of English* 16: 339–354.

Folta, B. P. 1979. *Effects of three approaches to teaching poetry to sixth grade students.* Unpublished Ph.D. diss., Purdue University, West Lafayette, IN.

Frost, R. 1923. *New Hampshire: A poem with notes and grace notes.* New York: Henry Holt.

Glenn, R. 1969. *Relating the subcultural world of the teenager to literature.* Ph.D. diss., Dissertation Abstracts International.

Heard, G. 1989. *For the good of the earth and sun: Teaching poetry.* Portsmouth, NH: Heinemann.

————. 1999. *Awakening the heart: Exploring poetry in the elementary and middle school.* Portsmouth, NH: Heinemann.

Hecht, S. N. 1978. *The teaching of poetry in grades seven and eight—A survey of theory, practices, and materials.* Unpublished Ph.D. diss., Boston University School of Education.

Hopkins, L. B. 1987. *Pass the poetry please.* New York: HarperCollins.

Huettenmueller, E. R. 1973. *A multi-sensory approach to teaching poetry to sixth-grade students.* Unpublished Ph.D. diss., The Ohio State University, Columbus.

Ingham, R. O. 1980. *The poetry preferences of fourth and fifth grade students in a suburban school setting in 1980.* Unpublished Ph.D. diss., University of Houston, TX.

Johnson, S. 1973. *A survey of reading habits: Theme four, literature, National Assessment of Educational Progress.* Denver, CO: Educational Commission of the States.

Jordan, A. 1921. *Children's interests in reading* Contributions to Education No. 107. New York: Teachers College, Columbia University.

Kangley, L. 1938. *Poetry preferences in the junior high school.* Contributions to Education No. 758. New York: Teachers College, Columbia University.

Kennedy, X. J. 1981. "Go and get your candle lit!" An approach to poetry. *Horn Book Magazine* 57: 273–279.

Koch, K. 1970. Wishes, lies, and dreams: Teaching children to write poetry. *New York Times Review of Books* 14 (April 9): 17–28.

————. 1973. *Rose, where did you get that red? Teaching great poetry to children.* New York: Random House.

————. 1998. *Making your own days: The pleasures of reading and writing poetry.* New York: Scribner's.

Krogness, M. M. 1995. *Just teach me, Mrs. K.: Talking, reading, and writing with resistant adolescent learners.* Portsmouth, NH: Heinemann.

————. 1998. The POW in language power. *Ohio Reading Teacher* 32: 17–20.

Kutiper, K., and P. Wilson. 1993. Updating poetry preferences: A look at the poetry children really like. *Reading Teacher* 47: 28–35.

Kutiper, K. S. 1985. *A survey of the adolescent poetry preferences of seventh, eighth, and ninth graders.* Unpublished Ph.D. diss., University of Houston, TX.

Kyte, G. 1942. Children's reactions to fifty selected poems. *Elementary School Journal* 48: 331–339.

Larrick, N. 1971. *Somebody turned on a tap in these kids*. New York: Delacorte.

Lenz, L. 1992. Crossroads of literacy and orality: Reading poetry aloud. *Language Arts* 69: 597–603.

Livingston, M. C. 1973. *When you are alone / It keeps you capone: An approach to creative writing with children*. New York: Atheneum.

———. 1975. But is it poetry?: Part I. *Horn Book Magazine* 51 (November/December): 571–580.

———. 1976. But is it poetry?: Part II. *Horn Book Magazine* 52 (January/February): 24–31.

———. 1978. Beginnings. *Language Arts* 55: 346–354.

Longfellow, H. W. 1855. *The song of Hiawatha*. Boston: Ticknor and Fields.

———. 1863. *Tales of a wayside inn*. Boston: Ticknor and Fields.

MacKintosh, H. 1924. A study of children's choices in poetry. *Elementary English Review* 1: 85–89.

———. 1931. A critical study of children's choices in poetry. [Monograph]. *Studies in Education* 7. Iowa City: University of Iowa Press.

Matanzo, J., and J. Madison. 1979. A poem-a-day can make a difference. *Connecticut English Journal* 10: 410–430.

McCall, C. J. H. 1979. *A determination of children's interest in poetry resulting from specific poetry experiences*. Unpublished Ph.D. diss., University of Nebraska, Lincoln.

McClure, A. A. 1985. *Children's responses to poetry in a supportive literary context*. Unpublished Ph.D. diss., The Ohio State University, Columbus.

———. 1990. *Sunrises and songs: Reading and writing poetry in an elementary classroom*. Portsmouth, NH: Heinemann.

Nelson, R. 1966. Children's poetry preferences. *Elementary English* 43: 247–251.

Norvell, G. W. 1958. *What boys and girls like to read*. New York: Silver Burdett.

Painter, H. M. W. 1970. *Poetry and children*. Newark, DE: International Reading Association.

Perfect, K. A. 1999. Rhyme and reason: Poetry for the heart and head. *Reading Teacher* 52: 728–737.

Purves, A. C., and R. Beach. 1972. *Literature and the reader: Research in response to literature, reading interests, and the teaching of literature*. Urbana, IL: National Council of Teachers of English.

Redmond, A. S. 1978. *Children's response to metaphor in poetry*. Unpublished Ph.D. diss., University of Minnesota, Minneapolis.

Riley, J. W. 1916. *The complete works of James Whitcomb Riley in ten volumes, including poems and prose sketches, many of which have not heretofore been published; an authentic biography, an elaborate index and numerous illustrations in color from paintings*. Memorial ed. New York: Harper.

Rosen, C., and H. Rosen. 1973. *The language of primary school children*. London: Schools Council.

Rosenblatt, L. M. 1968. *Literature as exploration*. Rev. ed. New York: Noble and Noble.

Rosenblatt, L. M. 1978. *The reader, the text, the poem: The transactional theory of the literary work*. Carbondale, IL: Southern Illinois Press.

Sandburg, C. 1916. *Chicago poems*. New York: Holt.

Schulte, E. S. 1967. *The independent reading interests of children in grades four, five and six*. Unpublished Ph.D. diss., The Ohio State University, Columbus.

Shapiro, P. P., and B. J. Shapiro. 1972. An evaluation of poetry lessons with children from less advantaged backgrounds. *Educational Leadership* 30 (October): 55–59.

Siemans, L. 1996. Walking through the time of kids: Going places with poetry. *Language Arts* 73: 234–240.

Silverstein, S. 1974. *Where the sidewalk ends*. New York: HarperCollins.

———. 1981. *A light in the attic*. New York: HarperCollins.

Simmons, M. P. 1980. *Intermediate-grade children's preference in poetry*. Unpublished Ph.D. diss., University of Alabama, Tuscaloosa.

Sloan, G. D. 1975. *The child as critic: Teaching literature in the elementary school*. New York: Teachers College Press.

———. 1999. *But is it poetry?* Unpublished manuscript, Queens College, New York.

Snedaker, M. 1925. Ballads in the sixth grade literature program. *Elementary English Review* 2: 206.

Squire, J., and M. Beckerman. 1950. The release of expression. *Elementary English* 39: 145–149.

Stevenson, R. L. 1895. *A child's garden of verses*. New York: Scribner's.

Terry, C. A. 1972. *A national survey of children's poetry preferences in the fourth, fifth, and sixth grades*. Unpublished Ph.D. diss., The Ohio State University, Columbus.

Thom, C. 1979. *What teachers read to pupils in the middle grades*. Unpublished Ph.D. diss., The Ohio State University, Columbus.

University of Toronto Library. 1997a. *Representative poetry on-line: Selected poetry of Ernest Lawrence Thayer, 1863–1940* [computer file]. University of Toronto Library. Accessed: June 19, 2001. Available: www.library.utoronto.ca/utel/rp/authors/thayer.html

University of Toronto Library. 1997b. *Representative poetry on-line: William Blake, 1757–1827, "The Tyger"* [computer file]. Web Development Group, Information Technology Services, University of Toronto Library. Accessed: June 19, 2001. Available: www.library.utoronto.ca/utel/rp/poems/blake17.html

Verble, D. 1973. *A road not taken: An approach to teaching poetry*. Nashville: Tennessee Arts Commission.

Viorst, J. 1981. *If I were in charge of the world and other worries*. New York: Aladdin.

9

From *The Story of Mankind* to Studies of AIDS

A Hundred Years of Informational Books for Children

James Cross Giblin

Today, in 1900, there are about ten thousand vehicles in Europe that are self-moving. It is thought there are about three hundred such vehicles in the United States. They are usually called automobiles. . . .

The automobile is the coming vehicle. We shall soon see it in all our cities and along our country roads. It is safe, fast, comfortable, and to use and ride in one is a pleasure we all will want to enjoy. . . . So we may imagine the child of the twentieth century saying, "Good-by, Mr. Horse! We thank you for all you have done for us. Go back to your farm and live in peace and comfort. Do the work you can do, and please don't be offended if we prefer to go to ride without you." (Barnard 1900, 388–389)

Those prophetic remarks are from an article titled "The Automobile: Its Present and Its Future" by a writer named Charles Barnard. It appeared in the March 1900 issue of *St. Nicholas* magazine, the best-known and most respected children's periodical at the turn of the century.

St. Nicholas was directed toward children ages six and older, but its articles and stories made few concessions to the slower reader. The type size used was small, and the vocabulary—like that in the preceding excerpt—was by no means limited to simple words. In this, it was typical of the books that were written and published for children in the early years of the twentieth century. Although a few big-city libraries had children's rooms by this time, no book publisher as yet had established a separate children's book department. If a manuscript for children came into the house, it was processed by an adult editor, and many books became children's favorites almost by accident.

To the Macmillan Company goes the credit for launching, in 1919, the first department devoted exclusively to the publication of books for children. Heading the

A version of Chapter 9 appeared in the July/August 2000 issue of the *Horn Book Magazine* under the title "More Than Just the Facts." Used with permission of Horn Book. © 2003.

department was Louise Seaman, who had previously done publicity on adult books for Macmillan. Before that, Seaman had taught in a progressive school, and so she knew how curious children were about the world around them and how things worked. From the start, her list at Macmillan included a wide assortment of informational books. Among them were such titles as *Buried Cities* by Jennie Hall (1922), *Girls in Africa* by Erick Berry (1928), and *Men at Work*, written and illustrated by the eminent photographer Lewis Hine (1932). As she said late in her career, Seaman believed "there is a poetry in jet planes and space ships and atoms."

Recognizing a new market, many other publishers founded children's book departments in the 1920s and 1930s. But none of these departments published *The Story of Mankind,* the nonfiction book by Hendrik Willem van Loon that won the first Newbery Medal in 1922. It was issued by Horace Liveright, which usually published adult books.

One of the strongest supporters of van Loon's book was the influential head of children's services at the New York Public Library, Anne Carroll Moore. In fact, she had been actively involved in its development, for van Loon had shown her his manuscript chapter by chapter as he was writing it. Later Moore (1961) commented, "No boy is likely to skip . . . a single chapter of a history which makes the world he lives in seem so spacious, so teeming with human interest" (160). (One assumes she thought girls would like the book, too.)

Today, van Loon's five-hundred-page tome is likely to seem more of a curiosity than anything else. The author's enthusiasm for his subject can be infectious, and his line drawings—which appear on almost every page—are charming. But other aspects of the book strike a contemporary reader as old-fashioned, if not downright dated. The beginning of the foreword provides a good example of van Loon's writing style: "History is the mighty Tower of Experience, which Time has built amidst the endless fields of bygone ages. It is no easy task to reach the top of this ancient structure and get the benefit of the full view. There is no elevator, but young feet are strong and it can be done" (van Loon 1921, xxii).

In structuring the book, van Loon follows the standard historical route of his day. He begins the chronicle with prehistoric man, then moves on to Ancient Egypt, Greece, Rome, the Dark Ages in western Europe, the Renaissance, and concludes with the modern era. There is nothing in the book about the history of Africa, and the coverage of Asian civilizations is limited to just ten pages on Confucius and Buddha.

Most surprising of all, in a book of this scope, there is a "Historical Reading List" at the back, but no index! One wonders how young readers of the 1920s and later could use the book for research.

The Story of Mankind may have been awarded the first Newbery Medal, but it certainly didn't start a trend. In the years since 1922, only five other informational books have won the Newbery. And none of them was a history; instead, all five were biographies. The winning titles included *Invincible Louisa: The Story of the Author of "Little Women"* by Cornelia Meigs (published 1933, Newbery awarded in 1934); *Daniel Boone* by James Daugherty (published 1939, Newbery awarded in 1940); *Amos Fortune, Free Man* by Elizabeth Yates (published 1950, Newbery awarded in 1951); *Carry On, Mr. Bowditch* by Jean Lee Latham (published 1955, Newbery awarded in 1956); and *Lincoln: A Photobiography* by Russell Freedman (published 1987, Newbery awarded in 1988). It's interesting to note that the five subjects of these biographies were all Americans, and only one of them was a woman.

Children's nonfiction fared better when it came to the selection of Newbery Honor Books. There have been thirty of those over the years, eighteen of them biographies (including two of George Washington). But the scope of subject matter treated in the Honor Books has gradually broadened. In 1951, Jeanette Eaton's *Gandhi: Fighter without a Sword* (1950) became the first biography of a non-Western figure to be awarded a Newbery Honor. Science writing received overdue recognition when Katherine Shippen's *Men, Microscopes, and Living Things* (1955) made the honors list in 1956. And a book of African American history entered the winners' circle for the first time in 1969 when the Newbery committee voted an honor to Julius Lester's groundbreaking work, *To Be a Slave* (1968).

Looking back at the biographies that have won Newbery Medals or Newbery Honors, one is reminded of a question that was raised about children's biographies for much of the twentieth century, and that still has not been entirely resolved: Should biographies include fictionalized scenes and dialogue to interest young readers, or should they hew strictly to the facts?

Author Jean Lee Latham made no bones about where she stood on the matter. In her Newbery acceptance speech for *Carry On, Mr. Bowditch* (1955), she frankly described her winning book as "fictionalized biography" (Latham 1956, 286). And as late as 1986, when the seventh edition of *Children and Books* by Zena Sutherland and May Hill Arbuthnot appeared, that bible of children's literature tried to have it both ways: "Perhaps fictionalized biography is the best pattern of biography for young people," the authors write. "There is no doubt that dialogue based on facts, written by a scholar and an artist, brings history to life and re-creates living, breathing people, who make a deep impression on children" (447).

A series of juvenile biographies launched in 1932 had helped to create a climate of acceptance for the fictionalized approach. This was the Childhood of Famous Americans series, which enjoyed great popularity in the thirties and for many decades after that.

A typical biography in the series was *Ethel Barrymore: Girl Actress* by Shirlee P. Newman, published in 1966. The copy on the jacket flap calls the book a story, not a biography, and the text bears out that description. It is written almost entirely in dialogue, in short, fast-moving paragraphs. Here's a sample passage:

Tumbling off the bed, Ethel and her brother Lionel threw their arms about their grandmother's knees. "Is it time to go, Mummum?" Ethel cried, using her grandmother's pet name. "Is it time to go and see Mama and Papa on the stage?"

"It will soon be time." Mummum leaned down and hugged them close. Then she pushed them away gently, and smoothed her long skirts. "Are you going to the theater like that, Ethel? What would the newspaper say?"

Mrs. Drew held a make-believe newspaper in the air. "Philadelphia, Pennsylvania," she pretended to read. "Ethel Barrymore, daughter of actors Maurice Barrymore and Georgia Drew Barrymore, went to the theater last night in a long, pink nightie." (Newman 1966, 12–13)

True to the series title, 176 of the book's 200 pages deal with the subject's childhood, taking Ethel only up to her stage debut at age fourteen in a play with her grandmother. The rest of the actress's life is crammed into pages 177 to 192, and the book ends with Ethel's seventieth birthday celebration, ten years before her death at eighty in 1959.

Stopping before the end of the subject's life was common in children's biographies of an earlier time, and not just in those published in the Childhood of Famous Americans series. For example, in *Abraham Lincoln,* a picture-book biography by Ingri and Edgar Parin D'Aulaire that won the Caldecott Medal in 1940, there is no mention of Lincoln's assassination. On the book's last page, the president simply sits down to rest in his rocking chair following the end of the Civil War. Such endings were an attempt—which many today would call misguided—to shield young readers from the harsher realities of life and give them a happy ending no matter what.

Attitudes toward fictionalization changed dramatically by the late 1980s. Jean Fritz, noted for her groundbreaking young biographies of the founding fathers, writes: "Once a biographer has collected the facts, it is not a matter of coaxing up a story; it is a matter of perceiving the story line that is already there. . . . I need as much evidence as I can get, for I do not invent" (Fritz 1988, 759).

Russell Freedman, in his Newbery acceptance speech for *Lincoln: A Photobiography,* took an even stronger stand in favor of sticking to the facts and avoiding any sort of dramatization. "Many current biographies for children adhere as closely to documented evidence as any scholarly work," he said. "And the best of them manage to do so without becoming tedious or abstract or any less exciting than the most imaginative fictionalization" (Horn Book and Association for Library Service to Children 2001, 76). Later, referring specifically to *Lincoln,* Freedman added, "It certainly wasn't necessary to embellish the events in his life with imaginary scenes and dialogue. Lincoln didn't need a speech writer in his own time, and he doesn't need one now" (Horn Book and ALSC 2001, 78).

I would venture to say that most writers of biographies for children today—as well as the majority of librarians and teachers who evaluate the books for purchase—would agree with Freedman's position. As I've learned from writing such biographies as *Charles A. Lindbergh: A Human Hero* (Giblin 1997), the use of excerpts from a subject's letters, diaries, speeches, and interviews can give young readers a much clearer impression of his or her personality than any invented dialogue possibly could.

Along with the move away from fictionalization, there arose a demand in the 1980s that nonfiction authors provide detailed notes on their sources—not just in biographies but in all types of informational books. Besides a list of sources, the books that followed often included glossaries, tables of important dates, and suggestions for further reading. And unlike *The Story of Mankind,* every informational book was now expected to have an index.

The new emphasis on accuracy was only one of the trends that swept through the children's nonfiction field in the latter part of the century. After the Soviet Union rocketed a satellite, *Sputnik,* into space in the fall of 1957, Congress responded by passing the National Defense Education Act of 1958. Among other things, the act provided funds for the purchase of science books by school libraries. This led publishers large and small to initiate new series of science books for all age levels. Among the most creative was the Let's Read and Find Out series, launched by Thomas Y. Crowell in 1960.

Aimed at youngsters in kindergarten through second grade, the Let's Read and Find Out series was in many ways the nonfiction counterpart to Harper's I Can Read series of easy-to-read stories. It combined the work of such outstanding science writers as Franklyn Branley, Paul Showers, and Judy Hawes with the illustrations of topflight artists including Aliki, Ed Emberley, Nonny Hogrogian, and Paul Galdone. The result was a line of books that combined solid information with lively, colorful graphics, books that entertained young readers even as they educated them.

Before the Let's Read and Find Out series came along, many nonfiction authors and editors thought the best way to interest youngsters in science was to surround the facts with a fictional framework. The result was the publication of countless books with titles like "Johnny and Janey Visit a Sewage Disposal Plant." The Let's Read and Find Out series and others like it seemed to have put an end to this particular brand of nonfiction hybrid, which usually succeeded neither as fiction nor nonfiction. But it surfaced again in a fresh and imaginative way with Joanna Cole's series of stories called The Magic School Bus, proving that even an outworn approach can be given new vitality by the right author.

School and public libraries received fresh support from President Lyndon B. Johnson's Great Society program of 1964. The new financing benefited all types of children's books, but nonfiction—and not just science nonfiction—got a large slice of the pie. The Great Society coincided with the rise of the Civil Rights movement in the United States. The latter movement, in turn, spawned a new interest in black history and the heroic men and women who had played active parts in it. Once again, Crowell led the way with a series of biographies for young people about such prominent figures as Harriet Tubman, Frederick Douglass, Rosa Parks, and Paul Robeson, written by well-known black authors such as Alice Walker, June Jordan, and Eloise Greenfield.

As federal funds for libraries dwindled in the 1970s and 1980s, children's book publishers shifted their focus to the bookstore market. To attract consumers, picture books became more colorful and juvenile nonfiction more visual. Some of the new nonfiction titles, such as David Macaulay's imaginative books about construction techniques, *Cathedral* (1973), *City* (1974), and *Pyramid* (1975), were illustrated with detailed drawings. But most of the nonfiction books that caught people's eyes in the 1970s were produced on heavy, high-grade paper and illustrated with top-quality black-and-white or full-color photographs. So many of these photo-illustrated books were published that they soon acquired a generic name: the photo essay.

The name might be new, but photo-illustrated fact books had occupied a small but significant niche in children's literature for many years. Florence Fitch's *One God: The Ways We Worship Him* (1944) made effective use of photographs to portray the rituals of the major religions in America. *Discovering Design* by Marion Downer (1947) introduced children to the similar patterns found in nature and in art. *What's Inside?* by May Garelick (1955) depicted the gradual emergence of a gosling from its egg.

The genre came into its own, though, with the publication of such photo essays of the 1970s as *Small Worlds Close Up* by Lisa Grillone and Joseph Gennaro (1978), *The Hospital Book* by James Howe (1981), and *Journey to the Planets* by Patricia Lauber (1982). Books like these attracted readers with their inviting design layouts and dramatic photographs, then held the readers' attention with tightly written and sharply focused texts, laced with carefully chosen anecdotes.

The trend toward more visual nonfiction books grew and spread in the 1980s. No longer was it confined to books for younger children; now it extended to books for the elementary and middle school grades. Some of the books were illustrated with contemporary pictures, others—such as Russell Freedman's *Children of the Wild West* (1983)—with archival photographs. Planning the illustration approach and researching the pictures became an important part of the nonfiction writer's job, as I discovered when I was working on such books as *From Hand to Mouth* (1987) and *The Riddle of the Rosetta Stone* (1990). In some cases, as in the popular Dorling Kindersley series on everything from ancient Rome to whales, the visual concepts came first and the texts of the books were often little more than captions.

At the same time children's nonfiction was becoming more attractive, it was gathering more serious critical attention. New awards were established to honor the creators of nonfiction: the *Boston Globe–Horn Book* Award for Nonfiction; the Golden Kite Award for Nonfiction, given by the Society of Children's Book Writers and Illustrators; and the Orbis Pictus Award, presented by the National Council of Teachers of English. The *Washington Post*–Children's Book Guild Award honored a nonfiction writer for his or her body of work.

Newbery Award committees also showed an increased interest in nonfiction—especially the new brand of illustrated nonfiction. After singling out only one nonfiction title as a Newbery Honor Book in the entire decade of the 1970s, the committees of the 1980s chose three in quick succession: *Sugaring Time* by Kathryn Lasky in 1984 (published in 1983); *Commodore Perry in the Land of the Shogun* by Rhoda Blumberg in 1986 (published in 1985); and *Volcano: The Eruption and Healing of Mount St. Helen's* by Patricia Lauber in 1987 (published in 1986). Then, in 1988, as noted before, the Newbery Medal was awarded to *Lincoln: A Photobiography* by Russell Freedman. It was the first time a nonfiction book had won the coveted Newbery since 1956, thirty-two years earlier.

After two decades of innovation in the children's nonfiction field, the 1990s were largely a time of consolidation. Russell Freedman received Newbery Honors for two more biographies, *The Wright Brothers: How They Invented the Airplane* in 1992 (published in 1991) and *Eleanor Roosevelt: A Life of Discovery* in 1994 (published in 1993), and Jim Murphy was given an honor in 1996 for *The Great Fire* (published in 1995), about the disastrous Chicago fire of 1871. But no nonfiction book of the nineties was awarded the Newbery Medal.

All three honor winners reflected the high standards of design and illustration that had been established for children's nonfiction in the previous decade. As more and more titles appeared in oversize formats with striking photographs or colorful paintings as illustrations, the traditional boundaries between age groups broke down. No longer did children in the upper elementary and middle school grades reject picture-book nonfiction as "babyish." Heavily illustrated titles such as Diane Stanley and Peter Vennema's biography of Shakespeare, *Bard of Avon* (1992); Stanley's *Joan of Arc* (1998) and *Leonardo da Vinci* (1996); Seymour Simon's spectacular books about the planets (*Mercury,* 1992a, and *Venus,* 1992b, for example); and my own picture-book biographies of *George Washington* (1992) and *Thomas Jefferson* (1994) found as much—if not more—acceptance from sixth graders as they did from third graders.

There are several possible explanations for this change in attitude. The most obvious is that modern young people, accustomed to getting so much of their information from television and the Internet, want the same sort of emphasis on the visual in their books. A second theory is less positive. It suggests that the many youngsters reading below their grade level find the brief texts in nonfiction picture books easier to grasp. Whatever the explanation, it seems clear that the trend toward nonfiction picture books for older children will continue in the new millennium.

Another trend that is likely to endure is the willingness to discuss hitherto taboo topics in children's informational books. In recent years, nonfiction writers have explored in a frank, thoroughgoing manner such subjects as child abuse, teenage sex and pregnancy, abortion, homosexuality, and substance abuse. However, they frequently have encountered opposition from pressure groups of various stripes who believe that such books are unsuitable for children and young adults.

I was made vividly aware of this situation a few years ago when I was asked by a Texas school librarian what project I was currently working on. I told her about the book that eventually became *When Plague Strikes* (1995), a comparative study of three deadly diseases, the Black Death, smallpox, and AIDS. "Oh, good," the librarian said. "I'll probably be able to purchase that book for my library because you put AIDS in the context of those other diseases. Given the strong feelings in my community, I couldn't buy a book about AIDS alone."

Despite such hurdles, I'm convinced that nonfiction writers will continue to explore controversial subject matter in the twenty-first century. Sensitively handled, these explorations can be an effective counterbalance to all the exploitative programming that is readily available to young people today on television and the Internet. If the opponents of so-called unsuitable books could be made to realize this, they might end up embracing the very books they are trying so hard to ban.

An unresolved issue at the beginning of the new century is the long-range impact the Internet will have on book publishing, generally, and children's nonfiction, in particular. Some claim that the book as we know it cannot survive and that young people in the future will receive all the information they need from one form of electronic transmission or another, including electronic books. I find this hard to believe, remembering when, not so long ago, various experts predicted that television would soon replace the book.

In fact, television in many instances has whetted the public's appetite for informational books. One librarian after another has told me that when a television program focuses on a particular subject—say a National Geographic special on elephants—libraries experience a run on books about elephants in the weeks that follow. I have a hunch that something similar may happen in the case of the Internet. After obtaining a summary of the desired information on screen, the young person will turn to a book for a more in-depth treatment of the subject—a book that does not require an electrical outlet or battery to operate and that can be transported easily to any place the young person wants to sit and read it.

There seems to be a circularity about most things in life; what goes around comes around, as the saying goes. This chapter began with an excerpt from an article about the automobile that appeared in a 1900 issue of *St. Nicholas*. Now I'll end it with an excerpt from another article about the automobile. This one is titled "A Hundred Years of Wheels and Wings"; the author is Jim Murphy (2000), and the piece is included in a nonfiction anthology, *The Century That Was: Reflections on the Last One Hundred Years* (Giblin 2000).

Like its predecessor, Murphy's article is filled with intriguing facts and is written in the sort of clear, lively style that has always marked—and no doubt will continue to mark—the best informational writing for children. The piece is framed with an account of the doings of an actual Connecticut farmer. Here is how it begins:

In the spring of 1901, Connecticut farmer Abel Hendron hitched his team of horses to the wagon and began the seven-and-a-half-mile journey to town to pick up the plow that he had ordered in February. Ordinarily, it could take him anywhere from two to four hours to reach town and come home, not counting stops he might make along the way to chat with neighbors." (53)

And here is how the piece ends, some sixteen pages later:

If Abel Hendron took a ride to town today, he would probably drive a pick-up truck or an off-road four-wheel-drive vehicle. . . . Few things would slow his drive, certainly not mud or roads so rutted as to be impassable. . . . In all, his travel time for the round trip journey of fourteen miles might be a half hour to forty minutes. . . .

   Abel would probably be startled to learn that the auto had replaced the horse in the lives and hearts of most Americans, and that only a handful of determined farmers still used them for work. . . . He might even blink in disbelief if someone told him that tests were being done on cars that moved over roads without wheels. . . . But Abel Hendron considered himself a modern farmer. So he would have driven quite happily into the twenty-first century, ready for whatever new forms of transportation the future might hold. (Murphy 2000, 68–69)

Just as we will move into the future, ready for whatever new forms the transmission of information may take. And one of them, I'm convinced, will be an old familiar form: the children's nonfiction book.

References

Barnard, C. 1900. The automobile: Its present and its future. *St. Nicholas* 27 (March): 379–389.

Berry, E. 1928. *Girls in Africa*. New York: Macmillan.

Blumberg, R. 1985. *Commodore Perry in the land of the Shogun*. New York: Lothrop, Lee & Shepard.

Daugherty, J. H. 1939. *Daniel Boone*. New York: Viking.

D'Aulaire, I., and E. P. D'Aulaire. 1939. *Abraham Lincoln*. New York: Doubleday.

Downer, M. 1947. *Discovering design*. New York: Lothrop, Lee & Shepard.

Eaton, J. 1950. *Gandhi, fighter without a sword*. Illus. R. Ray. New York: William Morrow.

Fitch, F. M. 1944. *One God: The ways we worship Him*. New York: Lothrop, Lee & Shepard.

Freedman, R. 1983. *Children of the Wild West*. New York: Clarion.

———. 1987. *Lincoln: A photobiography*. New York: Clarion.

———. 1991. *The Wright brothers: How they invented the airplane*. New York: Holiday House.

———. 1993. *Eleanor Roosevelt: A life of discovery*. New York: Clarion.

Fritz, J. 1988. Biography: Readability plus responsibility. *Horn Book* 64 (November/December): 759–760.

Garelick, M. 1955. *What's inside?* Illus. R. Jakobsen. New York: W. R. Scott.

Giblin, J. C. 1987. *From hand to mouth, or, How we invented knives, forks, spoons, and chopsticks, & the table manners to go with them.* New York: Crowell.

————. 1990. *The riddle of the Rosetta Stone: Key to ancient Egypt.* New York: Crowell.

————. 1992. *George Washington: A picture book biography.* Illus. M. Dooling. New York: Scholastic.

————. 1994. *Thomas Jefferson: A picture book biography.* Illus. M. Dooling. New York: Scholastic.

————. 1995. *When plague strikes: The Black Death, smallpox, AIDS.* Illus. D. Frampton. New York: HarperCollins.

————. 1997. *Charles A. Lindbergh: A human hero.* New York: Clarion.

————. 2000. *The century that was: Reflections on the last one hundred years.* New York: Atheneum.

Grillone, L., and J. Gennaro. 1978. *Small worlds close up.* New York: Crown.

Hall, J. 1922. *Buried cities.* New York: Macmillan.

Hine, L. W. 1932. *Men at work: Photographic studies of modern men and machines.* New York: Macmillan.

Horn Book and Association for Library Service to Children. 2001. *The Newbery and Caldecott Medal books, 1986–2000: A comprehensive guide to the winners.* Chicago: American Library Association.

Howe, J. 1981. *The hospital book.* Illus. M. Warshaw. New York: Crown.

Lasky, K. 1983. *Sugaring time.* Illus. C. G. Knight. New York: Macmillan.

Latham, J. L. 1955. *Carry on, Mr. Bowditch.* Illus. J. O. H. Cosgrave. Boston: Houghton Mifflin.

————. 1956. Newbery acceptance speech. *Horn Book* 32 (August): 283–292.

Lauber, P. 1982. *Journey to the planets.* New York: Crown.

————. 1986. *Volcano: The eruption and healing of Mount St. Helens.* New York: Bradbury.

Lester, J. 1968. *To be a slave.* Illus. T. Feelings. New York: Dial.

Macaulay, D. 1973. *Cathedral: The story of its construction.* Boston: Houghton Mifflin.

————. 1974. *City: A story of Roman planning and construction.* Boston: Houghton Mifflin.

————. 1975. *Pyramid.* Boston: Houghton Mifflin.

Meigs, C. 1933. *Invincible Louisa: The story of the author of "Little Women."* Boston: Little, Brown.

Moore, A. C. 1961. *My roads to childhood: Views and reviews of children's books.* Boston: Horn Book.

Murphy, J. 1995. *The great fire.* New York: Scholastic.

———. 2000. A hundred years of wheels and wings. In *The century that was: Reflections on the last one hundred years,* ed. J. C. Giblin, 53–69. New York: Atheneum Books for Young Readers.

Newman, S. P. 1966. *Ethel Barrymore, girl actress.* Indianapolis: Bobbs-Merrill.

Shippen, K. B. 1955. *Men, microscopes, and living things.* New York: Viking.

Simon, S. 1992a. *Mercury.* New York: Morrow Junior Books.

———. 1992b. *Venus.* New York: Morrow Junior Books.

Stanley, D. 1996. *Leonardo da Vinci.* New York: Morrow Junior Books.

———. 1998. *Joan of Arc.* New York: Morrow Junior Books.

Stanley, D., and P. Vennema. 1992. *Bard of Avon: The story of William Shakespeare.* Illus. D. Stanley. New York: Morrow.

Sutherland, Z., M. H. Arbuthnot, and D. L. Monson. 1986. *Children and books.* 7th ed. Glenview, IL: Scott Foresman.

van Loon, H. W. 1921. *The story of mankind.* New York: Boni & Liveright.

Yates, E. 1950. *Amos Fortune: Free man.* Illus. N. S. Unwin. New York: E. P. Dutton.

10

Nonfiction

A Genre Comes of Age

Evelyn B. Freeman

- A large urban school district sponsors an all-day workshop on informational books for a hundred elementary school literacy coordinators.

- Professional articles in journals about informational books and biographies increase; books for educators specifically on nonfiction appear; conferences feature sessions on nonfiction children's literature.

- Various literary awards to honor nonfiction children's books are started such as the Orbis Pictus Award of the National Council of Teachers of English, the nonfiction category in the *Boston Globe–Horn Book* Awards, and the American Library Association's Robert F. Sibert Informational Book Award.

- David Macaulay's *The Way Things Work* has sold more than 2.5 million copies and has been translated into nineteen languages.

These are some recent highlights in children's nonfiction literature that reflect changes within this genre in the twentieth century. Nonfiction has traditionally been considered the stepchild genre within children's literature, lacking in the recognition and popularity of fiction and picture books. It has suffered from negative stereotypes that have characterized nonfiction books as boring and difficult to read. Yet as we enter the twenty-first century, the image of nonfiction is rapidly changing and its popularity with children is rising. When we trace the development of nonfiction literature for children during the twentieth century, several themes emerge that represent the major landmarks. This chapter discusses some of the key changes in nonfiction children's literature—informational books and biography—during the twentieth century and focuses on the following areas: an increased emphasis on authenticity and research; an engaging writing style and corresponding view of nonfiction as literature; a variety of formats to present information; book design; informational picture books and picture-book biographies; evidence of humor; blended genres; and the visibility of informational books and biography in the elementary classroom.

Increased Emphasis on Authenticity and Research

Invincible Louisa: The Story of the Author of "Little Women" by Cornelia Meigs (1933) was the first biography to receive the Newbery Medal. Considered an authentic biography, it is illustrated with black-and-white photographs of Louisa's home and family members. Meigs provides acknowledgments of the sources she consulted in researching the biography. At the end of the book is a chronology of dates in Alcott's life and an index. Similarly, in the most recent biography to receive the Newbery Medal, *Lincoln: A Photobiography* by Russell Freedman (1987), black-and-white archival photographs illustrate the book, sources are noted, and an index is provided. If we look only at these two fine examples of children's biography, we may not realize the progression of children's biography as it has moved away from fictionalization toward more authenticity and accuracy.

Biography for children in the twentieth century included many fictionalized works in which authors took license to create dialogue, dramatize various events, and indicate thoughts of the subject that the author inferred or assumed but cannot document. For example, the Newbery Award–winning *Carry On, Mr. Bowditch* (Latham 1955) is a fictionalized biography of Nat Bowditch, the self-taught navigator. Although a highly readable and well-researched book, it contains invented dialogue and other aspects of fictionalization and lacks any acknowledgment of sources or research material. The 1940 Newbery Medal recipient, *Daniel Boone* (Daugherty 1939), creates an idealized Boone with fictionalized dialogue and assumed thoughts as well as negative stereotypes of Native Americans in text and illustrations. In 1982, Jo Carr wrote an article, "What Do We Do about Bad Biographies?" and commented on the generally poor quality of biography for children, which created larger-than-life heroes with no human frailties.

Informational books also show this change in the increased emphasis on careful research. Milton Meltzer has written informational books for children for more than forty years and has set a high standard for meticulous research, use of primary sources, and accuracy in presentation. He explains, "Much of my work has to do with letting people of the past speak their own voices. As much as possible, to tell their stories through what the scholars call 'primary evidence' " (Meltzer 1994, 63).

Although many informational books in the earlier decades of the twentieth century were carefully researched, no mention of sources was included in them. Sometimes an acknowledgment appeared such as in Sonia Bleeker's books on Native Americans. For instance, in *Indians of the Longhouse: The Story of the Iroquois* (Bleeker 1950), she writes, "Thanks are due to Dr. William N. Fenton, Bureau of American Ethnology, Smithsonian Institution, Washington, D.C., for reading and criticizing the manuscript" (5). This brief acknowledgment contrasts sharply with the extensive bibliography in Rhoda Blumberg's *The Great American Gold Rush* (1989), which contains a page of primary sources and a separate list of secondary sources.

In university children's literature courses, conference presentations, and articles on nonfiction, the criteria of accuracy and authenticity are mentioned first when evaluating children's informational books. Children's literature college textbooks further delineate these important criteria and advise readers to check for the author's credentials and qualifications, the inclusion of a reference list, and the clear distinction between fact and opinion.

Writing Style

As the twentieth century unfolded, the writing style of informational books paralleled that found in encyclopedias of that era. This straightforward style did not attempt to arouse curiosity and interest, engage the reader, use descriptive or figurative language, or tell a story. Yet many authors of nonfiction for children view themselves as storytellers and point out that they are telling a story, a true story, but one as interesting and engaging as a fictional one. Rhoda Blumberg, author of award-winning informational books, stated, "Stories are enchanting, and for me true stories—from history— are the most enchanting" (Sibert 1995, 66).

An example of a riveting true story is the Newbery Honor book, *The Great Fire* by Jim Murphy (1995). Murphy meticulously researched the Chicago fire of 1871, consulting many primary sources, such as letters written by individuals who experienced the fire, a book about the fire written in 1871, and archival photographs. He organizes this informational book by following the lives of actual individuals during the fire. His writing style is compelling, descriptive, and reads like a novel: "The wind coming off the prairie had been strong all day, sometimes gusting wildly, and leaves scuttled along the street; the sound of laughter and fiddle music drifted through the night" (13).

Writers have employed other narrative techniques to engage young readers. In the 1940s, Millicent Selsam began writing science informational books for children. In *Egg to Chick* (1946), she poses questions within the text such as, "What makes an egg grow into an animal?" (12). In *Bulbs, Corms, and Such* (1974), she addresses the reader as *you*: "You probably have planted seeds and watched new plants grow from them" (5). First paragraphs of informational books can pique interest and motivate readers to continue reading. Award-winning author James Cross Giblin is well known for his engaging first paragraphs. For example, he begins *The Riddle of the Rosetta Stone: Key to Ancient Egypt* (1990): "The scene: The Egyptian Sculpture Gallery of the British Museum in London. The time: Now" (3).

A trend in writing style that has occurred in the past twenty-five years is the author's use of first-person narrative, a literary technique usually associated with fiction. Jim Brandenburg's conversational first-person narrative transports readers to join his Arctic adventure in *To the Top of the World: Adventures with Arctic Wolves* (1993). His fascinating account begins: "The leader of the wolf pack glanced back at me as I scrambled after him across the sea. . . . My heart pounded with excitement because I sensed something about this wolf, whom I had nicknamed Buster (after my father)" (1). Jill Krementz spent a year with Vivi Malloy, whose story is told in the photo essay *A Very Young Rider* (1977). Vivi's ten-year-old voice narrates this factual account of Vivi, her pony, and her goal of being a member of the United States Equestrian Team.

Another change in writing style is the increased evidence of highly descriptive and figurative language. In *Safari beneath the Sea: The Wonder World of the North Pacific Coast* (Swanson 1994), even the table of contents reflects an emphasis on language with such chapter titles as "Spineless Superstars" and "Far-Out Fish." Robert Burleigh creates vivid imagery in *Flight: The Journey of Charles Lindbergh* (1991) as he writes: "He moves through dense, curling fog, lit ghostly white by the moon" (n.p.).

Thus, nonfiction in the twentieth century evolved from a focus on merely reporting facts to crafting a true story and led more people to view nonfiction for children as literature comparable to fiction. Patricia Lauber (1992), author of many award-winning informational books, eloquently summarizes this emphasis on nonfiction as literature:

> I hope to show that it is possible to read science for pleasure, that a good science book touches the mind, the heart, the imagination. I hope to show that a well-written science book can stand up to literary evaluation, that it is part of our literature, that it is deserving of a place on reading lists and in classroom libraries. (15)

Variety of Formats

During the first half of the twentieth century, the format of children's informational books was generally dense, expository paragraphs. Informational books looked like biographies and novels of the time, with continuous pages of text. In 1977, *Ashanti to Zulu: African Traditions* (Musgrove 1976) received the Caldecott Medal. This landmark book presented information about twenty-six African tribes in both the text and the detailed illustrations by Leo and Diane Dillon. Each letter of the alphabet designated a different African tribe and presented specific information about that tribe accompanied by a magnificent illustration. This format contributed to children's ability to easily access facts. Today, the ABC format is widely used to convey information on a host of subjects from airplanes to zoo animals.

Writers of informational books now embrace a variety of formats by which to share material with readers. In addition to the ABC format, the use of counting books organized around a theme is also becoming more evident. The groundbreaking book for this format is *Moja Means One: Swahili Counting Book* (Feelings 1971) with Caldecott Honor illustrations by Tom Feelings. As with ABC concept books, this counting book paired each number with information about the people who speak Swahili.

In the 1960s, George Sanderlin wrote several children's books based on journals of famous individuals. For instance, in *Across the Ocean Sea: A Journal of Columbus's Voyage* (1966), he explains that "most of this book consists of selections from Columbus's *Journal* for his voyage of 1492–93" (xi). Almost thirty years later, Steve Lowe selected portions of Columbus's journal to craft the informational picture book *The Log of Christopher Columbus* (1992). By presenting selections from an individual's own journal, young readers can identify with the events that are retold from a very personal perspective. Will Steger shares his diary entries to help readers follow his trek across the Arctic in *Over the Top of the World* (Steger and Bowermaster 1997). The journals of other famous historical figures have also been edited in a format appropriate for a child audience. In *Off the Map: The Journals of Lewis and Clark* (Roop and Roop 1993), the important journey of Meriwether Lewis and William Clark is told in their own words through journal entries.

The question and answer format provides children easy access to information. In *If Your Name Was Changed at Ellis Island* (1993), author Ellen Levine poses a question every two or three pages and then answers it. For example, "What was Ellis Island?" or "Would you go straight to Ellis Island when you arrived in New York Harbor?" Other examples of this format are *New Questions and Answers about Dinosaurs* (Simon 1990) and *Dinosaur Questions* (Most 1995).

An increase in types of access features (Kerper 1998) enables readers to gain information in multiple ways. These features, which may include table of contents, index, glossary, timelines, and sidebars, provide authors unique venues to share material with readers. If we review Aliki's *William Shakespeare and the Globe* (1999), we can see the many formats that convey information within a single book. First, the table of contents is organized like a playbill, listing the various acts and scenes within each act. So, Act One includes one scene, "Childhood," while Act Two has three scenes. Illustrations are captioned, and often they include facts and ideas not presented in the main text. Famous quotes from Shakespeare's plays are interspersed throughout the book. Illustrated captioned insets provide additional facts, such as the inset about Richard Burbage and the Earl of Southampton. A detailed map within the text shows London and the countryside during Shakespeare's time. There is a diagram of the Globe Theatre, a chronology of Shakespeare's life, a complete list of his plays and poems, an illustrated two-page spread of "Words and Expressions," and a page with "Sites to Visit" in London and Stratford-upon-Avon.

Book Design

The look of nonfiction books evolved and changed during the twentieth century. Technological advances led to innovative design, prevalence of full color, and computer-enhanced visuals. Beverly Kobrin (1995) points out that "a generation or so ago, illustrations were almost always black and white; pages of photographs were assembled in sections far from the words they pictured; and design and layout were pedestrian" (341). Today, bright color photographs attract readers' attention, a range of media is used to illustrate informational books and biography, and covers of books invite readers to open the pages.

The design of Seymour Simon's *Sharks* (1995) exemplifies the shift in informational books' appearance and the attention to visually appealing covers and designs. As readers turn the title page, a double-page spread of underwater color photographs of sharks swimming greets them. On each double-page spread, one side is filled with text and the other is a full-page color photograph, some of which almost jump off the page, like the teeth of the sand tiger shark.

Bush (1995) discusses photography in nonfiction for children, pointing out that "distinctive photography in children's nonfiction began to flourish in the 1960s, and through the following decades many skilled photographers have developed a personal body of work either in collaboration with writers or in illustrating books they have also written" (520). Jill Krementz was the first woman photographer for the *New York Herald Tribune* before she began creating her landmark children's book series about "A Very Young. . . ." These photo essays follow the life of a child who is engaged in riding, skating, dancing, acting, and other activities.

Photographer George Ancona brought his considerable talent to collaboration with others, most notably Joan Anderson, with whom he created such books as *The First Thanksgiving Feast* (1984) reenacted at Plimouth Plantation, before writing and photographing his own books such as *Powwow* (1993). Well-known writer-photographer collaborations in children's nonfiction include Kathryn Lasky and Christopher Knight (*The Weaver's Gift,* 1980), Dorothy Hinshaw Patent and William Muñoz (*Eagles of America,* 1995), Diane Hoyt-Goldsmith and Lawrence Migdale (*Hoang Anh: A Vietnamese-American Boy,* 1992), and Brent Ashabranner and Paul Conklin (*Gavriel and Jemal: Two Boys of Jerusalem,* 1984).

Other developments regarding photography as illustrations in informational books have also occurred. In addition to contemporary photographs, the inclusion of archival photographs has also become more evident. Russell Freedman, James Cross Giblin, Jim Murphy, and others are especially known for their thoughtful choice of archival photographs. These authors carefully research the photographs that are selected for the text. Technology has also influenced the nature of photographs used to illustrate books. In "Photography Note" for *The Brain: Our Nervous System,* Seymour Simon (1997) explains to young readers: "Scientists are using fantastic new machines that peer inside the human body to picture the invisible . . . many of these images were taken by various kinds of scanners, which change X-ray photos into computer code to make clear, colorful graphics. The computer-enhanced pictures of planets beamed back to Earth from distant space use a similar technique" (n.p.).

Another trend in book design is the size of the book so that informational books and biographies are no longer limited to 5¼ by 8 inches in size. Books by Edwin Tunis in the 1950s and 1960s such as the Newbery Honor title *Frontier Living* (1961) featured an oversized format. This oversized format received additional attention with the awarding of the Caldecott Honor book to David Macaulay's *Cathedral* (1973) and *Castle* (1977) and the publication of Peter Spier's *People* (1980). Today, informational books come in all shapes and sizes, with both horizontal and vertical orientations.

Illustrations for informational books and biographies are rendered in a wide variety of media, including paintings, pen-and-ink drawings, cartoons, and mixed media. In the 1960s, Leonard Everett Fisher wrote and illustrated a series of books on colonial craftspeople. For instance, in *The Glassmakers* (1964), striking black-and-white scratchboard illustrations accompany the text. More than thirty years later, Fisher is still writing and illustrating informational books and biographies but has expanded the media in which he works with acrylic paintings in *Marie Curie* (1994) and sepia-tone illustrations in *Anasazi* (1997). The evolution and expansion of the art in informational books and biographies relate closely to the next change to be discussed: the increase in informational picture books and picture-book biographies.

Informational Picture Books and Picture-Book Biographies

As the twentieth century progressed, we witnessed a steady increase in informational picture books and picture-book biographies. In addition, the number of nonfiction books specifically geared for primary-aged children expanded. In the early 1960s, Aliki wrote and illustrated titles for the Let's Read and Find Out Science Book series of Thomas Crowell Publishers. The audience for this series was children in the primary grades. In addition to informational books, Aliki also began crafting picture-book biographies in the early 1960s such as *The Story of William Penn* (1964).

Husband and wife collaborators Ingri and Edgar Parin D'Aulaire wrote the first picture-book biography, *Abraham Lincoln* (1939), which was awarded the 1940 Caldecott Medal. They continued to write picture-book biographies with such titles as *Benjamin Franklin* (1950) and *Columbus* (1955). More than fifty years later, this fine tradition was carried on by Diane Stanley, assisted by husband Peter Vennema, who has crafted biographies illustrated with Stanley's luxurious, detailed paintings, including *Charles Dickens: The Man Who Had Great Expectations* (1993) and *Bard of Avon: The Story of William Shakespeare* (1992).

Most recently, a picture-book biography, *Snowflake Bentley* (Martin 1998), was awarded the Caldecott Medal. Mary Azarian's woodcuts, hand tinted with watercolors, join seamlessly with the text to tell the life of Wilson Bentley, who photographed snowflakes and revealed that no two flakes are alike. In addition to the art of Azarian, the book is also illustrated with Bentley's snow crystal photographs.

Informational picture books have a history of recognition as Caldecott Honor books. In 1942, H. C. Holling's *Paddle to the Sea* (1941) was named an Honor Book. Although by today's standards the book's extensive fictionalization may not classify it as an informational book, the book is a geographically accurate expedition through the Great Lakes to the Atlantic Ocean. David Macaulay's works in the 1970s are certainly landmarks in terms of the blending of text and illustration to convey information. His detailed pen-and-ink drawings led to Caldecott Honor designations for *Cathedral* (1973) and *Castle* (1977).

Another landmark in the development of informational picture books was the appearance of the wordless books of Japanese artist Anno, who tells a true story completely through pictures. For instance, in *Anno's Britain* (1982), readers join a lone traveler as he visits the British countryside, watches a parade in front of Big Ben, and enjoys a stroll around Trafalgar Square. Similarly, John L. Goodall's wordless informational picture books, set in England, are social histories. *The Story of Main Street* (1987) traces the changes in an English main street from medieval times to the present day.

Probably the most prolific author of the informational picture book for young children is Gail Gibbons who has shared text and pictures on a wide range of topics and concepts since the late 1970s. Kvilhaug (1995) discusses Gibbons's life and work: "From boats to clocks, from gas stations to recycling, Gibbons takes a common object or process and breaks it down to easily digestible pieces, using bright, flat color and innovative design" (271). Other author-illustrators who are known for their informational picture books are Peter Spier and Aliki. Author David Adler has paired with several illustrators to write the picture-book biography series for Holiday House, which includes such titles as *A Picture Book of Amelia Earhart* (1998) and *A Picture Book of Frederick Douglass* (1993).

Evidence of Humor

Although children's nonfiction suffers from an unfortunate stereotype of being serious in tone, examples abound of humorous and whimsical informational books and biographies. Facts are fun, and many authors have used humor effectively in sharing information with young readers.

Though Jean Fritz is often credited with raising the standards for accuracy in biography for children, she also is known for her clever and witty treatment of her subjects. Since the publication of *And Then What Happened, Paul Revere?* (1973), Fritz has chronicled human beings who, although famous, possess the same foibles as others. She researches little-known tidbits about people's lives, conveying them to young readers in a lighthearted, conversational tone. For example, she writes: "Paul spent the summer sitting around, cleaning his rifle and polishing his sword. And swatting flies. There were thousands of flies at Lake George that summer" (12).

Vicki Cobb invites readers to engage in science activities and experiments through her unique and humorous books. More than thirty years ago, she wrote *Science Experiments You Can Eat* (1972), pointing out to readers how the recipes for various foods illustrate a scientific concept or principle. For example, the recipe for Borscht Cocktail allows readers to understand food suspension and how to separate suspended particles. Cartoon-like illustrations by Peter Lippman add to the book's light tone.

Blended Genres

A recent and controversial trend in informational books centers on the blending of genres in which informational books also include fantastic or fictional elements. The popular Magic School Bus series developed by science writer Joanna Cole and illustrated by Bruce Degen has shown children how much fun it can be to learn about science. However, these facts are shared through the eyes of fictional Ms. Frizzle and her class who travel in a magic school bus as they learn about the waterworks, the human body, the solar system, and other topics. Cole and Degen provide explanations at the conclusion of each book to indicate the fantastic elements. This series has been praised for opening the world of science to young readers and helping them delight in the joys of discovery.

Although most well known for his Arthur books, Marc Brown also has written and illustrated informational books with his wife Laurene Krasny Brown that present material on serious and important topics in a lighthearted, child-oriented way. Rather than people, dinosaurs are the main characters, introducing a fantasy element to these books. In *Dinosaurs Divorce: A Guide for Changing Families* (1986), the simple text, appropriate for primary children, is enhanced through illustrations featuring personified dinosaurs. For instance, in the section "Living with Stepparents," the text reads, "Pick a name for your stepparent that you find easy to use and your stepparent is comfortable with," and the illustration shows a young dinosaur holding a clipboard, standing near his stepmother. The paper on the clipboard lists the words "Stepmom, extra mom Julie, and mom-Julie."

Math also can be described through humor and playful language. Popular illustrator Steven Kellogg has created Marvelosissimo, the mathematical magician, and riotous illustrations for David Schwartz's jovial text in *How Much Is a Million?* (1985) and *If You Made a Million* (1989). These informational math books delight readers and enable mathematical concepts to come alive in a vibrant way.

Although popular with children, these blended texts have been criticized for their potential to confuse children who may not be able to differentiate fact from fiction. Many fear that children will be misled, confused, and learn inaccurate information.

Visibility of Informational Books and Biography

Within the past decade, informational books and biographies increased their visibility in the elementary classroom. Two landmark professional books, *Matters of Fact: Aspects of Non-Fiction for Children* by Margery Fisher (1972) and *Beyond Fact: Nonfiction for Children and Young People* edited by Jo Carr (1982), were devoted exclusively to the nonfiction genre, but a paucity of professional literature on informational books and biographies existed prior to the 1980s.

The literature-based reading movement in the 1980s included an emphasis on literature across the curriculum and sparked professional attention in publications and professional presentations on informational books and biographies. More book chapters and journal articles discussed ways to integrate books of all genres in the curriculum. Research studies focused specifically on informational books (Pappas 1991, 1993; Robb 1994) and teacher-researcher articles describing how nonfiction was shared with children in classrooms (Duthie 1994; Guth 1992) were published in educational journals.

In 1988, the National Council of Teachers of English started the Committee on Using Nonfiction in the Elementary Language Arts Classroom, which was followed by the establishment of the Orbis Pictus Award in 1989 (see Table 10.1). The committee edited a volume that focused exclusively on the genre, *Using Nonfiction Trade Books in the Elementary Classroom: From Ants to Zeppelins* (Freeman and Person 1992). Other books devoted to this genre also appeared in the 1990s, such as *Nonfiction for Young Adults: From Delight to Wisdom* (Carter and Abrahamson 1990), *Nonfiction for the Classroom* (Meltzer 1994), *Using Nonfiction in the Classroom* (Burke and Glazer 1994), and *Making Facts Come Alive: Choosing Quality Nonfiction Literature K–8* (Bamford and Kristo 1998).

Teachers are writing articles and presenting at conferences on ways they have integrated nonfiction into their classrooms. For instance, in the preface to *True Stories: Nonfiction Literacy in the Primary Classroom* (1996), first-grade teacher Christine Duthie shares, "Young nonfiction readers move beyond 'encyclopedia text,' and young writers beyond 'the facts' to view nonfiction as a unique genre rich in possibilities" (v).

Table 10.1
The Orbis Pictus Award for Outstanding Nonfiction for Children

2003 Pam Muñoz Ryan. *When Marian Sang: The True Recital of Marian Anderson: The Voice of a Century.* Illus. B. Selznick. Scholastic.
Honor Books
    Jane O'Connor. *Emperor's Silent Army: Terracotta Warriors of Ancient China.* Viking.
    Russell Freedman. *Confucius: The Golden Rule.* Illus. F. Clement. Arthur A. Levine Books.
    John Fleischman. *Phineas Gage: A Gruesome but True Story About Brain Science.* Houghton Mifflin.
    Raymond Bial. *Tenement: Immigrant Life on the Lower East Side.* Houghton Mifflin.
    Wendie C. Old. *To Fly: The Story of the Wright Brothers.* Illus. R. A. Parker. Clarion.
2002 Susan Campbell Bartoletti. *Black Potatoes: The Story of the Great Irish Famine, 1845–1850.* Houghton Mifflin.
Honor Books
    Mark Kurlansky. *The Cod's Tale.* Illus. S. D. Schindler. Penguin Putnam.
    Barbara Kerley. *The Dinosaurs of Waterhouse Hawkins: An Illuminating History of Mr. Waterhouse Hawkins, Artist and Lecturer.* Illus. B. Selznick. Scholastic.
    Doreen Rappaport. *Martin's Big Words: The Life of Dr. Martin Luther King, Jr.* Illus. B. Collier. Hyperion Books for Children.
2001 Jerry Stanley. *Hurry Freedom: African Americans in Gold Rush California.* Crown.
Honor Books
    James Cross Giblin. *The Amazing Life of Benjamin Franklin.* Scholastic.
    David A. Adler. *America's Champion Swimmer: Gertrude Ederle.* Gulliver Books.

(Continued)

Table 10.1(*Cont.*)

Diane Stanley. *Michelangelo*. HarperCollins.

Jim Arnosky. *Wild and Swampy: Exploring with Jim Arnosky*. HarperCollins.

Osceola Mays and Alan Govenar. *Osceola: Memories of a Sharecropper's Daughter*. Jump at the Sun.

2000   Ruby Bridges and Margo Lundell. *Through My Eyes*. Scholastic.

Honor Books

Sylvia A. Johnson. *Mapping the World*. Atheneum.

Walter Dean Myers. *At Her Majesty's Request: An African Princess in Victorian England*. Scholastic.

Susanna Reich. *Clara Schumann: Piano Virtuoso*. Clarion Books.

Sy Montgomery. *The Snake Scientist*. Illus. N. Bishop. Houghton Mifflin.

Steve Jenkins. *The Top of the World: Climbing Mount Everest*. Houghton Mifflin.

1999   Jennifer Armstrong. *Shipwreck at the Bottom of the World: The Extraordinary True Story of Shackleton and the Endurance*. Crown.

Honor Books

Anita Lobel. *No Pretty Pictures: A Child of War*. Greenwillow.

Robert Burleigh. *Black Whiteness: Admiral Byrd Alone in the Antarctic*. Illus. W. L. Krudop. Atheneum.

Thom Holmes. *Fossil Feud: The Rivalry of the First American Dinosaur Hunters*. Messner.

Steve Jenkins. *Hottest, Coldest, Highest, Deepest*. Houghton.

1998   Laurence Pringle. *An Extraordinary Life: The Story of a Monarch Butterfly*. Illus. B. Marshall. Orchard.

Honor Books

Walter Wick. *A Drop of Water: A Book of Science and Wonder*. Scholastic.

Arthur Dorros. *A Tree Is Growing*. Illus. S. D. Schindler. Scholastic.

Jerry Stanley. *Digger: The Tragic Fate of the California Indians from the Missions to the Gold Rush*. Crown.

James Cross Giblin. *Charles A. Lindbergh: A Human Hero*. Clarion.

Wilborn Hampton. *Kennedy Assassinated: The World Mourns. A Reporter's Story*. Candlewick.

1997   Diane Stanley. *Leonardo da Vinci*. Morrow.

Honor Books

Russell Freedman. *The Life and Death of Crazy Horse*. Holiday House.

Rhoda Blumberg. *Full Steam Ahead: The Race to Build a Transcontinental Railroad*. National Geographic Society.

Mary Pope Osborne. *One World, Many Religions: The Ways We Worship*. Knopf.

1996   Jim Murphy. *The Great Fire*. Scholastic.

Honor Books

Penny Colman. *Rosie the Riveter: Women Working on the Home Front in World War II*. Crown.

Laurence Pringle. *Dolphin Man: Exploring the World of Dolphins*. Photography by Randall S. Wells. Atheneum.

1995   Diane Swanson. *Safari Beneath the Sea: The Wonder World of the North Pacific Coast*. Sierra.

Honor Books

Russell Freedman. *Kids at Work: Lewis Hine and the Crusade against Child Labor*. Clarion.

Jennifer Owings Dewey. *Wildlife Rescue: The Work of Dr. Kathleen Ramsay*. Boyds Mills.

Patricia C. McKissack and Frederick L. McKissack. *Christmas in the Big House, Christmas in the Quarters*. Scholastic.

(*Continued*)

1994   Jim Murphy. *Across America on an Emigrant Train*. Clarion.
Honor Books
>   Bruce Brooks. *Making Sense: Animal Perception and Communication*. Farrar, Straus and
>   Giroux.
>   Jim Brandenburg. *To the Top of the World: Adventures with Arctic Wolves*. Walker.

1993   Jerry Stanley. *Children of the Dust Bowl: The True Story of the School at Weedpatch Camp*.
Crown.
Honor Books
>   Pat Cummings. *Talking to Artists*. Bradbury.
>   Molly Cone. *Come Back, Salmon*. Sierra.

1992   Robert Burleigh. *Flight: The Journey of Charles Lindbergh*. Philomel.
Honor Books
>   Walter Dean Myers. *Now Is Your Time: The African-American Struggle for Freedom*
>   HarperCollins.
>   Pam Conrad. *Prairie Vision: The Life and Times of Solomon Butcher*. HarperCollins.

1991   Russell Freedman. *Franklin Delano Roosevelt*. Clarion.
Honor Books
>   Normee Ekoomiak. *Arctic Memories*. Holt.
>   Patricia Lauber. *Seeing Earth from Space*. Orchard.

1990   Jean Fritz. *The Great Little Madison*. Putnam.
Honor Books
>   Rhoda Blumberg. *The Great American Gold Rush*. Bradbury.
>   Patricia Lauber. *The News about Dinosaurs*. Bradbury.

Note: The Orbis Pictus Award was established in 1989 with the first award given in 1990 by the National Council of Teachers of English to promote and recognize excellence in nonfiction writing. The award is named in commemoration of the book *Orbis Pictus* (*The World in Pictures*) by Bishop Johann Amos Comenius. It was originally published in 1657 and is considered to be the first informational book written specifically for children. For additional information, please visit the Orbis Pictus Award Web site: http://www.ncte.org/elem/pictus/.

Conclusion

   This chapter has described some of the key changes that have occurred as children's nonfiction, informational books, and biographies developed during the twentieth century. We can see how this genre has evolved to be vibrant and growing within the field of children's literature. It is a genre that has come of age. At the beginning of the twenty-first century, however, children's nonfiction literature can look forward to many new landmarks and milestones. The impact on publishing of rapid changes in technology, the increased access to the Internet as a source of information for children, and the recent attention regarding the importance of children reading nonfiction texts are forces that will influence the evolution of nonfiction in the coming decades. Although the first Newbery Medal was awarded to a nonfiction title, *The Story of Mankind* (van Loon 1921) and several informational books have been named Newbery Honor books, no informational book (as distinct from biography) since the first Newbery has yet received the highest honor in children's literature. We eagerly await the day when everyone recognizes nonfiction as literature, worthy of the highest honors we can bestow.

References

Adler, D. A. 1993. *A picture book of Frederick Douglass.* Illus. S. Byrd. New York: Holiday House.

———. 1998. *A picture book of Amelia Earhart.* Illus. J. Fisher. New York: Holiday House.

Aliki. 1964. *The story of William Penn.* Englewood Cliffs, NJ: Prentice Hall.

———. 1999. *William Shakespeare and the Globe.* New York: HarperCollins.

Ancona, G. 1993. *Powwow.* San Diego: Harcourt Brace Jovanovich.

Anderson, J. 1984. *The first Thanksgiving feast.* Illus. G. Ancona. New York: Clarion.

Anno, M. 1982. *Anno's Britain.* New York: Philomel.

Ashabranner, B. K. 1984. *Gavriel and Jemal: Two boys of Jerusalem.* Illus. P. Conklin. New York: Dodd Mead.

Bamford, R. A., and J. V. Kristo. 1998. *Making facts come alive: Choosing quality nonfiction literature K–8.* Norwood, Mass.: Christopher-Gordon.

Bleeker, S. 1950. *Indians of the longhouse: The story of the Iroquois.* Illus. A. Kerr. New York: Morrow.

Blumberg, R. 1989. *The great American gold rush.* New York: Bradbury.

Brandenburg, J. 1993. *To the top of the world: Adventures with Arctic wolves.* New York: Walker.

Brown, L. K., and M. T. Brown. 1986. *Dinosaurs divorce: A guide for changing families.* Boston: Little, Brown.

Burke, E. M., and S. M. Glazer. 1994. *Using nonfiction in the classroom.* New York: Scholastic.

Burleigh, R. 1991. *Flight: The journey of Charles Lindbergh.* Illus. M. Wimmer. New York: Philomel.

Bush, M. 1995. Photography in nonfiction for children. In *Children's books and their creators,* ed. A. Silvey, 520–522. Boston: Houghton Mifflin.

Carr, J., ed. 1982. *Beyond fact: Nonfiction for children and young people.* Chicago: American Library Association.

Carr, J., ed. 1982. What do we do about bad biographies? In *Beyond fact: Nonfiction for children and young people,* ed. J. Carr, 118–129. Chicago: American Library Association.

Carter, B., and R. F. Abrahamson, eds. 1990. *Nonfiction for young adults: From delight to wisdom.* Phoenix, AZ: Oryx.

Cobb, V. 1972. *Science experiments you can eat.* Illus. P. J. Lippman. New York: Harper & Row.

Daugherty, J. H. 1939. *Daniel Boone.* New York: Viking.

D'Aulaire, I., and E. P. D'Aulaire. 1939. *Abraham Lincoln.* New York: Doubleday.

———. 1950. *Benjamin Franklin.* Garden City, NY: Doubleday.

———. 1955. *Columbus*. Garden City, NY: Doubleday.

Duthie, C. 1994. Nonfiction: A genre study for the primary classroom. *Language Arts* 71: 588–595.

———. 1996. *True stories: Nonfiction literacy in the primary classroom*. York, ME: Stenhouse.

Feelings, M. L. 1971. *Moja means one: Swahili counting book*. Illus. T. Feelings. New York: Dial.

Fisher, L. E. 1964. *The glassmakers*. New York: Franklin Watts.

———. 1994. *Marie Curie*. New York: Macmillan.

———. 1997. *Anasazi*. New York: Atheneum Books.

Fisher, M. T. 1972. *Matters of fact: Aspects of non-fiction for children*. New York: Crowell.

Freedman, R. 1987. *Lincoln: A photobiography*. New York: Clarion.

Freeman, E. B., and D. G. Person, eds. 1992. *Using nonfiction trade books in the elementary classroom: From ants to zeppelins*. Urbana, IL: National Council of Teachers of English.

Fritz, J. 1973. *And then what happened, Paul Revere?* Illus. M. Tomes. New York: Coward-McCann.

Giblin, J. 1990. *The riddle of the Rosetta Stone: Key to ancient Egypt. Illustrated with photographs, prints, and drawings*. New York: Crowell.

Goodall, J. S. 1987. *The story of a main street*. New York: McElderry.

Guth, N. D. 1992. Get real, teacher! What happens when at-risk middle-school readers become involved with nonfiction. In *Using nonfiction trade books in the elementary classroom: From ants to zeppelins,* ed. E. B. Freeman and D. G. Person, 17–25. Urbana, IL: National Council of Teachers of English.

Holling, H. C. 1941. *Paddle to the Sea*. Boston: Houghton Mifflin.

Hoyt-Goldsmith, D., and L. Migdale. 1992. *Hoang Anh: A Vietnamese-American boy*. Illus. L. Migdale. New York: Holiday House.

Kerper, R. M. 1998. Choosing quality nonfiction literature: Features for accessing and visualizing information. In *Making facts come alive: Choosing quality nonfiction literature K–8,* ed. R. A. Bamford and J. V. Kristo, 55–74. Norwood, MA: Christopher-Gordon.

Kobrin, B. 1995. Information books. In *Children's books and their creators,* ed. A. Silvey, 341–344. Boston: Houghton Mifflin.

Krementz, J. 1977. *A very young rider*. New York: Knopf.

Kvilhaug, S. K. 1995. Gail Gibbons. In *Children's books and their creators,* ed. A. Silvey, 270–272. Boston: Houghton Mifflin.

Lasky, K. 1980. *The weaver's gift*. Illus. C. G. Knight. New York: Frederick Warne.

Latham, J. L. 1955. *Carry on, Mr. Bowditch*. Illus. J. O. H. Cosgrave. Boston: Houghton Mifflin.

Lauber, P. 1992. The evolution of a science writer. In *Using nonfiction trade books in the elementary classroom: From ants to zeppelins,* ed. E. B. Freeman and D. G. Person, 11–16. Urbana, IL: National Council of Teachers of English.

Levine, E. 1993. *If your name was changed at Ellis Island.* Illus. W. Parmenter. New York: Scholastic.

Lowe, S., ed. 1992. *The log of Christopher Columbus: The first voyage, spring, summer, and fall 1492.* Illus. R. Sabuda. New York: Philomel.

Macaulay, D. 1973. *Cathedral: The story of its construction.* Boston: Houghton Mifflin.

———. 1977. *Castle.* Boston: Houghton Mifflin.

Martin, J. B. 1998. *Snowflake Bentley.* Illus. M. Azarian. Boston: Houghton Mifflin.

Meigs, C. 1933. *Invincible Louisa: The story of the author of "Little Women."* Boston: Little, Brown.

Meltzer, M. 1994. *Nonfiction for the classroom: Milton Meltzer on writing, history, and social responsibility.* New York: Teachers College Press.

Most, B. 1995. *Dinosaur questions.* San Diego: Harcourt Brace.

Murphy, J. 1995. *The great fire.* New York: Scholastic.

Musgrove, M. 1976. *Ashanti to Zulu: African traditions.* Illus. L. Dillon and D. Dillon. New York: Dial.

Pappas, C. C. 1991. Fostering full access to literacy by including information books. *Language Arts* 68: 449–462.

———. 1993. Is narrative "primary"? Some insights from kindergarteners' pretend readings of stories and information books. *Journal of Reading Behavior* 25: 97–129.

Patent, D. H. 1995. *Eagles of America.* Illus. W. MuZoz. New York: Holiday House.

Robb, L. 1994. Second graders read nonfiction: Investigating natural phenomena and disasters. *New Advocate* 7: 239–252.

Roop, P., and C. Roop. 1993. *Off the map: The journals of Lewis and Clark.* Illus. T. Tanner. New York: Walker.

Sanderlin, G. W. 1966. *Across the ocean sea: A journal of Columbus's voyage.* Illus. L. Kubinyi. New York: Harper & Row.

Schwartz, D. M. 1985. *How much is a million?* Illus. S. Kellogg. New York: Lothrop, Lee & Shepard.

———. 1989. *If you made a million.* Illus. S. Kellogg. New York: Lothrop, Lee & Shepard.

Selsam, M. 1946. *Egg to chick.* Illus. B. Wolff. New York: Harper & Row.

Selsam, M. E. 1974. *Bulbs, corms, and such.* Illus. J. Wexler. New York: William Morrow.

Sibert, M. F. 1995. Rhoda Blumberg. In *Children's books and their creators,* ed. A. Silvey, 65–66. Boston: Houghton Mifflin.

Simon, S. 1990. *New questions and answers about dinosaurs.* Illus. J. Dewey. New York: Morrow.

———. 1995. *Sharks.* New York: HarperCollins.

———. 1997. *The brain: Our nervous system.* New York: William Morrow.

Spier, P. 1980. *People.* Garden City, NY: Doubleday.

Stanley, D., and P. Vennema. 1992. *Bard of Avon: The story of William Shakespeare.* Illus. D. Stanley. New York: William Morrow.

———. 1993. *Charles Dickens: The man who had great expectations.* New York: William Morrow.

Steger, W., and J. Bowermaster. 1997. *Over the top of the world: Explorer Will Steger's trek across the Arctic.* New York: Scholastic.

Swanson, D. 1994. *Safari beneath the sea: The wonder world of the North Pacific Coast.* Photographs by the Royal British Columbia Museum. San Francisco: Sierra Club Books for Children.

Tunis, E. 1961. *Frontier living.* New York: Crowell.

Van Loon, H. W. 1921. *The story of mankind.* New York: Boni & Liveright.

11

Reflections

Julius Lester

It is rather startling to be asked to reflect on literature for black children in the twentieth century and to realize that one's life has covered sixty years of that century. Although startling, it is also exhilarating to be able to look back over such an expanse of time and see from where one has come.

So, my remarks are in the manner of personal reflections since I am not a scholar of African American children's literature who could give you a survey of the evolution of that literature in the twentieth century. Though some of what I say might apply to the black experience generally, please understand that the black experience is exceedingly complex and no individual can speak for all of it.

I was born in 1939, grew up in Kansas City, Kansas, and Nashville, Tennessee, and spent parts of summers at my maternal grandmother's in Arkansas. I do not remember any books from childhood except "Jack and the Beanstalk" and *Little Black Sambo* (Bannerman 1900), which I remember primarily because it made me feel ashamed.

The forties and fifties were not pleasant decades for blacks, and I am uncomfortable around white people who get nostalgic for the fifties. I am not nostalgic for segregation, for the "No Colored Allowed" signs that covered the landscape like litter on the smooth green grass of a park. I am not nostalgic for a time when my life was in danger if I raised my eyes and they accidentally met those of a white girl or woman. Black men and boys were lynched for this during my growing-up years.

Though I do not remember specific books, I remember reading, as if the act of reading was more important than what was being read. As I recall, I read biographies, history, and geography, and I realize now that each subject area took me out of my immediate environment. Through biographies I could be someone else, and in books about history and geography I could live in another time and place. Those now-forgotten books gave me an emotional knowledge that a world bounded by the white heat of hatred was not the only reality. Somewhere my eyes could not then penetrate were dreams and possibilities.

The mystery and miracle of a book are found in the fact that it is a solitary voice penetrating time and space to go beyond time and space and alight for a moment in that place within each of us that is also beyond time and space. And what is really wonderful about a book is that it does not have to be "great" literature to work its magic on you. So, although I can't remember all the books I read as a child, I do remember the comic books with much affection. My father brought home comic books in a cardboard box, a hundred at a time. I remember the comic book shop he would take me to where I swapped comics two for one. In comics my imaginative mind was nurtured. Every child yearns for the power of a superhero or the wizardry of a sorcerer, and that yearning was especially poignant for at least one black child in the forties and fifties.

My other memory of childhood reading is rather macabre. I read countless issues of such magazines as *True Police Stories* and *Police Gazette*. They were pulp magazines that recounted in graphic detail the true stories of lurid murders. The stories were accompanied by crime scene photographs of the murder victims. This is what I read avidly at age eight. Why I did so will become clearer in a few moments.

In the early fifties, my family moved from Kansas to Tennessee, and there I discovered that blacks were permitted in only one library—the "colored" branch, as it was referred to then. It was on the other side of town from where I lived, an hour or more one way by public transportation. So, my only access to books was the bookmobile that came to my neighborhood every Friday evening. Its stock of books was not only limited in number but consisted primarily of westerns and mystery novels discarded from the white libraries. So, through much of my adolescence, I read almost nothing but westerns and Perry Mason mysteries (see Gardner 1933) and would read two to six every weekend.

I marvel at the wisdom of my parents. They never questioned or derided what I read. I am astounded that they bought the magazines and comic books for me since they were devoid of literary merit. But maybe my parents understood on some primal level what I was doing, though I did not.

I grew up in a violent world. Segregation was a psychological and spiritual violence, not only in its many restrictions on where we could live, eat, attend school, and go at night. Segregation violated the very premise of my existence by decreeing that I was inferior to the white majority by the mere fact that I had been born black. There was also the continual threat of physical retribution and even death if you looked at a white man in what he considered the wrong way or if he didn't like your attitude. There was also the actual physical violence in my neighborhood. I will not recite the deaths from stabbings or shootings or speak of classmates imprisoned for rapes they did not commit. I will not recite the deaths of classmates from accidental fires or car accidents. Suffice it to say that I grew up in conditions in which fear and death were neighbors, and if you weren't careful, they could sneak through your back door and be sitting at the dinner table, knife and fork in their hands, and a paper napkin tucked in their shirt.

What does a child do who is exposed daily to such violence, who confronts the force of death even before he can spell the word? I was an adult before I understood that my reading of comic books and murder magazines, westerns and mysteries was an attempt to neutralize and withstand the violence intrinsic to my dailiness. In reading about violence, I found a way to isolate and objectify it, to see it as separate from me. Reading about it also reassured me that violence was not unique to my neighborhood and not only did it exist in other places, it existed at other times. And, yes, it was also reassuring to read that white people died, too. Reading about violence was also like a vaccination, in which I immunized myself against that which sought to harm me.

I am thankful my parents did not impose literary judgments on me but left me alone to read what I wanted to. They trusted me to educate my soul as I saw fit, though I did not know that was what I was doing.

There were no children's books in my childhood nor in those of any black children I knew. Perhaps that is because we did not have childhoods. Nothing so illustrates for me the gap between blacks and whites of my generation than the fact that I have still not read some of the recognized and much-loved children's books of my white friends such as *Winnie-the-Pooh* (Milne 1926) and *Charlotte's Web* (White 1952). Thus, it is not surprising that the February 23, 1970, issue of *Publishers Weekly* included an article by me titled "The Kinds of Books We Give Children: Whose Nonsense?" (Lester 1970, 86–88). I would not say today that the books children are given are nonsense, and there are certainly far more books that are reality based than when I was a child. So, what changed between my childhood and the one my granddaughter will grow into?

Clearly, one of the major transformative events of the twentieth century was the Civil Rights movement of the 1960s. Through its attacks on the institution of segregation and the psychohistorical phenomenon we know as racism, the way in which all Americans, black and white, thought about race began to change. Blacks began to have some reality as human beings to white Americans, and blacks began to have a new reality for themselves as they rediscovered their historical and racial past.

The writing of *To Be a Slave* (1968) came out of a personal need to understand my racial past and restore respect and dignity to lives that had been robbed of these by being designated as slaves. A thirtieth anniversary edition of the book was published in 1998, and I would be remiss if I did not acknowledge the fact that the book's longevity owes much to the members of the 1969 Newbery committee who accorded *To Be a Slave* status as one of two Honor books that year. It was only the second Newbery Honor given a book by a black author and the first since 1949.

I mention this not as an advertisement for myself but to draw attention to a new consciousness emanating from the very influential American Library Association. Because blacks are a numerical minority, we are dependent on the majority to change its perception of itself and thus its perception of us, and as I wrote in the introduction to the anniversary edition of *To Be a Slave*, "History is not just facts and events. History is also a pain in the heart and we repeat history until we are able to make another's pain in the heart our own."

So, if the first change in consciousness was a consequence of the Civil Rights movement, the second change was a response by a significant enough number of whites in publishing, schools, and libraries to make this change concrete. In doing so, they ushered in what I think of as a golden age for African American books. Certainly, more books and more quality books about and by African Americans have been published in the past thirty years than in all the years of the republic's history. Not enough credit has been given to the editors, teachers, and librarians who have demanded and continue to demand such books as essential for the health of the nation as a whole.

But it must be said that black writers may face special problems in the complex writer–editor relationship. Despite an editor's openness to publishing black books and even his or her understanding of black history and culture, there are times when the editor's value system may be at odds with that of a black writer's attempt to communicate black culture. And I won't begin to talk about editors and especially copy editors who have no ear for black speech rhythms or knowledge of black speech.

The story I am about to relate appeared in print some years back, and I learned subsequently that some readers were assuming that the editor mentioned was Phyllis Fogelman, then editor in chief of Dial Books for Young Readers and now publisher of her own imprint at Penguin Putnam. So, I want to make it clear at the outset that I do not recall the name of the editor to whom I will be referring, do not even recall what she looked like, and after her encounter with me, there is a good chance that she changed careers.

The editor and I met to discuss the manuscript of the first volume of my retelling of the Uncle Remus stories, *Tales of Uncle Remus: The Adventures of Brer Rabbit* (1987). It was our first time working together, and it was apparent immediately that we had conflicting conceptions of what a tale on the page should be.

She objected to the contemporary references, the changes in verb tense from past to present and past again, sometimes in the same paragraph. She especially objected to what she considered "sexism" in some of the stories. For example in the story "Brer Rabbit and the Mosquitoes," Brer Rabbit courts Brer Wolf's daughter, and I had written the following:

Brer Wolf's daughter, who had always thought Brer Rabbit was kind of cute, put on her mascara and eyeliner and whatever else it is that the women put on their face. She squeezed herself into a pair of jeans four sizes too small. Have mercy! And she put on a pink halter top! When Brer Rabbit saw her, he thought he'd died and gone to heaven. (Lester 1987, 125)

My editor found this especially objectionable and exploitative of women.

It proved to be a long and arduous afternoon and, for me, an exceptionally lonely one. I sat in her tiny office as we went through the manuscript, page by page, and I had to defend myself from each of her queries regarding voice and language. In 1969, I had submitted my manuscript "Black Folktales" for publication and had it rejected by a publisher because of the contemporary references I had put into some of the stories. I saw nothing incongruous with God reading *TV Guide,* for example, but that was because I had grown up in a culture in which God did all kinds of extraordinary things that had not made their way into the Bible. So, I took the manuscript to another publisher and *Black Folktales* has been in print continuously for thirty years.

If not for the acceptance *Black Folktales* had received, I might have acceded to the editor's pressure. But I knew that to do so would be to betray those black people from whose lives the stories had come. My responsibility was to them as their descendent.

The editor feared that the contemporary references would make the book outdated, and she pointed to Italo Calvino's *Italian Folktales* (1980) as the model of what my *Uncle Remus* books should be.

But I was not interested in creating a work of literature. Folktales exist in time, and the *Uncle Remus* tales as told by Joel Chandler Harris (1880) are filled with references that are scarcely understood now. His use of references contemporary to his time did not injure the stories. Quite the contrary. They communicated something of the lives of the storytellers, and even though a story is told by one person only, the story being told is not one person's story.

Not only did my editor want me to delete the contemporary references, she did not think that the inconsistencies in grammatical usage would communicate to white readers. I told her they weren't supposed to. But what was the harm in asking whites to read stories written in language with which they were not intimately familiar, I wanted to know. The stories would communicate to anyone. That the language carried nuances and evoked memories that would be available primarily to blacks merely gave the stories an added dimension.

The most bitter point of disagreement remained the references she considered "sexist." I told her that my narrator could not refer to "halter tops" if some women didn't wear them. How did describing what some women wore make it "sexist"? The problem was that my editor considered women who wore halter tops to be "unliberated," and she was insisting that I rewrite history and culture to satisfy her version of white feminism. To those who have read any of my retellings of the *Uncle Remus Tales,* it is clear that I prevailed.

I recount this story not to cast aspersions on editors and publishing. Rather, I think my experience brings me to the heart of an issue that arose in the last two decades of the twentieth century and which certainly carries over into the twenty-first, and that is the issue of multiculturalism.

If multiculturalism is going to be truly meaningful, then it has to mean more than publishing and placing into school curricula books by African American, Native American, Hispanic, and Asian writers and illustrators. In some instances, multiculturalism represents a challenge to Western cultural assumptions about how a sentence is put together, about the representation of voice on the printed page, about what a story is, even. History is not the same to those of us on whom it has trod, and therefore it should shock or surprise no one if the voices in which we write history are sometimes tense with anger, sometimes sting with rage. And I know that I am not the only black writer who has had confrontations with editors who tried to tone down our language to make it more "acceptable" to white people.

Multiculturalism is difficult because it means that whites must give up some degree of control over what is expressed and how it is expressed, over what children are exposed to. Multiculturalism is not Euro-American culture with a tan. It is an invitation to whites to enter the human family instead of standing off to the side looking down their noses at the rest of us.

But multiculturalism is also fraught with dangers. Under the banner of multiculturalism there are some writers who maintain that those not born into the particular group cannot tell its stories or write about its people. In the past few years, a form of tyranny seems to have arisen in some children's literature circles whereby many white librarians and teachers hesitate to express an opinion—positive or negative—about a book by a minority writer for fear that they will be accused of being racist. In the May/June 1999 issue of the *Horn Book Magazine,* editor Roger Sutton confronts this issue when he admits that when Carolivia Herron's book *Nappy Hair* (1997) came into the office, no one wanted to review it because "we didn't know if we were allowed to like it" (260). He goes on to describe the dilemma of whites who are "in no position to evaluate something that had nothing to do with their experience" (260).

But that is the position white editors, teachers, and librarians are in, and quite frankly it is not ethical for minority writers to treat literature as their exclusive private property. Imagine the outrage from blacks should a group of white writers claim that being black disqualifies blacks from writing about whites.

Multiculturalism is a two-way street. If the proponents want others to accept multiculturalism's challenge to Western cultural norms and relinquish power and control, the proponents cannot move into what is now a power vacuum and usurp the same power they detest. If multiculturalism is going to have integrity, then it must run the risk that others are going to be so excited by a tale that they will want to tell it, and in the process of doing so, they will do things with the tale that will, indeed, violate the culture from which it came. Indeed, the tale might be Disneyfied into a colorful and tuneful sentimentality. That is the risk of living in a democracy.

The only way to control the tales of one's culture are to never tell them outside one's group. But once one puts stories into a book, the story is available to anyone who can read and there isn't a damned thing you can do about what that person does with it.

But as Roger Sutton says in the conclusion to his *Horn Book* editorial: "To encourage diversity of viewpoint is to admit conflict" (Sutton 1999, 261). Multiculturalists cannot have it both ways; that is, demand that their viewpoints be included while simultaneously seeking to squelch the viewpoints of anyone who disagrees with them.

Let's be honest. None of us has a good idea of what multiculturalism is. We in America are attempting something that has not been attempted in world history. We have created a nation with a population that includes people from practically every country on the globe, and the grand adventure of the twenty-first century is figuring out how we can all live together while simultaneously cherishing and sharing the unique customs and ways of our particular groups. Right now, we don't have a clue how we should do this, so some of us get very anxious and nervous and concerned about doing the absolutely correct thing so we will not offend anyone. And others of us are afraid of being offended and exploited because we have been exploited so many times in the past that we want to put a great wall around our cultures and let in only those of whom we approve.

As we grapple with challenges humans have not grappled with before, it is all right to be confused. It is all right to make mistakes. It is all right to simply not know what the right thing to do—if, if we are agreed that what we want in our lives and thus, our literature, is the inclusion of as wide a variety of the human experience as possible.

The twentieth century brought us to the threshold of this wonderful possibility, this vision of a humanity that will acknowledge its commonalities and cherish and respect its cultural differences. This new century invites us to make this vision a reality.

References

Bannerman, H. 1900. *The story of little black Sambo.* London: Grant Richards.

Calvino, I. 1980. *Italian folktales.* 1st American ed. New York: Harcourt Brace Jovanovich.

Gardner, E. S. 1933. *The case of the velvet claws.* New York: William Morrow.

Harris, J. C. 1880. *Uncle Remus, his songs and his sayings: The folk-lore of the old plantation.* New York: D. Appleton.

Herron, C. 1997. *Nappy hair.* Illus. J. Cepeda. New York: Knopf.

Lester, J. 1968. *To be a slave.* Illus. T. Feelings. New York: Dial.

———. 1969. *Black folktales.* Illus. T. Feelings. New York: R. W. Baron.

————. 1987. *Tales of Uncle Remus: The adventures of Brer Rabbit.* Illus. J. Pinkney. New York: Dial.

————.1970. The kinds of books we give children: Whose nonsense? *Publishers Weekly,* February 23, 86-88.

Milne, A. A. 1926. *Winnie-the-Pooh.* Illus. E. H. Shepard. London: Methuen.

Sutton, R. 1999. "Now, why's he got to come back to that?" *Horn Book Magazine* 75, no. 3 (May/June): 260–261.

White, E. B. 1952. *Charlotte's web.* Illus. G. Williams. New York: Harper & Row.

12

African American Children's Literature in the Twentieth Century

Vivian G. Johnson and
Jonella A. Mongo

Over the past hundred years, the evolution of African American children's literature has been on a long and slow journey. Compared with other social and political advancements of African American culture, African American children's literature is still in the infancy stage. Just think, shortly after the end of the Civil War people could count on their fingers the number of books written by and for African Americans, and most books in publication did not feature African American characters. Those books that did include African Americans characters often featured stereotypical and derogatory portrayals. Now, although literature in general has grown significantly, topics concerning African American children have somehow remained stagnant.

This chapter discusses the development of African American children's literature from the early 1900s to 2000, reviewing some of the major African American authors and illustrators of these books. The crucial role literature plays in exposing children to positive images that reflect the family life of their culture and ethnic group is emphasized. Finally, the chapter examines future trends of this particular genre of children's literature.

African American Publications in the Early to Mid-1900s

A trend in African American children's literature emerged in the early 1900s, when several African Americans founded or purchased publishing firms (Joyce 1986). Writings by African Americans during this period reflected the advancement of the middle-class, educated black person. In many of the stories published, the theme was vocation and avocation. Often the literature was "oppositional" and contradicted a theme, motif, or stereotype (Harris 1990). It was a time of social and political change that greatly influenced the lives of black Americans. This was reflected in many of the early publications of the 1900s, particularly in biographies of prominent African Americans.

W. E. B. Du Bois began to question the pictorial depictions of African Americans often found in children's books and magazines. From January 1920 through December 1921, Du Bois and Augustus Dill published *The Brownies' Book,* a monthly magazine for children, edited by an African American female writer, Jessie Faust. One of the goals of *The Brownies' Book* was to render positive visual representations of children of color and convey meaningful messages. During its short circulation period, the magazine provided positive images and textual information about the experiences of African Americans through photographs of children from all over the United States (Harris 1984; Johnson 1988; Johnson-Feelings 1996). In addition to *The Brownies' Book,* Du Bois and Dill also published two African American biographies in 1921, *Unsung Heroes* by Elizabeth Ross Haynes and *A Child's Story of Dunbar* by Julia Henderson (Johnson 1988; Johnson-Feelings 1996).

A few more advances were made in African American children's literature during the 1930s. African American historian Carter G. Woodson established Negro History Week in February and also published Helen A. Whitings's *Negro Folk Tales* (1938), which was adopted for use in several schools (Harris 1992). Other efforts were made to present positive images of African Americans in children's literature. *Shuttered Windows* (Means 1938) was considered one of the more realistic depictions of African Americans (Baker 1975; Williams and Caver 1995). The same was true for *Tobe* (Sharpe 1939), in which photographs were used to accurately portray the characters. These were two books that had powerful characters and intact nuclear family relationships, including the presence of a father.

The first picture book noted for having black and white children playing together was *Two Is a Team* (Beim and Beim 1945) whose illustrator was African American. When this book first appeared, it was welcomed because it did not mention the cultural and racial background of the two boys who worked together to solve a problem. These types of portrayals depicted "a 'mutuality'—egalitarian and intimate relationship that involved the disclosure of unique information and shared experiences" (Pescosolido, Grauerholz, and Milkie 1997, 451) that did not exist in other picture books for children.

Later criticism of this type of children's literature relegated it into the "melting pot" category, a category that by its nature makes no distinction between the races and limits acknowledgment of the presence of African Americans in the literature (Sims-Bishop 1983). Two other books published during this period were also considered worthy of recognition. *My Dog Rinty* (Tarry and Ets 1946) was one of the high-quality books that featured photographs of urban life and blacks in professional positions (Baker 1975). In the story *By Secret Railway* (Meadowcroft 1948), an African American family assisted slaves without the help of European Americans.

Almost twenty years after Du Bois voiced his concerns, negative images of African Americans were once again challenged by the 1941 publication of the first edition of the National Council of Teachers of English's (NCTE) *We Build Together: A Reader's Guide to Negro Life and Literature for Elementary and High School Use* (Rollins 1941). Rollins spearheaded the effort that resulted in this pamphlet listing seventy-two titles of acceptable books about African Americans for school-age children. A second edition of the NCTE publication *We Build Together* (Rollins 1948) highlighted ninety children's books that portrayed African Americans positively and realistically. The increase from seventy-two to ninety was still dismal.

Pescosolido, Grauerholz, and Milkie (1997) found that there was a decline in the appearance of African American characters from the late 1930s through the late 1950s. The miniscule appearances were largely as "secondary, peripheral and subordinate characters" (460). One book, *The Rooster Crows: A Book of American Rhymes and Jingles* (1945) written and illustrated by Maud and Miska Petersham—the 1946 Caldecott Medal winner—was challenged by the National Association for the Advancement of Colored People (NAACP). This book contained four pages of illustrations depicting African American children with "great buniony feet, coal black skin, and bulging eyes (in the distance, a dilapidated cabin with a black, gun-toting, barefoot adult)" (Larrick 1965, 65). Years of complaints about this type of portrayal led publishers to delete the offensive illustrations. A new edition of the book was released in 1964 with only white children appearing in the pictures (Larrick 1965; Pescosolido et al. 1997; Williams and Caver 1995). Not only was the lack of positive and realistic representation of African Americans in children's books an issue, but the limited representation was as well, a pattern that continued into the following two decades. The period from the late 1950s through 1964 had "nearly zero representation" of African Americans in children's picture books. "Black characters and interracial images were systematically excluded from children's picture books" (Pescosolido et al. 1997, 458).

"Nicodemus, Auntie, and Baby." From *Nicodemus and the Newborn Baby*, by Inez Hogan.

Books published during the 1950s were mostly biographies and fictionalized biographies, and few of these were about living African Americans. Bontemps, author of sixteen books, wrote about the Fisk Jubilee Singers, George Washington Carver, and Frederick Douglass. It was interesting that *Amos Fortune, Free Man* by Yates (1950), a fictionalized biography of an African American, won the Newbery Award, even though it was noted as being "condescending" and the African appeared almost "subhuman upon his arrival in America" (Williams and Caver 1995, 18).

African American Children's Literature from the Mid-1960s

African Americans were portrayed in more picture books during the 1960s. One of the first books to portray African Americans in an urban setting, in contrast to the many rural settings, was Ezra Jack Keats's *Snowy Day* (1962), which received the 1963 Caldecott Medal. This picture book was not without controversy. The African American mother was pictured as having a huge figure clad in a "gaudy yellow plaid dress" (Larrick 1965, 65) reminiscent of some of the typical "mammy" figures depicted in picture books published in earlier years (Miller 1986; Sims-Bishop 1982; Thompson and Woodard 1972).

By 1965, African Americans had almost disappeared from the illustrations in children's picture books. Nancy Larrick, former president of the International Reading Association and an educator, reported on a survey of more than five thousand trade books published in 1962, 1963, and 1964 and solicited responses to a questionnaire from publishers of trade books for children. The results documented that the availability of African American literature was dismal. Only 349 (6.7 percent) of the books published over a three-year period included the African American experience in the text or illustrations. Nancy Larrick's 1965 article drew attention to the disparity in the number of books for children about African Americans, but more important, the 1965 civil unrest in Watts drew attention to the disenchantment felt by many African Americans. Prior to the Civil Rights movement, publications of illustrated literature with African American content were limited, and those that were available contained negative and stereotypical images of the African American culture (Bingham 1970; Phillips 1995).

Pescosolido and associates (1997) reported that the level of racial conflict in the 1960s United States correlated with the low percentage of books portraying at least one black person (including books featuring only black people). Although the Voting Rights Act was signed in 1965, it did little to guarantee what was wanted most, equal opportunities for African Americans. As Larrick (1965) states, "Integration may be the law of the land, but most of the books children see are all white" (65). From 1966 to 1968, civil unrest took place in Chicago, Cleveland, Newark, Detroit, and Boston. The assassination of Dr. Martin Luther King Jr. in 1968 ended the dream for many who had followed his philosophy of nonviolence. Several other factors added to the frustration that sparked the national call for blacks to demand equal treatment "by any means necessary." According to a report completed in 1968 by the Kerner Commission, the cause of the continued problems for blacks was directly related to "white racism" (Hughes et al. 1995). This racial and economic inequality permeated the world of children's literature, not just in terms of available books, but in terms of who was writing, illustrating, publishing, and getting publicity for their works. African Americans in positions to push for and to make changes in the world of children's book publishing began to do so.

In 1969, the idea for the Coretta Scott King Award was born through the diligence of librarians Mabel McKissick and Glyndon Greer, along with publisher John M. Carroll. This award was created to honor the accomplishments of African American authors and illustrators who historically had not been recognized. It is presented to the authors of children's books that "best promote cultural awareness and the contribution of all people to the realization of the American Dream" (Smith 1994, x). The first award was presented to George Ford for his illustrations in *Ray Charles,* a biography, written by Sharon Bell Mathis (1973). The Coretta Scott King Award continues to validate the works of African American authors and illustrators whose goal is to present authentic depictions and convey positive images of the African American experience in books written for children.

African American Children's Literature in the 1970s

The early 1970s were a time when more children's books about African Americans were published. Results of Chall's 1979 replication of Larrick's 1965 study indicate that the highest number of children's books about African Americans was published between 1973 and 1974 (Chall et al. 1979). Six hundred eighty-nine (14.4 percent) books included African Americans in text and illustrations, with twenty-eight of them within contemporary urban settings as opposed to rural settings. The increase in the number of publications often is attributed to the social and political changes affecting African Americans that took place in the United States during the early 1970s (Pescosolido et al. 1997). Many of the picture books published in the 1970s merely reintroduced African American characters by reissuing books with black children in place of white children in the illustrations.

The publications during this period helped to increase the visibility of African Americans in children's picture books, yet many of those very same books often were criticized also. Many of the images in these books depicted blacks outside the United States and in folk literature (Pescosolido et al. 1997). Also at issue was the content. According to Sims-Bishop (1982), "The literary quality of many of them is poor enough to suggest that had they not been timely, they might not have been published at all" (30). This sentiment was expressed early during the onslaught of literature published about African Americans. According to Latimer and associates (1973), some literature available in the 1970s even aggravated the racism in America.

The 1970s was also a time to begin publishing literature that, according to Sims-Bishop (1982), was written to encourage non–African Americans to "develop empathy, sympathy, and tolerance for African American children and their problems" (17). These books were written from the point of view of white characters and had a paternalistic or patronizing attitude toward the black characters. Some of the picture books of this period ignored all differences except physical ones: skin color and other racially related physical features. A need for children's books that accurately depicted authentic African American experiences for children still existed. Julius Lester in an open letter to the *New York Times Book Review*'s children's book editor George Woods wrote the following: "I must address myself to Blacks, to write books that hopefully will give black children the strength and pride that have been deliberately kept from them. . . . I want black children to have that black sense of self on which to build. When you come right down to it, they have nothing else" (Woods and Lester 1970, 34).

By the middle of the 1970s, the number of children's books published about or with African American characters stabilized at about 20 to 30 percent per year (Pescosolido et al. 1997). African American writer Lucille Clifton made a major contribution to books for younger children during the 1970s. *The Boy Who Didn't Believe in Spring* (Clifton 1973a) and *Don't You Remember?* (Clifton 1973b) were a prelude to her series of picture books featuring Everett Anderson. His experiences in typical family situations were shared in *Everett Anderson's Friend* (Clifton 1976) and *Everett Anderson's Nine Month Long* (Clifton 1978). Clifton also published *Amifika* (Clifton 1977), a story about a young boy wondering whether his father will remember him after a long absence from home. *The Lucky Stone* (Clifton 1979) opens the window on the extended family with a relationship between a great-grandmother and her great-granddaughter (Johnson 1988).

Novels about the African American experience were prevalent in the 1970s as well. Virginia Hamilton wrote *M. C. Higgins, the Great* (1974), about the life in African American Appalachia, and *The Planet of Junior Brown* (1971), focused on diverse students and lifestyles in American education. Sharon Mathis's older characters faced crucial issues in *A Teacup Full of Roses* (1972) and *Listen for the Fig Tree* (1974). Walter Dean Myers's book, *It Ain't All for Nothin'* (1978), presented "the murky side of inner city life where children must bear grown-up responsibilities" (Williams and Caver 1995, 21).

African American Children's Literature in the 1980s

By 1980, publications of African American children's literature began to dwindle. According to Rollock (1984/1989), approximately 2,000 children's books were published per year, with an average of only 25 (1.3 percent) noted in 1984 and 34 (1.7 percent) in 1989 about African Americans. This decrease, according to Rudine Sims-Bishop (personal communication 1997), could be attributed to the more conservative political climate in the United States during the 1980s and, to some extent, the absorption of smaller publishing companies by larger publishing houses.

The political climate had changed and 29 percent of African Americans were below the poverty level compared to 8 percent of European Americans. Those blacks who were employed were more than likely to be found in skilled labor positions. In response to the continued racism and inequality present in the United States, sixteen major black organizations were formed to help resolve some of the problems plaguing the African American community (Hughes et al. 1995). More widespread attention to social issues affecting African Americans filtered down to the children's literature community.

Some authors and illustrators began to produce children's books that featured an authentic picture of African American experiences. Conversely, others maintained the status quo. Some of the children's books published during the 1980s had the melting pot theme that first appeared in the 1940s. These books focused on integration and were written from the point of view of black characters. In picture books, illustrations were the only indicators of the racial or ethnic identities of the characters. However, these books were still considered essential during this time period. Although not without some fault in illustrations and text, these "socially conscious" and melting-pot-themed children's books afforded readers some insight into the experiences of African Americans and provided an awareness of shared values and experiences (Sims-Bishop 1982).

The 1980s brought about an emergence of some "culturally conscious" children's fiction. These books reflected experiences indicative of growing up African American in the United States. Elements in the text, not just the pictures, make it clear that the book consciously sought to depict a fictional African American life experience. At minimum, this means that the major characters are African American, the story is told from their perspective, the setting is an African American community or home, and the text includes some means of identifying the characters as black—physical description, language, cultural traditions, and so forth (Sims-Bishop 1982).

These stories reflected the diversity found among all family systems: single parent, two parents, extended family, and multigenerational households. Access to such books would help children to better understand their own family interactions and those of other children. Examples of these children's books include Lucille Clifton's *My Friend Jacob* (1980); *The Patchwork Quilt* written by Valerie Flournoy and illustrated by Jerry Pinkney (1985); John Steptoe's books, *Daddy Is a Monster . . . Sometimes* (1980) and *Mufaro's Beautiful Daughters* (1987); and *Willie's Not the Hugging Kind* (1989) by Joyce Barrett. The culturally conscious theme is also found in picture books such as *Cornrows* by Camille Yarbrough (1979), *My Mama Needs Me* (1983) by Mildred Pitts Walter, *Mirandy and Brother Wind* by Patricia McKissack (1989), *Tar Beach* by Faith Ringgold (1991), and Sharon Bell Mathis's *The Hundred Penny Box* (1975).

In the 1970s, authors and illustrators had responded to the cries for recognition from the disenfranchised African Americans. In the 1980s, they now responded to the need for the experiences of the African American family and community to be reflected in children's books. Even with changes in the pictorial depictions and themes in children's books about African Americans, the number of books published remained low.

African American Children's Literature in the Early 1990s

Children's books that featured African Americans engaged in activities unique to their cultural experiences were more visible in the early 1990s. The number of books published remained small but increased from those available in the 1980s. Sims-Bishop (1990) reports that between 2,500 and 3,500 books were published yearly, and less than 2 percent of these books were about African Americans. Cobb (1995) surveyed approximately fifty-four publishing firms and found that from 1989 through 1991 there were 104 children's books about African Americans published. According to statistics reported by Horning, Kruse, and Schliesman (2001), 4,500 children's books were published in 1994, but only 166 (3.7 percent) were about African Americans.

One of the positive factors about African Americans featured in children's books published in the 1990s is that there were more positive pictorial images of black Americans and their experiences are accurately represented. The themes most prevalent in these contemporary realistic fiction picture storybooks revolve around interactions with family and friends and community activities with neighbors. Many of the stories written with African Americans as primary characters have focused on the family as a central part of the story's plot. Contemporary realistic fiction children's books give many views of family life, sensitive explorations into the relationships of family members, and occasions to observe how normal daily activities become the focus for memorable stories (Buchoff 1995).

"Holding Aunt Carolyn's baby, Carl." From *Something Beautiful,*
by Sharon Dennis Wyeth and illustrated by Chris K. Soentpiet.

This is also reflected in Sims-Bishop's (1994) description of culturally specific fiction. The themes that appear in culturally specific fiction reflect the experiences of growing up in a nonwhite culture group and detail the specific daily living experiences that are recognizable by members of that group. During the 1990s, more stories were published in various formats that began to reflect the diversity of family styles within the African American culture than had been done in earlier years.

Until the 1990s, infant board books—sturdily constructed for easy handling by babies and toddlers—rarely depicted African American characters. Publishing companies recruited popular African American authors of picture books to write for an even younger audience during this decade. In 1991, the writing and illustrating team of Eloise Greenfield and Jan Spivey Gilchrist produced a series of four books, *Big Friend, Little Friend* (1991a), *Daddy and I* (1991b), *I Make Music* (1991c), and *My Doll, Keisha* (1991d). Recent board books by Andrea and Brian Pinkney highlight the cultural norms of African American family life: *I Smell Honey* (1997a), *Pretty Brown Face* (1997b), *Shake, Shake, Shake* (1997c), and *Watch Me Dance* (1997d) are examples of quality board books that are now available to educators and parents interested in reading aloud to the very young child.

Many of the books published in the 1990s have themes relevant to the African American community as well, and quite a few specifically focus on the heritage and pride associated with the experiences of being black. The diversity in children's literature published during the 1990s is evident in books such as Dakari Hru's *The Magic Moonberry Jump Ropes* (1996). In this story, an African American uncle, sporting dreadlocks and wearing a dashiki, presents his nieces with a magical rope he purchased in Africa. *Mimi's Tutu* (1996) by Tynia Thomassie has vivid images of nuclear and extended family members playing African musical instruments and dancing. Other books are available with illustrations of African Americans engaged in culturally related activities such as Kwanza and Juneteenth celebrations.

In a discussion of the many facets of children's literature and cultural diversity, author Mildred Pitts Walter writes: "To the African-American children I bring characters that are in the home, in the street, and in the institutions, act and react the way they do. They see and hear themselves, their relatives, and their friends, and can form opinions about who they really are" (Cameron et al. 1992, 32).

The 1990s were a time of positive images of African Americans "in their home, in the street, and in the institutions, acting and reacting the way they do" (Cameron et al. 1992, 32) in children's books. It is possible that some of this is directly related to an awareness of the need to be sensitive to the messages that children's books may convey.

Current Trends in African American Children's Literature

Previous figures from the Cooperative Children's Book Center (CCBC) note that of the 4,500 books published in the United States in 1996, approximately 172 were specifically about African or African American history, culture, or peoples. In 1995, only 167 were published, an increase of one from the 166 published in 1994. The 216 books about African Americans published in 1997 represent the highest number published from 1994 to 2000. There was a decline to 183 in 1998, even fewer in 1999 with 150, and the number is slowly decreasing. In the year 2000, of the 5,000 to 5,500 books published, about 147 were about African American characters (Horning et al. 2001). Despite the dismal report, many of those books published reflect accurate portrayals of African American life and culture. Diversity among African Americans is more visible— pictorial images mirror the different hues of lifelike faces.

Many of the books focus on issues that are true to the experiences of *all* children. A book such as Jacqueline Woodson's *We Had a Picnic This Sunday Past* (1997) is a wonderful depiction of a family gathering. It sounds and looks like the family reunion many children experience. *Something Beautiful* (Wyeth 1998) features characters from various cultures helping a young girl understand beauty. In her latest book, *Darkness before Dawn* (2001), Sharon Draper takes readers deeper into the lives of familiar characters from *Forged by Fire* (1997) and *Tears of a Tiger* (1994). Walter Dean Myers and Christopher Paul Curtis, in books such as *Monster* (Myers 1999) and *Bud, Not Buddy* (Curtis 1999), continue to present strong African American male characters. In *Born in Sin* (2001), author Evelyn Coleman deals with the myth of African Americans and swimming. *Two Mrs. Gibsons* (Igus 1996), *Plain City* (Hamilton 1993), and *The World of Daughter McGuire* (Wyeth 1994) feature biracial characters coping with their two worlds.

Conclusion

Despite the historically derogatory and stereotypical depiction of some earlier publications, positive portrayals of African Americans emerged in both the illustrations and text of later-twentieth-century children's books. Seeing African American children respond enthusiastically to depictions that reflect their own experiences validates the struggle of authors and illustrators to create different images. Chall and her colleagues (1979), while studying blacks in the world of children's books, found studies that support the contention that literature has the power to affect self-concept and worldview. Attitudes about others can be reinforced or clarified through exposure to children's literature. Sims-Bishop (1983) writes that books have the power to promote favorable attitudes and foster positive behavior on the part of the reader. Moreover, she voices concern about the potential of children's literature to influence readers' attitudes about themselves and others. Using children's literature to increase social awareness is at the core of arguments about black images and authentic African American experiences as mirrored in children's fiction. This mirror is instrumental in helping develop positive self-images in African American children whose lives had been invisible in the literature.

There is a great responsibility and an obligation to create environments in which children of all ethnicities are made aware of the diversity that exists in the United States. *All* ethnic groups should be accurately portrayed in the literature that is presented to children.

References

Baker, A. 1975. The changing image of the black in children's literature. *Horn Book Magazine* 51: 79–88.

Barrett, J. D. 1989. *Willie's not the hugging kind.* Illus. P. Cummings. New York: Harper & Row.

Beim, L., and J. Beim. 1945. *Two is a team.* Illus. E. Crichlow. New York: Harcourt Brace.

Bingham, J. M. 1970. A content analysis of the treatment of Negro characters in children's picture books 1930–1968. Ph.D. diss., Michigan State University, East Lansing. *Dissertation Abstracts International* 31, no. AAG70204372411.

Buchoff, R. 1995. Family stories. *The Reading Teacher* 49: 230–233.

Cameron, A., K. Narahashi, M. P. Walter, and D. Wisniewski. 1992. The many faces in children's books. *School Library Journal* 38: 28–33.

Chall, J. S., E. Radwin, V. French, and C. Hall. 1979. Blacks in the world of children's books. *The Reading Teacher* 32: 527–533.

Clifton, L. 1973a. *The boy who didn't believe in spring.* Illus. B. Turkle. New York: E. P. Dutton.

———. 1973b. *Don't you remember?* Illus. E. Ness. New York: E. P. Dutton.

———. 1976. *Everett Anderson's friend.* Illus. A. Grifalconi. New York: Holt, Rinehart and Winston.

————. 1977. *Amifika.* Illus. T. DiGrazia. New York: E. P. Dutton.

————. 1978. *Everett Anderson's nine month long.* Illus. A. Grifalconi. New York: Holt, Rinehart and Winston.

————. 1979. *The lucky stone.* Illus. D. Payson. New York: Delacorte.

————. 1980. *My friend Jacob.* Illus. T. DiGrazia. New York: E. P. Dutton.

Cobb, J. B. 1995. Images and stereotyping of African Americans and Hispanic Americans in contemporary children's fiction. Paper presented at the 40th Annual Meeting of the International Reading Association, April 30–May 5, Anaheim, CA.

Coleman, E. 2001. *Born in sin.* New York: Atheneum.

Curtis, C. P. 1999. *Bud, not Buddy.* New York: Delacorte.

Draper, S. M. 1994. *Tears of a tiger.* New York: Atheneum.

————. 1997. *Forged by fire.* New York: Atheneum.

————. 2001. *Darkness before dawn.* New York: Atheneum.

Flournoy, V. 1985. *The patchwork quilt.* Illus. J. Pinkney. New York: Dial.

Greenfield, E. 1991a. *Big friend, little friend.* Illus. J. S. Gilchrist. New York: Black Butterfly Children's Books.

————. 1991b. *Daddy and I.* Illus. J. S. Gilchrist. New York: Black Butterfly Children's Books.

————. 1991c. *I make music.* Illus. J. S. Gilchrist. New York: Black Butterfly Children's Books.

————. 1991d. *My doll, Keisha.* Illus. J. S. Gilchrist. New York: Black Butterfly Children's Books.

Hamilton, V. 1971. *The planet of Junior Brown.* New York: Macmillan.

————. 1974. *M. C. Higgins, the great.* New York: Macmillan.

————. 1993. *Plain City.* New York: Blue Sky.

Harris, V. J. 1984. The Brownies' book: Challenge to the selective tradition in children's literature. Opinion Papers, University of Illinois, Urbana-Champaign.

Harris, V. J. 1990. African American children's literature: The first one hundred years. *Journal of Negro Education* 59: 540–555.

————. 1992. African-American conceptions of literacy: A historical perspective. *Theory into Practice* 31: 276–286.

Horning, K. T., G. M. Kruse, and M. Schliesman. 2001. *Children's books by and about people of color published in the United States: Statistics gathered by the Cooperative Children's Book Center* [online]. Cooperative Children's Book Center, University of Wisconsin-Madison. Accessed: August 2001. Available: www.education.wisc.edu/ccbc/pcstats.htm

Hru, D. 1996. *The magic moonberry jump ropes.* Illus. E. B. Lewis. New York: Dial.

Hughes, L., M. Meltzer, C. E. Lincoln, and J. M. Spencer. 1995. *A pictorial history of African Americans.* 6th ed. New York: Crown.

Igus, T. 1996. *Two Mrs. Gibsons.* Illus. D. Wells. San Francisco: Children's Book Press.

Johnson, D. A. 1988. For the children of the sun: What we say to Afro-American youth through story and image. Ph.D. diss., Yale University, Hartford, CT. *Dissertation Abstracts International* 50, no. AAG89176961345.

Johnson-Feelings, D., ed. 1996. *The best of the Brownies' book.* New York: Oxford University Press.

Joyce, D. F. 1986. Changing book publishing objectives of secular black book publishers, 1900–1986. *Book Research Quarterly* 2: 42–50.

Keats, E. J. 1962. *The snowy day.* New York: Viking.

Larrick, N. 1965. The all white world of children's books. *Saturday Review of Literature* 48: 63–65, 84–85.

Latimer, B. I., M. Gruen, D. Holden, A. Cosby, J. Newman, and M. Todd, eds. 1973. *Starting out right: Choosing books about black people for young children, pre-school through third grade.* Washington, DC: Day Care and Child Development Council of America.

Mathis, S. B. 1972. *Teacup full of roses.* New York: Viking.

———. 1973. *Ray Charles.* Illus. G. C. Ford. New York: Crowell.

———. 1974. *Listen for the fig tree.* New York: Viking.

———. 1975. *The hundred penny box.* Illus. L. Dillon and D. Dillon. New York: Viking.

McKissack, P. 1989. *Mirandy and Brother Wind.* Illus. J. Pinkney. New York: Knopf.

Meadowcroft, E. L. M. 1948. *By secret railway.* Illus. H. C. Pitz. New York: Crowell.

Means, F. C. 1938. *Shuttered windows.* Illus. A. Sperry. Boston: Houghton Mifflin.

Miller, J. 1986. Black images in American children's literature. In *Masterworks of children's literature—The twentieth century,* vol. 8, ed. W. T. Moynihan, M. E. Shaner, and J. Cott, x, 333. New York: Stonehill/Chelsea House.

Myers, W. D. 1978. *It ain't all for nothin'.* New York: Viking.

———. 1999. *Monster.* Illus. C. A. Myers. New York: HarperCollins.

Pescosolido, B., E. Grauerholz, and M. Milkie. 1997. Culture and conflict: The portrayals of blacks in U.S. children's picture books through the mid and late twentieth century. *American Sociological Review* 62: 443–464.

Petersham, M. F., and M. Petersham. 1945. *The rooster crows: A book of American rhymes and jingles.* New York: Macmillan.

Phillips, K. B. 1995. A comparative content analysis of illustrated African American children's literature published between 1900–1962 and 1963–1992. Ph.D. diss., University of Oklahoma, Norman. *Dissertation Abstracts International* 56, no. AAI95323601933.

Pinkney, A. D. 1997a. *I smell honey.* Illus. J. B. Pinkney. San Diego: Harcourt Brace.

———. 1997b. *Pretty brown face.* Illus. J. B. Pinkney. San Diego: Harcourt Brace.

———. 1997c. *Shake, shake, shake.* Illus. J. B. Pinkney. San Diego: Harcourt Brace.

————. 1997d. *Watch me dance*. Illus. J. B. Pinkney. San Diego: Harcourt Brace.

Ringgold, F. 1991. *Tar beach*. New York: Crown.

Rollins, C. H., ed. 1941. *We build together: A reader's guide to Negro life and litera-ture for elementary and high school use*. Chicago: National Council of Teachers of English.

————. 1948. *We build together: A reader's guide to Negro life and literature for ele-mentary and high school use*. Rev. ed. Chicago: National Council of Teachers of English.

Rollock, B., ed. 1984/1989. *The black experience in children's books*. New York: New York Public Library.

Sharpe, S. G. 1939. *Tobe*. Illus. C. Farrell. Chapel Hill: University of North Carolina Press.

Sims-Bishop, R. 1982. *Shadow and substance: Afro-American experience in contem-porary children's fiction*. Urbana, IL: National Council of Teachers of English.

————. 1983. What has happened to the "all-white" world of children's books? *Phi Delta Kappan* 64: 650–653.

————. 1990. Walk tall in the world: African American literature for today's children. *Journal of Negro Education* 59: 556–565.

————, ed. 1994. *Kaleidoscope: A multicultural booklist for grades K–8*. Urbana, IL: National Council of Teachers of English.

Smith, H. M. 1994. *The Coretta Scott King Awards book: From vision to reality*. Chi-cago: American Library Association.

Steptoe, J. 1980. *Daddy is a monster . . . sometimes*. Philadelphia: Lippincott.

————. 1987. *Mufaro's beautiful daughters: An African tale*. New York: Lothrop, Lee & Shepard.

Tarry, E., and M. H. Ets. 1946. *My dog Rinty*. Illus. A. Alland and A. Alland. New York: Viking.

Thomassie, T. 1996. *Mimi's tutu*. Illus. J. S. Gilchrist. New York: Scholastic.

Thompson, J., and G. Woodard. 1972. Black perspective in books for children. In *The black American in books for children: Readings in racism,* ed. D. MacCann and G. Woodard, 39–51. Metuchen, NJ: Scarecrow.

Walter, M. P. 1983. *My mama needs me*. Illus. P. Cummings. New York: Lothrop, Lee & Shepard.

Whiting, H. A. 1938. *Negro folk tales for pupils in the primary grades*. Illus. L. M. Jones. Washington, DC: Associated Publishers.

Williams, M. T., and H. B. Caver. 1995. African-Americans in children's literature— From stereotype to positive representation. In *The all-white world of children's books and African American children's literature,* ed. O. Osa, 13–31. Trenton, NJ: Africa World Press.

Woods, G., and J. Lester. 1970. Black and white: An exchange. In *The black American in books for children: Readings in racism,* ed. D. MacCann and G. Woodard, 28–35. Metuchen, NJ: Scarecrow.

Woodson, J. 1997. *We had a picnic this Sunday past.* Illus. D. Greenseid. New York: Hyperion Books for Children.

Wyeth, S. D. 1994. *The world of Daughter McGuire.* New York: Delacorte.

———. 1998. *Something beautiful.* Illus. C. K. Soentpiet. New York: Bantam Doubleday Dell.

Yarbrough, C. 1979. *Cornrows.* Illus. C. M. Byard. New York: Coward McCann & Geoghegan.

Yates, E. 1950. *Amos Fortune: Free man.* Illus. N. S. Unwin. New York: E. P. Dutton.

13

Native Americans in Children's Books of the Twentieth Century

Debbie A. Reese

If someone is asked to name a Native American (or American Indian) author of children's books, Joseph Bruchac, of the Abenaki tribe, is likely to be at the top of the list. Readers should note Bruchac's tribe (Abenaki); Native Americans prefer to be identified by a specific tribe rather than *Native American* or *American Indian* when possible. Bruchac has written numerous children's books about Native Americans. His work spans several genres: *The Story of the Milky Way* (Bruchac and Ross 1995) is traditional literature, *The Heart of a Chief* (1998b) is contemporary realistic fiction, *Arrow over the Door* (1998a) is historical fiction, *Crazy Horse's Vision* (2000) is biography, and *Bowman's Store* (1997) is his autobiography. What is not well known in the field of children's literature is Bruchac's role in mentoring aspiring Native authors. Indeed, he is recognized as the single most important force in the nation in publishing and promoting the work of emerging Native American writers (Lerner 1994). Bruchac was instrumental in establishing the Returning the Gift festival in 1992. Held in Norman, Oklahoma, it was conceived as a gathering at which Native authors could share their work and talk with or mentor aspiring Native American authors. It evolved into an annual Returning the Gift festival and the formation of several organizations whose goals are to publish the work of Native authors and provide beginning authors with mentors. Native American authors who serve as mentors include Leslie Marmon Silko (Laguna Pueblo), whose *Ceremony* (1977) is widely used in high school classrooms, and Sherman Alexie (Spokane/Coeur d'Alene). Also serving as mentors are Gayle Ross (Cherokee), known for her picture-book retellings of traditional literature and oral storytelling and, of course, Bruchac. In addition to the festival, Bruchac established the Greenfield Review Press, a small publishing house devoted to publication of Native authors. Without question, Bruchac has been significant, not only for his own writing, but also for his efforts to mentor and promote the work of other Native authors.

Historical Development of the Literature: The First Ninety Years

Most readers of this chapter are familiar with Silko, Ross, and Alexie's names as authors whose works are used today, at the start of the twenty-first century, in class-rooms from kindergarten through college. Poised as we are at the end of the twentieth and beginning of the twenty-first century, many of us recognize the work of these Native authors, but what about the early 1900s? Were there Native authors writing for children then?[1] How were Native Americans presented in books published in the first half of the twentieth century?

The later half of the century saw a growing awareness of debates such as bias, insider-outsider perspective, voice, appropriation, and stereotyping. However, Native American children voiced that awareness nearly a hundred years ago, in 1908. What follows is a quote from a Native American child, printed in *What the White Race May Learn from the Indian* (James 1908). The child, a student at an Indian school, was speaking to the author:

When we read in the United States history of white men fighting to defend their families, their homes, their corn-fields, their towns, and their hunt-ing-grounds, they are always called "patriots," and the children are urged to follow the example of these brave, noble, and gallant men. But when Indians—our ancestors, even our own parents—have fought to defend us and our homes, corn-fields, and hunting-grounds they are called vindictive and mer-ciless savages, bloody murderers, and everything else that is vile. You are the Indians' friend: will you not some time please write for us a United States history that will not teach us such wicked and cruel falsehoods about our forefathers because they loved their homes enough to fight for them—even against such powerful foes as you have been. (25)

Early Native American authors shared these concerns. Scholars of Native Ameri-can literature identify Charles Alexander Eastman (Santee Sioux) and Zitkala Sa (Yankton Sioux) as the best known of the early Native American authors (Ruoff 1991; Wiget 1994). These early authors attempted to correct the common notion that Indians were primitive, bloodthirsty savages who attacked innocent settlers—notions Native children were keenly aware of, as evidenced by the preceding quote—by working to replace negative stereotypes left over from colonial conquest with positive ones that critiqued modern society by promoting a positive, antimodernist understanding of Na-tive American culture in their writing for youth (Deloria 1998). Thus, the image of the bloodthirsty savage was joined by one of a romantic, heroic Indian.

Most of the early literature is autobiographical in nature, and those who were most successful wrote using the European American autobiographical model that doc-uments the author's life story, rather than one based on the tribal oral narrative tradi-tion that consists of "brief stories, descriptive passages, and images [that] tumble out one after another with *very* few explicit connections or transitions" (Brumble 1994, 182). Eastman's *Indian Boyhood,* published in 1902 by Little, Brown and Company, was a favorite among "citybound Anglo youth" in Boy Scout programs and the "In-dian hobbyist" movement (Wiget 1994, 54). It contains autobiographical sketches first printed in *St. Nicholas,* a popular magazine for children (Peyer 1994). Zitkala Sa (also known as Gertrude Bonnin), a Yankton Sioux woman, was an author, musician, and political activist. In 1901, she published *Old Indian Legends,* a collection of Iktomi trickster stories. Sneve (1995a) describes the stories as "good" Indian stories because themes are about a free child of nature or the Indian as brave and courageous. These stories were well received and often used in schools (Sneve 1995a, xv). In stark contrast are Zitkala Sa's "bad" Indian stories, which were critical essays of assimilationist educational programs, forced Christianity, and the treatment of Indian children at Carlisle Indian Industrial School. These essays, initially published in *Atlantic Monthly* and *Harper's,* were negatively received. Eventually, several were published together in *American Indian Stories* (Hafen 1996; Zitkala [1921] 1985). Both of Zitkala Sa's books are marketed today to child and adult readers (Hafen 1996; Picotte 1985).

Two other Native Americans who wrote children's books prior to the 1950s include Luther Standing Bear (Lakota) and E-Yeh-Sure (Isleta Pueblo). Standing Bear's *My Indian Boyhood* (1931) is primarily autobiographical, but he also wrote two other books that described traditional Lakota culture: *My People, the Sioux* (1928) and *Land of the Spotted Eagle* (1933). In 1939, William Morrow published *I Am a Pueblo Indian Girl,* written by E-Yeh-Shure (Blue Corn), a thirteen-year-old girl from Isleta Pueblo whose book is usually listed under her English name, Louise Abeita. In simple prose, information about various aspects of Pueblo Indian life and culture are presented from the author's perspective as a young girl. Several artists who studied at the Dorothy Dunn studio in Santa Fe, New Mexico, in the 1930s did the watercolor illustrations for *I Am a Pueblo Indian Girl* (see the illustration). One of the artists, Allan Houser, eventually became world renowned for his work. In 1992, President George Bush awarded Houser the National Medal of Arts.

"Hair washing." From *I Am a Pueblo Indian Girl,* by E-Yeh-Shure.

In addition to the aforementioned books and stories, the United States Bureau of Indian Affairs was engaged in publishing books about Native Americans. During the 1940s, the Bureau of Indian Affairs published the Navajo, Sioux, and Pueblo book series, most of them written by noted author Ann Nolan Clark, who is not herself Native American. Major publishing houses later reprinted some of the books, which were originally written for use in the U.S. Government Boarding and Day Schools that served Navajo, Sioux, and Pueblo Indian children. Known as the "Indian Life Readers," some of the books included English text but also the native language spoken by the children at the school. Most of the illustrations for the books were done by Native artists who, like Allan Houser, went on to become world-class artists. *In My Mother's House* (Clark 1941a) was selected to receive distinction as a Caldecott Honor book. The book started out as a booklet titled "Home Geography," written by Clark and illustrated by her students at Tesuque Pueblo Day School in New Mexico. In it was "an account of life in Tesuque Pueblo, as it is influenced by environmental factors" (Bader 1976, 161). Pueblo artist Velino Herrera did the watercolor illustrations for *In My Mother's House.*

With Navajo artist Hoke Denetsosie, Clark wrote the Little Herder series, which included *Little Herder in Autumn/Áakéedgo na'nilkaadí yázhí* (1940b), *Little Herder in Spring/Dáago na'nilkaadí yázhí* (1940c), *Little Herder in Summer/Shiigo na'nilkaadí yázhí* (1942a), and *Little Herder in Winter/Haigo na'nilkaadi yázhí* (1942b). Of particular interest is Denotsosie's attention to authenticity as reported in Bader (1976) quoting from Denetsosie's self-authored artist profile:

The nature of the series, being concerned with Navajo life, called for illustration genuine in every sense of the word. I had to observe and incorporate in pictures those characteristics which serve to distinguish the Navajo from other tribes. Further, the setting of the pictures had to change to express local changes as the family moved from place to place. The domestic animals raised by the Navajo had to be shown in a proper setting just as one sees them on the reservation. The sheep could not be shown grazing in a pasture, nor the horses in a stable, because such things are not Navajo. (162)

Other titles in the series written by Clark include *Little Boy with Three Names: Stories of Taos Pueblo* (1940a), illustrated by Tonia Lujan; *The Pine Ridge Porcupine/Wazi ahanhan p'ahin k'un he* (1941b), *There Still Are Buffalo* ([1942] 1992), *Brave against the Enemy/Toka wan itkokip* (1944), and *The Singing Sioux Cowboy/Lak'ota Pteole Hoksila Lowansa. Woundspe T'okahe* (1947), all illustrated by Andrew Standing Soldier; and *Who Wants to Be a Prairie Dog/Háisha T'aá Kad Dloo Silii* (1940d), illustrated by Andrew Van Tsihnahjinnie. Some titles were not written by Clark. They include *Little Man's Family/Diné Yázhi Báatchíní* (1940), written and illustrated by James Byron Enochs, and *Field Mouse Goes to War/Tusan Homichi Tuwvoöta* (1944), by Edward A. Kennard, illustrated by Hopi artist Fred Kabotie.

From the 1950s until 1968, very few Native authors were published (Ruoff 1991). D'Arcy McNickle's (Cree Salish) historical fiction novel for middle school readers, *Runner in the Sun,* was published in 1954. The novel follows Salt, a teen who leads his people from their cliff-dwelling village to a valley where water is more abundant. In 1960, Pablita Velarde's (Santa Clara Pueblo) *Old Father, the Storyteller* was published. It is a collection of stories told to her by her grandfather. Velarde, also a world-renowned artist, did the illustrations for the book and provided information regarding the symbolism of elements she included in the illustrations. The collection includes "Turkey Girl," a story that resembles the European version of Cinderella, but that ends differently. In "Turkey Girl," there are consequences for failing to follow through on commitments. Others (Peggy Pollack and Joe Hayes) have retold the story of Turkey Girl and changed it in ways that make it less a Pueblo Indian story and more of a fairy tale. In contrast, Velarde's is worth reading for the insider perspective she provides. *Old Father, the Storyteller* was republished by Clear Light Press in the late 1980s.

During the 1970s, a magazine for children was published by the American Indian Historical Society. Titled *The Wee Wish Tree,* it contained short stories, poems, and essays written by Native American authors and Native American children. A landmark book published during this time is Simon Ortiz's (Acoma) *The People Shall Continue* (1977). The prose poem chronicles the history of Native Americans from creation to the present day and includes content often omitted or glossed over in other narratives about the settlement of the United States. Thus, the reader learns about forced removal of Native peoples from their homelands, the development of boarding schools, and the alliances formed in the 1960s among and between peoples of color.

During the 1970s, the Council on Interracial Books for Children (CIBC) was instrumental in promoting the work of Rosebud Sioux author Virginia Driving Hawk Sneve. Her works of fiction include three chapter books: *The Chichi Hoohoo Bogeyman* (1975), *When Thunders Spoke* (1974), and *High Elk's Treasure* (1972).

The Closing Decade

In the 1990s, publication of books written by Native authors increased significantly. In this decade, several Native authors wrote fiction and nonfiction for children. A few wrote several books and became widely known, while others were not as prolific. In combination, however, their work represents a growing body of literature for children that presents authentic stories about Native Americans.

Michael Dorris's (Modoc) works of historical fiction include *Sees Behind Trees* (1996), *Guests* (1994), and *Morning Girl* (1992). Each is noteworthy, but *Sees Behind Trees* is especially valuable for its treatment of women. In most works of historical fiction, females are marginalized as beasts of burden of no significance. Recent scholarship has revealed a different picture. The role of women in Native tribes was one of great import. Dorris presents this to us in the character of Otter, the tribe *weroance,* who controls the comings and goings of the people and presides over important events. Further discussion of Native women in historical fiction can be read in "Representations of Native American Women and Girls in Children's Historical Fiction" in Lehr's *Beauty, Brains and Brawn* (Reese 2001).

Virginia Driving Hawk Sneve, whose works of fiction were published in the 1970s, wrote a series of nonfiction books for Holiday House. Titled the First Americans series, it has been well received, primarily for the style and scope of coverage in each book. Each one opens with a creation story from the tribe the book is about and ends with information about the tribe in the present day. There are currently nine books in the series, all written by Sneve: *The Apaches* (1997), *The Cherokees* (1996a), *The*

Cheyennes (1996b), *The Hopis* (1995b), *The Iroquois* (1995c), *The Navajos* (1993a), *The Nez Perce* (1994a), *The Seminoles* (1994b), and *The Sioux* (1993b).

Gayle Ross's (Cherokee) traditional stories include *How Rabbit Tricked Otter and Other Cherokee Trickster Stories* (1994), *How Turtle's Back Was Cracked* (1995), and *Legend of the Windigo: A Tale from Native North America* (1996). Ross, a storyteller, is careful to describe the ways in which she adapts and modifies stories she tells. Hearne (1999) favorably compares Ross's source note for the Windigo story with that of Douglas Wood in his story of the Windigo (1996).

Artist and storyteller Virginia Stroud (Cherokee) has written three books for children and young adults: *Doesn't Fall Off His Horse* (1994), *The Path of the Quiet Elk: A Native American Alphabet Book* (1996), and *A Walk to the Great Mystery* (1995). Stroud collaborates with Bruchac and Ross, providing the artwork for some of their books.

Luci Tapahonso (Navajo) wrote two picture books for children, both of which provide rich information about the Navajo people. The first, *Navajo ABC, a Diné Alphabet Book* (1995), includes words in English and Diné, while *Songs from Shiprock Fair* (1999) provides substantive information about a tribal fair. Poems from her *Blue Horses Rush In* (1997) can be used with middle and high school students.

There are many other Native authors whose work has not received much attention. Joseph McLellan's (Ojibwe) series of picture books that feature Nanabosho, the Ojibwe trickster, are based on his oral tellings of Nanabosho stories; Bernelda Wheeler's (Cree) picture books are outstanding stories about modern-day Native American children; and Michael Lacapa's (Apache/Hopi/Tewa) books are also compelling. Joseph Bruchac has been prolific, as noted in the opening pages of this chapter. The work of several authors is discussed in the "Authors to Watch" section of this chapter, including Cynthia Leitich Smith (Creek), Jan Waboose (Anishinabe), and Cheryl Savageau (Abenaki/Metis).

Controversy and Debate

For the most part, the history of children's literature about Native Americans is problematic in multiple ways. Studies indicate that most books contain inaccuracies, stereotypes, and bias (Byler 1982; Moore and Hirschfelder 1977; Reese 2001). Problems range from erroneous depictions of the tribe being represented, to suggestions that Native American culture ceased to exist, to portrayals of Native Americans as savage, romantic, or heroic and possessing superhuman qualities. The majority of these books are not written by Native American authors, which leads to the debate over authenticity and insider/outsider perspective.

There are some writers who are not Native who have written noteworthy books about Native Americans. Paul Goble's retellings of traditional Native stories are quite good. (It should be noted, however, that some critics have challenged his Iktomi series for his appropriation and interpretation of the voice of Iktomi.) Goble's research, artistic skills, and the time spent with Native people contribute to the accuracy of his work and his ability to provide readers with stories that resound with Native readers. However, Goble's retellings are the exception. Most authors do library research but do not visit reservations and interact with Native people enough to understand what it means to create works that authentically embody a Native American perspective. Some recent examples illuminate the problems that can occur if authors do not take time to read or consult with Native Americans to learn about their concerns with the ways in which Native cultures are presented.

Native American cultures are often linked with environmentalist themes about caring for the environment. In 1991, Dial published *Brother Eagle Sister Sky: A Message from Chief Seattle*. This book features illustrations by Susan Jeffers and text that is attributed to Seattle, a nineteenth-century leader of the Suquamish and Duwamish people of the Pacific Coast. The book became a best-seller, but it is problematic in several ways. The book is set in a contemporary period, as shown by the presence of a modern-day family that appears to be European American. In contrast, the illustrations of Native Americans show them only in traditional clothing, while in other instances, they are presented in a transparent manner, presumably suggesting a spiritual presence. The material culture of Seattle and his people is based on their geographic location, but Jeffers's illustrations predominantly reflect a Plains culture rather than one of the northwest coast. The speech presented in the book is one oft attributed to Seattle, but represents only a small segment of a much larger one he gave when his people were forced from their traditional lands. A concern for the environment is not the theme of his speech. Moreover, the actual text Jeffers used is more akin to one used in a 1971 television program about the northwest rain forest than Seattle's actual speech. Mendoza and Reese (2001) provide an extended analysis of the book.

Several other popular books also have received close readings. Lynne Reid Banks's series *The Indian in the Cupboard* (1980) has been challenged for her presentation of Native American culture. Native scholar Rhonda Harris Taylor's (2000) case study of the reviews for the series and analysis of its content points out the problems with the books. Angela Cavendar Wilson's analysis of Native children's responses to Laura Ingalls Wilder's *Little House on the Prairie* has gained attention from many quarters, including a television segment that ran on Nickelodeon's kid news program, *Nick News*. Still others have written about inaccuracy and bias and the outrage Native Americans express at Ann Rinaldi's whitewash of the Native American boarding school experience in her book *My Heart Is on the Ground: The Story of Nannie Little Rose*, a title in Scholastic's Dear America series of historical fiction diaries (Atleo et al. 1999; Thompson 2001).

Much of this criticism is new, reflecting the greater involvement of Native Americans in the arena of literary criticism and children's literature. Books that once received awards from the literary establishment are receiving a "second look" and falling far short of their previous acclaim. McDermott's *Arrow to the Sun* (1974) has been criticized for its portrayal of Pueblo culture and spirituality (Reese and Caldwell-Wood 1997), and Speare's *Sign of the Beaver* (1983) and Dalgliesh's *Courage of Sarah Noble* (1954) have been analyzed for negative depiction of Native women (Reese 2001).

In addition to literary analysis, there is greater attention to the identity of authors who claim to be Native American. America's history is replete with stories of European Americans who adopted Native American ways of living. In the twentieth century, however, the motives for posing as Native have changed as individuals sought to exploit the romantic appeal of Native Americans for their own commercial gain. This has increased to the degree that a major reference, the *Encyclopedia of North American Indians* (Hoxie 1996), includes an entry titled "Fakes and Imposters" (Lynn-Sherow 1996). It includes a discussion of two authors whose claims to Native American identity have been challenged: Jamake Highwater (1977), author of *Anpao*, and

Forest Carter (1976), author of *Education of Little Tree* (Justice 2000). In her 1997 article "The Indians America Loves to Love and Read: American Indian Identity and Cultural Appropriation," Shanley goes into great detail documenting Highwater's claim, while Justice provides detailed discussion of Carter's claim in his 2000 article "A Lingering Miseducation: Confronting the Legacy of Little Tree."

Trends

Several trends in the literature about Native Americans are noteworthy. First, many Native authors writing for children got their start by writing for an adult readership. Second, Native authors who write for children are writing about modern-day Native people as opposed to stories rooted in the oral tradition. As they do, a third trend emerges. The topics they write about in their fiction deal with issues modern-day Native Americans are confronted with. Finally, Native authors are exploring the photo essay as a format for sharing information about their cultures. Each of these trends is described in the following paragraphs.

Several Native authors whose children's books are well known started out writing for adult readers. Michael Dorris wrote *Yellow Raft in Blue Water* (1987) prior to his works of historical fiction mentioned earlier. Louise Erdrich wrote *Beet Queen* (1986), *Love Medicine* (1984), and *Tracks* (1988) prior to her children's books *Grandmother's Pigeon* (1996) and later *Birchbark House* (1999), a critically acclaimed work of historical fiction that was nominated for the National Book Award. Erdrich plans to follow *Birchbark House* with two other works of historical fiction. Joy Harjo's poetry and her band, Poetic Justice, were well established before her picture book *Good Luck Cat* (2000) was published. N. Scott Momaday, author of Pulitzer Prize–winning *House Made of Dawn* (1968), wrote *Circle of Wonder: A Native American Christmas Story* in 1994. Luci Tapahonso wrote several volumes of poetry, including *Breeze Swept Through* (1987), before writing her children's books. Perhaps their success in the adult market provided them (and the publishing houses) with an entrée not extended to Native authors who start out writing for children. It may be that other Native authors who write for the adult market will follow their lead.

With greater frequency, Native authors are writing fiction about modern-day Native people, as opposed to traditional stories. There is also an effort to provide a balanced picture that includes women in central ways. Some of this fiction includes political content on issues such as gaming, stereotypes, and the use of Native American imagery as mascots for sports teams. As other Native authors become published, it may be that this trend will continue, or that other emerging issues such as land claims and treaty rights will be addressed.

Historical events that have received little attention in the past are now being explored. One example is the boarding school experience of Native people in the United States. Two recent children's books on the topic have been problematic: critical reviews of Rinaldi's *My Heart Is on the Ground: The Diary of Nannie Little Rose* and Cooper's *Indian School* (1999) can be read online at www.oyate.org, in the "Books to Avoid" link. Publishers seeking manuscripts about boarding schools would be well advised to seek out Native people who can write such stories based on their own or a grandparent's experiences at the schools. One such book is Shirley Sterling's *My Name Is Seepeetza* (1992). Though not written for children, two books about the boarding school experience that can be used with middle school and young adult readers include K. Tsiannina Lomawaima's (Hopi) *They Called It Prairie Light: The Story of Chilocco Indian School* (1994) and Brenda Child's (Chippewa) *Boarding School Seasons: American Indian Families 1900–1940* (2000).

Another example is *Battlefields and Burial Grounds* (1994), a children's work of nonfiction written by two Pawnee men, Roger C. and Walter R. Echo-Hawk. The book describes the efforts of Native Americans to recover remains of their ancestors from museum holdings for reburial on tribal lands.

Finally, more Native authors are writing nonfiction books in the form of photo essays. One example is the We Are Still Here series of photo essays published by Lerner Publications, each of which profiles contemporary Native American children (Horning, Kruse, and Schliesman 2001). The series has been well received by critics for its focus on contemporary Native American children and the ways their tribal heritage is portrayed as a vibrant part of their daily lives. At present, there are ten titles in the series. Each book focuses on a specific tribe. Other Native Americans are bringing forward photo essays similar to these. Among them is LaVera Rose (1999), a Lakota author who wrote *Grandchildren of the Lakota,* and Marcie Rendon (1996), who did *Pow Wow Summer.* Additional information can be found in the March 2000 issue of *Multicultural Review* in the informative essay titled "Photo Essays of American Indian Children" by Beverly Slapin (28).

Authors to Watch

Creek author Cynthia Leitich Smith has published two books in the last few years, both featuring contemporary Native protagonists and their families. In the picture book *Jingle Dancer* (2000), readers learn about Jenna and her efforts to secure the tin cones necessary to make a traditional dress to wear at a powwow. In the story, readers meet members of Jenna's family, including her aunt, who is a lawyer. The watercolor illustrations are beautifully rendered and do a fine job of illuminating the fact that modern-day Native American people drive cars, hold professional jobs, and live in houses much like the rest of non-Native America. Smith's second book, *Rain Is Not My Indian Name* (2001), is a work of fiction for middle school readers. It features Cassidy Rain, a young mixed-blood girl who is recovering from the loss of her mother and best friend. As readers come to know Cassidy Rain, Smith seamlessly provides a wealth of information about Native American culture in modern America. Tech-savvy Smith maintains a Web site about children's literature, but of most interest is the companion pages she has created to go along with *Rain Is Not My Indian Name.* Teachers and students will find them valuable not only for literature circle discussions, but also to enhance knowledge about various subjects from the novel. Some are lighthearted, such as links to *Star Trek* Web sites, but others are practical. These include the links to sites that help users create Web pages and the links to sites maintained by Native American tribes featured in the novel. The URL for the Web site is www.cynthialeitichsmith.com/rainisnotmyindianname.html. Smith's third book, *Indian Shoes* (2002), is a collection of short stories that features a contemporary Native boy and his grandfather.

Anishinabe author Jan Waboose also has made significant contributions. Her *Morning on the Lake,* published in 1997, is a heartwarming story about a child and his grandfather as they spend the day together, starting with a quiet morning on the lake. Her second book, *Sky Sisters,* published in 2000, is about two sisters and their nighttime walk through the frozen night to see the Sky Sisters, commonly known as the northern lights. Both are stories about modern-day Ojibway children.

Another name to watch for is Cheryl Savageau of the Abenaki/Metis tribes. Savageau writes poetry for older readers as well as picture books about contemporary Native children. Her first book, *Muskrat Will Be Swimming* (1996), was identified as a 1996 Notable Book for Children by the Smithsonian Institution, and she was recognized by Word Craft Circle as the 1997 Writer of the Year. She currently is working on another children's book and has used a short story, "Coyote and the Sleeping Monster," with middle school students during author visits. The story is published in an anthology titled *Spinning Tales, Weaving Hope* (Brody), published in 1991 by New Society Publishers. Her book of poems, *Dirt Road Home* (Savageau 1995), though not marketed as a children's book, contains poems that she's read aloud to grade school children in school settings.

Finally, Louise Erdrich, author of *Birchbark House* and *Grandmother's Pigeon,* plans to write additional novels about Omakayas, the protagonist of *Birchbark House.* Muscogee poet Joy Harjo wrote a delightful story, *The Good Luck Cat,* published in 2000, and it is possible she will write others.

Guidelines for Evaluating Children's Books about Native Americans

Today, there are several sets of guidelines teachers and librarians can use to evaluate books about Native Americans. The guidelines usually take the form of a set of questions intended to help the evaluator determine the presence of problems with bias and stereotyping. The roots of such guidelines go back to the Intergroup Education Movement of the 1940s and its efforts to promote positive relationships among racial and ethnic groups (Banks 1995). One approach was to provide children with stories about racially and ethnically diverse children that presented the subjects in a positive light, while simultaneously helping children detect error and bias in literature (Havighurst 1945). Helen Trager, a prominent member of the Intergroup Education Movement, wrote an article that was a survey and critical evaluation of well-known children's books. Trager's (1945) evaluation included examining the books to determine "whether the reader would come away with a favorable attitude toward or at least a better understanding of persons of other culture groups; or whether the reader's presumed prejudices would be deepened or perpetuated in spite of the author's good intention" (138). The article appeared in the November 1945 issue of *Childhood Education* and included a set of twelve questions she used in her evaluation (for example: "Is a particular way of life, a custom or tradition explained, or is it described with bias?" and "Do the illustrations help one to like the people in the story, or are they stereotyped, queer, or ugly?" [139]). The questions were broad in scope and could be applied to various cultural, racial, and ethnic groups. In 1948, the National Council of Teachers of English (NCTE) published Charlamae Rollins's book *We Build Together,* which was subtitled "A Reader's Guide to Negro Life and Literature for Elementary and High School Use." It contained a list of questions that teachers could use to discern the presence of bias in children's books with African American characters. In the decades to come, others would develop similar questions specific to a racial or ethnic group.

Among the earliest studies that looked critically at representations of Native Americans in children's books is Byler's *American Indian Authors for Young Readers: A Selected Bibliography,* published in 1973 by the Association on American Indian Affairs in New York. In the introductory essay to the bibliography, Byler describes a broad range of problematic depictions in children's books with Native American content. A few years later, a set of questions that reflect her essay was published by the Council on Interracial Books for Children in two of its books: *Unlearning Indian Stereotypes* (1977) and *Guidelines for Selecting Bias-Free Textbooks and Storybooks* (1980).

These questions evolved and gained greater currency over time. In 1991, the American Indian Library Association (an affiliate of the American Library Association) published *"I" Is Not for Indian: The Portrayal of Native Americans in Books for Young People,* by Naomi Caldwell-Wood and Lisa Mitten. The most useful and widely cited publication on Native American literature is Slapin and Seale's *Through Indian Eyes: The Native Perspective in Books for Children* (1998). Originally published in 1988, it is currently published by the American Indian Studies program at the University of California, Berkeley. *Through Indian Eyes* includes essays by noted authors such as Joseph Bruchac and Michael Dorris, critical reviews of children's books with Native American characters or themes, and a set of guidelines titled "How to Tell the Difference: A Checklist for Evaluating Books for Anti-Indian Bias." Items on the guidelines are enhanced by the use of illustrations and passages taken directly from children's books. Slapin and Seale are working on a second book, *The Broken Flute.*

The best resource for locating books by small presses and those published by mainstream publishers that have been carefully reviewed by individuals knowledgeable about Native culture is Oyate. Oyate's catalogue is available online (www.oyate.org); a hard copy can be obtained by writing to Oyate, 2702 Mathews St., Berkeley, CA 94702, by calling (510) 848-6700, or by e-mail: oyate@oyate.org.

Journals that publish studies of Native Americans in children's and young adult literature include *The New Advocate* and *Multicultural Review.* (Note: *The New Advocate* has recently ceased publication.) Scholars who have published research articles and book chapters on this topic include Naomi Caldwell, Jim Charles, Donnarae MacCann, Jean Mendoza, Debbie Reese, and Beverly Slapin.

Optimism for the Twenty-First Century

The outlook for the twenty-first century is one of optimism. Without a doubt, there is a great deal of work to be done. It is difficult to change expectations, especially when the mass media and society are so filled with savage, romantic, or outdated ideas of who Native Americans are. The closing decade of the twentieth century reflects a greater involvement of Native people in the writing, publishing, and criticism of literature about Native people than was the case in the first ninety years. There is, and will continue to be, resistance to their voices, but Native people have endured and persisted through hundreds of years of oppression and injustice, and they are bringing that same endurance and persistence to improving the literature that tells their stories.

Note

1. In this chapter, I focus primarily on Native authors. Although there are many other authors who write books about Native Americans, it is my position that the work of Native authors needs to be brought forward and highlighted. Native heritage is no guarantee of a work's authenticity. However, there are a great many Native authors whose work is not receiving the attention it can and should.

References

Atleo, M., N. Caldwell, B. Landis, J. Mendoza, D. Miranda, D. Reese, L. Rose, B. Slapin, and C. Smith. 1999. Fiction posing as truth: A critical review of *My Heart Is on the Ground: The Story of Nannie Little Rose, a Sioux Girl. Rethinking Schools* 13: 4, 14–16.

Bader, B. 1976. *American picturebooks from Noah's ark to the beast within.* New York: Macmillan.

Banks, J. A. 1995. Multicultural education: Historical development, dimensions, and practice. In *Handbook of research on multicultural education,* ed. J. A. Banks and C. A. M. Banks, 3–24. New York: Macmillan.

Banks, L. R. 1980. *The Indian in the cupboard.* Garden City, NY: Doubleday.

Brody, E., ed. 1991. *Spinning tales, weaving hope: Stories of peace, justice and the environment.* Philadelphia: New Society.

Bruchac, J. 1997. *Bowman's store: A journey to myself.* New York: Dial.

———. 1998a. *The arrow over the door.* Illus. J. Watling. New York: Dial.

———. 1998b. *The heart of a chief: A novel.* New York: Dial.

———. 2000. *Crazy Horse's vision.* Illus. S. D. Nelson. New York: Lee & Low.

Bruchac, J., and G. Ross. 1995. *The story of the Milky Way: A Cherokee tale.* Illus. V. A. Stroud. New York: Dial.

Brumble, D. 1994. Autobiographies by Indians. In *Handbook of Native American literature,* ed. A. Wiget, 178–183. New York: Garland.

Byler, M. G. 1973. *American Indian authors for young readers: A selected bibliography.* New York: Association on American Indian Affairs.

———. 1982. Introduction to American Indian authors for young readers. In *American Indian stereotypes in the world of children: A reader and bibliography,* ed. A. B. Hirschfelder, 34–45. Metuchen, NJ: Scarecrow.

Caldwell-Wood, N., and Mitten, L. A. (1991). *"I" is not for Indian: The portrayal of Native Americans in books for young people* [program of the ALA/OLOS Subcommittee for Library Services to American Indian People, American Indian Library Association]. American Indian Library Association. Accessed: 2/28/02. Available: www.nativeculture.com/lisamitten/ailabib.htm

Carter, F. 1976. *The education of Little Tree.* New York: Delacorte.

Child, B. J. 2000. *Boarding school seasons: American Indian families, 1900–1940.* Lincoln: University of Nebraska Press.

Clark, A. N. 1940a. *Little boy with three names. Stories of Taos Pueblo.* Illus. T. Lujan. Chilocco, OK: Chilocco Agricultural School Printing Department.

———. 1940b. *Little herder in autumn. Áakéedgo na'nilkaadí yázhí.* Illus. H. Denetsosie. Phoenix, AZ: Phoenix Indian School Printing Department.

———. 1940c. *Little herder in spring. Dáago na'nilkaadí yázhí.* Illus. H. Denetsosie. Phoenix, AZ: Phoenix Indian School Printing Department.

———. 1940d. *Who wants to be a prairie dog? Háisha t'aá kad dloo silii?* Illus. A. Van Tsihnahjinnie. Phoenix, AZ: Phoenix Indian School Printing Department.

———. 1941a. *In my mother's house.* Illus. V. Herrera. New York: Viking.

———. 1941b. *The Pine Ridge porcupine. Wazi ahanhan p'ahin k'un he.* Lawrence, KS: Haskell Institute Printing Department.

———. 1942a. *Little herder in summer. Shiigo na'nilkaadí yázhí.* Illus. H. Denetsosie. Phoenix, AZ: Phoenix Indian School Printing Department.

———. 1942b. *Little herder in winter. Haigo na'nilkaadí yázhí.* Illus. H. Denetsosie. Phoenix, AZ: Phoenix Indian School Printing Department.

———. [1942] 1992. *There still are buffalo.* Illus. S. Tongier. Santa Fe, NM: Ancient City Press.

———. 1944. *Brave against the enemy. Toka wan itkokip.* Lawrence, KS: Haskell Institute Printing Department.

———. 1947. *Singing Sioux cowboy. Lak'ota pteole hoksila lowansa: Wounspe tokahe.* Illus. A. Standing Soldier. Lawrence, KS: U.S. Indian Service.

Cooper, M. L. 1999. *Indian school: Teaching the white man's way.* New York: Clarion.

Council on Interracial Books for Children. 1977. *Unlearning "Indian" stereotypes: A teaching unit for elementary teachers and children's librarians.* New York: Racism and Sexism Resource Center for Educators, a division of the Council on Interracial Books for Children.

———. 1980. *Guidelines for selecting bias-free textbooks and storybooks.* New York: Council on Interracial Books for Children.

Dalgliesh, A. 1954. *The courage of Sarah Noble.* Illus. L. Weisgard. New York: Scribner's.

Deloria, P. J. 1998. *Playing Indian.* New Haven: Yale University Press.

Dorris, M. 1987. *A yellow raft in blue water.* New York: Henry Holt.

——— 1992. *Morning girl.* New York: Hyperion Books.

———. 1994. *Guests.* New York: Hyperion.

———. 1996. *Sees behind trees.* New York: Hyperion.

Eastman, C. A. 1902. *Indian boyhood.* New York: McClure Phillips.

Echo-Hawk, R. C., and W. R. Echo-Hawk. 1994. *Battlefields and burial grounds: The Indian struggle to protect ancestral graves in the United States.* Minneapolis, MN: Lerner Publications.

Enochs, J. B. 1940. *Little Man's family*. Díné yázhi ba'átchíní. Phoenix, AZ: Phoenix Indian School Printing Department.

Erdrich, L. 1984. *Love medicine. A novel*. New York: Holt, Rinehart and Winston.

Erdrich, L. 1986. *The beet queen: A novel*. New York: Holt, Rinehart and Winston.

———. 1988. *Tracks: A novel*. New York: Henry Holt.

———. 1996. *Grandmother's pigeon*. Illus. J. LaMarche. New York: Hyperion Books.

———. 1999. *The birchbark house*. New York: Hyperion Books.

Giblin, J. 1998. *Writing books for young people*. Expanded ed. Boston: Writer Inc.

Hafen, P. J. 1996. Zitkala Sa Gertrude Bonnin. In *Encyclopedia of North American Indians*, ed. F. E. Hoxie, 708–710. Boston: Houghton Mifflin.

Halsey, R. V. [1911] 1969. *Forgotten books of the American nursery: A history of the development of the American story-book*. Detroit, MI: Singing Tree.

Harjo, J. 2000. *The good luck cat*. Illus. P. Lee. San Diego: Harcourt Brace.

Havighurst, R. J. 1945. Caste and class in a democracy. *Childhood Education* 22, no. 3: 116–120.

Hearne, B. G. 1999. Swapping tales and stealing stories: The ethics and aesthetics of folklore in children's literature. *Library Trends* 47, no. 3: 509–528.

Highwater, J. 1977. *Anpao: An American Indian odyssey*. Illus. F. Scholder. Philadelphia: Lippincott.

Horning, K. T., G. M. Kruse, and M. Schliesman. 2001. *Children's books by and about people of color published in the United States: Statistics gathered by the Cooperative Children's Book Center* [online]. Cooperative Children's Book Center, University of Wisconsin-Madison. Accessed: August 2001. Available: www.education.wisc.edu/ccbc/pcstats.htm

Hoxie, F. E., ed. 1996. *Encyclopedia of North American Indians*. Boston: Houghton Mifflin.

James, G. W. 1908. *What the white race may learn from the Indian*. Chicago: Forbes & Company.

Justice, D. H. 2000. A lingering miseducation: Confronting the legacy of *Little Tree*. *Studies in American Indian Literatures* 12, no. 1: 20–36.

Kennard, E. A. 1944. *Field mouse goes to war. Tusan homichi tuwvöta*. Illus. F. Kabotie. Washington, DC: U.S. Indian Service Education Division.

Lerner, A. 1994. Joseph Bruchac. In *Handbook of Native American literature*, ed. A. Wiget, 401–405. New York: Garland.

Lomawaima, K. T. 1994. *They called it prairie light: The story of Chilocco Indian School*. Lincoln: University of Nebraska Press.

Lynn-Sherow, B. 1996. Fakes and imposters. In *Encyclopedia of North American Indians*, ed. F. E. Hoxie, 190–192. Boston: Houghton Mifflin.

McDermott, G. 1974. *Arrow to the sun: A Pueblo Indian tale*. New York: Viking.

McNickle, D. A. 1954. *Runner in the sun: A story of Indian maize.* Illus. A. C. Houser. Philadelphia: Winston.

Mendoza, J., and D. A. Reese. 2001. Examining multicultural picture books for the early childhood classroom: Possibilities and pitfalls. *Early Childhood Research and Practice* 3, no. 2.

Momaday, N. S. 1968. *House made of dawn.* New York: Harper & Row.

———. 1994. *Circle of wonder: A Native American Christmas story.* Santa Fe, NM: Clear Light.

Moore, R. B., and A. B. Hirschfelder. 1977. Feathers, tomahawks and tipis: A study of stereotyped "Indian" imagery in children's picture books. In *Unlearning "Indian" stereotypes: A teaching unit for elementary teachers and children's librarians,* ed. Council on Interracial Books for Children, 5–23. New York: Racism and Sexism Resource Center for Educators, a division of the Council on Interracial Books for Children.

Ortiz, S. J. 1977. *The people shall continue.* Illus. S. Graves. San Francisco: Children's Book Press.

Peyer, B. C. 1994. Charles Alexander Eastman. In *Handbook of Native American literature,* ed. A. Wiget, 231–237. New York: Garland.

Picotte, A. M. 1985. Foreword. In *Old Indian legends,* ed. Zitkala-Sa, xi–xviii. Lincoln: University of Nebraska Press.

Rees, D. 1984. *Painted desert, green shade: Essays on contemporary writers of fiction for children and young adults.* Boston: Horn Book.

Reese, D. A. 2001. Representations of Native American women and girls in children's historical fiction. In *Beauty, brains, and brawn: The construction of gender in children's literature,* ed. S. S. Lehr, 127–141. Portsmouth, NH: Heinemann.

Reese, D. A., and N. Caldwell-Wood. 1997. Native Americans in children's literature. In *Using multiethnic literature in the K–8 classroom,* ed. V.J. Harris, 155–192. Norwood, MA: Christopher-Gordon.

Rendon, M. R. 1996. *Powwow summer: A family celebrates the circle of life.* Illus. C. W. Bellville. Minneapolis, MN: Carolrhoda Books.

Rollins, C. H., ed. 1948. *We build together: A reader's guide to Negro life and literature for elementary and high school use.* Rev. ed. Chicago: National Council of Teachers of English.

Rose, L. 1999. *Grandchildren of the Lakota.* Illus. C. W. Bellville. Minneapolis, MN: Carolrhoda Books.

Ross, G. 1994. *How Rabbit tricked Otter and other Cherokee trickster stories.* Illus. M. Jacob. New York: HarperCollins.

———. 1995. *How Turtle's back was cracked: A traditional Cherokee tale.* Illus. M. Jacob. New York: Dial.

———. 1996. *The legend of the Windigo: A tale from native North America.* Illus. M. Jacob. New York: Dial.

Ruoff, A. L. B. 1991. *Literatures of the American Indian.* New York: Chelsea House.

Savageau, C. 1995. *Dirt road home: Poems.* Willimantic, CT: Curbstone.

———. 1996. *Muskrat will be swimming.* Illus. R. Hynes. Flagstaff, AZ: Northland.

Seattle. 1991. *Brother eagle, sister sky: A message from Chief Seattle.* Illus. S. Jeffers. New York: Dial.

Shanley, K. W. 1997. The Indians America loves to love and read: American Indian identity and cultural appropriation. *American Indian Quarterly* 21, no. 4: 675–702.

Silko, L. M. 1977. *Ceremony.* New York: Viking.

Slapin, B. 2000. Photo essays of American Indian children. *Multicultural Review* 9, no. 1: 28.

Slapin, B., and D. Seale. 1998. *Through Indian eyes: The native experience in books for children.* Los Angeles: American Indian Studies Center, University of California.

Smith, C. L. 2000. *Jingle dancer.* Illus. Y.-H. Hu. New York: Morrow Junior Books.

———. 2001. *Rain is not my Indian name.* New York: HarperCollins.

———. 2002. *Indian shoes.* Illus. J. Madsen. New York: HarperCollins.

Sneve, V. D. H. 1972. *High Elk's treasure.* Illus. O. Lyons. New York: Holiday House.

———. 1974. *When Thunders spoke.* Illus. O. Lyons. New York: Holiday House.

———. 1975. *The chichi hoohoo bogeyman.* Illus. N. Agard. New York: Holiday House.

———. 1993a. *The Navajos.* Illus. R. Himler. New York: Holiday House.

———. 1993b. *The Sioux.* Illus. R. Himler. New York: Holiday House.

———. 1994a. *The Nez Perce.* Illus. R. Himler. New York: Holiday House.

———. 1994b. *The Seminoles.* Illus. R. Himler. New York: Holiday House.

———. 1995a. *Completing the circle.* Lincoln: University of Nebraska Press.

———. 1995b. *The Hopis.* Illus. R. Himler. New York: Holiday House.

———. 1995c. *The Iroquois.* Illus. R. Himler. New York: Holiday House.

———. 1996a. *The Cherokees.* Illus. R. Himler. New York: Holiday House.

———. 1996b. *The Cheyennes.* Illus. R. Himler. New York: Holiday House.

———. 1997. *The Apaches.* Illus. R. Himler. New York: Holiday House.

Speare, E. G. 1983. *The sign of the beaver.* Boston: Houghton Mifflin.

Standing Bear, L. 1928. *My people, the Sioux.* Boston: Houghton Mifflin.

———. 1931. *My Indian boyhood.* Boston: Houghton Mifflin.

———. 1933. *Land of the spotted eagle.* Boston: Houghton Mifflin.

Sterling, S. 1992. *My name is Seepeetza.* Vancouver: Douglas & McIntyre.

Stroud, V. A. 1994. *Doesn't Fall Off His Horse.* New York: Dial.

———. 1995. *A walk to the great mystery.* New York: Dial.

————. 1996. *The path of the quiet elk: A Native American alphabet book*. New York: Dial.

Tapahonso, L. 1987. *A breeze swept through*. Albuquerque, NM: West End.

————. 1997. *Blue horses rush in: Poems and stories*. Tucson: University of Arizona Press.

————. 1999. *Songs of Shiprock Fair*. Illus. A. C. Emerson. Walnut, CA: Kiva.

Tapahonso, L., and E. Schick. 1995. *Navajo ABC: A Diné alphabet book*. Illus. E. Schick. New York: Macmillan.

Taylor, R. H. 2000. *Indian in the cupboard*: A case study in perspective. *International Journal of Qualitative Studies in Education* 13, no. 4: 371–384.

Thompson, M. K. 2001. A sea of good intentions: Native Americans in books for children. *Lion and the Unicorn* 25, no. 3: 353–374.

Trager, H. 1945. Intercultural books for children. *Childhood Education* 22, no. 3: 138–145.

Velarde, P. 1960. *Old father, the storyteller*. Globe, AZ: D. S. King.

————. 1989. *Old Father, the storyteller*. Santa Fe, NM: Clear Light.

Waboose, J. B. 1997. *Morning on the lake*. Illus. K. Reczuch. Toronto: Kids Can Press.

————. 2000. *Sky Sisters*. Illus. B. Deines. Toronto: Kids Can Press.

Wiget, A., ed. 1994. *Handbook of Native American literature*. New York: Garland.

Wood, D. 1996. *The Windigo's return: A north woods story*. Illus. G. Couch. New York: Simon & Schuster.

Zitkala, S. [1901] 1985. *Old Indian legends*. Boston: Ginn & Company.

————. [1921] 1985. *American Indian stories*. Washington, DC: Hayworth.

14

The Evolution of Historical Fiction for Children

Linda M. Pavonetti

If you are a youngster, say eleven or twelve years old, in 1902, what would you read on a stormy summer afternoon? Chances are, if you are a voracious reader—and because there are no televisions, video games, MP3 players, or DVDs, no malls, or movie theaters or even radios yet—you would have read Sir Walter Scott's *Ivanhoe* (1820), all of Howard Pyle's adventures, and even Louisa May Alcott's *Little Women* (1868) and *Little Men* (1871). If your parents care at all for your moral well-being, they will be protecting you from cheap modern page-turners such as *The Wonderful Wizard of Oz* (Baum 1900) and the tawdry Stratemeyer and Horatio Alger thrillers.

Chances are, if you are a boy in 1902, you might pick up *The Golden Galleon: Being a Narrative of the Adventure of Master Gilbert Oglander, and of How, in the Year 1591, He Fought under the Gallant Sir Richard Grenville in the Great Sea-Fight off Flores, on Board Her Majesty's Ship the* Revenge (Leighton 1900). Naval exploits are all the rage among your chums. If you are a girl, you might be rereading one of your favorites, Charlotte M. Yonge's *Richard the Fearless, or The Little Duke* (Yonge 1856), or if you're lucky, you might have a book by that new author that everyone one is secretly raving about—Joseph Altsheler—such as *In Hostile Red; A Romance of the Monmouth Campaign* (1900b) or *In Circling Camps; A Romance of the Civil War* (1900a). Your mother wants you to read *Polly's Secret: A Story of the Kennebec* (Nash 1902), but she always wants you to read those children's books. Why, just yesterday, your best friend—who had to sit in the parlor and read it aloud to her younger sister— told you that it was nothing but a "quaint story of a brave and lovable New England girl who kept a secret" (Sears 1925, 393).

At the turn of the twentieth century, literature for American children was still struggling to catch up with British publishing. Children, however, were relieved to "have been spared the 'good godly' books of the Puritans. The sin complex was all but gone in 1910—almost but not quite" (Smith 1963, 1). Note that the first *Children's Catalog* (Potter 1909) suggested more than one hundred tales of naval exploits for well-stocked children's libraries. And the adventure story—set in the past—was alive and well, although most readers never called it *historical fiction*.

This chapter summarizes the development, during the course of the twentieth century, of a separate genre of American children's historical fiction. Furthermore, it will put forth an emerging set of criteria triggered by librarians' and educators' need to neatly categorize and define the genre. The chapter specifically follows an issues approach based on social awareness and historical accuracy. Finally, the chapter examines some of the trends that existed during the twentieth century as well as those that may exist at the beginning of the twenty-first century.

Adventure Story or Historical Fiction?

Certainly, historical fiction was alive and well at the commencement of the twentieth century. "A rose by any other name is still a rose," but early in its existence horticulturalists may simply have called it a flower. Similarly, for the first several decades of the twentieth century, authors wrote historical fiction, it received awards, and children read it with relish. However, those who taught, shelved, and wrote about books for children considered historical fiction not as a separate genre, but as a type of adventure or fiction.

Cornelia Meigs edited a text that legitimized children's literature as a scholarly endeavor. *A Critical History of Children's Literature: A Survey of Children's Books in English from Earliest Times to the Present* (Meigs et al. 1953) did not so much define genres or discuss the educational value of books as to trace the history of children's reading matter from Caxton's *Aesop* (Caxton and Jacobs [1484] 1889) to the mid-twentieth century. *A Critical History* focused on the books children had read during the past 450 years as well as the authors who influenced these (pejoratively dubbed) "juveniles" and "toy books." Ruth Viguers, librarian and instructor at Simmons Library School, who contributed the historical fiction piece to *A Critical History of Children's Literature,* chose to title her chapter "Adventures in the Past" (482). This appears to represent the prevailing opinion that "adventure" was a broad-ranging designation that included contemporary adventures, historical adventures, and fanciful (fantasy) adventures. She did not define historical fiction as such, but instead subsumed it within adventure, noting that "the adventure story, after the folk tale, was probably the first form of literature that children took for their own. By its very nature it spoke to every age" (482).

May Hill Arbuthnot, one of the early mavens of university-based children's literature, also included historical fiction as a category of realistic stories in her first edition of *Children and Books* (1947). "Realistic stories for children are divided into many categories. There are innumerable stories about peoples of other lands and a growing body of historical novels for children" (361). Like Meigs, Arbuthnot looks back on a half century of children's books to make her recommendations. Her focus, however, is on teaching with books as compared to Meigs's scholarly analysis of children's books.

Anne T. Eaton, coauthor with Meigs and Viguers of *A Critical History of Children's Literature,* referred to historical fiction as "Stories Old and New" in her 1940 collection of essays, *Reading with Children* (Eaton 1940). Anne Carroll Moore was the first superintendent of Children's Work at the New York Public Library (from 1906 to 1941) and, beginning in 1918, author of the first sustained professional children's book criticism for *The Bookman*. Moore ([1939] 1961) referred to historical fiction as "books dealing with historical periods" (93) and designated them as books for older youths. In general, the term *historical fiction* rarely was applied to young people's books, and there was little differentiation among romances, adventures, histories, and stories.

When writing at the time, reviewers and critics also did not designate *as historical* those books that featured children of other lands—*Hans Brinker, or the Silver Skates* (Dodge 1865), *Heidi* (Spyri [1884] 1925), *The Good Master* (Seredy 1935), and *Young Fu of the Upper Yangtze* (Lewis 1932). "*Hans Brinker* and *Heidi*, like *Tom Sawyer* and *Little Women,* are not only among the first of the realistic books for older children but are still deservedly popular" (Arbuthnot 1947, 412). However, all of these books were cross-referenced in the chapter on realism—under the aegis of "Realism for Older Children: Forerunners" (600) as well as the subsequent chapter on historical fiction. In linking Alcott and Twain with other books in the same section—*Hans Brinker* and *Heidi*—Arbuthnot (1947) states that such nineteenth-century European imports "give American children authentic and exciting accounts of life in foreign lands and acquaint them with children who seem as real as the children next door" (412). Conversely, she denounces the caliber of American-produced books as superficially portraying people of other lands, highlighting the "picturesque at the expense of the usual" (414).

What Children Read: 1900–1950

By examining the Newbery Medal and Honor Award books and the authors and titles recommended at midcentury by Eaton, Moore, Arbuthnot, Meigs, Dora V. Smith, and the *Horn Book Magazine,* we may open a window onto the early-twentieth-century books that made up the bulk of public and school library collections, bookstores' stock, and parent or grandparents' gift selections. For such was the influence of a small group of particularly vocal reviewers, librarians, and educators that they could create a virtual canon of children's books. Possibly, this is attributable to the relative paucity of books, much less "good" books, published previous to World War II.

Imports were still considered the elite of children's books, and the majority of classic historic adventures originated in the British Isles or aspired to British heritage. Sir Walter Scott is held up as a paragon of historical writing and the inspiration for future generations of children's authors. "Scott was one of those writers whom children sought out on their own initiative" (Meigs et al. 1953, 105). Charlotte Yonge, one of the nineteenth century's most popular authors, wrote, "I may respect, admire, rely on other authors more, but my literary affection must ever be for Sir Walter!" (Coleridge 1903, as cited in Meigs et al. 1953, 173). A litany of Victorian writers read Scott throughout their lives, beginning when their parents presented his historical novels as a rite of passage—"a divine, far-off event to which all one's life seemed slowly moving" (Meigs et al. 1953, 173). It is difficult to imagine such modern enthusiasm for Scott's works, unless Harry Potter is inserted as protagonist. "In Scott's great stories, the remote and the real have reached just the balance that young readers love . . . there is no great complication of plot or subtlety of character that are difficult for young minds to follow" (Meigs et al. 1953, 106). *Ivanhoe* (1820), *Rob Roy* (1817), *Waverley* (1814), and *The Redgauntlet* (1824) were on every well-educated young person's must-read list—even into the mid–twentieth century.

Although Newbery winners and Honor books usually made up the majority of American recommendations, Viguers (1953) did not introduce them until after English historic adventures, consisting primarily of sea-faring exploits, medieval stories, European quests, and a short section on "England in Period Stories." The following titles, ranging from Scott's early-nineteenth-century volumes *Rob Roy* (1817) and

Redgauntlet (1824), to a single twentieth-century publication, *Jim Davis* (Masefield 1912), comprised a canon-like list of recommendations for twentieth-century readers. The remainder of the list included *Treasure Island* (Stevenson 1883), *Captains Courageous* (Kipling 1896), *Kidnapped* (Stevenson 1886), *Masterman Ready* (Marryat 1841) and *Mr. Midshipman Easy* (Marryat 1836), *Moby-Dick* (Melville 1851), *The Three Musketeers* (Dumas and Marquet 1844), and *The Count of Monte Cristo* (Dumas, Marquet, and Fiorentino 1846).

As mentioned earlier, children's literature critics—whether authors, librarians, reviewers, or academics—belonged to a small alliance at the beginning of the twentieth century. Frequently, members wore more than one hat. So it is not surprising that books written by some of those members received high praise from their fellows. Cornelia Meigs was such a woman: her books were lauded in virtually every mid-century resource. *Master Simon's Garden* (1916) was called "a landmark in children's literature" (Viguers 1953, 493). "Through [*Master Simon's Garden*] are woven the basic principles of the founding of America and the flowering of freedom and tolerance . . . a vivid interpretation of the most vital principles of democracy" (494). Arbuthnot presents Meigs's writing as exemplifying strong plots backed by strong themes. In the books that Arbuthnot recommends, such as *Clearing Weather* (Meigs 1928), *Master Simon's Garden* (Meigs 1916), and *The Willow Whistle and Other Stories* (Meigs 1931), Meigs "is interested not only in our historical past but also in the beginnings of ideas and their development" (Arbuthnot 1947, 399). Cornelia Meigs figured so prominently in children's literature during the middle years of the twentieth century that the September–October 1944 issue of the *Horn Book Magazine* focused on her and her books.

There are several historical fiction authors and books that received a majority of attention from all critics. In the main, these were the Newbery Award books. *Calico Bush* (Field 1931), *Johnny Tremain* (Forbes 1943), *Caddie Woodlawn* (Brink 1935), *Adam of the Road* (Gray 1942), and the Laura Ingalls Wilder Little House series (1932–1953) were everyone's first-line recommendations.

First among the homegrown favorites was Rachel Field, whose best-remembered book, *Calico Bush* (1931), "may well serve as a model of sound historical fiction" (Arbuthnot 1947, 398). *Calico Bush,* the 1932 Newbery Honor, is only one of the thirty-six books Field wrote and sometimes illustrated—not including her poetry or adult books—and was considered her "finest prose contribution to children's literature" (Arbuthnot 1947, 121).

Two other Newbery Award–winning authors were also highly regarded: Elizabeth Coatsworth and Walter D. Edmonds. Coatsworth's books, *Away Goes Sally* (1934), *Five Bushel Farm* (1939), and *The Fair American* (1940), use the past to illuminate the present world and its problems. Edmonds won the Newbery Award for his first children's book, *The Matchlock Gun* (1941), which portrays Indians attacking a mother and her baby while an older son shoots at them from the family's cabin. Although Arbuthnot hints that Edmonds's book is "a little incredible" (Arbuthnot 1947, 402), *The Matchlock Gun* today would and *should* be considered outrageous in its depiction of Native peoples.

When the scholarly writers recommended historical fiction set in Europe, Howard Pyle's *Otto of the Silver Hand* (1888) and *Men of Iron* (1892) occupied a central role. Although some of the early critics admitted that Pyle's medieval British dialogue confounded readers, they also believed that his battles made the struggle worthwhile. Regrettably, *Otto of the Silver Hand* still remains on many "recommended" and "classics" lists (Helbig and Perkins 1985) while its language continues to make this book unpalatable for modern readers—even adults. Research conducted by Wilson (1985) found that fifth- and sixth-grade students overwhelmingly disliked *Otto of the Silver Hand* and similar books because of the obsolete, arcane language.

Adam of the Road (Gray 1942), the 1943 Newbery Medal winner, with a weak plot and little conflict, is virtually the opposite of Pyle's nineteenth-century blood and gore. Like many of her peers, Gray was more interested in exposing her readers to distant surroundings and epochs. Gray's Newbery acceptance speech described what was uppermost in her mind as she created Adam and his world.

> I chose the thirteenth century for the period of my tale . . . and I sent Adam wandering down the highroad not only because as a minstrel he could enter into all the different kinds of medieval life, the abbey, the castle, the manor house, the inn, the fair, the university, but also and even more because along the highways he would find the simple folk of England . . . and know their kindness, their wisdom, their strength, and their laughter. (Gray 1943, 239–240)

Formulating Criteria

Contrary to current children's literature texts, long lists of criteria to assist teachers and librarians in differentiating "good" books from "bad" were relatively rare during the earlier part of the twentieth century. It was more normal for critics to recommend the books that they considered notable. However, criteria for children's historical fiction were often implicit in their discussions. "Such are some of the historical stories which have been adding their gold to the growing treasury of literature for children. Exciting, colorful, authentic, but above all full of life because their people are real, they become living experiences for boys and girls" (Viguers 1953, 507).

Sir Walter Scott, considered the father of historical romance by most adults of the early twentieth century, became the model for those who desired criteria for children's historical fiction. His personal guidelines assumed the following:

> Dignity should be preserved and grandiloquence avoided; . . . atmosphere . . . without extreme use of archaic terms; . . . strength is necessary but . . . melodrama should be avoided. . . . There should be proportion without sacrifice of detail and . . . *accuracy of background must not crowd out human interest*. (Scott, as cited in Smith 1953, 167)

Lillian H. Smith (1953) concludes her discussion of criteria by affirming that "in books of historical fiction for children there can be no question that *adventure* is the first requirement" (167).

On the surface, the principal goal of nineteenth-century historical fiction writers—to enlighten children—seems to have been discarded when the new twentieth-century criteria were selected. It was replaced by an emphasis on authenticity—a "responsibility to present the truth" (Viguers 1953, 507). The best of twentieth-century children's authors sought a "complete integrity of material, a result of their sound knowledge of a period, an understanding of human beings in any period, and great gifts of imagination" (Viguers 1953, 507).

Although Arbuthnot did not define historical fiction as a genre, she described her standards for good adventure stories set in the past: historically accurate primary plot details as well as background details; dynamic people, places, and problems; exciting and absorbing story lines in which historical facts are secondary to the action. Finally, she argues that the conflicts and difficulties of bygone times should shed light and provide options for modern life (Arbuthnot 1947). These criteria for historical fiction read much like the ones commonly suggested at the beginning of the twenty-first century.

The overarching benchmark for historical fiction dictated that "it gives us a profound sense of being part of a long chain of life that went on years before us and will go on years after us, with customs and events differing in many ways but man's problems and aspirations, his griefs [sic] and joys, remaining substantially the same" (Gray 1943, 239).

During the first four decades of the twentieth century, historical novels for children comprised a strong force even though Americans had not yet identified historical fiction as a genre, nor established structured criteria for writing and judging its worth. There were strong indications that these formalities were just over the horizon, along with World War II.

The Evolution of Modern Historical Fiction

The middle decades of the twentieth century brought about numerous changes in American society. Issues of criteria, voice, "political correctness," objectivity, and complexity became the topic of panel discussions, scholarly debate, and journal articles. New formats—picture storybooks, controlled-vocabulary series, diaries, journals, and epistolary novels took their place alongside the historical novels. As the twentieth century progressed, children's literature mirrored those shifts.

Through mid–twentieth century, much of the puritanical belief that children's literature should instruct, sanctify, and protect the reader remained. Historical fiction written during and immediately after World War II frequently carried a subtext of patriotism associated with the overwhelming sentiment of a nation at war. This was understandable, considering the relative youthfulness of the nation and its history of wars. World Wars I and II were recent scars that returning GIs wanted to forget.

Throughout discussions of historical fiction during the first half of the century, authors stressed themes of American values and principles. *Johnny Tremain* (Forbes 1943) was held up as the paragon of good historical fiction. Esther Forbes, the Pulitzer Prize–winning author of *Paul Revere and the World He Lived In* (1942), conceived of her Newbery Award winner as she researched and wrote the adult biography of Paul Revere. Here is a description of Forbes's procedure for writing her 1944 Newbery Medal book:

While Miss Forbes had been working on her *Paul Revere and the World He Lived In*, her imagination had been caught by the apprentice boys of Boston of that period and of the parts they had played in the Revolution, unknown boys whose activities may have changed the tide of events many times, yet who in history have won little of either honor or blame. So insignificant were they that most of them have been simply lost in the crowds of ordinary people who have no identity—yet for whom and by whom wars are fought. But Miss Forbes, one of those writers who must inevitably know why things are done, could not let these boys slip back into obscurity once she had seen them. She did not let them take the stage but put them off until *Paul Revere* was completed, when she felt she was free to "make up" something. Then she wrote *Johnny Tremain,* and so alive is Johnny, so real is Boston of Revolutionary times, that it is difficult to believe that Esther Forbes had "made up" anything at all. . . .

It is to this book [*Paul Revere and the World He Lived In*] that *Johnny Tremain,* which won the [1944] Newbery Medal, is closely related, and no doubt it is because of the vast and careful research done on *Paul Revere* that she was able to forget the period as history and, seemingly without effort, evoke Boston of Revolutionary times and the people who lived there in her first book for young people.

John Hancock, Sam Adams, Josiah Quincy, Paul Revere are no longer mere names in a history lesson. They are living people, with all the faults and failings of humans. . . . It is easy for the reader to identify himself with Johnny; he has so many faults but is at the same time so lovable. . . . His tongue was too quick and his courage often failed him, but the core of his being was strong and idealistic. (Viguers 1953, 500–501)

This passage exemplifies several important qualities of what was universally admired in historical fiction writing for children at midcentury. First, historical accuracy was a major concern. Whereas much of the earlier fiction was halfheartedly researched, new standards came into play. Not only were the major events assumed to be verifiable, but minor details—such as the weather, furniture, food, or the probability that a woman wore gloves or a hat—also required research. Forbes's writing not only brought Johnny—a fictional compilation of the many apprentices she read about—to life for readers, but also energized those actual historical figures that students learned about in their history books.

In thinking about the way Forbes's research for the adult biography informed her writing of *Johnny Tremain,* one could imagine her closing her file cabinet after completing *Paul Revere and the World He Lived In,* locking it, then leaning back in her chair to contemplate her next project. While her research remained in the locked cabinet, Forbes drew on her deep knowledge of the Boston that Johnny inhabited. She knew the streets, their inhabitants, homes, and shops intimately, but she never let that knowledge interfere with her plot. All the research informed her writing, but it stayed in the background. This type of accuracy became the norm for all historical fiction from *Johnny Tremain* forward. Reviewers at the midpoint of the twentieth century began to demand that people, places, and events should come alive; plot takes precedence over historical details and setting; and the problems of the past illuminate current situations. These points could have been an outline for Viguers's comments about Forbes's writing.

Katherine Paterson began her illustrious career by writing three volumes of historical fiction set in ancient Japan: *The Sign of the Chrysanthemum* (1973), *Of Nightingales That Weep* (1974), *The Master Puppeteer* (1975). More recently, she has explored New England, the Industrial Revolution, and slavery with *Lyddie* (1991) and *Jip: His Story* (1996), which won the 1997 Scott O'Dell Award for Historical Fiction. Paterson (1999) writes about the place of research in her books:

The more research you've done, the more you have to rewrite in order to
bury that research. . . . If the reader is impressed by the amount of research
the writer has done, then the writer has . . . failed. I want readers to be so
caught up in the story that he or she will race to the end of the book to find
out what happens to these people. (1430)

The War's Conclusion: Issues of Perspective

World War II ushered in a new era for American children's literature. At first, just
like the returning soldiers and their families, the literature clustered around home and
family. But when the United States emerged from its isolation, its citizens and its writers began examining their literary perspectives. Christopher Collier, co-recipient with
his brother of a 1975 Newbery Honor Award for their portrayal of a family's struggle
with their individual loyalties and beliefs in *My Brother Sam Is Dead* (Collier and Collier 1974), was one of the first to challenge other authors' depiction of war. He explained his opinion: "All written history is interpretation, and novelists present their
own historical interpretation whether they are conscious of it or not" (Collier 1976,
132). Collier challenged writers' infallible belief in American hegemony. He questioned their immutable stance that war can be represented in one-sided, right versus
wrong terms. "To present history in simple, one-sided—almost moralistic—terms, is
to teach nothing worth learning and to falsify the past in a way that provides worse than
no help in understanding the present or in meeting the future" (Collier 1976, 138).

In a study that analyzed thirty-two children's novels dealing with the American
Revolution, Taxel (1983) concluded, "Authors have drawn quite selectively from the
wide range of possible interpretations of the event" (80). Numerous issues, from the
place of blacks in the Revolution to the opposing political views of the colonists and
the royalists, never surfaced, or if they did, they were never treated as multifaceted
concerns. Taxel (1983) notes that the political viewpoints in his study's books, which
included both *Johnny Tremain* and *My Brother Sam Is Dead,* were probably influenced greatly by the political climate when they were written. "Anti-war sentiment is
visible in the novels written during the Vietnam War era" (78) when *My Brother Sam
Is Dead* appeared. He compares that to the books written post–World War I, which ex-
hibit none of those reactions, and concludes that "this discrepancy . . . probably says
more about the simplified, unambiguous style of writing at that time" (78). He further
indicates that books written concurrently with *Johnny Tremain* uphold America's "basic ideological values and beliefs" (78).

In the same vein, fewer historical fiction books won Newbery Awards during the
postwar years, and of the twenty-seven that did (25 percent of 110 books between 1940
and 1960) only six, *The Matchlock Gun* (Edmonds 1941), *Indian Captive: The Story of
Mary Jemison* (Lenski 1941), *Johnny Tremain* (Forbes 1943), *Rifles for Watie* (Keith
1957), *House of Sixty Fathers* (De Jong 1956), and *The Perilous Road* (Steele 1958),
focused on war. However, during this time period, a new trend arose—contemporary
realistic fiction books that explored the events of World War II and the postwar period.
Even more interesting is that eleven of these historical fiction award winners were
published between 1940 and 1944, which suggests they were begun before the United
States entered World War II. Historical fiction as a major force in children's literature
began a downward trend with the shift from America's unquestioned and unexamined

patriotism of the first half of the twentieth century to the post-Vietnam cynicism. Figure 14.1 illustrates the trend in the number of Newbery Awards presented to historical fiction. It is also illustrative of the influence of war on the genre.

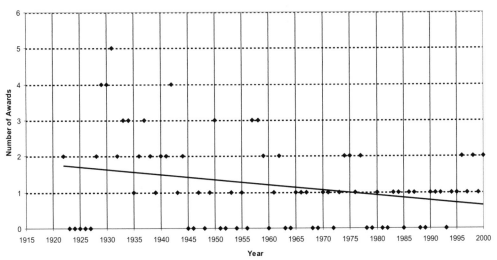

Figure 14.1. Distribution of historical fiction Newberry Award, 1922–2000.

Another related issue surfaced during the second half of the century. Should authors include everything their research discloses? Kathryn Lasky (1990), well-known author of numerous historical novels, railed about the disservice authors commit when they are not entirely truthful—by omitting information. She notes that there is historical fiction, but there is also "the fiction of history—a subtle but important difference. . . . One is an unveiling through literary means of a time, of an era, of people and events; the other is a falsification of the past, a cover up, an outright lie" (159).

Authorial Style: Issues of Language

One of the more thorny issues in writing historical fiction is the language. What constitutes "enough" historical language and what is too much? Joan W. Blos (1985) calls this the "Bunches of Hessians" syndrome: "Historical material and thought lack validity if expressed in modern phrases, idioms, or linguistic rhythms. 'Peering out of her bedroom window, Deeny saw *bunches of Hessians* heading for the green' " (39). A further complication is that no one really knows how people spoke in the past. Without tape recordings, the only indication of language is written language, which differs markedly from spoken dialogue.

How can authentic language flavor the passage? Kathryn Lasky wrote the following passage in *A Journey to the New World: The Diary of Remember Patience Whipple* (1996). "CAST—SPEW—SPOUT—PUKE—Hummy Sawyer and I are making a list of all the words for these wrathful contortions of our innards" (8). Is this too difficult? Read this sentence aloud to any group of fourth or fifth graders and their guffaws will ease your concerns.

Julius Lester appends an "Author's Note" to *Pharaoh's Daughter* (2000), his interpretation of the biblical story of Moses. Among other issues pertinent to writing historical fiction, Lester describes his struggle with the issue of language.

Writing about a civilization that existed more than three thousand years ago is a challenge, to put it mildly. Yet, because the Egyptians left a visual record in the numerous tomb paintings as well as written records, we know a lot about ancient Egypt. All the names used are authentic, and I have sought to be historically faithful throughout and in ways that will not always be obvious. For example, ancient Egyptians had no concept of time smaller than an hour. That is why no character here says, "Wait a minute," and there are no descriptions saying, "She paused for an instant." . . . The Egyptians did not have money, so I could not have a character ask, "How did you spend your day?" or use figures of speech using concepts involving payment, such as, "He paid a price for what he did." (Lester 2000, 169)

There is no magic formula, but when the language interferes with communication, the reader will have a problem. This is a delicate balance: enough authentic language to flavor the passage, but not interfere with comprehension. Early-twentieth-century historical fiction, like Victorian writing, inclined toward purple prose. Sentences were full of what Josephine Tey calls "writing forsoothly" or "gadzookery" (as cited in Sutcliff 1973, 307). As an example of this type of composition, Sutcliff (1973) writes, "Victorian writers, and even those of a somewhat later date . . . saw nothing ludicrous in 'Alas! fair youth, it grieves me to see thee in this plight. Would that I had the power to strike these fetters from thy tender limbs' " (307).

As the twentieth century progressed, writers became more aware of the sound of their writing—sometimes overcorrecting for past "gadzookery." Avi (2002) contends that "it's a balancing act. You create a style and invent a language that accommodates the difference. Metaphors and references have to be true to the period" (1609). Many critics are dubious about the value of historical fiction series, especially when it comes to authentic language. One character in the Dear America series from Scholastic is criticized for not maintaining the British affectations she assumes for the first three pages but uses only occasionally throughout the remainder of the book (Lindsay 1999). On the other hand, Patricia McKissack (1997) has been lauded for her even-handed application of dialect in *A Picture of Freedom: The Diary of Clotee, a Slave Girl.*

Issues of Voice: Political Correctness

One of the most far-reaching as well as controversial issues of the late twentieth century grew out of cultural sensitivity. The Civil Rights movement gave historically suppressed people a voice, and many used that voice to correct inaccurate portrayals of their history. Historical fiction had omitted not only black soldiers, cowboys, merchants, and explorers, but also the role of women had been diminished; Native Americans were portrayed as heathen savages; Asian, Latino, Hispanic, and numerous other groups were ignored or stereotyped. Outside of negative images, there was a virtual void of historical fiction about them. Because it is commonly believed that readers need to see themselves in their books to truly connect with the text, this became a major point of contention. Children's literature scholars argued that one of the primary functions of historical fiction was to overcome the flatness of history by inserting the reader into the story. "To try and conceive . . . what it *felt* like to sit down in a crinoline, or wear armour, or share a bed-place six feet square with three other passengers in a transatlantic sloop in the eighteenth century" (Aiken 1985, 81).

African American authors led the way, and others followed. They realized that history books covered the facts of slavery, but they could share their family stories of the pain of slavery, of a whip across the back, of spouses and children sold and never seen again. Laurence Yep (1989), two-time Newbery Honor winner for *Dragon's Gate* (1993) and *Dragonwings* (1975), alludes to the value of family stories in his historical fiction.

> Adult history is full of dry discussions of abstractions, such as runaway inflation. But that was just a concept to me until I heard about how my paternal grandmother in China would have to pack a small suitcase full of paper currency just to buy a box of matches. When one hears such anecdotes, the theoretical becomes all too real. (318)

Katherine Paterson (1994) notes that "political correctness" is a slippery term she can't define. She also admits that no matter how she tries, "I cannot rid myself of all bias. As carefully as I research, as sensitively as I try to write, as hard as I try not to impose my own beliefs . . . there is no way I can eliminate myself entirely" (89).

When her editor discussed writing a book in honor of the 1992 Columbus quincentennial commemoration, Jane Yolen (1992b) suggested she look for a Native American author "remembering the concerns of my black colleagues, though I have always felt it's the writer's job to put on the clothes of his or her characters, whether or not the skin, religion, gender, nationality, or pathology are his or her own" (236). As she pondered writing the book that became *Encounter* (1992a), she questioned whether a Cherokee, Iroquois, or any other Native American could write about a destroyed people any better than she, the child of European Jews.

> What good is a writer if she is not able—with careful research, total empathy, and great admiration—to assume the mantle of her characters. . . . A writer's duty . . . is to get inside a character, heart and mind and blood and skin and bone. I do not have to commit a murder to write a murder mystery nor be in love to write a love poem. I need to find that murderer—and that lover—inside myself. (Yolen 1992b, 237–238)

Other authors have added their voices to the fracas—Kathryn Lasky, Joyce Hansen, Diane Stanley (Sipe 1997)—and to date, there is no resolution to this issue. Walter Dean Myers responded in a speech to questions about assuming a female point of view in *At Her Majesty's Request: An African Princess in Victorian England* (Myers 1999) that he does not want to be restricted to writing only what he knows. Limiting authors to their own world would sound the death knell of historical fiction.

Issues of Genre: Categorization

How to distinguish historical fiction from contemporary realistic fiction is one of the most passionately discussed elements of historical fiction. One definition holds that authors must set the text before their birth (Drabble 1985). Frances Temple's *The Ramsey Scallop* (1994), set in fourteenth-century Europe, occurred more than five hundred years before her birth, while John Ritter's *Choosing Up Sides* (1998) occurred a mere fifty years before his.

Another alternative is that books set more than two generations in the past qualify as historical fiction (Fleishman 1971). Anything set in the present or the immediate past generation would therefore be considered modern realistic fiction.

Both of these definitions—before the author's birth, and more than two generations in the past—present problems. The first excludes all novels that have stood the test of time and thus, because of their age, have moved from the category of contemporary realistic fiction into historical fiction. This would exclude books such as Louisa May Alcott's *Little Women* (1868), Laura Ingalls Wilders's Little House books (1932–1953), and Marie McSwigan's *Snow Treasure* (1942). All were written as either realistic fiction or as remembrances of the author's childhood and thus would be excluded by the "before-their-birth" rule.

Fleishman (1971) presents a counterargument to this concept. He references an essay on historical fiction written in 1901 by Brander Matthews. In it, Matthews states that Walter Scott, who is to historical fiction as "Shakespeare to English tragedy" (Drabble 1998, 464) " 'attempted the impossible,' since one can't step outside one's own time, and the 'really trustworthy historical novels are those which were a-writing while the history was a-making' " (Fleishman 1971, xv). Thus, Alcott's, Wilders's, and McSwigan's novels would be the ideal examples of historical fiction.

The "two-generation" rule is even more problematic because we must ask, *Whose generations?* Is the forty- to sixty-year time span that comprises two generations determined by the Library of Congress? By librarians shelving books in public or school libraries? Or by teachers who are themselves barely one generation old by Fleishman's rule? When the youthful reader is taken into consideration, generations become much shorter. An adult may remember vividly what happened forty to sixty years previously. A child's memory barely stretches ten years, especially when we are speaking of historical events instead of personal markers. For most students, the Gulf War is as much history as the Civil War. Therefore, the "two-generation" rule assumes one meaning in children's and young adult literature and quite a different significance in adult books.

So how do we differentiate between a contemporary novel and a historical novel? In many instances the difference lies in the purpose and the use. Historical fiction books are those that an *author* writes to provide a contrast between past and present times. Karen Cushman (1994) exemplifies this type of writing. Whether counting the lice she picks from her body, or resenting the marriage her father has arranged, the young noblewoman in *Catherine, Called Birdy* (1994) is a perfect foil for teens who find twenty-first-century life trying. Leon Garfield (1988) expresses this notion quite elegantly. "When we look back, we can recognize ourselves, whether in doublet, [or in] toga. . . . It is this shock of recognition that is the very stuff of historical fiction. History becomes a mirror in which we see ourselves . . . as others see us" (738). Asking, "What is the author's purpose for writing within this specific framework?" frequently will help to distinguish between historical and contemporary realistic fiction.

Not all historical fiction provides situations that contrast with or even relate to readers' lives. Authors may wish to provide information about a specific historical situation that is outside a readers' experience. Robert Westall's *Gulf* (1992) is such a book. Few readers will personally relate to twelve-year-old Andy who exists in alternative *real worlds* when asleep. Although all of the situations Westall provides for his protagonist occur during the child's lifetime, they would be historical events for today's readers. Consequently, some librarians or teachers may choose to call *Gulf* historical fiction, although it could easily be identified as fantasy or contemporary realistic fiction.

When we examine the uses for historical fiction, especially in the classroom, we may expand the time frame to include books that accentuate differences between current times and a time period previous to a *reader's* memory or experience (whenever that may be). By so doing, these books provide experiences from history that may illuminate or suggest alternative solutions to problems in the reader's life. *Ramona and Her Father* (Cleary 1977) may have been written more than twenty years ago—which may be outside teachers' reading life spans as well as students' physical life spans—but the experiences are so similar to current family life that it would remain modern realistic fiction. However, Trudy Krisher's powerful young adult novel *Spite Fences* (1994) qualifies as historical fiction even though it occurs in 1960—within the previous generation's lifetime. This is because students may read it in conjunction with studying the Civil Rights movement in the South, an experience that they (and the author) would need to research in order to understand.

Issues of Curriculum and Format: Historical Fiction in School

One of the biggest trends in the final decade of the twentieth century was historical fiction in picture storybooks. There are several reasons for this phenomenon: Whereas historical fiction was relegated to older readers during the first half of the century, at the end of the century it was considered suitable and even necessary for younger children to learn about their predecessors.

However, children have little understanding of history since their own life experiences are so brief. This is especially obvious when talking with younger children. Often, kindergarten students will begin a statement—in all seriousness—with, "When I was little . . ." Lack of historical perspective should not exclude even the youngest preschoolers from listening to and enjoying historical fiction as a read aloud. Historical stories for young children, published previous to the late 1980s, focused on one or two notable individuals, and this has continued. Because of the recent movement to align curricula, especially through literature-based instruction, authors and illustrators have begun producing a bounty of accessible historical fiction in short, easy- to-read formats as well as beautifully illustrated picture storybooks. Some of these historical offerings for young children are set in a generalized past era. Others extend a simplified view of historical problems and events. Many still feature renowned historical characters. Because these stories are for novice and emergent readers, they require less description and more carefully plotted action. Ideally, they should also provide any background information needed to inform young readers' expanding historical schema. Historical fiction for young children often has emphasized exciting people in history, possibly introduced by the mass media—knights, pirates, Vikings, soldiers, pioneers—whether these characters are real or invented.

Not all of these picture storybooks involve famous battles or leaders. Jan Brett, a perennial favorite with primary and preschool students, deviated from her normal folktale format to produce *The First Dog* (1988), possibly one of the most simplified introductions to prehistoric man. Author George Ella Lyon and illustrator Peter Catalanotto collaborated to create *Who Came Down That Road?* (1992), a historical fiction picture storybook that demonstrates the bond between each of us and our individual and collective histories. A mother responds to her preschool son's insistent questioning with a litany of people, animals, and even spirits who preceded them on the path that stretches ahead of them. Catalanotto's dreamy watercolor illustrations preview each step back in time, so that even before children turn the pages, they can predict the next connection to the past. *The House on Maple Street,* written by Bonnie Pryor and illustrated by Beth Peck (1987), is similar in that it portrays how the present moment is connected to the past and the past affects what occurs in the future.

Advances in technology are another potential reason for the proliferation of historical fiction in picture storybook format. Adults and children alike marvel at their beauty. Illustrations for *N. C. Wyeth's Pilgrims,* text by Robert San Souci (1991), are some of the most striking artwork—although not historically flawless—available in children's literature. The illustrations are actually photographs of the murals Wyeth created between 1940 and 1945 for the Metropolitan Life Insurance Company. San Souci's text and "Author's Note" indicate the history of Thanksgiving, some of the information he gleaned from exhaustive research, and the errors in Wyeth's murals. More history than historical fiction, this book remains one of the most beautiful presentations of the Pilgrims' landing in Plymouth.

Along with the beauty that the picture storybook facilitates, it provides a forum for excerpts from older historical stories and poems. Carol Ryrie Brink's poem *Goodie O'Grumpity,* originally published in 1937, has been reissued with extraordinary linocut illustrations by Ashley Wolff (1994). Wolff's depiction of girls' skirts sweeping dangerously close to the cooking fire enables even the youngest reader to visualize the differences between today's homes—with modern stoves and raised-hearth fireplaces—and those of colonial America. Wolff explains how she used clues in Brink's poem about Goody O'Grumpity's baking a cake for hungry children to determine when Goody lived and how to portray her. Because of her on-site research at Plimoth Plantation, Wolff's illustrations accurately represent life in colonial America.

One of the most surprising reasons for the proliferation of historical fiction in picture storybook format is that older students no longer shun these books. Teachers also have discovered that all age groups of students can benefit from the visual context picture storybooks provide. A current trend in illustrated books specifically targets young adult audiences—especially middle school and older. *Encounter* (Yolen 1992a) pairs well with another complex picture storybook, David Macaulay's *Ship* (1993). Both are more appropriate for an older audience. These books work well with Michael Dorris's *Morning Girl* (1992) and provide contrast with Peter Sis's *Follow the Dream: The Story of Christopher Columbus* (1991) and other more traditional views of Columbus's influence in the New World.

New issues about the American Revolution and early republic are represented more by novels, both for early readers and more mature readers, than picture storybooks. In *George Washington's Cows* (1994), Caldecott medalist David Small renders a humorous glimpse into a White House that never was. Even though it provides little of historical significance, young children invariably laugh at Small's caricature and poetic burlesque of Washington's problems. *Katie's Trunk* (Turner 1992) presents a child's view of a preliminary skirmish at the beginning of the Revolution. What makes this an interesting addition to the body of literature about the Revolutionary War is that Katie and her family are Tories and the men who raid their house are the rebels. This is a great counter to the majority of anti-British texts.

Although most of Jean Fritz's books are historical biography, *George Washington's Breakfast* (1969) is a charming pastiche of history and fiction. A twentieth-century boy, George Washington Allen, questions what General George Washington ate for breakfast. He researches and won't give up until he discovers a book written by a contemporary of Washington's. Although *George Washington's Breakfast* is an illustrated book instead of a picture storybook, the simple text makes a great read aloud that new readers also can enjoy on their own. In the same category, Robert Lawson contributes two biographical fictions, *Ben and Me* (1939) and *Mr. Revere and I* (1953). The hilarious psuedobiography of Ben Franklin is narrated by his good mouse Amos, while Paul Revere's story is told by his horse. Both contain enough history to make them worthwhile for developing a historical sense in youngsters.

Authenticity in Illustration

In her Caldecott acceptance speech for *Ox-Cart Man* (Hall 1979), Barbara Cooney discussed the importance of authenticity in artistically developing a book's setting. Her insights remind us that picture storybook authors and illustrators have a double responsibility for accuracy—in the text as well as in the illustrations.

First of all, I had to establish *exactly* when the story could have happened. "When" is very important to an illustrator because the sets (the landscape and architecture) must be accurate; so must the costumes, the props, the hairdos, everything.

To begin, I tackled the road that the Ox-Cart Man would have followed. This, I found out, would have been one of the early New Hampshire turnpikes, one which opened to traffic in 1803. This was a toll road. . . . Every year thousands of carts and wagons passed this way until the railroads arrived in 1847 and commerce took to the rails.

Next, I investigated Portsmouth and Portsmouth Market to ascertain what buildings would have been there between 1803 and 1847. The main difficulty here was that Portsmouth buildings, including the Market, had a bad habit of periodically burning down. It was a puzzle trying to figure out what was where and when.

What finally determined the date was the Ox-Cart Man's beard. I wanted him to have a lovely red beard. . . . The story, therefore, had to happen between 1803 and 1847, when the turnpikes were busy, at a time when the brick market building in Portsmouth was standing, and when beards were in fashion. Thus, the date of 1832 was settled upon. (Cooney 1980, 381–382)

Katherine Paterson speaks of such obsession with detail when she wrote *Lyddie* (1991). She spent days tracking down the exact date in 1846 when the ten-hour workday petition came to the Massachusetts legislature. Books can rise to the top or fall flat on the quality of the author's research. An anachronism in the illustrations—a musical instrument made from an alloy that did not exist—can hurt an otherwise good product. Writing or illustrating historical fiction forces the author and illustrator to become "a historical detective" (Anderson 2001).

Conclusion

Arbuthnot (1947) concludes her treatment of historical fiction with an extensive discussion of the educational trend to include such texts in the curriculum. She reminds teachers that they should not allow attempts to correlate all of their literature to their social studies program, but her outlook for historical fiction concludes on a rather upbeat note: "Fortunately, this field has attracted outstanding authors and has yielded an unusually high proportion of stories" (p. 397). The increased focus on historical fiction may in part be due to the 1982 inauguration of an award for Historical Fiction (see Table 14.1). Scott O'Dell, who received the 1961 Newbery Award for *Island of the Blue Dolphins* (1960) as well as three additional Newbery Honors for his historical fiction writing, established this award "to encourage other writers—particularly new authors—to focus on historical fiction . . . to increase the interest of young readers in the historical background that has helped to shape their country and their world" (Hall 2003).

Arbuthnot's (1947) statistics indicate that publishers produced more than two hundred books about South America in a two- to three-year period. Her caution remains relevant: "Some of these books about other lands are up to date and authentic,

Table 14.1

The Scott O'Dell Award for Historical Fiction

2002	Mildred D Taylor. *The Land*. Phyllis Fogelman Books.
2001	Janet Taylor Lisle. *The Art of Keeping Cool*. Richard Jackson/Atheneum.
2000	Miriam Bat-Ami. *Two Suns in the Sky*. Front Street/Cricket Books.
1999	Harriette Robinet. *Forty Acres and Maybe a Mule*. Jean Fritz/Atheneum.
1998	Karen Hesse. *Out of the Dust*. Scholastic.
1997	Katherine Paterson. *Jip, His Story*. Lodestar/E. P. Dutton.
1996	Theodore Taylor. *The Bomb*. Harcourt, Brace.
1995	Graham Salisbury. *Under the Blood-Red Sun*. Delacorte.
1994	Paul Fleischman. *Bull Run*. HarperCollins.
1993	Michael Dorris. *Morning Girl*. Hyperion.
1992	Mary Downing Hahn. *Stepping on the Cracks*. Clarion.
1991	Pieter Van Raven. *A Time of Trouble*. Charles Scribner's Sons.
1990	Carolyn Reeder. *Shades of Gray*. Macmillan.
1989	Lyll Becerra de Jenkins. *The Honorable Prison*. Lodestar/E. P. Dutton.
1988	Patricia Beatty. *Charley Skedaddle*. William Morrow.
1987	Scott O'Dell. *Streams to the River, River to the Sea*. Houghton Mifflin.
1986	Patricia MacLachlan. *Sarah, Plain and Tall*. Harper & Row.
1985	Avi. *The Fighting Ground*. Lippincott.
1984	Elizabeth George Speare. *The Sign of the Beaver*. Houghton Mifflin.

Note: In 1982, well-known children's historical fiction author Scott O'Dell established the Scott O'Dell Award for Historical Fiction. To be eligible for the award, a book must be published by a U.S. publisher for children or young people; it must be set in the Americas, and it must be written in English by a U.S. citizen. No award was given in 1982 or 1983. Since 1984, the award has been presented each year. For additional information, please visit the Scott O'Dell Award Web site: www.scottodell.com/sosoaward.html.

but many others are superficial and do not portray foreign countries fairly or adequately" (414). In 1947, when she raised the issues of historical fiction written for curricular purposes and accurate portrayal of world cultures, Arbuthnot may have fired the first shots in a battle that continues to rage at the beginning of the twenty-first century.

It is impossible to separate social awareness from historical accuracy. It is even arguable that one necessarily precedes the other. What applies to children's historical fiction, however, is that "truth varies with authors' and readers' perspectives, that are in turn conditioned by historically changing socioeconomic circumstances" (Cai 1992, 288). Within those confines we hope to see ever improving accuracy in children's historical fiction.

References

Aiken, J. 1985. Interpreting the past. *Children's Literature in Education* 16, no. 2: 67–83.

Alcott, L. M. 1868. *Little women.* New York: Little, Brown.

———. 1871. *Little men: Life at Plumfield with Jo's boys.* 1st American ed. Boston: Roberts Brothers.

Altsheler, J. A. 1900a. *In circling camps; a romance of the Civil War.* New York: D. Appleton.

———. 1900b. *In hostile red; A romance of the Monmouth campaign.* New York: Doubleday Page.

Anderson, L. H. 2001. The writing of *Fever, 1793. School Library Journal* 47, no. 5: 44–45.

Arbuthnot, M. H. 1947. *Children and books.* Chicago: Scott Foresman.

Avi. 2002. The *Booklist* interview: Avi. *Booklist* 98, no. 18: 1609.

Baum, L. F. 1900. *The wonderful wizard of Oz.* Illus. W. W. Denslow. Chicago: G. M. Hill.

Blos, J. W. 1985. The overstuffed sentence and other means for assessing historical fiction for children. *School Library Journal* 32: 38–39.

Brett, J. 1988. *The first dog.* San Diego: Harcourt Brace Jovanovich.

Brink, C. R. 1935. *Caddie Woodlawn.* New York: Macmillan .

———. [1937] 1994. *Goody O'Grumpity.* Illus. A. Wolff. New York: North-South Books.

Cai, M. 1992. Variables and values in historical fiction for children. *New Advocate* 5, no. 4: 279–291.

Caxton, W. [1484] 1889. *The fables of Aesop: As printed by William Caxton in 1484 with those of Avian, Alfonso and Poggio,* J. Jacobs, ed. London: D. Nutt.

Cleary, B. 1977. *Ramona and her father.* Illus. A. Tiegreen. New York: Morrow.

Coatsworth, E. J. 1934. *Away goes Sally.* Illus. H. Sewell. New York: Macmillan.

———. 1939. *Five bushel farm.* Illus. H. Sewell. New York: Macmillan.

———. 1940. *The fair American.* Illus. H. Sewell. New York: Macmillan.

Collier, C. 1976. Johnny and Sam: Old and new approaches to the American Revolution. *Horn Book Magazine* 52: 132–138.

Collier, J. L., and C. Collier. 1974. *My brother Sam is dead*. New York: Four Winds.

Cooney, B. 1980. Caldecott Medal acceptance. *Horn Book Magazine* 56: 378–382.

Cushman, K. 1994. *Catherine, called Birdy*. New York: Clarion.

De Jong, M. 1956. *The house of sixty fathers*. New York: Harper.

Dodge, M. M. 1865. *Hans Brinker, or the silver skates*. New York: Scribner's.

Dorris, M. 1992. *Morning Girl*. New York: Hyperion.

Drabble, M. 1985. *The Oxford companion to English literature*. 5th ed. Oxford: Oxford University Press.

———. 1998. *The Oxford companion to English literature,* 5th ed., 2nd rev. Oxford: Oxford University Press.

Dumas, A., and A. Marquet. [1844] 1846. *The three musketeers*. Trans. William Barrow. Paris: Baudry.

Dumas, A., A. Marquet, and P. A. Fiorentino. 1846. *The count of Monte Cristo*. New York: Burgess Stringer.

Eaton, A. T. 1940. *Reading with children*. New York: Viking.

Edmonds, W. D. 1941. *The matchlock gun*. New York: Dodd Mead.

Field, R. 1931. *Calico bush*. Illus. A. Lewis. New York: Macmillan.

Fleishman, A. 1971. *The English historical novel: Walter Scott to Virginia Woolf*. Baltimore: Johns Hopkins University Press.

Forbes, E. 1942. *Paul Revere and the world he lived in*. Boston: Houghton Mifflin .

———. 1943. *Johnny Tremain*. Boston: Houghton Mifflin.

Fritz, J. 1969. *George Washington's breakfast*. New York: Coward-McCann.

Garfield, L. 1988. Historical fiction for our global times. *Horn Book Magazine* 64: 736–742.

Gray, E. J. 1942. *Adam of the road*. Illus. R. Lawson. New York: Viking.

———. 1943. History is people. In *Newbery Medal books: 1922–1955,* ed. B. M. Miller and E. W. Field, 236–241. Boston: Horn Book.

Hall, D. 1979. *Ox-cart man*. Illus. B. Cooney. New York: Viking.

Hall, H. R. 2003. *The Scott O'Dell Award for Historical Fiction*. Accessed 8/11/03. Available: www.scottodell.com/sosoaward.html

Helbig, A., and A. Perkins. 1985. *Dictionary of American children's fiction, 1859–1959: Books of recognized merit*. Westport, CT: Greenwood.

Keith, H. 1957. *Rifles for Watie*. New York: Crowell.

Kipling, R. 1896. *Captains courageous*. Garden City, NY: Nelson Doubleday.

Krisher, T. 1994. *Spite fences*. New York: Delacorte.

Lasky, K. 1990. The fiction of history: Or, What did Miss Kitty really do? *New Advocate* 3, no. 3: 157–166.

———. 1996. *A journey to the New World: The diary of Remember Patience Whipple.* New York: Scholastic.

Lawson, R. 1939. *Ben and me: A new and astonishing life of Benjamin Franklin as written by his good mouse, Amos.* Boston: Little, Brown.

———. 1953. *Mr. Revere and I: Being an account of certain episodes in the career of Paul Revere, Esq., as recently revealed by his horse, Scheherazade, late pride of His Royal Majesty's 14th Regiment of Foot.* Boston: Little, Brown.

Leighton, R. 1900. *The golden galleon: Being a narrative of the adventure of Master Gilbert Oglander, and of how, in the year 1591, he fought under the gallant Sir Richard Grenville in the great sea-fight off Flores, on board her Majesty's ship the* Revenge. New York: A. L. Burt.

Lenski, L. 1941. *Indian captive: The story of Mary Jemison.* Philadelphia: Lippincott.

Lester, J. 2000. *Pharaoh's daughter: A novel of ancient Egypt.* San Diego: Silver Whistle/Harcourt.

Lewis, E. F. 1932. *Young Fu of the upper Yangtze.* Illus. K. Wiese. Philadelphia: John C. Winston.

Lindsay, N. 1999. Packaging the past. *School Library Journal* 45, no. 7: 34–35.

Lyon, G. E. 1992. *Who came down that road?* Illus. P. Catalanotto. New York: Orchard.

Macaulay, D. 1993. *Ship.* Boston: Houghton Mifflin.

Marryat, F. 1836. *Mr. Midshipman Easy.* London: Saunders & Otley.

———. 1841. *Masterman ready; or, The wreck of the Pacific: Written for young people.* New York: D. Appleton.

Masefield, J. 1912. *Jim Davis.* New York: F. A. Stokes.

McKissack, P. 1997. *A picture of freedom: The diary of Clotee, a slave girl.* New York: Scholastic.

McSwigan, M. 1942. *Snow treasure.* New York: E. P. Dutton.

Meigs, C. 1916. *Master Simon's garden: A story.* New York: Macmillan.

———. 1928. *Clearing weather.* Boston: Little, Brown.

———. 1931. *The willow whistle and other stories.* New York: Macmillan.

Meigs, C., A. T. Eaton, E. Nesbitt, and R. H. Viguers. 1953. *A critical history of children's literature: A survey of children's books in English.* New York: Macmillan.

Melville, H. 1851. *Moby-Dick, or, The Whale.* New York: Harper.

Moore, A. C. [1939] 1961. *My roads to childhood: Views and reviews of children's books.* Boston: Horn Book.

Myers, W. D. 1999. *At her majesty's request: An African princess in Victorian England.* New York: Scholastic.

Nash, H. A. 1902. *Polly's secret: A story of the Kennebec.* Boston: Little, Brown.

O'Dell, S. 1960. *Island of the blue dophins.* Boston: Houghton Mifflin.

Paterson, K. 1973. *The sign of the chrysanthemum*. New York: Crowell.

———. 1974. *Of nightingales that weep*. New York: Crowell.

———. 1975. *The master puppeteer*. New York: Crowell.

———. 1991. *Lyddie*. New York: E. P. Dutton/Lodestar.

———. 1994. Cultural politics from a writer's point of view. *New Advocate* 7, no. 2: 85–91.

———. 1996. *Jip: His story*. New York: E. P. Dutton/Lodestar.

———. 1999. Historical fiction: Some whys and hows. *Booklist* 95, no. 15: 1430–1431.

Potter, M. E., ed. 1909. *Children's catalog: A guide to the best reading for young people based on twenty-four selected library lists*. Minneapolis, MN: H. W. Wilson.

Pryor, B. 1987. *The house on Maple Street*. Illus. B. Peck. New York: William Morrow.

Pyle, H. 1888. *Otto of the silver hand*. New York: Scribner's.

———. 1892. *Men of iron*. New York: Harper & Brothers.

Ritter, J. H. 1998. *Choosing up sides*. New York: Philomel.

San Souci, R. D. 1991. *N. C. Wyeth's pilgrims*. Illus. N. C. Wyeth. San Francisco: Chronicle.

Scott, W. 1814. *Waverley; or, 'Tis sixty years since*. 2d ed. Edinburgh: Printed by J. Ballantyne for A. Constable.

———. 1817. *Rob Roy*. New York: H. M. Caldwell.

———. 1820. *Ivanhoe: A romance*. 2d American ed. Philadelphia: M. Carey & Son.

———. 1824. *Redgauntlet: A tale of the eighteenth century*. Philadelphia: A. Sherman.

Sears, M. E., ed. 1925. *Children's catalog: A dictionary catalog of 4100 books with analytical entries for 863 books*. 3d rev. and enlarged ed. New York: H. W. Wilson.

Seredy, K. 1935. *The good master*. New York: Viking.

Sipe, L. R. 1997. In their own words: Authors' views on issues in historical fiction. *New Advocate* 10, no. 3: 243–258.

Sis, P. 1991. *Follow the dream: The story of Christopher Columbus*. New York: Knopf.

Small, D. 1994. *George Washington's cows*. New York: Farrar, Straus and Giroux.

Smith, D. V. 1963. *Fifty years of children's books, 1910–1960: Trends, backgrounds, influences*. Champaign, IL: National Council of Teachers of English.

Smith, L. H. 1953. *The unreluctant years: A critical approach to children's literature*. Chicago: American Library Association.

Spyri, J. [1884] 1925. *Heidi*. New York: Grosset & Dunlap.

Steele, W. O. 1958. *The perilous road*. New York: Harcourt Brace.

Stevenson, R. L. 1883. *Treasure Island*. London: Cassell.

———. 1886. *Kidnapped; being the memoirs of the adventures of David Balfour in the year 1751*. London: Cassell.

Sutcliff, R. 1973. History is people. In *Children and literature: Views and reviews,* ed. V. Haviland, 305–312. Glenview, IL: Scott Foresman.

Taxel, J. 1983. The American Revolution in children's fiction. *Research in the Teaching of English* 17, no. 1: 61–83.

Temple, F. 1994. *The Ramsay scallop*. New York: Orchard.

Turner, A. W. 1992. *Katie's trunk*. Illus. R. Himler. New York: Macmillan.

Viguers, R. H. 1953. The golden age 1920–1950. In *A critical history of children's literature: A survey of children's books in English,* ed. C. Meigs, 427–605. New York: Macmillan.

Westall, R. 1992. *Gulf*. New York: Scholastic.

Wilder, L. I. 1932–1953. Little house series. Illus. H. Sewell. New York: Harper & Row.

Wilson, P. J. 1985. Children's classics: A reading preference study of fifth and sixth graders. Ph.D. diss., University of Houston, Texas. *Dissertation Abstracts International* 47, no. 02: 0454A.

Yep, L. 1975. *Dragonwings*. New York: Harper & Row.

———. 1989. The green cord. *Horn Book Magazine* 65, no. 3: 318–322.

———. 1993. *Dragon's gate*. New York: HarperCollins.

Yolen, J. 1992a. *Encounter*. Illus. D. Shannon. San Diego: Harcourt Brace Jovanovich.

———. 1992b. Past time: The writing of the picture book *Encounter*. *New Advocate* 5: 234–239.

Yonge, C. M. 1856. *Richard the Fearless, or, The little duke*. New York: D. Appleton.

15

A Long Way from Pleasantville

Lois Lowry

My grandmother died long before I was born.

That did not affect me, really, in any way, because my grandfather, by the time I came along, had remarried; and so I grew up with a grandmother.

But it did mean that from time to time, my sister and I, as children, went with our mother to the cemetery in our small town so that she could visit her own mother's grave.

Wandering nearby when I was still quite young, I discovered a grave that interested me much more than my late grandmother's. A large granite tombstone was engraved with the phrase "Babes in the Wood" and the names of three children, sisters, who had all died on the same day, many years before. (I think there were flowers and bunnies engraved as well, but perhaps my memory has embellished the marker and given it a kind of Hallmark card quality that it didn't actually have.)

With my mother's permission, I would take a flower or two from my own grandmother and deposit it at the base of the little girls' tombstone. I think I pictured them resting there together the way sisters might snuggle, hugging one another, in a bed. Death didn't enter my picture. It was to me a little the way Beth's death had been in *Little Women* (Alcott 1868): there on one page, gone on the next. Maybe a whispered farewell. Then *poof,* like an extinguished candle. Babes in the Wood.

When we left the cemetery, we would ride home, mother driving our 1937 Chevrolet carefully through the clean and quiet streets of our town, to the neighborhood where we lived: a neighborhood of picket fences, jolly mailmen, cheerful servants, and playful puppies.

It was the same neighborhood that I had read about in first grade: Dick and Jane and Baby Sally, romping with Spot and Puff on the greenest of grass. It was the neighborhood I read about in every book I had: a regular Pleasantville of a town.

There was such a sense of familiarity: the stern but kindly grandfathers; the hardworking, affectionate servants; the helpful and cheery playmates; the cheeky bullies eager for reform. I found them in *The Five Little Peppers* (Sidney 1881), *Rebecca of Sunnybrook Farm* (Wiggin 1903), *The Bobbsey Twins* (Hope 1904), *Elsie Dinsmore* (Finley 1867), *Pollyanna* (Porter 1940).

179

And a series about a little girl named Honey Bunch (for example, Thorndyke 1923a, 1923b, 1923c).

Let me share with you a scene describing Thanksgiving in Honey Bunch's house, in Honey Bunch's town:

> She and Mother began that very day to get ready for Thanksgiving. They went to market together and Mother told the butcher what kind of turkey she wanted and he promised to send her a nice one the day before Thanksgiving. Then Mother and Honey Bunch bought nuts and raisins and cranberries and apples and oranges and a great yellow pumpkin that Honey Bunch thought was too pretty to cook.

While Honey Bunch and her mother are busy shopping, her father—known as "Daddy Morton"—is busy, too. He is preparing a Thanksgiving basket for someone who is never named but is referred to, throughout the book, as "the little lame boy." Daddy Morton carefully opens walnuts, removes the nuts, inserts dimes, and carefully reglues the walnut shells, so that the lame boy will be surprised by the coins.

"Did the little lame boy like his basket?" Honey Bunch asks her father, later.

> "To be sure he did," said Daddy Morton. "I left him eating grapes and looking at the rest of the things when I came away. . . ."
> Every year Mrs. Morton invited three old ladies who lived in an old ladies' home to come to Thanksgiving dinner. They were sisters and their names were Miss Anna, Miss Mary, and Miss Bertha Anderson. Mother told Honey Bunch that they were not exactly poor and they were not hungry; they were well taken care of in the home.
> "But they are lonely, for they have no one of their own to love them," she said. "No nice daddy, no little girl. I like them to come and be happy with us, and Daddy does, too."

Her Thanksgiving seemed so commonplace, so much like my own. The lovable grocer: we had our Mr. Barnhart, at the neighborhood corner store. The noblesse oblige; we, too, gave food to the less fortunate, though with less special attention than Daddy Morton's dimes-in-walnuts trick.

We even had our three old-lady sisters at Thanksgiving: my three great-aunts, dressed in silk and smelling of talcum and cologne.

It was only much, much later, looking back on my Pleasantville memories, that I assessed the differences. I remembered the gap in our family, the lack. No Daddy Morton. My own father was in the Pacific, then. My mother had a new baby, a son my father had never seen. She read the war headlines and listened to the evening news with a sense of fear and anguish that my sister and I felt but didn't completely comprehend.

The loving, busy cook in my grandmother's kitchen, each Thanksgiving, had a family of her own: children and grandchildren who lived in another part of town, a less pleasant part of Pleasantville. Who cooked *their* dinner? And why didn't I wonder about it when I was a little girl?

The three great-aunts? Thanksgiving, I realized as an adult, was the only time I ever saw them together. Yes, they were sisters, but estranged by a dispute over a long-ago inheritance; they never spoke to each other during the rest of the year.

The Babes in the Wood? The gravestone decorated with bunnies? I learned their story, too, when I was older. Their bodies, bullets in their heads, had indeed been found in the woods outside our town. They had been murdered by their mother and her lover.

So much for Pleasantville.

Years later, I would use as an epigraph to my book *Autumn Street* (1980) a quotation from e e cummings ([1973] 1991): "along the brittle treacherous bright streets of memory comes my heart" (305).

There was an orphanage in my town. It was called, euphemistically, "The Children's Home," but we all knew what that meant. With my blinders firmly in place—and glued there by the books I loved—I envied orphans. *The Secret Garden* (Burnett 1911) and Sara Crew in *A Little Princess* (Burnett 1905) told me that they often had rich benefactors with country estates; and sometimes their long-lost fathers reappeared, smiling and laden with gifts. I could see for myself, peering through the fence, that there was enviable play equipment on the grounds of the place in my own town where orphans lived.

They came to my school because it was the one nearest the orphanage. We all—even the teachers, if my memory isn't too treacherous—actually referred to those children as "orphans" and made certain allowances for their differences. Relying on institutional drivers, they were often tardy and always forgiven.

But no one played with them. They couldn't linger after school for the jump-rope and hopscotch games. They weren't invited to birthday parties because, of course, they couldn't come.

A boy named Frederick was in my first-grade class. A resident of the Children's Home, he sat silently in the back and was taken for granted, until the day that he and I became linked in an odd excursion.

My first-grade teacher was the daughter of a professor at the local college. He had—I only learned the details of this as an adult—asked his daughter for two children, a gifted child and a slow learner, to be used in a demonstration before a large class in child psychology.

And so, six years old, wearing my best dress, I found myself standing on a stage beside the professor at his lectern. Frederick, wearing *his* best clothes, stood on the other side. Terrified—and mystified, too, by being there—I looked out at a sea of faces.

I was supposed to be the gifted child. My mother, many years after the event, still groaned with the humiliation of it. "You were *bright*," she said defensively. "But how would anybody know that? You wouldn't open your mouth!"

It was true. I remember it. I hung my head, looked at the floor of the stage, went mute, and refused to answer the professor's questions.

Frederick, the slow learner, the orphan, answered loudly, at length, with embellishment and wry humor. He worked the crowd and beamed with his own success.

My mother read aloud to us at home. How fortunate we were, for that. Our school had no library, used no fiction. I doubt if many of the children in my classes had, at home, the crowded bookcases that my family did, or the tradition.

I have a photograph—it appears in my memoir *Looking Back* (1998)—of my mother, age six, wearing a white dress, being read to by her mother.

I liked to think that the book was *The Secret Garden,* which my mother had loved as a child, and which she read to me.

No photograph exists of my mother reading to her children because the family photographer, my dad, was overseas for the duration of the war.

And no photograph exists of me reading to my children, because *I* was the family photographer.

But there is a photograph, also in *Looking Back,* of my daughter Kristin, eleven or so, lying on the back of her horse, reading a book. Not great horsemanship. But it was a gentle horse. And it looks as if it must have been a great book. Kristin, grown now, a mother herself, says that it may well have been *The Secret Garden.*

When my sister and I were still young, my mother read *The Yearling* (Rawlings [1933] 1938) to us, a chapter a night, sitting in the hallway between our bedrooms. On those spring nights in 1945, with my own father far away on an island in the Pacific (the same island, though we did not know it then, where the atomic bomb would soon be loaded onto a plane), my mother sat quietly in that hallway and read of the boy named Jody. I remember, still, how the light fell on her, on her hair, and I watched from my bed in the darkened room. She had a clear and expressive voice. Within a few chapters I began to identify with Jody Baxter, who even looked like me: skinny and blond. I took his side—made it *my* side, too—when his mother scolded him. I walked beside him through the swamp, hunting dogs at our heels, Jody's and mine, while we watched his father track the huge bear they called Old Slewfoot.

One night my mother read the chapter—it's Chapter 14 (Rawlings [1933] 1938, 158)—which concludes with Jody, the boy, sitting on the floor leaning against his father's bed through a long night. His father, bitten by a rattlesnake, is struggling to live. (You may remember that immediately after being bitten, Jody's father shoots a deer, rips it open, and uses the still-warm liver to draw the venom from his own wound. Later they realize that the deer had had a fawn.)

It seemed to Jody that he was alone with his father. . . . If he kept awake, and labored for breath with the tortured sleeper, breathing with him and for him, he could keep him alive. He drew his breath as deep as the ones his father was drawing *(and I, listening, drew the same long, labored breath).* It made him dizzy. He was light-headed and his stomach was empty. He knew he would feel better if he should eat, but he could not swallow. He sat down on the floor and leaned his head against the side of the bed. . . .

He recalled the triangular head [of the snake], the lightning flash of its striking, the subsidence into alert coils. His flesh crawled. It seemed to him he should never be easy in the woods again. He recalled the coolness of his father's shot, and the fear of the dogs. He recalled the doe and the horror of her warm meat against his father's wound. He remembered the fawn. . . . The fawn was alone in the night, as he had been alone. . . . It had lain hungry and bewildered through the thunder and rain and lightning, close to the devastated body of its [mother], waiting for the stiff form to arise and give it warmth and food and comfort. [Jody] pressed his face into the hanging covers of the bed and cried bitterly. *(And I, listening to my mother read that sentence, pressed my own face into my pillow in anguish for the fictional boy who somehow had become merged into one with me.)*

"He was torn with hate for all death and pity for all aloneness," *my mother read, and began to cry.*

And I knew, though I was only in fourth grade, that my mother, too, was torn with hate for death and pity for aloneness—and that it had to do not with rattlesnakes or fawns, but with the war that had taken my father from us. It had to do with humanity and all of us, and it was a very, very long way from Pleasantville.

Not long after that, I picked up a book called *A Tree Grows in Brooklyn* (Smith 1943). I moved from Jody Baxter's lonely swampland in northern Florida to Francie Nolan's life in the teeming immigrant streets of New York. They were both real worlds to me: worlds inhabited by cruelness and eccentricity, but also populated by courage and by the deeply human connections that people feel for one another.

The world of literature opened up for me then. When I was eleven, we moved from Pennsylvania to Tokyo. We couldn't take much with us; and so we sorted and selected. I donated all of my Bobbsey Twins, all the Nancy Drews, Honey Bunch and all of her ilk to the public library in my town. I never looked back. I left Pleasantville behind.

In two weeks, I will return to that town. I've been invited to celebrate the 100th birthday of the library there: the same library that gave me *The Yearling* and *A Tree Grows in Brooklyn* and which began my literate life.

I think the town will probably look like Pleasantville—beautiful, historic college town, with tree-shaded streets. But I know now that the streets hid secrets, as such streets always have.

I wonder now about the boy named Frederick who sat in the back of the classroom each year, friendless and silent, except for his one day of glory at my expense, in first grade. Might his days have been different if someone had read *Maniac Magee* (Spinelli 1990) to him? Or *Holes* (Sachar 1998)?

When I came, rather late, at forty, to the writing of children's books, I tried—subconsciously—to make amends for the shallow, blinded view I had had of childhood.

My first book, *A Summer to Die* (1977), wrestled with the issues of grief and guilt from which children are not exempt. Perhaps this was a kind of apology to the Babes in the Wood, an acknowledgment that their deaths had nothing to do with butterflies and bunnies. My sister, still young herself, was by then buried very near them.

In *Autumn Street* (1980) I tried to address the accepted racism, including that of my own family, in that town at that time.

In the numerous Anastasia books (*Anastasia Krupnik*, 1979, for example; see references for a complete list), I've tried to show realistic family life with all its squabbling and uncertainty and also with the one essential truth of most contemporary families: that they consist of flawed people loving and forgiving each other day after day, year after year.

It was no accident that in *The Giver* (1993) I re-created the essence of Pleasantville: its seductive sense of order, its courtesies and platitudes, its shadowed corners and deeply hidden secrets.

The letters that I receive each day from young readers tell me of their own realities.

"We're going to Disney World when my dad is on parole."

"My mom has a wig cuz of chemo."

"My dad is getting married again and she is my cousin but it's okay because she's removed."

I think of Daddy Morton fastidiously hiding dimes in walnut shells for a little lame boy. Today's kids, so many of them crippled by circumstances, don't need patronizing coinage. They need the companionship and solace that a world of good and honest books provides.

References

Alcott, L. M. 1868. *Little women; or, Meg, Jo, Beth and Amy.* New York: Little, Brown.

Burnett, F. H. 1905. *A little princess; being the whole story of Sara Crewe, now told for the first time.* New York: Scribner's.

———. 1911. *The secret garden.* 2d ed. New York: F. A. Stokes.

cummings, e. e. [1973] 1991. along the brittle treacherous bright streets. In *e.e. cummings: Complete poems 1904–1963,* ed. G. J. Firmage, 305. New York: Liveright.

Finley, M. 1867. *Elsie Dinsmore.* New York: M. W. Dodd.

Hope, L. L. 1904. *The Bobbsey twins.* New York: Grosset & Dunlap.

Lowry, L. 1977. *A summer to die.* Boston: Houghton Mifflin.

———. 1979. *Anastasia Krupnik.* Boston: Houghton Mifflin.

———. 1980. *Autumn Street.* Boston: Houghton Mifflin.

———. 1981. *Anastasia again!* Boston: Houghton Mifflin.

———. 1982. *Anastasia at your service.* Boston: Houghton Mifflin.

———. 1984. *Anastasia, ask your analyst.* Boston: Houghton Mifflin.

———. 1985. *Anastasia on her own.* Boston: Houghton Mifflin.

———. 1986. *Anastasia has the answers.* Boston: Houghton Mifflin.

———. 1987. *Anastasia's chosen career.* Boston: Houghton Mifflin.

———. 1991. *Anastasia at this address.* Boston: Houghton Mifflin.

———. 1993. *The giver.* Boston: Houghton Mifflin.

———. 1995. *Anastasia, absolutely.* Boston: Houghton Mifflin.

———. 1998. *Looking back: A book of memories.* Boston: Houghton Mifflin.

Porter, E. H. 1940. *Pollyanna, the glad book.* New York: Grosset & Dunlap.

Rawlings, M. K. [1933] 1938. *The yearling.* New York: Scribner's.

Sachar, L. 1998. *Holes.* New York: Farrar, Straus and Giroux.

Sidney, M. 1881. *The five little Peppers and how they grew.* New York: Lothrop, Lee & Shepard.

Smith, B. 1943. *A tree grows in Brooklyn.* New York: Harper & Brothers.

Spinelli, J. 1990. *Maniac Magee.* Boston: Little, Brown.

Thorndyke, H. L. 1923a. *Honey Bunch: Her first days on the farm.* New York: Grosset & Dunlap.

————. 1923b. *Honey Bunch: Her first visit to the city*. New York: Grosset & Dunlap.

————. 1923c. *Honey Bunch: Just a little girl*. Illus. W. S. Rogers. New York: Grosset & Dunlap.

Wiggin, K. D. S. 1903. *Rebecca of Sunnybrook farm*. Boston: Houghton Mifflin.

16

The Role of Family in the Novels of Lois Lowry

Sylvia M. Vardell

"Happy families are all alike, but every unhappy family is unhappy in its own way," claimed Russian writer Leo Tolstoy. Russell (2001) states, "Family stories— also called domestic stories—have been around since Victorian days" (210). He cites two prominent examples commonly regarded as milestone books in children's literature:

> Louisa May Alcott's *Little Women* (1868), one of the earliest family stories . . . [is] a realistic portrayal of mid-nineteenth-century American family life with all its ups and downs. . . . Among the best of the early domestic stories is the series by the Canadian writer Lucy Maud Montgomery, beginning with *Anne of Green Gables* (1908). (Russell 2001, 210)

Happy families were a staple in the children's literature of the early to mid-twentieth century. "Optimism is reflected in the views of the children and families depicted in American children's books of the late 1930s through the beginning of the 1960s" (Norton 1995, 85). Unhappy families, however, gradually appeared in children's novels with more frequency. Russell (2001) claims, "Modern social realism may trace its roots back to the best-known coming-of-age stories, Mark Twain's (1885/1982) *The Adventures of Huckleberry Finn*" (213).

Researchers who have analyzed children's literature over time have identified the 1960s, 1970s, and 1980s as decades in which traditional social, family, and personal values appeared to be changing—children were becoming more outspoken, independent, and critical of adults (Norton 1995, 88).

Russell (2001) points out that "in the second half of the twentieth century, the domestic story for older readers moved further away from its romantic beginnings" (213); as examples he cites the novels *Where the Lilies Bloom* by Bill and Vera Cleaver (1969), *The Great Gilly Hopkins* by Katherine Paterson (1978), and *Homecoming* by Cynthia Voigt (1981), which all pivot around issues of death, poverty, and abandonment.

But in contrast, contemporary novels about families also have explored the lighter moments of everyday life. "A common feature of many domestic stories, and one seen from the very beginning, is their humorous tone. . . . Beverly Cleary, Betsy Byars, and Lois Lowry have written exceedingly popular domestic stories filled with laughter" (Russell 2001, 212). Indeed, modern family stories often balance humor and pathos, the mundane details and the life-changing crisis in ways that reflect real life as many people live it. The novels of Newbery Award–winning author Lois Lowry, in particular, reflect these changing attitudes toward family, the conflicts and struggles of unhappy families, as well as the complexities and challenges facing modern "happy" families.

This trend toward the inclusion of family and parent characters as essential to the narrative and in the depiction of a variety of types of family characters in children's novels is in itself relatively recent (Taylor 1996). In the early part of the twentieth century, children's novels provided a "secure escape," according to Goforth (1998), in which "parents were not necessarily well-developed characters, but remained in the background providing safety and security if needed" (150).

In the past two decades, society and its norms have changed. . . . In the Western world, one of the fastest changing social norms is that of the family in which father goes out to work and mother is at home. Though still in existence, this family no longer stands as the measure by which all other family styles are judged. The number of families in which both parents are in the labor force and the number of single-parent families are increasing. (Kinman and Henderson 1985, 885)

Harriet the Spy by Louise Fitzhugh (1964) signaled a turning point in novels for young people (Jacobs and Tunnell 1996; Tomlinson and Lynch-Brown 1995). Here was a girl protagonist who was sometimes unhappy and outcast, and whose well-to-do and busy parents seemed to neglect her. Many contemporary novels that followed, especially the "problem novels," reflected more complicated and challenging aspects of modern life, such as children coping with divorce, disease, death, and other real-life issues. Kortenhaus and Demarest (1993) also found a more even distribution of both genders in their analysis of child characters in central roles in books published after 1970. "Contemporary realistic fiction tends to serve as the bellwether for what is acceptable subject matter in children's books . . . changes in the content of children's literature typically appear first in this genre and then spread to others" claim Jacobs and Tunnell (1996, 92). This quality also makes the genre susceptible to censorship, as authors tackle taboos that adults who select books for children may find uncomfortable. "Today, children's literature reflects the variety of philosophies of childhood and child-raising techniques held by adults" (Goforth 1998, 152); some adults may yearn for books that reflect the pre-1960s era of a supposed safe and secure environment, with benign and homogeneous parent characters. A close examination of the children's novels of the late twentieth century reveals that families are nearly as varied as the child protagonists in children's literature are. In some cases, parent characters were given traditional gender roles but still emerge as richly drawn individuals within the narrative. In other examples, the parent characters bend gender expectations in unique ways (Vardell 2001).

When children read children's books, they read to identify with protagonists close to their own age. Some authors portray these characters within the context of a family in a way that makes them integral to the narrative. Their interactions help the reader to see the dynamic growth of the young hero or heroine. The challenge is to incorporate adult characters in the story in ways that seem real and believable to both children and adults. The temptation is to inject elements into the characterization of adult characters that are didactic, hoping to sneak in a message about growing up. These emerge as the weakest of literary characters and children's responses are often negative or apathetic. Fortunately, the best books avoid this trap. The families depicted in the novels of Lois Lowry sampled here are interesting literary characters in their own right. They may not always include the best parents or role models, but they are always interesting book characters. They communicate a fascinating array of family arrangements, reflecting an increasing reality for most of America's children: a world of working parents, struggling single parents, and caring adults who are surrogate parents. "Clearly, children's literature now presents a greater range and more realistic representations of family diversity" (Norton 1995, 94).

Families in current children's novels are not always so loving, positive, or traditional, however. "Divorce, broken homes, alcoholism, child abuse, and same-sex relationships—all nearly absent from books written 30 years ago—are now widely treated in children's realistic fiction" (Temple et al. 1998, 272). Families also may be important to the story in *negative* ways, abusing or abandoning their children and setting in motion stories of survival or healing (Apseloff 1992). These stories may be difficult to read and share because adults often are inclined to want to shelter young readers from pain and suffering. It is important to remember, however, that many children today experience such pain and suffering firsthand and may find comfort, release, and recognition through literature. And, for those children whose lives are more "comfortable," they may find that reading about characters who are experiencing extreme difficulties helps promote a deeper understanding and empathy. It may be painful to read about negative family structures, but we are well aware that they exist in the real world.

In addition, "parent" characters in recent fiction are not just the child's birth parents anymore. Many novels for young people portray adult caregivers that are not the protagonist's parents but are important and pivotal story characters. Some stories weave together a variety of adult characters as supporting players in the child's growing up experience. As the African proverb confirms, "It takes a village to raise a child." Mann (1999) found different role models allow children to see that many kinds of people can serve this function. It also can be comforting to those students who are not part of a nuclear family because they realize that people other than parents can be role models; they show compassion and give comfort to the main characters of the stories but are never themselves the main characters. Mann (1999) continues:

The role models also convey a great deal of understanding for what the children are dealing with and never trivialize their issues or concerns. Students are able to see that someone does understand them and care about them. . . . Students need relationships with adults to be able to tap into the wisdom and strength that is there. (n.p.)

The novels of Lois Lowry stand as a body of work significant in their genres, style, and content. Not only has Lowry been awarded the Newbery Award twice for her distinguished contribution to writing for children, but her work is very popular with young readers as well. In addition, one of the hallmarks of her writing is the characterization of family in her stories. She creates rich parent characters that shape the narrative as well as the lives of their children. She provides glimpses of several different kinds of family structures, including traditional, extended, blended, and single-parent families. In addition, her protagonists and their families grapple with very real struggles in life, including war, prejudice, death, loss, and separation.

Traditional Families

"Not until relatively recently has childhood become the time for the close family interaction that we are familiar with today" (Norton 1995, 76). Lowry provides an excellent example of family intimacy in her series of books about the character Anastasia Krupnik. Here, precocious Anastasia lives with her artist mother, poet and professor father, and new brother Sam, when he arrives. One critic calls the series a "delightfully honest and upbeat look at the little upheavals of family life" (Broome 1985, n.p.). Another states, "Fans will still enjoy the familial warmth and comforting goofiness of the Krupniks" (Stevenson 1995, 20). From the death of a beloved grandmother to the birth of her younger brother, Anastasia copes with changes in life within the context of a loving and stable family unit.

In the first book in the series, *Anastasia Krupnik* (1979), Anastasia complains about the impending arrival of a new baby, "I'm the only one in the whole world, for pete's sake—the whole world including even my parents—who thinks that I'm important enough to be the only kid in the family" (Lowry 1979, 21). But, by the end of the novel, she concludes with another one of her lists of "Things I Love" and "Things I Hate."

Things I Love! . . .

My Late Grandmother

My Parents

Babies (esp. Sam). (Lowry 1979, 114)

Each of the Anastasia books maintains this balance between the humor and pathos that grow out of ordinary life situations in many families.

In Lowry's very first novel for children, *A Summer to Die* (1977), "The family relationships are closely, often humorously, observed. . . . Meg learns important lessons about the inevitability of death, the stranglehold of convention, and honest values. The writing is beautifully unobtrusive, yet bracing and compelling" (Hobbs 1979, 224–225). The tone of the story and its conclusion, however, are darker and deeper as the family copes with the death of one of its daughters, a traumatic event based on Lowry's own life experiences: " 'This is a hard thing to explain, Meg, but Molly is handling this thing very well by herself. She needs us, for our love, but she doesn't need us for anything else now.' He swallowed hard and said, 'Dying is a very solitary thing. The only thing we can do is be there when she wants us there' " (Lowry 1977, 105). The bond of the loving and supportive family is clearly communicated and serves as a firm foundation for the crisis and change that must follow.

Consider also the Newbery Award–winning *Number the Stars* by Lois Lowry (1989), a historical novel set during Hitler's occupation of Denmark. The protagonist is a ten-year-old girl whose Christian family has also suffered the death of the oldest daughter. Still, they hide Annemarie's Jewish friend and participate in the Resistance. Annemarie's parents (as well as other adults) are important characters as the story evolves, interacting with the children as caring and protective parents, but as also as co-conspirators.

At the conclusion of the story, "Annemarie's parents told her the truth about Lise's death at the beginning of the war. 'She was part of the Resistance, too' Papa had explained. 'Part of the group that fought for our country in whatever ways they could' " (Lowry 1989, 129–130). This family models strength, compassion, and courage. Though it may be wartime that forces them to become equals with each other and with their children, they clearly communicate the dignity of the individual and the connectedness of community.

In *Find a Stranger, Say Goodbye* (Lowry 1978), the teenage protagonist is seeking out her birth mother in a story that depicts a family's love and openness to their daughter's need for the truth. "Lowry allows her readers to experience the emotional side of adoption from three different perspectives; the childless couple, the adopted child, and the birth mother. This is a great plus for anyone interested in the whole picture" (DiNuzzo et al. 2000, n.p.). The book begins with this note to Natalie from her adoptive parents.

The box contains all the documents we have. They are very few, and your search, I'm afraid, will be a difficult and perhaps a painful one. You are mature, sensitive, and responsible. We wish you success in whatever journeys you make in these next three months. But we want you to know, also, that what you find is not important to us. You are our daughter, and our friend as well. We love you for being Natalie, and that's all that matters to us. (Lowry 1978, 32)

Natalie proceeds in her quest and learns much about herself as she finds her birth mother. "Natalie pictured her saying breezily, 'Darling, I'm going to have to dash' to the photographer after he had taken the picture, the way she had said the same thing to Natalie once, and left her sitting there alone, bewildered, remembering the smile" (Lowry 1978, 186).

In the end, Natalie is at peace about who she is and about what her family means to her, both her birth mother and her adoptive parents. Again, the tension between making our way as individuals and depending on our families for our identity and reality is sensitively handled.

So, thought Natalie, . . . that's what it all boils down to.

> You have to sort everything out.
> You have to figure out what you want to hold onto.
> You have to acknowledge what is and what was.
> And sometimes what never was, at all.
> And you have to relinquish things. (Lowry 1978, 187)

Finally, a nuclear family is also portrayed in Lowry's second Newbery winner, *The Giver* (1993). Both parents are present in this Utopian fantasy; however, the traditional roles are reversed. The mother is a judge, the father a "Nurturer," or nursery worker. "His mother moved to her big desk and opened her briefcase; her work never seemed to end, even when she was at home in the evening" (Lowry 1993, 19). Both parents are active participants in their children's lives, as mandated by the "perfect" society, but the father's role as a "professional parent" provides more opportunities for connections with children. "The newchild, Gabriel, stirred and whimpered, and Father spoke softly to Lily, explaining the feeding procedure as he opened the container that held the formula and equipment" (25). It is his dilemma in caring for the newborn baby Gabriel, in fact, which becomes the impetus for his son Jonas's daring and courageous act at the conclusion of the book. Neither of his parents, however, serves as the role models Jonas needs. Instead, it is another man, the Giver, who genuinely nurtures and guides Jonas, helping Jonas discover his own unique path. Is Lowry suggesting that there is no such thing as "perfect parents" or that sometimes we need to go outside of our family unit for the nurturing and support we need to grow up? Both, perhaps.

> This is a fantasy novel that does what fantasy at its best can do: make us see reality all the more clearly. The questions it asks about the cost of love, the structure of the family, the role of painful memories, the nature of the perfect society are all timely. But most of all, the novel examines what it is that makes us human. (Schmidt 1993, 14–15)

Even Lowry's novels with "traditional families" show families grappling with the complex tension between being a unique individual while also being part of the human family.

Extended Families

> Many books still portray strong family ties and stress the importance of personal responsibility and human dignity, but the happy, stable unit of the earlier literature is often replaced by a family in turmoil as it adjusts to a new culture, faces the prospects of surviving without one or both parents, handles the disruption resulting from divorce, or deals with an extended family, exemplified by grandparents or a foster home. (Norton 1995, 89)

Lois Lowry has also created stories in which the family characters include more adults or children than simply one set of parents and their offspring. One example with a generally light and humorous tone is *Taking Care of Terrific* (1983b). The protagonist, Enid Crowley (call her "Cynthia"), lives a fairly privileged life including two parents and a housekeeper/nanny.

> My mother hired Mrs. Kolodny years ago—fourteen, to be exact—when I was born. Mrs. Kolodny lives in our house, and she is supposed to keep track of things here; she is supposed to keep track of me. Most of the time it is the other way around. Mrs. Kolodny is one of the flakiest people I have ever met. In fourteen years, my mother has never noticed this. (Lowry 1983b, 9)

Enid continues describing her family life: "But some nights all three of us are home for dinner. Then Dad doesn't read, and Mom doesn't scrutinize my skin, hair, teeth, and clothes for flaws. Mrs. Kolodny wears a clean white apron; she sets the table with grandmother's silver and lights candles. We have *Conversation*" (Lowry 1983b, 41).

Enid is bored and ends up with a baby-sitting job for another wealthy family. She cares for Joshua Warwick Cameron IV (call him "Tom Terrific") and creates an extension of her family circle that includes a sarcastic friend, Seth, an African American gentleman nicknamed "Hawk," and several homeless women who live in Boston's Public Garden. "Although the plot seems incredible, the book as a whole is somehow satisfying" writes critic Karen Jameyson (1983).

> The Boston setting is vividly evoked, and the diverse cast of characters adds variety and flavor to the narrative. But the strength lies, as it does in the Anastasia books . . . in the author's ability to create a strong heroine whose determination and humorous outlook override her confusion and difficulties. (310)

These strong female characters are also a consistent component of Lowry's novels, offering a distinctive point of view about the family dynamics. Trites (1997) claims in *Waking Sleeping Beauty, Feminist Voices in Children's Novels* that "books which empower girls to recognize and claim their subject positions empower the entire culture, for our society can only grow stronger as we teach our children to be stronger" (137). As Enid begins to carve out an identity for herself outside her family, she does so within an extended circle of other adults and children. These relationships force her to take on new leadership roles that had not been necessary in the more intimate context of her nuclear family.

In another contemporary realistic novel, *Us and Uncle Fraud* (Lowry 1984), the nuclear family of sisters, brothers, mother, and father extends to include a visiting uncle. Here, Lowry captures the give-and-take of sisters and brothers with humor and understanding—both between adult siblings, Mother and Uncle Claude, and between the children, Louise and Marcus (and Tom and Stephanie). She "creates a superb companionship between brother and sister" (Hoopes 1985, 65). As Mother and Uncle Claude interact, he asks her,

> "Hallie, don't you remember when you and I were children?"
> She laughed, "Yes. You were full of nonsense, Claude, and you still are."
> "Dreams, Hallie. I was full of dreams."
> She was silent. Finally she said, "What have they brought you? Nothing."
> "Ah, Hallie, don't say that, not to me. I still pursue them. That's why I'm a traveling man—always will be. Nothing wrong with that."
> "No," she sighed, "I guess not. But I don't want you filling my children's heads with craziness, Claude."
> I could hear his chair scrape the floor as he pushed it back and stood up.
> "Dreams, Hallie. I'm simply putting dreams into their heads." (Lowry 1984, 41–42)

Lowry treats her family characters as individuals and their relationships grow out of their unique personalities. She also creates families with varying connections between mothers, fathers, uncles, aunts, and brothers, and sisters.

Sibling relationships play an important part in how individuals feel about themselves and how they relate to other people. . . . Sibling interaction often serves as a model for people in associating friends, new acquaintances, mates, and their own children, and in relating to society in general. (Rudman 1995, 11)

The portrayal of sibling relationships in many of Lowry's books is also a consistent story element. This kinship affects the family dynamic in interesting ways. The presence of the uncle, in this case, helps the characters look inward and place greater value on their family bond. At the book's conclusion, Louise reflects,

And we knew now, really, that Claude had lied; but we accepted that, because Claude was different, because he was part of our family, and because he loved us. Downstairs, we could hear Father muttering as he turned the pages of the paper, and Mother's low, expressive voice as she read a bedtime story to Stephanie. All around us, the house throbbed with the regular sounds of family life and of the love that bound us together, despite our flaws. The recognition of that was Claude's real gift—and, as Claude had said, it was a priceless one. But fragile? Claude was wrong about that. It was not fragile at all. (Lowry 1984, 147–148)

In Lowry's autobiographical novel, *Autumn Street* (1980), the family includes a mother and two daughters living with maternal grandparents while the father is away fighting during World War II. The African American housekeeper, Tatie, and her grandson, Charles, are also part of the protagonist, Elizabeth's, close circle. In fact, she often feels more connected to them than to her own very proper sister, Jessica, her preoccupied mother, her stiff and starchy step-grandmother, and even her beloved grandfather, after his debilitating stroke. As she worries about her mother's pregnancy and impending delivery, she offers a heartfelt, if reluctant prayer, "Gawd bless Jessica and Grandfather and Grandmother, I'm sorry I don't like Grandmother very much it isn't her fault because she never had babies of her own, I'll wash every night and I'll say my prayers every night, Gawd, if you don't let Mama or Daddy die, Amen" (Lowry 1980, 36–37).

As critic Zena Sutherland (1980) observes, "Lowry has most adroitly woven . . . familial relationships into a story that has nuance, depth, poignancy, and insight: through Elizabeth's memories, she gives a child's candid, painful view of fear and love" (57–58). Carol Otis Hurst (2000a) notes, "There is racial prejudice and even murder and its attendant guilt and suspicion in this taut, memorable book" (n.p.). These intergenerational, interracial relationships form a network of connection that show children and adults interacting as human beings, not just as parents and offspring.

At the end of the book, the family is grieving the death of the young boy, Charles. Elizabeth also has been deathly ill, and as she recovers, her father returns from the war. She says,

The first thing I saw on my seventh birthday was my father. He stood in the doorway, wearing the uniform that I remembered, smiling at me; and I remembered his smile, I remembered his face, I remembered in a rush all the things about my father that I had thought gone forever. When he walked toward my bed, it was slowly, and I saw that he was leaning on a cane. The sight made me curiously happy; it linked him to my grandfather, redeeming the dignity of the old man who now sat slumped and helpless in the house he had always commanded. Somehow the cane, and my father's slow, uneven steps, gave a continuity to the world and made it seem firm enough to hold me once again. (Lowry 1980, 181–182)

The world can be a scary place, and only our "impossible promises" to our families and loyal friends provide comfort and connection, "as nourishing and necessary as the sunlight that comes" (Lowry 1980, 188).

Blended Families and Single-Parent Families

Gallo (1997) reported an increase in the incidence of single-parent families in children's novels of the 1980s and early 1990s.

Family constellations have been changing rapidly since the beginning of the twentieth century. Class differences, ethnic differences, economic circumstances, the "sexual revolution," a dramatic rise in single-parent families, a movement from the concept of the parent-as-authority to a more flexible and permissive role, the influence of media such as film and television, and the opening of more and more options for lifestyle have all influenced the design and function of the family. (Rudman 1995, 74)

Rudman continues her description of these twentieth-century family groupings:

In the past decade, books have depicted a number of family constellations in addition to the nuclear. Single-parent families with either mothers or fathers as heads of the household, extended families, communes, single parent mothers who were never married, blended families with multiples of step-parents and step-siblings, same-sex parents, and families where children are living with relatives other than their parents appear with some degree of frequency. (74)

Several of Lois Lowry's novels include these kinds of blended and single-parent families.

In *Switcharound* (1985), *The One Hundredth Thing about Caroline* (1983a), and *Your Move, JP!* (1990), Lowry presents a trilogy of family stories that show children whose birth parents have divorced, whose father is largely absent, and who then recreate a new family relationship with their father, his second wife, and their children. These complicated adjustments are an ordinary part of daily life for many modern children. In studying contemporary novels for children, Rudman (1995) found many young protagonists experience deep inner conflicts.

They imagine that if they had done their job as "good children" their parents would still be together. These children may worry about whether their parents will continue to love and care for them, fret about being deserted by the remaining parent and about never again seeing their absent parent. They often worry about being supplanted in their parents' affections, and they question their own self-worth. (56)

Although the divorce is not an ongoing issue in these novels, it is an important part of the established relationships between the children and their parents. At the beginning of *Switcharound,* Caroline complains about her father, "The point is . . . he doesn't really care anything about us. *Twice* we went there to visit—twice in nine years—and both times it was just for a week, and both times it was *boring*. And now he says he wants us for a whole summer? No way" (Lowry 1985, 3). But by the end of the summer together, she reports back to her mother,

"Dear Mom," Caroline wrote. "I'm sorry I haven't written all week. Forget everything I said in my first letter, anyway. Everything is all switched around. . . . Now that everything is switched around, J. P. and I actually like Des Moines quite a bit. Wait till you see the shirts that we will bring back to New York at the end of the summer." (Lowry 1985, 117–118)

"Through a light, witty story, Lois Lowry teaches that hasty judgments can be wrong, and even relatives deserve to be given the benefit of the doubt" (Nix 1985, 64). Interestingly enough, the stereotyped gender expectations the father and stepmother have for Caroline and J. P. at the beginning of the story (*she* will baby-sit, *he* will help with Little League) get turned around, and this leads to the happy resolution within the new blended family. Norton (1995) confirms, "Unsurprisingly, a prominent theme in children's literature has been the changing relationships of children within the family" (78).

Rabble Starkey (1987) represents a different kind of family unit. As Rabble says,

"Me and Sweet-Ho [her mother], we was just hired help at the Bigelows. We didn't own a house or even pay rent. We just lived in two-rooms-and-a-bath up over the Bigelows' garage and held our breath tight every time Mr. Bigelow idled his Plymouth so the fumes drifting up through the floor and seeping through our braided rug wouldn't knock us flat dead." (Lowry 1987, 6)

Rabble and her mother are more like sisters than mother and daughter. And gradually, Sweet-Ho's relationship with Mr. Bigelow takes on more and more of a wife's role while his own wife is hospitalized for depression. Rabble and her mother talk about Rabble's distant dad, "We had talked about it lots, at night before we went to sleep, and we had decided long ago that we wouldn't be seeing Ginger Starkey again probably ever. Twelve years he'd been gone and no word" (Lowry 1987, 17–18).

Betsy Hearne (1987) summarizes that as these two families (one without a father, one with an absent mother) live and work together to care for each other, "Rabble discovers it is love, not convention, that shapes a family, and love can come from many directions and take many forms" (3–4). Critic Carol Otis Hurst (2000b) observes:

Many kinds of love are present in this thoughtful sometimes tragic and sometimes humorous book: the romantic love for Ginger that sweeps Sweet Ho off her feet when she is a young teenager; also romantic but founded on mutual respect is the love between Sweet Ho and Mr. Bigelow; family love is obviously present in the relationship between Rabble and her mother and between Mr. Bigelow and Veronica and Gunther. The friendship between Rabble and Veronica is another kind of love and then there's the love of Norman for Veronica which might be a kind of puppy love. (n.p.)

From this base of security and affection, both Rabble and Sweet-Ho gain the strength and confidence to move out on their own. As they discuss Rabble's two favorite books one night, Rabble remarks, " 'I'm just now realizing that they're both about the same thing. About all kinds of loving, and about saying goodbye, and about moving on to where more things are in store.' 'They're about growing older,' Sweet-Ho said. 'And growing up' " (Lowry 1987, 190–191).

Conclusion

These are important issues in the examination of families in children's fiction today. These are brave authors who are tackling these diverse perspectives and experiences. As highly acclaimed Australian author Mem Fox (1993) states, "From my point of view there's a great danger in writers being cooped up alone, cocooned from the prevailing movements of our time. . . . Writers and publishers should acknowledge society's fast-changing attitudes about women, people of color, the elderly, and minorities. Being unaware is dangerous and arrogant" (87–88).

Families in recent children's novels are looking more and more like real people in real life: nurturing, neglectful, loving, lost, hardworking, hardly noticing—a mixed bag. They make for interesting reading.

Families disintegrating and re-forming are part of life for today's children, and the candor with which authors address painful issues such as death, divorce, intolerance, abuse, and neglect in the late twentieth century reflects an awareness that children feel the pain of such changes as deeply as adults do. Yet for children, family is still a crucial factor in survival. The bonds of affection and concern; the warmth and shelter of home and its inhabitants, be they many or few; the depth of love and the tenacity that holds families together through hard times; and the thread that ties one generation to the next—these are themes that resonate through much of our best fiction and that keep stories alive from one generation to the next. (Carlson 1995, 231)

As Lowry has said in her autobiographical photomemoir, *Looking Back: A Book of Memories* (1998), "Looking back together, telling our stories to one another, we learn how to be on our own" (174). This tension between being on your own and being part of a family, being independent and being interconnected, is one of the most distinctive features of the writing of Lois Lowry. Whether it's the "traditional" family unit or extended, blended, or single-parent families, Lowry creates believable characters in a human context. Unlike many contemporary novels for young people in which the grown-ups disappear so the child protagonists can become more grown up, Lowry does not segregate the child population. She shows us a world in which the human family includes both adults and children, brothers and sisters, strong girls and sensitive men, as well as rich, poor, black, Jewish, homeless, and educated people—all interacting in ways that are authentic and true.

References

Alcott, L. M. 1868. *Little women; or, Meg, Jo, Beth and Amy.* New York: Little, Brown.

Apseloff, M. F. 1992. Abandonment: The new realism of the eighties. *Children's Literature in Education* 23, no. 2: 101–106.

Broome, J. 1985. *From the critics: A review of* Anastasia on Her Own *by Lois Lowry.* Barnes & Noble. Accessed: March 1, 2002. Available: www.barnesandnoble.com/

Carlson, D. B. 1995. Family stories. In *Children's books and their creators,* ed. A. Silvey, 228–231. Boston: Houghton Mifflin.

Cleaver, V., and B. Cleaver. 1969. *Where the lilies bloom.* New York: HarperCollins.

DiNuzzo, T., J. Moran, H. Pedersen, C. Yurgelonis, and K. E. Vandergrift. 2000. *Review of* Find a Stranger [Kay E. Vandergrift's Web site]. Accessed: March 1, 2002. Available: scils.rutgers.edu/~kvander/lowry.html

Fitzhugh, L. 1964. *Harriet, the spy.* New York: Harper & Row.

Fox, M. 1993. Men who weep, boys who dance: The gender agenda between the lines in children's literature. *Language Arts* 70, no. 2: 84–88.

Gallo, E. M. 1997. *A content analysis of the family structure in children's literature for the periods between 1955–1970 and 1980–1995.* Kent, OH: Kent State University. ERIC Document Reproduction Service No. ED412556.

Goforth, F. S. 1998. *Literature and the learner.* Belmont, CA: Wadsworth.

Hearne, B. 1987. Families shaped by love, not convention. *Christian Science Monitor,* May 1, pp. 3–4 B.

Hobbs, M. 1979. Review of *A summer to die. Junior Bookshelf* 43, no. 4: 224–225.

Hoopes, L. L. 1985. Review of *Us and Uncle Fraud. Christian Science Monitor,* March 1, p. 65.

Hurst, C. O. 2000a. *A review of* Autumn street *by Lois Lowry* [Web site]. Carol Otis Hurst. Accessed March 1, 2002. Available: www.carolhurst.com/newsletters/21cnewsletters.html

———. 2000b. *A review of* Rabble Starkey *by Lois Lowry* [Web site]. Carol Otis Hurst. Accessed March 1, 2002. http://www.carolhurst.com/newsletters/21cnewsletters.html

Jacobs, J. S., and M. O. Tunnell. 1996. *Children's literature, briefly.* Englewood Cliffs, NJ: Merrill.

Jameyson, K. 1983. Review of *Taking care of Terrific* by Lois Lowry. *Kirkus Reviews* 51, no. 6: 310.

Kinman, J. R., and D. L. Henderson. 1985. An analysis of sexism in Newbery Award Medal books from 1977–1984. *The Reading Teacher* 38, no. 9: 885–889.

Kortenhaus, C. M., and J. Demarest. 1993. Gender roles and stereotyping in children's literature: An update. *Sex Roles: A Journal of Research* 28, nos. 3 and 4: 219–232.

Lowry, L. 1977. *A summer to die*. Boston: Houghton Mifflin.

———. 1978. *Find a stranger, say goodbye*. Boston: Houghton Mifflin.

———. 1979. *Anastasia Krupnik*. Boston: Houghton Mifflin.

———. 1980. *Autumn Street*. Boston: Houghton Mifflin.

———. 1983a. *The one hundredth thing about Caroline*. Boston: Houghton Mifflin.

———. 1983b. *Taking care of Terrific*. Boston: Houghton Mifflin.

———. 1984. *Us and Uncle Fraud*. Boston: Houghton Mifflin.

———. 1985. *Switcharound*. Boston: Houghton Mifflin.

———. 1987. *Rabble Starkey*. Boston: Houghton Mifflin.

———. 1989. *Number the stars*. Boston: Houghton Mifflin.

———. 1990. *Your move, JP!* Boston: Houghton Mifflin.

———. 1993. *The giver*. Boston: Houghton Mifflin.

———. 1998. *Looking back: A book of memories*. Boston: Houghton Mifflin.

Mann, K. 1999. *Role models in Newbery Award winning books* [listserv]. Child Lit Listserv. Accessed: April 19, 1999. Available: CHILD_LIT@EMAIL.RUTGERS.EDU

Montgomery, L. M. 1908. *Anne of Green Gables*. New York: Grosset & Dunlap.

Nix, K. 1985. A trio to tickle the funny bone. *Christian Science Monitor,* November 11, p. 64.

Norton, D. E. 1995. *Through the eyes of a child: An introduction to children's literature.* 4th ed. Englewood Cliffs, NJ: Merrill.

Paterson, K. 1978. *The great Gilly Hopkins*. New York: HarperCollins.

Rudman, M. K. 1995. *Children's literature: An issues approach*. 3d ed. White Plains, NY: Longman.

Russell, D. L. 2001. *Literature for children: A short introduction*. 4th ed. New York: Longman.

Schmidt, G. 1993. A review of *The giver* by Lois Lowry. *Five Owls* 8, no. 1: 14–15.

Stevenson, D. 1995. A review of *Anastasia absolutely. Bulletin of the Center for Children's Books* 9, no. 9: 20–21.

Sutherland, Z. 1980. A review of *Autumn street* by Lois Lowry. *Bulletin of the Center for Children's Book* 34, no. 3: 57–58.

Taylor, A. 1996. Where have all the parents gone? The place of parents in children's literature. *Emergency Librarian* 24, no. 1: 20–22.

Temple, C. A., M. G. Martinez, J. Yokota, and A. Naylor. 1998. *Children's books in children's hands: An introduction to their literature*. Boston: Allyn and Bacon.

Tomlinson, C. M., and C. Lynch-Brown. 1995. *Essentials of children's literature.* 2d ed. Boston: Allyn and Bacon.

Trites, R. S. 1997. *Waking Sleeping Beauty: Feminist voices in children's novels.* Iowa City: University of Iowa Press.

Twain, M. [Samuel Clemens]. 1982. *The adventures of Huckleberry Finn.* New York: Scholastic. Original edition 1885, Chicago: C. L. Webster.

Vardell, S. 2001. Parent characters in children's novels: Lessons learned. In *Beauty, brains, and brawn: The construction of gender in children's literature,* ed. S. S. Lehr, 162–175. Portsmouth, NH: Heinemann.

Voigt, C. 1981. *Homecoming.* New York: Atheneum.

17

Young Adult Literature Comes of Age

Michael Cart

In preparing these remarks I've done my share of musing—and more—about how we can connect the history of young adult literature with its future. Each time my thoughts have strayed in this direction I have—perhaps inevitably—recalled "Peabody's Improbable History," episodes of which were my favorite feature of the *Rocky and Bullwinkle Show,* that classic of TV animation, which debuted in 1959.

The eponymous Mr. Peabody was a bow-tie-and-glasses-wearing talking dog. In each episode he and his pet boy, Sherman, stepped into their fabulous way-back machine and rocketed back into the dim recesses of history to offer us rapt viewers their own fractured version of one seminal event after another.

Suppose for a moment that we could join them and rocket back in time in our own search for the inception of young adult literature. What year would be our target? Would it be 1868, the year when both Louisa May Alcott's *Little Women* and Horatio Alger Jr.'s *Ragged Dick* were published? Or would it be1885 when the hands-down, no-competition great American novel *Huckleberry Finn* appeared? Or would it be, perhaps, 1904? That was the year when G. Stanley Hall, founder of the American Psychological Association, published his seminal two-volume work *Adolescence: Its Psychology*. Or how about 1930 when the American Library Association issued its first recommended list of "Books for Young People"? Or 1942 when Frank Sinatra first stepped onto the stage of the Paramount Theater in New York and set swooning bobby-soxers' hearts a-flutter? Or . . .

Well, don't tell Mr. Peabody I said this, but the truth is that no matter how many years we visited, we would never find that eternally elusive single, definable, discernable moment in which we might witness the birth of young adult literature. For young adult literature was not born. Instead, like some of the more venerable items in my refrigerator, it evolved! And not in isolation, either: young adult literature evolved in concert with and in response to the very concept of the adolescent, the teenager, the young adult, the embodied idea that there was a separate and distinct period of personal development between childhood and adulthood. This new landscape of life, this terrain of transition, did not begin to emerge until the turn of the twentieth century, however. Before then one moved directly from childhood into adulthood and that transition took place the day you first went to work.

"Up until the 1930s," Grace Palladino (1996) tells us in her *Teenagers: An American History,* "most teenagers worked for a living on farms, in factories, or at home, whatever their families required at the time" (5).

It was not until the Great Depression caused the job market to dry up—along with most of the state of Oklahoma—that children stopped going to work and, instead, started going to high school. Consider that in 1900 only 6 percent of Americans graduated from high school. By 1910, that percentage had increased—but barely—to 15 percent. And yet, by 1930, the first year of the Depression, almost half of America's adolescents—fourteen- to eighteen-year-olds—were enrolled in high school. By 1936, the number had grown to 65 percent, and by 1939, arguably the last year of the Depression, a robust 75 percent were in high school.

Significantly, they did not spend their entire day studying. They began developing a social life, too. It was in September 1936 that *Scholastic Magazine*—even then a fixture of the classroom—began running a brand new column; it was called "Boy Dates Girl."

In 1942, a scant six years later, this new reality of adolescent life found expression in the publication of Maureen Daly's *Seventeenth Summer,* a book that some—including Margaret Alexander Edwards, the patron saint of young adult librarians—have called the *first young adult novel.*

I must point out, however, that this book was not published for teens. As Ms. Daly herself heatedly pointed out in *Twentieth-Century Young Adult Writers,* her words sizzling on the page, "*Seventeenth Summer,* in my intention and at the time of publication, was considered a full adult novel and published and reviewed as such" (Berger 1994, 170).

Though not as important to the evolution of what came to be called young adult literature, an earlier novel, Rose Wilder Lane's *Let the Hurricane Roar,* also must be mentioned. It was published in 1933 as an adult novel by Longmans Green. Yet only a few months later the publisher was describing it in ads as the first in a series of promised "junior novels."

Two other 1930s junior novels (a term even more patronizing than "young adult") also must be mentioned as evidence of the emergence of a new kind of novel that was neither a children's book nor an adult book but, rather, a book targeted at a new audience, high school students. One, published in 1938, was *The Iron Duke* by the sportswriter John R. Tunis, who was mightily surprised when his publisher, Alfred Harcourt, explained that he had written a "juvenile." The second, published in 1936, was Helen Boylston's *Sue Barton: Student Nurse.*

Writing in the November 13, 1954, *Saturday Review,* Margaret A. Edwards recalled publisher Little, Brown's bemusement at receiving Boylston's manuscript. "While it was not a piece of literature" (I'll say it wasn't!), "it was an entertaining story which did not fit into any category. It was too mature for children and too uncomplicated for adults. In the end Little, Brown took a chance and published the story. And the dawn of the modern teen-age story came up like thunder" (88).

I'm afraid that Mrs. Edwards overstated her point a wee bit; however, there is no doubt that Boylston and Tunis helped set the stage for Maureen Daly's debut and for the authentic young adult novels that would follow, though they would not appear for another twenty-five years.

But I'm ahead of myself. Let us return to the 1940s. Two years after *Seventeenth Summer* was published, the magazine *Seventeen* debuted. Cause and effect? Perhaps. At any rate, the year was 1944; America was at war, and adolescents—now officially called "teenagers"—were finding part-time jobs to support their new role as consumers. As Palladino (1996) notes, a bit wryly, one hopes, "No matter what we profess to believe about teenagers and their vital importance to the future, we tend to value them most as consumers" (xi).

As if to prove this, *Seventeen,* within months of its debut, had hired a research company, Benson and Benson, to conduct a market survey of its readers. Called "Life with Teena" (I wince), the findings, *Seventeen* asserted, demonstrated that "Teena has money of her own to spend and what her allowance and pin money earnings won't buy her parents can be counted on to supply. For our girl Teena won't take no for an answer when she sees what she wants in *Seventeen*" (Palladino 1996, 104).

The perhaps self-fulfilling lessons of the 1940s were summed up late in the decade by another market researcher, a man named Eugene Gilbert, founder of the Youth Marketing Company, who stated, "Our salient discovery is that within the past decade (i.e., the 1940s) teenagers have become a separate and distinct group in our society" (Palladino 1996, 110).

Book publishers, of course, had already begun capitalizing on that idea. The extraordinary success of *Seventeenth Summer* spawned countless junior romances. Among the first was Betty Cavanna's *Going on Sixteen* (1946), whose teenage protagonist, Julie Ferguson, breathlessly reports having "just last month read a newspaper account of a book written by a girl of seventeen" (89). (Yes, Maureen Daly was seventeen when she began writing her famous first novel.)

Another romance writer who rivaled Cavanna in popularity was Rosamond Du Jardin, whose first junior novel was published in 1949. Its title? *Practically Seventeen.* Do I smell a trend?

Even if it were a trend, publishers, at first, approached it cautiously and even a bit defensively. It wasn't enough to offer readers simple diversion, it seems in retrospect. These novels also were to offer a kind of didactic direction. Consider that the dust jacket of *Going on Sixteen* promised "numerous useful tips on how to overcome shyness and how to become 'part of things' " (Cavanna 1946), while the dust jacket of *Practically Seventeen* was even more extravagant—in its language, if not its claims. Here's a sample paragraph: "In recent years, permanent recognition and popularity have been accorded the 'junior novel'—the story that records truthfully the modern girl's dream of life and romance and her ways of adjusting to her school and family experiences. *Practically Seventeen* is such a book—as full of life as the junior prom" (Du Jardin 1949).

With Daly, Cavanna, and Du Jardin in the lead, a parade of other specialists in romance language followed; among them: Anne Emery, Janet Lambert, Jessica Lyon, and James L. Summers. It was not until 1950 that a new writer, Mary Stolz, demonstrated that elements of romance could be incorporated into fiction that was not only engaging but also artful; indeed, her third novel, *The Sea Gulls Woke Me,* which was published in 1951, remains among the most important novels in the early history of young adult literature.

Though I've been focusing on romance, don't think for a minute that girls had all the fun in the 1940s. John R. Tunis published an even dozen memorable sports novels during his second decade of writing. Robb White and the great Howard Pease were industriously producing fast-paced action/adventure novels for boys, and in 1948 *Hot*

Rod Magazine debuted. Within five years, Henry Gregor Felsen had produced two car classics: *Hot Rod* (1950) and *Street Rod* (1953). At about the same time, Robert A. Heinlein began writing about space rods, his *Rocket Ship Galileo* being published in 1947.

Clearly, there was no shortage of published product to be consumed by this new reading audience, but one wonders, in retrospect, how—well, nutritious it was. Teen novels of the forties and fifties were, for the most part, formulaic genre fiction—fast food in a dust jacket. And the world they presented had about as much to do with reality as a wistful *Saturday Evening Post* cover. Was every teenager in America really white? Did every teenager in America really live in a wholesome small town in a rambling, tree-shaded, two-story house surrounded by a picket fence? Did every teenager really have worries no larger than getting a date to the junior prom or making the team? As one who lived through those years, I think not. And I also think authors and publishers patronized teenagers by producing only books that suggested this was reality.

Though in marketing terms these books were targeted at teens, in literary terms, they remained—with a few anomalous exceptions—children's books. It would take a sexual and social revolution—otherwise called the 1960s—before a true young adult literature would begin to emerge.

In the meantime, an adult novel was published that showed the way. J. D. Salinger's *The Catcher in the Rye,* published in 1951, introduced the themes of adolescent angst, alienation, and anomie that would define the category of literature that emerged in the late sixties. It also introduced, in Holden Caufield's unforgettably idiosyncratic voice, the first-person narrative that would become the genre's signature. Moreover, its thematic treatment of the loss of innocence would help the junior novel through its own rite of passage from children's literature appendage to independent literary form.

Before we discuss that, brief attention should be given to one of those anomalies I mentioned previously: a novel written by the king of the car books, Henry Gregor Felsen. It was *Two and the Town*. Published in 1952, it was the first and, for many years, the only novel to acknowledge that teenagers were—shudder—sexual beings; the first to contemplate what, in real life, might follow the chaste goodnight kiss after a date with Judy. This was revolutionary stuff and further treatment of the topic had to await the arrival of the sexual revolution of the sixties, and even then it wouldn't be until 1975—and the publication of Judy Blume's still controversial *Forever*—that the hard-edged reality would be acknowledged that sex did, indeed, obsess and perplex teens every bit as much, if not more, than their parents. Welcome to the real world.

It was the desire to write about that real world that inspired a teenager in Tulsa, Oklahoma, to produce a novel that would visit a sea-change on conventional fiction for young adults, as they had, by that time, come to be called, the American Library Association's Young Adult Services Division having been formed in 1958. The teenager was S. E. Hinton and the novel was *The Outsiders* (1967).

Reflecting on her literary field of choice in the August 27, 1967, *New York Times Book Review,* Hinton wrote, "The world is changing, yet the authors of books for teen-agers are still 15 years behind the times. In the fiction they write, romance is still the most popular theme, with a horse-and-the-girl-who-loved-it coming in a close second. Nowhere is the drive-in social jungle mentioned. In short, where is the reality?" (Hinton 1967b, 26). For enthralled teenagers, it was to be found in the pages of *The*

Outsiders and also, I hasten to add, in the pages of *The Contender,* Robert Lipsyte's first young adult novel published in that same extraordinary year of 1967.

Together these two bold innovators held up mirrors to the real world, and what they reflected wasn't necessarily pretty—teen gangs, class warfare, violence, dead-end lives, urban mean street settings, drug use—but it was visceral and it was *real!*

Hinton and Lipsyte and, yes, Paul Zindel and John Donovan whose first novels—*The Pigman* and *I'll Get There, It Better Be Worth the Trip*—were published in 1968 and 1969, respectively, were the first to set aside the shibboleths, the taboos that had hobbled and stunted young adult literature in terms of subject and style throughout the forties and fifties.

If readers were ready for reality, so were writers. The explosion of new talent that characterizes the seventies justifies its being called young adult literature's first golden age. Consider that of the eleven winners, to date, of the Margaret A. Edwards Lifetime Achievement Award in young adult literature, six began their writing careers in the seventies. You know their names: Richard Peck, Robert Cormier, Lois Duncan, M. E. Kerr, Walter Dean Myers, and Judy Blume. Others who emerged in this golden decade include Robin McKinley, William Sleator, Felice Holman, Robert Newton Peck, Sandra Scoppettone, Barbara Wersba, Sue Ellen Bridgers, Terry Davis, Harry and Norma Fox Mazer, Zibby Oneal, and Ouida Sebestyan. And thanks to innovative work by Myers, Julius Lester, Rosa Guy, Alice Childress, Virginia Hamilton, and Mildred Taylor, black faces and the African American experience began appearing in young adult fiction for the first time, too.

Of course, innovation breeds less talented imitation and that is why the seventies are also remembered as the decade of the problem novel; that is, the one-dimensional, ripped-from-the-headlines work of social realism in which character, setting, style, and plot are sacrificed to an almost expository treatment of the single, social problem of the week—drugs, alcohol abuse, parental divorce, family dysfunction, abortion, and—well—you name it.

Perhaps young adults became sated with too much reality or perhaps it was simply market factors that caused it, or perhaps it was an infectious presidential nostalgia for the good old days; whatever the causes, the reality of the eighties was the resurgence of romance. The content of the new romance differed scarcely at all from the old. The difference was in its presentation. The eighties brand came in the form of original paperback series. Readers no longer looked for the names of favorite authors but, instead, of favorite series—Wildfire, Caprice, Sweet Dreams, First Love, Wishing Star and—above all—Sweet Valley. Another difference: readers no longer looked for their latest reading fix in libraries but, instead, in chain bookstores strategically located in the new home away from home for America's teens: the neighborhood shopping mall. Publishers had finally discovered what *Seventeen Magazine* discovered in the 1940s: kids are consumers. Now, publishers are not stupid. They had known this fact of life as long as any other producer of consumables. That they hadn't targeted teens before was simply a reflection of another reality: teens historically have not bought hardcover books. These have always been purchased for them by adults—typically, librarians and teachers and—very occasionally—parents. It was the shrinking of institutional budgets—another appalling reality of the eighties—that inspired publishers to cultivate this new market. And, despite a significant decline in the teen population that began in 1977 and continued to 1992, they managed this very successfully by introducing a new format—the original paperback series for young adults. The 1980s was *the* great decade of the publishing of the paperbacks, what has become the format of choice for young adult consumers.

The same was not true of hardcover publishing, however, which diminished dramatically in the 1980s. Nevertheless, stimulated by infusions of new talent such as Francesca Lia Block, Bruce Brooks, Brock Cole, Chris Crutcher, Ron Koertge, Cynthia Voigt, and Virginia Euwer Wolff, it did not disappear altogether. However, by 1990, its health was anything but robust.

In fact, writing in the March/April 1990 issue of the *Horn Book Magazine,* Connie Epstein noted that "some editors, marketing directors, and subsidiary rights directors, have been wondering whether the young adult novel was ready for burial and certainly most would agree that the genre is in turmoil" (237).

Turmoil . . . and transformation. Like T. H. White's Merlin, young adults seemed, in the early nineties, no longer to be aging but "youthening" instead. It was the judgment of a panel of five editors at a 1994 American Library Association (ALA) program that young adult literature had somehow turned into middle school literature, targeted exclusively at readers in grades six through eight. Somehow, *Seventeenth Summer* had become *Fourteenth Summer.*

What had happened, of course, was that publishing, responding to the growing middle school movement in dear America, had followed the perceived market. At the same time, the manageably sized mall bookstores had turned into behemoth superstores that shelved so-called young adult books in their children's departments. I say "so-called" because the books bearing this label were actually ones published for eleven- to thirteen-year-olds. Now, technically, these are young adults, since the Young Adult Library Services Association defines YAs as persons aged twelve to eighteen. But the new, nearly exclusive focus on the younger end of the age range transformed the traditional high school audience into what editor Marc Aronson, one of the ALA panelists, called "this strange no person zone" (Cart 1996, 162).

This was a bitter irony for those who believed in the power of literature to redeem lives at risk. For at the same time that serious young adult literature appeared to be dying, America's teenagers were becoming the most at-risk generation in our nation's history. They were dying, too. Never before had they been more in need of literature that was relevant to their emotional and intellectual needs; literature that gave marginalized kids faces and, thereby, the assurance that they were not alone; literature that, in its unsparing realism and creative candor, showed teenagers a way they might not be but that too many of their peers were and that, in the showing, taught them empathy and compassion, wisdom of the heart. And what were we giving them? *Goosebumps* and *Fear Street.*

And yet . . . and yet: A funny thing happened on the way to the wake. Scarcely five years later we were in the midst of a second golden age of young adult literature. What on earth happened? Well, there is no one single cause, but a number of salutary changes contributed to this phenomenon. First, in 1992 demographics did an about-face. For the first time in fifteen years the teenage population showed an increase, and, in the years since, teens have become the fastest-growing segment of the U.S. population and will continue to be until the year 2011. Institutional budgets began recovering. In 1998, in California alone, $200 million suddenly became available to schools for the purchase of books. A number of caring editors began taking creative risks, and publishers began rediscovering older young adults, redefining them in the process. If, as one editor asserted in 1994, "young adult" stopped at age fourteen, it now doesn't stop until age twenty-two or even twenty-four. Publishers have discovered what is now called "the MTV demographic," those of us who are aged fifteen to twenty-five. This has been wonderfully liberating for writers who now have greater freedom than ever before to address "edgy" material in novels for the older end of this new demographic and to introduce ambiguity artfully into their increasingly complex treatments of the real lives of today's teenagers. Young adult literature has become more sophisticated than ever before in subject, style, and tone, and the product is, increasingly, being cross-marketed to both teen and adult audiences. The quintessential example of this new "cross-over" writer is Francesca Lia Block. Not only the content but also the design of young adult books is becoming increasingly sophisticated in both hardcover and paperback formats. Look at the Tempest imprint from Avon Books for a good example, or look at HarperCollins's newly repackaged edition of Francesca Lia Block's 1994 novel *The Hanged Man* or *Dangerous Angels* (1998), the omnibus collection of her five Weetzie Bat novels. Or check out the banner headline in the spring–summer 1999 Aladdin Paperbacks catalog that trumpeted "Introducing a sophisticated new format for young adult literature."

Do I make too much of this? I think not. Consider that such super(book)store chains as Barnes & Noble and Borders have announced the creation of authentic—that is to say, "separate"—young adult areas in their new stores. Meanwhile, the online bookstores, especially Amazon.com, have begun devoting special "virtual" areas to young adult books, where reviews, features, and author interviews are posted. Perhaps the most telling sign of all, though, is the national media's discovery of the renascence of young adult literature. During the first few months of 1999, feature articles about the phenomenal revival of YA literature have appeared in the *Wall Street Journal* and in such magazines as *Time, Brill's Content,* and *Book.*

Along with the exposure has come a certain amount of editorial hand-wringing. The March 24, 1999, *Wall Street Journal* article, for example, led with this sentence: "Books aimed at teenagers, like teen movies and music before them, are increasingly turning R-rated." An accompanying photo caption dubbed YA books "Risqué Reading" (Reilly 1999, p. B1).

Before anyone takes this too seriously, please remember that it's hyperbole that catches the eye and controversy that sells newspapers.

A far more sensible and thoughtful take on the new young adult literature is David Spitz's article in the July 19, 1999, issue of *Time.* After acknowledging that this new wave is being dubbed "bleak books," Spitz concludes, "Teen books may not be able to compete with the visuals of *The Matrix,* but they do provide a few hours of what teens may need most: time to think. And there's nothing bleak about that" (79).

It has taken twenty-five years, but the rest of the young adult book world has finally caught up with Robert Cormier who, in his 1974 novel *The Chocolate War,* first took teen readers into the heart of darkness and turned the lights on. In the process, young adult literature has finally come of age. And high time, too! For the result is the appearance of such essential books as Melvin Burgess's *Smack* (1998), Brock Cole's *The Facts Speak for Themselves* (1997), Chris Lynch's *Whitechurch* (1999), Norma Fox Mazer's *When She Was Good* (1997), Walter Dean Myers's *Monster* (1999), Han Nolan's *Dancing on the Edge* (1997), Virginia Walter and K. Roeckelein's *Making Up Megaboy* (1998), Laurie Halse Anderson's *Speak* (1999), and Ellen Wittlinger's *Hard Love* (1999), to name but a few.

Such books speak with integrity about the real lives of real young adults lived in the real world. That they also speak with art is evidenced, I think, by the fact that the granters of the glittering prizes, the annual book awards, are taking notice. In 1998, the prestigious *Los Angeles Times* Book Awards added a new category: young adult fiction. The National Book Foundation restored its long moribund award in the category of books for young readers in 1996. In each of the three years since, the award has gone to a young adult novel. And, closest and dearest to my heart, the American Library Association has just established the Michael L. Printz Award to be given annually to the best young adult book of the year, *best* being defined solely in terms of literary merit. This is the first award for young adult literature that is based solely on literary merit. It is, thus, an announcement to the world that young adult literature has come of age. To those who have always held that the phrase "young adult literature" was a contradiction in terms, an oxymoron, if you will: no longer! Young adult literature is now a viable literary form that can be taught and that can be analyzed using the same sophisticated literary tools and techniques that we have traditionally applied only to the established—and sometimes dusty—adult classics of the established literary canon.

The man for whom this award is named—the late Mike Printz—was for many years the librarian at Topeka West High School in Topeka, Kansas, where he was an early and stalwart champion of young adult literature. The establishment of this award says so much about the current condition of young adult literature. Consider that it can be awarded not only to a work of fiction but to a nonfiction book, as well, and you have evidence that this is a golden age of nonfiction, too. It can be presented to a work of poetry, to an original anthology, to a graphic novel, to a book originally published in another country—for this is a golden age of young adult literature not only in these United States but in countries around the world, from England to Australia, from Canada to New Zealand!

As for the future, well, unfortunately, there was no "way-forward" setting on Mr. Peabody's wonderful machine, so all I can do, in attempting to connect the past and the future, is to make a few educated guesses. For one, I anticipate that the current revival will continue at least to the year 2010 when the current upswing in the teen population will peak. I also look for more sophisticated means of marketing and promoting YA books involving the media and the Web. I wouldn't be surprised to see more original publication taking place in paperback format as the line dividing young adults and old adults continues to blur. And I believe that publishers will belatedly begin giving faces to one of the last remaining invisible segments of the teen population, gay and lesbian young adults.

What a wonderful time it is to be involved with young adult literature. And what a wonderful time, too, to promote and defend and speak out about the essential place such literature has in the lives of today's teens.

We cannot permit young adult literature ever again to come so close to being silenced as it was in the early nineties. Everyone who cares about literature and everyone who cares about young people has a dead-serious responsibility to focus attention on, support, and defend the very best, the most courageously outspoken and bluntly honest of young adult books. By doing so, we strengthen its voice; we amplify its opportunity to be heard by those who most need to hear it: the most at-risk-ever young adults themselves.

References

Alcott, L. M. 1868. *Little women*. New York: Little, Brown.

Alger, H. 1868. *Ragged Dick or, Street life in New York with the bootblacks*. Boston: Loring.

Anderson, L. H. 1999. *Speak*. New York: Farrar, Straus and Giroux.

Berger, L. S. 1994. *Twentieth-century young adult writers*. Detroit, MI: St. James.

Block, F. L. 1994. *The hanged man*. New York: HarperCollins.

———. 1998. *Dangerous angels: The Weetzie Bat books*. New York: HarperCollins.

Blume, J. 1975. *Forever . . .* New York: Simon & Schuster.

Boylston, H. D. 1936. *Sue Barton, student nurse*. Boston: Little, Brown.

Burgess, M. 1998. *Smack*. New York: Henry Holt.

Cart, M. 1996. *From romance to realism: Fifty years of growth and change in young adult literature*. New York: HarperCollins.

Cavanna, B. 1946. *Going on sixteen*. Illus. J. Gretzer. Philadelphia: Westminster.

Cole, B. 1997. *The facts speak for themselves*. Arden, NC: Front Street.

Cormier, R. 1974. *The chocolate war*. New York: Pantheon.

Daly, M. 1942. *Seventeenth summer*. New York: Dodd Mead.

Donovan, J. 1969. *I'll get there, it better be worth the trip*. New York: Harper & Row.

Du Jardin, R. N. 1949. *Practically seventeen*. Philadelphia: Lippincott.

Edwards, M. A. 1954. The rise of teenage-reading. *Saturday Review* 37 (November 13): 88–89, 95.

Epstein, C. C. 1990. A publisher's perspective. *Horn Book Magazine* 66: 237–241.

Felsen, H. G. 1950. *Hot rod*. New York: E. P. Dutton.

———. 1952. *Two and the town*. New York: Scribner's.

———. 1953. *Street rod*. New York: Random House.

Hall, G. S. 1904. *Adolescence: Its psychology and its relations to physiology, anthropology, sociology, sex, crime, religion and education*. New York: Appleton.

Heinlein, R. A., and T. W. Voter. 1947. *Rocket ship Galileo*. New York: Scribner's.

Hinton, S. E. 1967a. *The outsiders*. New York: Viking.

———. 1967b. Teen-agers are for real. *New York Times Book Review,* August 27, 26–29.

Lane, R. W. 1933. *Let the hurricane roar*. New York: Longmans Green.

Lipsyte, R. 1967. *The contender*. New York: Harper & Row.

Lynch, C. 1999. *Whitechurch*. New York: HarperCollins.

Mazer, N. F. 1997. *When she was good*. New York: Scholastic/Arthur A. Levine.

Myers, W. D. 1999. *Monster*. Illus. C. A. Myers. New York: HarperCollins.

Nolan, H. 1997. *Dancing on the edge*. San Diego: Harcourt Brace.

Palladino, G. 1996. *Teenagers: An American history*. New York: Basic Books.

Reilly, P. M. 1999. Luring today's teen back to books. *Wall Street Journal,* March 24, pp. B1+.

Salinger, J. D. 1951. *The catcher in the rye*. Boston: Little, Brown.

Spitz, D. 1999. Reads like teen spirit. *Time* 154 (July 19): 79.

Stolz, M. 1951. *The sea gulls woke me*. New York: Harper.

Tunis, J. R. 1938. *The iron duke*. New York: Harcourt Brace.

Twain, M. 1885. *Adventures of Huckleberry Finn Tom Sawyer's comrade*. New York: C. L. Webster.

Walter, V., and K. Roeckelein. 1998. *Making up Megaboy*. New York: DK Ink.

Wittlinger, E. 1999. *Hard love*. New York: Simon & Schuster.

Zindel, P. 1968. *The Pigman*. New York: Harper & Row.

18

Evolution to Revolution

Young Adult Literature Charts
Its Own Course

Teri S. Lesesne

I was convinced in my teenage years that one day I would become a nurse. It seems a steady diet of Sue Barton and Cherry Ames will do that to you. Those two females were the only role models in books that I encountered growing up when I did. As Michael Cart so eloquently points out in the preceding chapter, young adult literature had not yet come of age when I was an adolescent. What was available for readers like me back then? Romances and career books seemed to dominate. It was also a period of didacticism in literature, a time in which teens were patronized or caricaturized. S. E. Hinton's *The Outsiders* (1967) was still years in the future; Paul Zindel and Robert Cormier were still writing for adult audiences. Young adult literature (YA) was still in its early, evolutionary state.

How have we arrived at the place where YA exists today, a time in which the designation seems healthier than ever, a time in which YA literature is fulfilling the promises made by its earliest catalysts, a time in which YA literature is revolutionary? We need only look at the history and patterns of development in children's literature to better understand the history and development of its adolescent counterpart. Past trends in children's literature parallel what Michael Cart so aptly describes in his historical description of YA literature. Perhaps by looking back at the history of literature for younger readers we can see more clearly the history of literature for older readers.

In the Beginning

From time immemorial, books for children reflected the philosophical, educational, and sociological theories of childhood. Because children were not viewed as significantly different from adults until the nineteenth century, there was no real reason for a separate literary classification for children's books. The earliest children's books were those never really intended for youngsters, therefore. They were books written for adults who then gave them to children in order to instruct them. These

211

books of godly learning included fables and other instructive stories whose morals would train miniature adults to be good boys and girls. As Jackson (1989) notes, "Parents wanted their children to be taught . . . the skills, habits, virtues, and graces likely needed to gain success" (2). After all, society's view of children was that they were tabula rasa, blank slates that required learned adults to "write" knowledge onto them. Thus, early books given to children were instructional in nature. Books had one chief purpose: to inform. Instruction, didactic instruction, was the intent of these early children's books. *Pilgrim's Progress* (Bunyan 1678) and *The Book of Curtesye* (Caxton 1477) and the like were used to instill virtues in children, the virtues of hard work, good deeds, and perfect obedience. The cautionary and didactic nature of the tales told to children also may have been because of the extremely high mortality rate (about 50 percent prior to the nineteenth century) and the pressure to make certain that short lives were lived in accordance with the rules of the society. In fact, many of the early children's books concerned themselves with how to live a good life and gain glory. The overtly pious nature of the books was purposeful. Some writers and publishers, however, ventured to break the mold as we progressed into the late nineteenth century.

The latter years of the nineteenth century were a turning point in children's literature and marked the beginnings of its first golden age. During this time a little girl named Alice followed a rabbit down a hole, Jo March began writing about her family, a secret garden was uncovered, Dorothy landed in Oz, and a new direction in literature for children emerged. Here was literature for children that did not have to instruct or inform; it could simply entertain.

Thus, children's literature evolved in three phases. The first phase were the books meant to "preach" to children; John Cotton's (1656) *Spiritual Milk for Boston Babes in Either England* is a good example. Subtitled *Drawn Out of the Breasts of Both Testaments for Their Souls Nourishment: But May Be of Like Use to Any Children,* the implication of the nature of the book is crystal clear. Children's literature went on to "teach" children with books such as *Aesop's Fables* (Caxton and Jacobs [1484] 1889), *Orbis Pictus* (Comenius 1659), and other similar volumes. Finally, children's literature could "reach" its audience and give it a rip-roaring good read. Enter *Alice in Wonderland* (Carroll and Tenniel 1865) and her followers such as *Little Women* (Alcott 1868). How does literature for adolescents follow in these phases?

YA Follows the Path

Like their younger counterparts, teens were not seen as a separate entity for many years. Just when adolescence emerged as a distinct age group is something experts argue about, as Michael Cart discusses in the previous chapter. Donelsen and Nilsen ([1980] 2001) place the beginning point around the time of the Civil War, when the dime and domestic novels surfaced. The American Psychological Association would be comfortable with the date of 1904, the American Library Association with 1930, and some scholars with the 1942 publication of Daly's *Seventeenth Summer* (Cart 1996). Still others would point to the 1960s and the novels of S. E. Hinton, Lipsyte, Zindel, and a handful of others. However, the debate about books for this age group began to rage in the 1970s. It is during this tumultuous time that YA literature began to emerge with its own conventions, styles, issues, and criticism.

So, how has this literature for young adults mirrored the development of children's literature? Despite the fact that YA literature is a relatively recent phenomenon, there are some interesting parallels. We have seen the three phases of children's literature—preach, teach, and reach—reflected in the development of literature for older readers.

Preach and Teach

If we look at the early books in the young adult field, we see a propensity toward didacticism, direction, and instruction. While the works of Betty Cavana and Rosamond Du Jardin may be a bit better at disguising the message than, say John, Cotton's *Spiritual Milk for Boston Babes* (1656), the intent is still there: offer books that patronize teens, especially females. Keep the story soft and palatable, pabulum for the teen's nourishment if you will. The romance novels offered for teen reading in the days preceding the realism of Hinton and others painted the portrait of what was expected of a good girl (and boy, for that matter). Here were the virginal young women who went out on dates or sought careers. They were always on the lookout for Mr. Right, the young man who would place them on a pedestal and worship them from afar. Even would-be sleuths such as Nancy Drew (Keene 1930) relied on their male counterparts for rescue and redemption.

The career books were no better; they, too, preached to readers. There were accepted careers for women, chief among them nursing. Women could work outside of the home, but there were more than glass ceilings in the novels featuring Sue Barton (Boylston 1936) and Cherry Ames (Wells 1943). Sue and Cherry would gladly surrender their new careers if Mr. Right came along. Wife and mother would easily replace nursing and other professions. Career novels for girls fall more into the "teach" phase of development. In Sue Barton and Cherry Ames, young girls found the role models to follow. Young heroines forged career paths. The stories were still squeaky clean. Sue and Cherry were pursuing careers, yes, but they were hardly liberated women. Nonetheless, Ames and Barton were a step in the right direction.

Let's not neglect the young male teens of this time period. As Michael Cart has already noted, there was precious little to offer for the adolescent male. Felsen's car books (i.e., *Hot Rod* [1950])and *Street Rod* [1953] and the like) were perhaps the parallel for the romance novels of the time. After all, taking care of a car involved a commitment, didn't it? What about other books for boys? What topics were paramount within the pages of those books? Sports, certainly, appear to be a topic of some interest. Tunis's stories, such as *The Iron Duke* (1938), were a heartbeat away from the Dave Porter and other series books from the Edward Stratemeyer Syndicate (1905). Young men received programming similar to their female counterparts. Their lives were to be led in accordance with the Boy Scout oath: clean, thrifty, brave, and pure. Books read by teens prior to the groundbreaking books of the late 1960s fell easily into either the preach or teach phase of development. However, the 1960s did not signal the end of didacticism in YA literature.

Even in the groundbreaking *Mr. and Mrs. BoJo Jones* by Ann Head (1967), readers were to learn an important lesson: teen sexual behavior has horrendous consequences. Not only are July and BoJo doomed because of their sexual behavior, their "immoral act" is punished more severely when their baby dies. Shades of *Pilgrim's Progress* and the martyrs of John Bunyan. July and BoJo might well have been named

Adam and Eve. Books for teens were beginning to explore new territory; however, there were still some taboos in the field.

Books That Reach

The decade of the 1970s saw much progress in terms of breaking boundaries and challenging the roles of the "good" boy and girl. Robert Cormier's *The Chocolate War* (1974) did much to push the envelope. Here was a novel in which there were no traditional heroes and heroines. Jerry and Goober are as flawed as Archie and Leon (although not as evil, we could argue). *The Chocolate War* went one step further: the ending was not the traditional Hollywood underdog-defeats-brute. Instead, Cormier allows Jerry to be pummeled by Emil Janza, to suffer a brutal beating. Is Jerry defeated? Is Cormier telling readers that life will ultimately knock them down? That was and continues to be the debate about this touchstone novel. Cormier helped pave the way for others who were to come onto the scene in the next two to three decades. *The Chocolate War* took Cormier from the ranks of adult audiences and into the YA field. Cormier's uncompromising honesty in telling a story reinforced the transformation begun by Hinton's *The Outsiders* (1967) and Zindel's *The Pigman* (1968). Adult characters were either absent or so greatly flawed that they could not come to the rescue of the teen protagonist. Instead, the teens operated on their own, made their own way through life's challenges. Taboos began to fall: religion, drugs and alcohol, sex.

Other important works emerged in the 1970s. Some illustrate the pendulum swing from the new realism back to a more didactic approach. *Go Ask Alice* (1971) by Anonymous (in reality, Beatrice Sparks penned this fictional diary of a teen drug addict) wowed young readers. The fact that it was created by an adult whose purpose was to scare teens from drug use somehow is lost in the riveting nature of Alice's battle against addiction. Here are traces of the preach and teach aspects of literature for young adults.

Other books negotiated uncharted waters with less of a didactic tone. Judy Blume's *Are You There God? It's Me, Margaret* (1970) (which curiously moved from a YA novel to an intermediate novel in the intervening years) talked about topics probably only whispered and giggled about at slumber parties: menstruation and breasts and bras. *House of Stairs* (1974) by William Sleator portrayed the government not as a benign entity but as a system willing to expend the lives of innocent teens for its own research. *Home Before Dark* (1976) by the brilliant Sue Ellen Bridgers talked about the rivalry between women in the same household; Richard Peck's *Are You in the House Alone?* (1976) explored acquaintance rape before that term truly came into common use. This new realism would surely lead to grittier books in the 1980s, right? Once again, YA literature mirrored the progress and development of literature for children. It had taken some important steps forward; now it was time for a step back.

A Step Back

The 1980s, while marking the debut of some significant authors such as Chris Crutcher, Bruce Brooks, Chris Lynch, and Gary Paulsen among others, also marked the surge of the romance novels for female teens. Francine Pascal's Sweet Valley High (1983) series and all of the spin-offs and wannabe imitators did much to negate the progress forged by Hinton, Cormier, Peck, and others. Suddenly, young women were once again faced with the highly moralistic and didactic in the guise not of Cherry Ames and Sue Barton, but in the form of Jessica and her twin sister, Elizabeth. What was expected of good girls in these romances? Simply put: chastity, loyalty, and beauty. In many ways, Jessica and Elizabeth's characters harken back to Nancy Drew and her friends. Fun is to be found only in groups; adults are not nearly as perceptive as teens. Moreover, anyone can be pretty and popular as long as they have the right clothes and makeup. Individuality is something to be avoided if a girl is to have a good time and fit in with the crowd.

What is heartening about this decade, though, is the fact that books for boys become more abundant. These are not the hot-rod books of the previous generations. Here are gritty books that provide readers with action and adventure and introspection. This signals a giant leap forward in the field of YA literature marked by the achievements of a handful of authors who were willing to break the rules and push against the boundaries.

Gary Paulsen's *Hatchet* (1987), still a favorite among teen readers, provided the action and adventure that male readers craved. The teen protagonist of *Hatchet,* Brian, is a rather naïve individual at the outset of the novel. He is upset about his parents' separation and looking forward to spending some time with his father. When the plane in which he is a passenger crashes, killing the pilot, Brian is forced to learn how to survive on his own. Armed with only a hatchet, a parting gift from his mother, Brian manages to do more than survive. He is changed by his experiences with nature. Paulsen's work mirrors other great adventure authors such as Jack London. His hero is frightened and ignorant at the outset of the story. Through his growing respect for nature, the hero learns to live cooperatively with the elements. This introspective life changes the protagonists in Paulsen's novels deeply. Readers need only trace the development of Brian through the sequels to *Hatchet*: *The River* (Paulsen 1998), *Brian's Winter* (Paulsen 1996), and *Brian's Return* (Paulsen 1999) to see evidence of this. Perhaps Paulsen's work, then, is indicative of the philosophy of Rousseau and the writing of Defoe and others of an earlier time in children's literature. Man is at his best when he is in harmony with nature.

Interestingly, when Paulsen announced his intention to write books for boys, he was advised by someone in the industry *not* to write books for boys. He was told that boys do not read. When Paulsen asked why boys were not reading, the answer was that there were no books for them. Talk about a catch-22! Thankfully, Paulsen ignored the advice and went on to write dozens of novels, garnering a few Newbery Honor Awards, the Margaret A. Edwards Award from the American Library Association which is given in recognition of lifetime achievement in the field of YA literature, and a host of other accolades.

Another author whose work for boys altered the landscape of YA literature is Chris Crutcher. Sports may be a part of Chris Crutcher's stories, but to label him as a sports writer is to do him a disservice. Through the pages of novels such as *The Crazy Horse Electric Game* (Crutcher 1987) and *Stotan!* (Crutcher 1986), Crutcher explored the world of young people whose lives were not those of the movies and TV sitcoms. Here were teens who were abused and outcast, kids who needed lots of help, kids who certainly did not fit the mold of the preach and teach novels of the past. Crutcher, too, has been the recipient of the Margaret A. Edwards Award for his contributions to the field of YA literature as well as the National Council of Teachers of English (NCTE) Intellectual Freedom Award. His honest examination of the lives of adolescents in his novels has earned him a much-deserved reputation as a writer without compromise. His stories reach readers who might never encounter themselves in the pages of a book otherwise.

Chris Lynch burst onto the scene with novels that examined the darker side of the human condition in the latter half of this decade. Like Crutcher, many of Lynch's characters face obstacles not of their own making. These young men deal with absent or abusive parents, cruel enemies among their peers, and countless other challenges. Yet, somehow, each manages to find salvation of sorts. *Gypsy Davey* (Lynch 1994a), *Iceman* (Lynch 1994b), and *The Shadow Boxer* (Lynch 1993) proved that it is possible for those dealt a tough hand by life to survive. Lynch, though, was not content to become celebrated as an author of dark coming-of-age novels. *Slot Machine* (Lynch 1995) and its sequel *Extreme Elvin* (Lynch 1999) as well as the hilarious He-Man-Woman-Hater's Club series (Lynch 1997) demonstrates the power of humor in tough situations. Thanks to Elvin Bishop, teens can once again laugh at themselves.

Bruce Brooks's Newbery Honor book, *The Moves Make the Man* (1984), also shows how powerful a narrative can be. The stunning stream-of-consciousness style Brooks brought to this tale of an unlikely friendship between Bix and Jerome moved the field forward. YA literature could challenge readers stylistically in a way it had not yet done. Brooks cleared the path for others to follow, and follow they did.

Perhaps one other name must be mentioned as crucial to the development of YA literature in the 1980s. Don Gallo, a professor of YA literature, had a brilliant idea. He asked YA writers of distinction to contribute an original short story to a collection he would edit. These stories would bring the young adult designation into the twentieth century. They would also assist teachers looking for some way to breathe life into a curriculum top heavy with dead white male writers. Before Gallo's idea, short stories written specifically for YA readers were virtually nonexistent. Despite the fact that secondary school curricula dictated a study of the short-story genre, textbooks contained little that excited and interested contemporary readers. Gallo's first collection, *Sixteen* (1984), and the dozen or more that would follow, reminded us that there are other genres to explore in YA literature. Other genres still lingered in the children's literature domain, waiting for their coming of age. Poetry, drama, and nonfiction would soon be included in what was to become the golden age of YA.

The 1980s did see some remarkable books for YA readers. What are some of the landmark books of this decade? Who were the important writers in the field? These were the questions Dr. Don Gallo and Dr. Ted Hipple posed to some of their colleagues. Gallo asked his colleagues to list the authors they felt were the most important ones in the field of YA literature. From the list of nominations, then, he asked these same colleagues to rank order the authors.

Gallo's survey netted a list of the top YA authors in 1988 (Gallo 1989). These authors may be found in Table 18.1. Hipple asked experts in the YA field to nominate the titles they believed to be the most influential novels of the decade. In other words, what YA novels from the 1980s should every English teacher know? The results of Hipple's survey may be found in Table 18.2.

Table 18.1

Important YA Authors in Rank Order

1. S. E. Hinton	2. Paul Zindel	3. Richard Peck
4. Robert Cormier	5. M. E. Kerr	6. Katherine Paterson
7. Judy Blume	8. Sue Ellen Bridgers	9. Virginia Hamilton
10. Madeleine L'Engle	11. Robert Newton Peck	12. Robert Lipsyte
13. Norma Klein	14. Scott O'Dell	15. Paula Danziger
16. Norma Fox Mazer	17. Paula Fox	18. Zibby Oneal
19. Maureen Daly	20. Ouida Sebestyen	21. Lloyd Alexander
22. Lois Duncan	23. Ursula LeGuin	24. Rosa Guy
25. William Sleator	26. Bette Greene	27. Jane Yolen
28. Harry Mazer	29. Robin Brancato	30. Mary Stolz
31. Laurence Yep	32. Isabelle Holland	33. Nat Hentoff

Source: Taken from D. R. Gallo, "Who are the most important YA authors?" *ALAN Review* 16 (Spring 1989): 18–20.

Table 18.2

Best YA Novels of the 1980s in Rank Order

1. *Hatchet* (Paulsen 1987)	2. *Fallen Angels* (Myers 1988)
3. *Permanent Connections* (Bridgers 1987)	4. *Jacob Have I Loved* (Paterson 1980)
5. *The Goats* (Cole 1987)	6. *Dicey's Song* (Voigt 1982)
7. *Fade* (Cormier 1988)	8. *Chinese Handcuffs* (Crutcher 1989)

Source: Taken from T. Hipple, 1992. "Have you read . . .?" (Part 4), *English Journal* 81(7): 91.

A Golden Age

By the end of the 1980s, many experts feared that YA literature had reached its peak. YA publishing seemed to be on the decline, and some were pronouncing the death of this category of literature, barely a half century old. Just when YA literature was being given the last rites and pronounced dead, a surge of adrenaline brought it back to life. The 1990s, as Michael Cart notes, was a renaissance of the genre. YA novels began to appear alongside the more traditional selections in new literature anthologies. Poetry and nonfiction and drama began to emerge from the shadow of children's literature and assumed a place in the YA arena.

Mel Glenn's novels in poetry form did much to bring a new appreciation of poetry to teen readers. From *Who Killed Mr. Chippendale? A Murder Mystery in Poems* (1996) to *The Taking of Room 114: A Hostage Drama in Poetry* (1997b) and *Jump Ball: A Basketball Season in Poetry* (1997a), the boundaries of poetry began to expand. Karen Hesse's Newbery Medal–winning *Out of the Dust* (1997) helped redefine poetry for older readers, as did the delightful anthology edited by Naomi Shihab Nye and Paul Janeczko, *I Feel a Little Jumpy around You: A Collection of His and Her Poems in Pairs* (1996).

Strong female characters also came of age in the 1990s. The plucky heroines of *Out of the Dust* (Hesse 1997), *Shabanu* (Staples 1989), *The Ear, the Eye, and the Arm* (Farmer 1994), Newbery winner *The Midwife's Apprentice* (Cushman 1995), and *Hope Was Here* (Bauer 2000) are just a handful of examples of how far women have evolved since Cherry Ames and Sue Barton. Here are teens who speak their minds, who handle incredible adversity with dignity and, occasionally, humor. Here, indeed, are characters who can reach today's female readers because they are not simply representations of teen girls; they are fully realized, well-rounded women who can serve as role models to today's young women.

Another step forward in the 1990s was the expansion of the YA audience, which widened from a narrow middle school focus to include good YA for high school and even college-age readers. Hitherto, these older readers had been written off by the YA market. Most high school and college readers long ago moved on to adult books. Was there really a market for books for more sophisticated readers? Authors such as Francesca Lia Block and Rob Thomas seem to think so. The quirky magical realism created by Block in books featuring *Weetzie Bat* (1989) and her friends and family and the hip observations of the fully fleshed out characters of Rob Thomas (1996) appeal to readers who can see the ironic humor, who can differentiate between the real and the surreal, and who can discuss the serious topics addressed with rollicking good humor by these gifted writers. The American Library Association, in recognition of the fact that many teens read adult books, instituted the ALEX Awards for the most exemplary books written for adults but suitable for YA readers. Winners may be found at the American Library Association Web site: www.ala.org.

Perhaps the greatest barometer for the newly regained health of YA literature is the creation of the Michael L. Printz Award (see Table 18.3) from the American Library Association. The Printz Award, first given in 2000, honors an author for distinguished contribution to literature for young adults. Similar to the Newbery Award, this honor elevates the entire literary designation and offers renewed hope for its continued well-being. The Robert F. Sibert Informational Book Award will call similar attention to a long-overlooked genre. Created by the American Library Association (see the Web site www.ala.org for details and a list of winners) and presented for the first time in 2001, the Sibert Award honors the best in nonfiction for "children." Think of it as the Newbery for Nonfiction. No longer will nonfiction be relegated to something less than fiction. Only drama remains underexplored by YA authors. Perhaps the next decades will see an interest in new genres.

Though the 1990s are barely gone, two experts in the field have compiled lists of the best YA books of the decade. Ted Hipple, as he did for the 1980s, surveyed leaders in the field of YA literature, asking them to identify the best books of the decade. His list appears in Table 18.4. Michael Cart (2001) writes, "Future literary historians . . . will view the 1990s as one of the most significant and breathtakingly dramatic decades in the history of young adult literature," in the introduction to the fourteenth edition of *Books for You* (xv). His list of must-read books of the 1990s is found in Table 18.5.

Table 18.3
Michael L. Printz Award Books

2002   An Na. *A Step from Heaven*. Front Street.
    Honor Books
        Peter Dickinson. *The Ropemaker*. Delacorte.
        Jan Greenberg. *Heart to Heart: New Poems Inspired by Twentieth-Century American Art*.
            Abrams
        Chris Lynch. *Freewill*. HarperCollins.
        Virginia Euwer Wolff. *True Believer*. Atheneum.

2001   David Almond. *Kit's Wilderness*. Delacorte.
    Honor Books
        Carol Plum-Ucci. *The Body of Christoper Creed*. Harcourt Brace.
        Terry Trueman. *Stuck in Neutral*. HarperCollins.
        Carolyn Coman. *Many Stones*. Front Street.
        Louise Rennison. *Angus, Thongs, and Full Frontal Snogging*. HarperCollins.

2000   Walter Dean Myers. *Monster*. HarperCollins.
    Honor Books
        Laurie Halse Anderson. *Speak*. Farrar, Straus and Giroux.
        David Almond. *Skellig*. Delacorte.
        Ellen Wittlinger. *Hard Love*. Simon & Schuster.

Note: The Michael L. Printz Award is presented annually to a book that exemplifies literary excellence in young adult literature. It is named for a Topeka, Kansas, school librarian who was a long-time active member of the Young Adult Library Services Association. For additional information, please visit the Michael L. Printz Award Web site: www.ala.org/yalsa/printz/index.html.

Table 18.4
Best YA Novels of the 1990s in Rank Order

1. *The Giver* (54 votes; Lowry 1993)	2. *Out of the Dust* (43 votes; Hesse 1997)
3. *Holes* (23 votes; Sachar 1998)	4. *Make Lemonade* (22 votes; Wolff 1993)
5. *Ironman* (18 votes; Crutcher 1995)	6. *The Watsons Go to Birmingham, 1963* (18 votes; Curtis 1995)
7. *Harry Potter and the Sorcerer's Stone* (17 votes; Rowling 1998)	8. *Walk Two Moons* (16 votes; Creech 1994)
9. *Staying Fat for Sarah Byrnes* (16 votes; Crutcher 1993)	10. *Freak the Mighty* (13 votes; Philbrick 1993)
11. *When She Was Good* (11 votes; Mazer 1997)	12. *Deliver Us from Evie* (10 votes; Kerr 1994)

Source: Taken from T. Hipple, 2000. "Have you read . . .?" *English Journal* 89(4): 138.

Table 18.5
Significant Young Adult Books of the 1990s

Nothing but the Truth (Avi 1991)	*We All Fall Down* (Cormier 1991)
What Hearts (Brooks 1992)	*The Giver* (Lowry 1993)
Shizuko's Daughter (Mori 1993)	*Gypsy Davy* (Lynch 1994a)
Baby Bebop (Block 1995)	*Parrot in the Oven: Mi Vida* (Martinez 1996)
The Facts Speak for Themselves (Cole 1997)	*Blood and Chocolate* (Klause 1997)
Whirligig (Fleischman 1998)	*Holes* (Sachar 1998)
Monster (Myers 1999)	*Speak* (Anderson 1999)
Hard Love (Wittlinger 1999)	

Source: Taken from M. Cart, "Foreword: A Brief History of Young Adult Literature." In *Books for You: An Annotated Book List for Senior High,* 4th ed., p. xxiv. Urbana, IL: National Council of Teachers of English, 2001.

What's Next?

Crystal ball, anyone? Where will YA literature go in the twenty-first century? What impact will the online bookstores and online publishing have on the next generation of readers? Will books become obsolete? Will we be taking a palm-sized computer to bed with us instead of a book? What trends will be next? What frontiers are still to be explored?

In *Radical Changes: Books for Youth in a Digital Age,* Eliza Dresang (1999) points to three significant changes in YA literature in the past decade: changing forms and formats, changing perspectives, and changing boundaries. Some recent noteworthy books indicate how these changes have reshaped YA literature.

Monster (1999) by Walter Dean Myers is one example of a YA novel that is illustrative of these changes. The film script format of the book and the seemingly hand-written diary entries are indicative of the changing form and format of the literature. Though epistolary novels are certainly not a new literary form, they are a relatively recent addition to YA literature. *Speak* (1999) by Laurie Halse Anderson is a fine example of this type of change as well, with its nonsequential organization and nonlinear plot.

The changing perspectives type of radical change is evident in Frank's *Life Is Funny* (2000), a novel that follows a dozen characters from junior to senior high and graduation. This use of multiple perspectives, previously unheard voices, and frank presentation of the reality of the lives of the characters all bring a fresh face to YA literature.

The final radical change, changing boundaries, is certainly a hallmark of the books we will continue to see in the years to come. Unresolved endings (*is* Jerry Renault defeated in *The Chocolate War*? What happens to Jonas at the end of *The Giver*?), new settings and subjects, and increasingly complex character portrayal wait on the horizon. The first glimmers of this new dawn in YA literature are beginning to gleam. *Freewill* (2001) by Chris Lynch, Chris Crutcher's *Whale Talk* (2001), and *Give a Boy a Gun* (2000) by Todd Strasser mark what may become another zenith in our category. What does the future hold? Where will YA books lead readers? Though my crystal ball is a bit cracked, I am willing to speculate that the future of young adult literature, still in its infancy, is full of the same promise as the lives of its audience.

References

Alcott, L. M. 1868. *Little women*. New York: Little, Brown.

Almond, D. 1999. *Skellig*. New York: Delacorte.

———. 2000. *Kit's wilderness*. New York: Delacorte.

Anderson, L. H. 1999. *Speak*. New York: Farrar, Straus and Giroux.

Anonymous. 1971. *Go ask Alice*. New York: Simon & Schuster.

Avi. 1991. *Nothing but the truth: A documentary novel*. New York: Orchard.

Bauer, J. 2000. *Hope was here*. New York: G. P. Putnam's Sons.

Block, F. L. 1989. *Weetzie Bat*. New York: Harper & Row.

———. 1995. *Baby be-bop*. New York: HarperCollins.

Blume, J. 1970. *Are you there God? It's me, Margaret*. Englewood Cliffs, NJ: Bradbury.

Boylston, H. D. 1936. *Sue Barton, student nurse*. Boston: Little, Brown.

Bridgers, S. E. 1976. *Home before dark*. New York: Knopf.

———. 1987. *Permanent connections*. New York: Harper & Row.

Brooks, B. 1984. *The moves make the man*. New York: Harper & Row.

———. 1992. *What hearts*. New York: HarperCollins.

Bunyan, J. 1678. *The pilgrim's progress from this world, to that which is to come: Delivered under the similitude of a dream wherein is discovered, the manner of his setting out, his dangerous journey; and safe arrival at the desired countrey*. London: Printed for Nath Ponder.

Carroll, L., and J. Tenniel. 1865. *Alice's adventures in Wonderland*. London: Macmillan.

Cart, M. 1996. *From romance to realism: Fifty years of growth and change in young adult literature*. New York: HarperCollins.

———. 2001. Foreword: A brief history of young adult literature. In *Books for you: An annotated booklist for senior high*, 14th ed., ed. G. K. Beers and T. S. Lesesne, xv–xxiv. Urbana, IL: National Council of Teachers of English.

Caxton, W. 1477. *The booke of curtesye*. Westminster/London: W. Caxton.

Caxton, W., and J. Jacobs, eds. [1484] 1889. *The fables of Aesop: As printed by William Caxton in 1484 with those of Avian, Alfonso and Poggio*. London: D. Nutt.

Cole, B. 1987. *The goats*. New York: Farrar, Straus and Giroux.

———. 1997. *The facts speak for themselves*. Arden, NC: Front Street.

Coman, C. 2000. *Many stones*. Asheville, NC: Front Street.

Comenius, J. A. 1659. *John Amos Commenii Orbis Sensualium Pictus: Hoc est omnium fundamentalium in mundo rerum et in vita actionum pictura et nomenclatura.* Trans. C. Hoole. London: Kirton.

Cormier, R. 1974. *The chocolate war.* New York: Pantheon.

————. 1988. *Fade.* New York: Delacorte.

————. 1991. *We all fall down.* New York: Delacorte.

Cotton, J. 1656. *Spiritual milk for Boston babes in either England: Drawn out of the breasts of both Testaments for their souls nourishment: But may be of like use to any children.* Cambridge, MA: Printed by Samuel Green for Hezekiah Vsher at Boston in New-England.

Creech, S. 1994. *Walk two moons.* New York: HarperCollins.

Crutcher, C. 1986. *Stotan!* New York: Greenwillow.

————. 1987. *The crazy horse electric game.* New York: Greenwillow.

————. 1989. *Chinese handcuffs.* New York: Greenwillow.

————. 1993. *Staying fat for Sarah Byrnes.* New York: Greenwillow.

————. 1995. *Ironman.* New York: Greenwillow.

————. 2001. *Whale talk.* New York: Greenwillow.

Curtis, C. P. 1995. *The Watsons go to Birmingham, 1963.* New York: Delacorte.

Cushman, K. 1995. *The midwife's apprentice.* New York: Clarion.

Daly, M. 1942. *Seventeenth summer.* New York: Dodd Mead.

Donelson, K. L., and A. P. Nilsen. [1980] 2001. *Literature for today's young adults.* 6th ed. New York: Longmans.

Dresang, E. T. 1999. *Radical change: Books for youth in a digital age.* New York: H. W. Wilson.

Farmer, N. 1994. *The Ear, the Eye, and the Arm.* New York: Orchard.

Felsen, H. G. 1950. *Hot rod.* New York: E. P. Dutton.

————. 1953. *Street rod.* New York: Random House.

Fleischman, P. 1998. *Whirligig.* New York: Henry Holt.

Frank, E. R. 2000. *Life is funny.* New York: DK Ink.

Gallo, D. R. 1989. Who are the most important YA authors? *ALAN Review* 16 (Spring): 18–20.

————, ed. 1984. *Sixteen: Short stories by outstanding writers for young adults.* New York: Delacorte.

Glenn, M. 1996. *Who killed Mr. Chippendale? A mystery in poems.* New York: Lodestar.

————. 1997a. *Jump ball: A basketball season in poems.* New York: Lodestar/E. P. Dutton.

————. 1997b. *The taking of Room 114: A hostage drama in poems.* New York: Lodestar.

Head, A. 1967. *Mr. and Mrs. BoJo Jones.* New York: G. P. Putnam's Sons.

Hesse, K. 1997. *Out of the dust.* New York: Scholastic.

Hinton, S. E. 1967. *The outsiders.* New York: Viking.

Hipple, T. 1992. "Have you read . . . ?" Part 4. *English Journal* 81(7): 91.

———. 2000. "Have you read . . . ?" *English Journal* 89(4): 138.

Jackson, M. V. 1989. *Engines of instruction, mischief, and magic: Children's literature in England from its beginnings to 1839.* Lincoln: University of Nebraska Press.

Keene, C. 1930. *The secret of the old clock.* New York: Grosset & Dunlap.

Kerr, M. E. 1994. *Deliver us from Evie.* New York: HarperCollins.

Klause, A. C. 1997. *Blood and chocolate.* New York: Delacorte.

Lowry, L. 1993. *The giver.* Boston: Houghton Mifflin.

Lynch, C. 1993. *Shadow boxer.* New York: HarperCollins.

———. 1994a. *Gypsy Davey.* New York: HarperCollins.

———. 1994b. *Iceman.* New York: HarperCollins.

———. 1995. *Slot machine.* New York: HarperCollins.

———. 1997. *Johnny Chesthair.* New York: HarperCollins.

———. 1999. *Extreme Elvin.* New York: HarperCollins.

———. 2001. *Freewill.* New York: HarperCollins.

Martinez, V. 1996. *Parrot in the oven: Mi vida.* New York: HarperCollins.

Mazer, N. F. 1997. *When she was good.* New York: Scholastic/Arthur A. Levine.

Mori, K. 1993. *Shizuko's daughter.* New York: Henry Holt.

Myers, W. D. 1988. *Fallen angels.* New York: Holt, Rinehart and Winston.

———. 1999. *Monster.* Illus. C. A. Myers. New York: HarperCollins.

Nye, N. S., and P. B. Janeczko. 1996. *I feel a little jumpy around you: A book of her poems and his poems collected in pairs.* New York: Simon & Schuster.

Pascal, F., and K. William. 1983. *Double love.* Sweet Valley High no. 1. New York: Bantam.

Paterson, K. 1980. *Jacob have I loved.* New York: Crowell.

Paulsen, G. 1987. *Hatchet.* New York: Bradbury.

———. 1996. *Brian's winter.* New York: Delacorte.

———. 1998. *The river.* New York: Bantam Doubleday.

———. 1999. *Brian's return.* New York: Delacorte.

Peck, R. 1976. *Are you in the house alone?* New York: Viking.

Philbrick, W. R. 1993. *Freak the mighty.* New York: Scholastic/Blue Sky Press.

Plum-Ucci, C. 2000. *The body of Christopher Creed.* San Diego: Harcourt.

Rennison, L. 2000. *Angus, thongs and full-frontal snogging: Confessions of Georgia Nicolson.* New York: HarperCollins.

Rowling, J. K. 1998. *Harry Potter and the sorcerer's stone.* New York: Scholastic/Arthur A. Levine.

Sachar, L. 1998. *Holes*. New York: Farrar, Straus and Giroux.

Sleator, W. 1974. *House of stairs*. New York: E. P. Dutton.

Staples, S. F. 1989. *Shabanu: Daughter of the wind*. New York: Knopf.

Strasser, T. 2000. *Give a boy a gun*. New York: Simon & Schuster.

Stratemeyer, E. 1905. *Dave Porter at Oak Hall, or, The schooldays of an American boy*. Illus. H. M. Brett. Boston: Lothrop, Lee & Shepard.

Thomas, R. 1996. *Rats saw God*. New York: Simon & Schuster.

Trueman, T. 2000. *Stuck in neutral*. New York: HarperCollins.

Tunis, J. R. 1938. *The iron duke*. New York: Harcourt Brace.

Voigt, C. 1982. *Dicey's song*. New York: Atheneum.

Wells, H. 1943. *Cherry Ames, student nurse*. New York: Grosset & Dunlap.

Wittlinger, E. 1999. *Hard love*. New York: Simon & Schuster.

Wolff, V. E. 1993. *Make lemonade*. New York: Henry Holt.

Zindel, P. 1968. *The pigman*. New York: Harper & Row.

19

Children's Books in the Classroom

Milestones and Memories of the Literature-Based Revolution

Marjorie R. Hancock

Children's literature assumed a variety of often-contradictory roles in the elementary classroom during the twentieth century. At times, especially while the whole language movement flourished, children's books were a mainstay of reading, language arts, and cross-curricular learning. At other times their significance as instructional tools was questioned. Although few twentieth-century educators would deny that children's literature motivates and improves children's reading skills, proponents of standardized testing and basal reading systems attempted to relegate literature—read aloud, sustained silent reading, and free reading programs—to a subordinate role in favor of skill and drill. For a time, authentic literature disappeared from bookshelves when Dick and Jane held sway; later, trade books replaced primers and filled classroom and school libraries with innovative, prize-winning novels and glorious picture storybooks. Recently children's literature has shared the spotlight with emerging technologies. Throughout this period, however, children's literature continued to touch hearts, inspire young readers, provide teachers the foundation for creative instruction, and survive almost every educational trend of the century.

This chapter serves as a retrospective journey through the century, particularly the last half of the twentieth century, and the continuously changing role of literature in the elementary classroom. The chapter chronologically blends literature-based milestones and memories from four stages of my own life as student and educator: years as a child in an elementary classroom in the 1950s; university elementary teacher preparation in the 1960s; an elementary teaching career in the 1970s and 1980s; and current experience as a professor of language arts and children's literature in the 1990s. The purpose of the chapter is to follow, discuss, reflect on, and linger over the literature-based trends, issues, milestones, and memories of the emerging role of literature in the elementary classroom.

Recognition and Foundations of Literature

The first half of the twentieth century laid the groundwork for the gradual infusion of literature into elementary classrooms. Recognition of children's literature as its own literary entity was a first step in providing the impetus for a fresh perspective on quality books for children. The first Newbery Award, initiated in 1922, honored the most distinguished contribution to American literature for children—*The Story of Mankind* by Hendrik Willem Van Loon (1921). The Caldecott Medal, first presented in 1938, honored the illustrator of the most distinguished American picture book—*Animals of the Bible, A Picture Book* illustrated by Dorothy P. Lathrop (Fish 1937). Although the topics and tone of these award-winning titles expanded throughout the century, the Newbery and Caldecott awards raised standards of excellence in literature for children and increased the level of awareness of children's books.

Children's book publishing also assisted in paving the way for literature's eventual journey into the elementary classroom. The addition of children's departments to publishing firms indicated the importance of a special literature for the young. In 1924, the *Horn Book Magazine* dedicated its pages exclusively to reviews and discussions on children's books. Public libraries increasingly began to staff children's rooms with quality selections for the emergent and established child reader.

The 1930s and 1940s saw about 1,000 books published for children each year. During recent years, however, those numbers have grown to over 6,000 books annually. But the most impressive changes related to children's books have occurred as a result of the slow, steady, and progressive meshing of children's literature into the instructional fabric of the elementary classroom. The dynamic alliance between children's literature and classroom instruction provides the focus of this chapter. The historical chronology of educational trends parallels the meandering journey of a half century of children's literature and its evolving role in the elementary classroom.

Read-Aloud Memories of the Fifties

During my precious years as an inquisitive child in an elementary classroom during the 1950s, my single, most vivid memory of children's literature is the read aloud. School days were filled with basal readers, flash cards, textbooks, workbook pages, handwriting practice, and quiet time in our isolated desks. But after lunch each day, my classmates and I anticipated the loving read-aloud voice of Mrs. Dunne, poised to fill our souls and spirits beyond their academic needs. Even as a ten-year-old, I realized how literature, in stark contrast to instructional materials, could touch my own life and expand my zeal for reading. Each day we third graders relished the continuing adventures of *The Boxcar Children* (Warner 1942), as Henry, Jessie, Violet, and Benny found treasures in the dump, shared creative meals on the blue tablecloth, and reunited with their loving grandfather. As our teacher turned the last page of that book, she included an invitation to seek out the public library (no library in our school) where similar journeys through literature awaited us—*Strawberry Girl* by Lois Lenski (1945), *Miss Hickory* (1946) by Carolyn Sherwin Bailey, *Caddie Woodlawn* (1935) by Carol Ryrie Brink, and *Johnny Tremain* by Esther Forbes (1943). These titles paved my way to independent reading, and the characters became my treasured companions on my personal journey through children's books.

For most of us who attended school in the 1950s, children's literature was indeed a luxury. Read alouds of literature bestowed a reward for working hard all morning, but little thought was attributed to their value as motivation for reading itself. Occasionally, poetry provided text for memorization purposes, but the enjoyment of language, rhyme, or imagery remained shrouded in words. Teachers housed literature on a private shelf, never borrowed, and rarely placed into the hands of a child. Learning to read with literature, becoming readers through children's books, and learning to love books never crossed the mind of most educators during that decade. Although Dick and Jane portrayed the ideal American family and dominated the reading program, few teachers or school libraries provided access to the sparse number of published children's books. Literature offered something you did when all the required schoolwork was complete, never intended for lifelong enjoyment or the curricular focus of the school day. Though May Hill Arbuthnot's *Children and Books* (1957) provided a critical analysis of genres of children's literature, it did little to bring teachers, children, and books together in an elementary setting.

In spite of a steady diet of progressively challenging, but nonmotivating, basal readers, many children like myself grew up wanting to be teachers. The drill and practice worksheets, the dusty blackboard, and the sharpened red pencils did little to attract us to the profession. But the promise of reading books aloud to future students kept our teaching dreams alive. The thought of sharing Marguerite de Angeli's *The Door in the Wall* (1949) with sixth graders or mesmerizing a fifth-grade class with Elizabeth George Speare's *The Witch of Blackbird Pond* (1958) ignited my desire to become a teacher.

Becoming a Teacher in the Sixties

I entered a teacher preparation program at Northern Illinois University, formerly a Normal School, in 1965, just as the Elementary and Secondary Education Act was passed. Suddenly, school libraries became a reality before my eyes, fulfilling the desire to teach in a classroom with hundreds of accessible children's books just down the hall. Assigned a regular library visit each week, children in my second-grade practicum experience actually browsed library shelves and checked out books such as Maurice Sendak's *Where the Wild Things Are* (1963) and Robert McCloskey's *Time of Wonder* (1957) to read and savor on their own. Children kept those books on the corners of their desks steadfastly ready to read during free time. The desire to teach grew stronger with each trip down that hallway to the school library.

Teacher preparation in the 1960s, for the most part, focused primarily on teaching like we were taught, but a few rebellious professors dared to require paperback texts such as *Using Literature with Young Children* (Jacobs 1965) or *Teaching Literature in the Elementary School* (Odland 1969) in language arts and reading methods courses. Reading aloud, storytelling, choral speaking, and dramatizing stories and poems yielded cutting-edge instructional methods. Professors with doctorates from progressive East Coast universities emphasized the potential of literature to provide variety and motivation to elementary students. For me, the department of library science rather than the college of education housed the required children's literature course and teaching collection. I recorded annotations for *The Snowy Day* by Ezra Jack Keats (1962), *Swimmy* by Leo Lionni (1963), and *Sam, Bangs & Moonshine* by Evaline Ness (1966) in my course card file, but included limited connections between books and the classroom. However, the course delivered a clear message that literature paved the way into children's hearts, providing a genuine desire to read. This philosophy charged teachers with the dual task of encouraging children to choose reading as a free-time activity and turning elementary students into lifelong readers. Although the actual links between literacy instruction and literature remained an unarticulated secret, the course's hidden agenda mandated the strong presence of "library books" in a child's life during those early elementary years.

Dr. Charlotte Huck of The Ohio State University had the greatest influence on children's literature and its role in the elementary classroom in the 1960s. Her first edition of *Children's Literature in the Elementary School* with Doris Young (1961) gave educators permission to do what they longed to do—to bring books and children together in an educational setting in meaningful ways. The unique "Using Literature with Children" section of the book suggested utilizing real books with real children in real ways. Now in its seventh edition, *Children's Literature in the Elementary Classroom* (Huck et al. 2001) continues to have an impact on the direction of literature-based classrooms. Charlotte Huck maintains the strength of her initial influence bringing teachers and books together through the countless doctoral students, "The Attic Rats," she nurtured in her premier children's literature program.

Literature as a Subversive Activity

The end of the 1960s brought my first teaching position at $7,200 per year and the unexpected reality of the classroom. Assigned to teachers in heterogeneous groups, children in my first-year classroom consisted of a challenging "high-ability" group of fifth graders inappropriately paired with a "low-ability" group of sixth graders. Using the basal readers seemed essential to survival; after all, it was what everyone else used. Yet read-aloud literature provided the single thread that wove us together for at least twenty minutes per day. I remember reading aloud chapter books such as E. L. Konigsburg's *From the Mixed-Up Files of Mrs. Basil E. Frankweiler* (1967) and passing the tissue box during Fred Gipson's *Old Yeller* (1956). During that first year, skeptical mentors and a questioning administrator carefully scrutinized my teaching. They challenged whether the time spent reading aloud warranted the instructional time I traded to do it. My principal often secretly listened in over the intercom to monitor my fledgling teaching, but I often wondered if he really wanted to hear the next chapter of Madeline L'Engle's *A Wrinkle in Time* (1962). I had waited a "lifetime" to read aloud to my students, and no one was going to convince me that time for instruction was more valuable than my voice bringing life and meaning to words on a page of a good children's book.

Individualized Reading through Literature

With the onset of the 1970s came the trend toward individualized reading instruction. Perhaps for the first time, teachers valued readers as individuals with unique literature preferences, varied reading abilities, and diverse instructional needs. Not every child needed to be on the same page of the same basal at the same time. For many teachers like myself, individualized reading became an SRA (Science Research Associates) box with color-coded cardboard cards with fiction and nonfiction reading selections, comprehension and vocabulary checks, and skills practice. Ironically, these kinds of individualized reading programs defined comprehension questions through single correct answers that left no option for individual interpretation of the text. Individualized reading often meant the clinical use of specialized equipment to facilitate reading fluency. Much time passed before resources for individualized reading gradually turned to authentic trade books in most classrooms.

The prominence of book awards, both at the national and state level, served as an impetus to independent reading in the 1970s and beyond. The announcement of each year's Newbery Medal and Honor books brought forth chapter book titles for children and teachers to read together and then to pursue as independent reading. *Roll of Thunder, Hear My Cry* by Mildred Taylor (1976) brought deeper understanding of children of color to our culturally encapsulated students, while *My Brother Sam Is Dead* by the Colliers (1974) invited us to integrate our read-aloud choices with our social studies curriculum. The same was true for younger children as the Caldecott Medal and Honor books found their way into classroom read alouds and eventually into the hands of eager children. Schoolchildren became aware of what the gold or silver medal stickers meant on the front cover of a book as they hugged Gerald McDermott's *Arrow to the Sun* (1974) and Verna Aardema's *Why Mosquitoes Buzz in People's Ears* (1975) when they located these familiar titles on the library shelves. State-level book awards, many established in the 1970s, provided additional lists of books to be read by children or by teachers to children with the promise of casting a vote for a favorite title. The 1970s established a continuing momentum toward independent reading of quality literature in the elementary setting.

The arrival of the paperback book to the school scene created a boon for the individualized reading program. The advent of paperback book clubs made multiple copies of inexpensive books available to children and schools. Some librarians refused to purchase paperbacks for the permanent library collection, citing poor construction and abbreviated shelf life as reasons for their skepticism. Some even feared children might "steal" books because of the reduced size of a paperback book. Classroom teachers, however, determined to place books in the hands of children (and in a constant quest for bonus points), reveled in such paperback book clubs as Troll, Scholastic, and Arrow. I can still remember the much-anticipated arrival of the Scholastic book club box and the celebrated unpacking of *Summer of the Swans* (Byars 1970), *M. C. Higgins the Great* (Hamilton 1974), and *The Westing Game* (Raskin 1978). Reading centers and classroom collections flourished, and, for the first time, many children were able to afford a book purchase of their own. Children's bookstores were not yet common, so accessibility through the convenience of paperback clubs provided a major turning point in independent reading.

Through the 1970s, reading instruction emphasized refining individual reading skills of those who already could read, but little attention was paid to aspects of early reading or struggling readers. Besides Jeanne Chall's (1967) "Great Debate" and Dolores Durkin's (1966, 1974) insights into children who read early, there continued to be a tug-of-war between phonics and whole-word instruction for beginning reading. Yet fresh ideas, gathered internationally, provided a new perspective for the teaching of early reading. Literature finally gained an instructional foothold in the primary (pre-K–2) classroom—one which it would sustain and maintain for the remainder of the century.

Early Literacy, Literature, and Young Children

A growing interest in young children's reading in the late 1970s focused American attention on work in the British primary schools and the infant schools of New Zealand. A developmental approach to and acceptance of individual differences in learning to read changed the way American educators viewed early literacy. While "reading readiness" heralded the battle cry of the 1950s and 1960s, exposure to literature at an early age provided a stepping stone toward the gradual, individual acquisition of literacy as a new decade approached.

Don Holdaway's (1979) *Foundations of Literacy* showcased the importance of the early lap reading experience with parents. Talking about the book, pointing to words, inviting children to join in on repeated readings—all these techniques seemed effective in preparing children as readers. Re-creating the lap experience for early literacy instruction in school required "big books." Teachers modeled reading while children joined in as familiarity fostered reading confidence. Children then retold stories and even dictated experiences to the teacher on large chart paper, often resulting in class big book formats with children's sentences and illustrations.

The predictable format of *The Very Hungry Caterpillar* (Carle 1969), for example, now appeared in a 18-inch-by-30-inch format, replicating the proportion, the exact text, and the same illustrations and die cuts of the original trade book. This book follows a caterpillar through each day of the week as he eats one, two, then three types of certain foods not meant for caterpillar consumption. The familiarity of numbers and days of the week help children "read" this well-loved predictable book. The "shared book experience" consisted of the teacher guiding a whole class lesson complete with word pointing, repeated readings, student predictions, and gradual internalization of words and phrases. Through read-aloud repetition and growing comprehension, children eventually learned to "read," and their confidence and self-esteem soared. "Little book" copies of big books allowed children to share the joys of being a reader with parents in the home setting.

As with any effective idea, publishers quickly latched on to this popular trend. Authentic literature with predictable/patterned text began to be reproduced in big book formats. By the late 1980s, however, overly ambitious textbook publishers created big book predictable texts based on contrived, rhymed text—not authentic literature. Almost overnight, all big books were not created equal as quantity confronted quality. Format-disguised, inauthentic text and illustrations challenged the exclusive use of authentic children's books as the basis of early reading instruction. Naïve teachers devoured every big book to share with their children, diluting the impact of real literature. Many teachers ignored cautions by children's literature advocates in their desperate effort to use these popular big books. Unknowingly, some teachers actually abandoned the spirit of both the original big books and real literature in favor of the readily available publisher and "Big Book Club" clones.

The burning desire to know more about early reading and writing ignited as first-generation college baby boomers began to raise their own children. A new concept showcased as emergent literacy (Teale and Sulzby 1986) defined the reading and writing behaviors of young children that precede and develop into conventional literacy. The influence of storybook reading, the home literacy environment, the connections between oral and written language, and the early scribbling-writing phenomenon all took center stage as literature provided the key to early school success. More children's bookstores began to appear as parents purchased classic storybooks they had experienced during their own childhood. *Goodnight Moon* (Brown 1947) and *Charlotte's Web* (White 1952), for example, experienced a resurgence of popularity as parents read aloud to their preschool children. A renewed market for children's books—parents—provided a strong incentive to keep classic children's books in print.

Simultaneously, the work of New Zealand's Marie Clay (1979) was gaining attention in this country as it focused on how good readers learned to read. Marie Clay transferred what she learned about good readers' acquisition of literacy to at-risk, struggling readers. Her "Concept of Print" diagnostic tool provided early detection of "at-risk" behavior. She worked individually with struggling readers with "little books" published in Australia and New Zealand featuring repetitive, familiar text. Clay observed children as they learned to read these books fluently, documenting their strategies and word recognition through running records. Clay's Reading Recovery™ program involved extensive training in which teachers became astute observers of the individual reading process. Reading and rereading of leveled books assured reader success. Later, the Reading Recovery program came to the United States and became well established and respected as a literature-based intervention model directed toward at-risk children.

The emphasis on attention to reading even before school began was the thrust of the 1980s. Researchers focused on the plight of early readers and the role of early storybook reading as an initial gateway to literacy (Snow and Ninio 1986). If book experiences did not occur in the home environment (Heath 1982), the school assumed the responsibility to provide that literacy-rich environment through exposure to quality children's books. The fear of losing children as readers during the early years prompted important research in the area of early literacy (Strickland and Morrow 1989) and directed attention from a "reading readiness" model to an "emergent literacy" model built on authentic literature as a precursor of literacy.

The Call to Read More Books, More Often, and More Globally

Becoming a Nation of Readers (Anderson 1985) focused the nation's attention on the fact that children spend less and less time reading outside of school. Fifth graders read four minutes a day outside of school, suggesting children must be given more time inside of school for self-selected reading. Communities believed that children were neither learning to read adequately nor choosing to read independently. Educators viewed basal reading series as limited in scope and lacking the essence of classic and contemporary children's literature. Anderson's report evolved into an educational focus on comprehension, reading aloud to children, independent reading of books throughout the day, and fewer worksheets. *Becoming a Nation of Readers* paved the way for the century's greatest infusion of literature into the classroom and may have been paramount in starting the literature-based "revolution" (McGee 1992). Award-winning books such as Patricia MacLachlan's *Sarah, Plain and Tall* (1985), Jerry Spinelli's *Maniac Magee* (1990), and Lois Lowry's *Number the Stars* (1989) quickly found their way into paperback editions and became the foundation of sustained silent reading time in classrooms. Real literature became the bait for luring children back to choosing reading as a free-time activity both at school and at home.

Paralleling the trend toward the use of authentic reading materials in the classroom was the explosion in the publication of children's books. The 1980s witnessed the publication of almost 3,000 children's titles in the early part of the decade with an increase to almost 6,500 titles by the decade's end. Quantity was accompanied by the recognition of the value of literature in the elementary classroom. During the 1980s, the Children's Literature Assembly of the National Council of Teachers of English established the Notables Children's Books in the Language Arts award, resulting in an annual list of thirty titles for K–8 children that focused on language, participation, and response (McClure and Kristo 1996). For example, teachers accessed the 1988 list to share the flowing language of Bill Martin Jr. and John Archambault's *Listen to the Rain* (1988), to gain student participation in Paul Fleischman's *Joyful Noise: Poems for Two Voices* (1988), or to elicit responses to Ann Cameron's *The Most Beautiful Place in the World* (1988). This prestigious list continues to affect teachers' choices for reading-writing-responding connections in elementary classrooms.

Another publication phenomenon of the 1980s was the growing recognition of and need for quality multicultural literature. This paralleled our nation's growing awareness of the infusion of cultures into our own nation and our increasing access to a global society. Although initiated in 1970, the Coretta Scott King Award experienced increased interest in the 1980s as the quality and quantity of multicultural literature grew to meet the needs of a diverse school culture. This award honors one African American author and one African American illustrator annually for outstanding inspirational and educational contributions to children's literature. At first, some teachers reluctantly introduced titles such as John Steptoe's *Mufaro's Beautiful Daughters* (1987) and Mildred Taylor's *The Friendship* (1987) into their read-aloud agenda. With growing acceptance and respect, Patricia McKissack's *Mirandy and Brother Wind* (1989) and folktales from Virginia Hamilton's *The People Could Fly* (1985) became classroom favorites. With more reading time, children readily chose Valerie Flournoy's *Patchwork Quilt* (1985) and Mildred Pitts Walter's *Justin and the Best Biscuits in the World* (1986) for independent reading. Often considered a new genre of children's literature, multicultural literature helped children see themselves in the books they read. Multicultural literature in the classroom contributed greatly to children's understanding of their classmates, their community, and their world.

The direct infusion of more and better literature into the school program became the phenomenon of the 1980s. The result of combining real literature with meaningful, authentic reading and writing activities in the classroom provided the educational foundation and initial thrust that became the basis of the whole language movement.

Whole Language—Whole Literature

An explosion in the publication of children's books and teacher support of literature-based programs and language-centered instruction paralleled the rise of the whole language movement (Cullinan 1992). Defined by Kenneth Goodman (1986) in *What's Whole in Whole Language,* this grassroots literacy movement emphasized the use of authentic children's literature as the basis of reading and writing programs, supported the integration of school subjects through the use of children's literature, and suggested the use of real reading and real writing across the curriculum through meaningful, functional activities. In extreme cases, teachers literally "threw out basal readers with the bath water" as zealous advocates of pure literature-based instruction reacted to a long-anticipated invitation that supported the use of authentic literature across the elementary curriculum. In other school settings, teachers stacked basals in closets or the basals collected dust on storage shelves as children's books became the exclusive means of teaching reading. In more cautious classrooms, teachers took a somewhat skeptical approach toward whole language and responded to astute publishers who produced literature-based basals in response to growing support for children's books as an instructional tool. Whole language was at first considered an exclusive club for those who were "real" professionals, who threw caution to the wind, and who were ready for dramatic change. In reality, whole language grew to represent a teaching philosophy—not merely a reading and writing program. From its inception, it provided an invitation into real language, real literature, and real instruction for children. Teachers challenged themselves to seek new understandings to inform their thinking about the links between reading, instruction, and literature.

The whole language movement resulted in three types of literature-based teachers (Huck 1996). First and foremost were those who avidly followed the philosophy of whole language and meaningfully and exclusively integrated trade books across the entire elementary curriculum. As a simple example, the whole language teacher in a primary classroom might share Patricia Polacco's *Thunder Cake* (1990) during reading and Seymour Simon's *Storms* (1989) during science. The whole language teacher in an intermediate classroom might have all children reading Karen Cushman's *The Ballad of Lucy Whipple* (1996) integrated with a social studies unit on the gold rush. These teachers reflected creativity, knew much about children's literature, and made valid connections between trade books and the existing curriculum. Many teachers desired to be this kind of teacher, but soon discovered they simply didn't know enough to function within such a philosophy. Most teachers, enthralled by the prospect of a literature-based curriculum, did their dedicated best to read professional journals and books, to meet with support groups within their schools, and to attend conferences where whole language sessions attained growing popularity.

The second group of literature-based educators exclusively used literature, but tended to balance its use in a way in which they previously used basal readers and textbooks. For example, children might locate vocabulary and write word definitions from *Tuck Everlasting* (Babbitt 1975). Readers still answered closed-ended comprehension recall questions relegated to basals, but now used *Bridge to Terabithia* (Paterson 1977) as a source for those responses. This whole language teacher eagerly purchased "novel study" packets filled with black-line masters of related exercises based on the content of the literature. Although these activities did not reflect whole language in the purest sense, they brought a balanced mode of literature-based instruction to their classrooms with exposure to both quality literature and skills instruction. These teachers gradually attained a comfortable and meaningful balance between authentic literature and more traditional reading instruction.

Aligned with this second group of literature-based educators, the literature-based movement witnessed programs in entire states. The California Reading Initiative afforded the choice of literature or the literature-based basal for reading instruction and issued lists of children's literature books for use in the classroom (California State Department of Education 1986). Unfortunately, a lack of money to support such an ambitious program and its top-down mandate created hurdles to optimal success. Many teachers had not had a children's literature course in their teacher education programs and they survived by applying basal techniques to children's literature (Gardner 1988).

Terms like the "basalization" and the "abuse" of children's literature (Hickman, Hepler, and Cullinan 1994) surrounded this type of literature-based instruction. These teachers were not to be faulted or demeaned; they were merely capitalizing on their love of literature, but relying on traditional methods of instruction. The time, dedication, and energy required to create new instruction from authentic text often seemed overwhelming. In many cases, they constructively supplemented their reading programs with authentic literature related to the author, illustrator, and title in the basal reader.

The third group of literature-based advocates were those that relied on the comfort and security of the new literature-based "anthologies." Knowing that their children were reading "real" literature within a basal program gave them sustenance and promise. They economized on planning as all comprehension questions, vocabulary, and strategic exercises appeared in a teacher's manual. Nevertheless, these cautious, conservative teachers warmed to literature but clung to traditional methods of instruction. They were not to be faulted since many schools supported a very cautious approach to whole language in the 1990s.

Whole language, in its truest sense, heartily supported the inclusion of children's literature across the curriculum and across literary genres. For the first time, master teachers began to see the connectedness of literature across content areas. A study of the Civil War, for example, might be accompanied by small-group reading of *Across Five Aprils* (Hunt 1964), *Charlie Skedaddle* (Beatty 1987), or *Shades of Gray* (Reeder 1989). Within the same Civil War study, students might write letters in the guise of young boys sent to war after listening to authentic voices in Jim Murphy's (1990) nonfiction account of *The Boy's War: Confederate and Union Soldiers Talk about the Civil War*. Portions of Russell Freedman's (1987) Newbery Award–winning *Lincoln: A Photobiography* could visually and verbally enrich the reenactment of the Civil War period.

During this period of integrated, literature-based instruction, the recognition of the nonfiction/informational genre accompanied the creation of the Orbis Pictus Award in 1990. Titles such as *Children of the Dust Bowl* by Jerry Stanley (1992) and *Safari beneath the Sea* by Diane Swanson (1994) naturally found their way into the existing curriculum. Teachers became aware of the continued effectiveness of the blending of genres across the entire curriculum, including mathematics. Thematic units, weaving a topic through all curricular areas and across all literary genres, became synonymous with literature-based instruction. Educators who planned and taught in this integrated, literature-based instructional mode experienced some of the most fulfilling teaching of the decade and perhaps of their careers, while literature-motivated children thrived as they noticed the relevance and connectedness of the content areas.

By the 1990s, there was a committed, dedicated interest in the use of children's literature in school programs. This trend evidenced itself through coverage of literature-based topics in conference presentations, professional journal articles, and published books, many written by teachers. Regie Routman's *Transitions* (1988) and Nancie Atwell's *In the Middle* (1987) began a frenzy of publications by Heinemann Educational Publishers as teachers' voices began to be solicited, heard, and valued over those of textbook publishers and university professors. Teachers viewed themselves as professionals, capable of making sound instructional decisions and more than willing to share their expertise with other educators. This trend has continued as teachers have become researchers, presenters, authors, and respected professionals at local, state, and national levels.

In the early 1990s, researchers conducted fresh studies on the effects of literature-based instruction on reading achievement, attitudes toward reading, and early entry into literacy (Galda and Cullinan 1991; McGee 1992; Tunnell and Jacobs 1989). The literature-based revolution remained alive and flourished with authentic literature as the basis of a student's understanding of story structure and writing process. It also promoted reading fluency and created avid readers. Not only did literature have a positive impact in the classroom, but a new generation of qualitative research studies in literature-based settings and with literature-based methods resulted in fresh ways of assessing instructional effectiveness.

Enriching the Literature Experience through Reader Response

Even as whole language gained momentum and began to revolutionize teaching in the1990s, a passionate voice cried out to teachers. Although Louise Rosenblatt (1938, 1978) had been speaking to educators for more than fifty years, the timeliness of her message blended perfectly with the philosophy of the whole language and the literature-based movements. As whole language advocated the inclusion of literature in the elementary classroom, teachers sought to enrich the literature experience rather than just "using" literature. Louise Rosenblatt's transactional theory of reader response (1978) provided the message teachers eagerly chose to embrace as they witnessed firsthand the uniqueness of each reader in their literature-based programs. The desire to blend the world of a literature-based classroom through authentic literature, meaningful response-based activities, and a variety of response options across literary genres and curricular areas opened teachers' minds to the eloquently articulated thoughts of Louise Rosenblatt.

The transactional theory of reader response supports teachers' desires to surround readers with quality children's literature experiences, resulting in the creation of life-long readers whose emotions and empathy fostered by literature will reach beyond reading to influence their view of humanity (Hancock 2000). The theory is built on the uniqueness of readers as they interact with literary text in personal ways. These personal literary interactions provide an outlet for written responses and oral conversations about literature to take place in the classroom. Rosenblatt's theory cast aside the dominance of the text and directed the spotlight to the vital role of the reader who brings life and light to the reading of a literary text. Rosenblatt's theory provided the transitional foundation for developing classroom practice through new methods of eliciting personal responses from children including response prompts, literature circles, reading and writing workshop, and literature response journals.

Teachers quickly learned that a detectable difference existed between "efferent" and "aesthetic" reading. Efferent reading implies information gleaned from the text; aesthetic reading requires personal feelings and emotions in response to the text. For example, Diane Stanley's picture-book biography of *Leonardo da Vinci* (1996) may inform readers that this Renaissance artist was born in 1452. But the same readers may also identify da Vinci's inventiveness and determination as admirable traits they see in their own life. Teachers realized that reading moves far beyond literal comprehension to relating events and characters from a book to the reader's own life. This opened new avenues for response in the classroom. The uniqueness of the individual response within the context of the literature replaced the traditional single correct answer to a comprehension question.

Louise Rosenblatt provided the theoretical underpinning for many well-accepted response-based options in today's elementary classroom. Response prompts (Kelly 1990), literature response journals (Hancock 1993), literature circles (Hill, Johnson, and Schlick Noe 1995), and other varied aspects of reader response (Holland, Hungerford, and Ernst 1993) all based their premises on the uniqueness of a reader's interaction with an individual text. In fact, as the new millennium turned, the most effective instructional methods in the schools focused on Rosenblatt's transactional theory and related response-based activities.

Response prompts began to provide guidance for young readers as teachers sought to delve into personal feelings. "What did you notice in the story?" "How did the story make you feel?" and "What does the story remind you of from your own life?" guided oral and written response to literature in younger children. Though children struggled at first with these open-ended invitations to respond, they gradually internalized these prompts as they became the framework for everyday interaction. Children applied these prompts to such dissimilar books as Eve Bunting's *Smoky Night* (1994), Peggy Rathmann's *Officer Buckle and Gloria* (1995), and Paul Zelinsky's *Rapunzel* (1997) with dynamic results. Children soon realized that their response did not need to match a predetermined, correct answer, but that their teacher valued the unique, genuine response from within each of them.

Literature response journals became an outlet for written responses to literature in the intermediate classroom. For example, students in a fifth-grade class select one of three Gary Paulsen titles—*The Haymeadow* (1992), *Hatchet* (1987), or *Brian's Winter* (1996)—and respond spontaneously in a journal format. Their written responses may be shared with a group of peers or a teacher for feedback and comments. The literature response journal purports to capture the ongoing thoughts and emotions of the reader during the process of reading, rather than following the completion of the book (Hancock 1993). Reflective teacher comments create momentum and variety in response, while reading peer journals inspires reading of other text set titles.

Literature circles or grand conversations (Eeds and Wells 1989) became an effective oral outlet for response to literature. For example, students may be reading thought-provoking titles such as Lois Lowry's *The Giver* (1993) or Karen Hesse's *Out of the Dust* (1997) and meeting for twenty minutes twice a week to discuss their thoughts, predictions, and personal connections. Each member of the group assumes a role (for example, discussion director, literary luminary, connector, illustrator, vocabulary enricher, or summarizer) (Daniels 1994) and shares independent thoughts and reflections. Teachers learned to listen, instead of talk, yet provided a framework for talk, verbal support, and direction when needed. This method of sharing literature proved effective and continues as a means of sharing response, particularly in intermediate and middle-level classrooms.

Reader response took a lasting hold on classroom practice as teachers and students alike found room for individual expression in its theoretical foundation. Reader response has assumed a comfortable role in primary classrooms also, as teachers learned that response is not unique to older readers, but to all successful readers who interact, connect, and relate to the books they read.

The Approach of the Twenty-First Century

The rise of the standards movement in the last half of the 1990s created a new challenge to the effective use of authentic literature in the classroom. The *Standards for the English Language Arts* (International Reading Association [IRA] and National Council of Teachers of English [NCTE] 1996) include comfortable phrases such as "classic and contemporary works," "fiction and nonfiction," and " a wide range of literature from many periods in many genres," which serve as an extended invitation to continue the use of authentic literature in the elementary classroom. In fact, the *Standards* support the use of multicultural literature across the curriculum as students "build an understanding of texts, themselves, and of the cultures of the United States and the world" (IRA and NCTE 1996, 3). Literature-based professionals have greeted the reaffirmation of literature at the national level with renewed enthusiasm. The standards invite us to share the newest nonfiction (*Hurry Freedom: African Americans in Gold Rush California* by Jerry Stanley [2000]), quality multicultural literature (*Virgie Goes to School with Us Boys* by Elizabeth Fitzgerald Howard [1999]), and contemporary fiction (*Because of Winn-Dixie* by Kate DiCamillo [2000]).

A response to blending literature-based reading and student accountability for comprehension has been the Accelerated Reader program. Children read from a list of preselected quality trade book titles that have been leveled to match independent reading ability. Following their reading, students take a computer-based comprehension quiz that tabulates results directly to the classroom teacher. Teachers report the Accelerated Reader program not only generates more reading and checks comprehension, but it provides sound support as a supplemental, motivational literature program.

Children's literature advocates continue their quality inclusion and infusion of literature in the context of national and state demands. Some states retain standards that directly value literature and literature response (Kansas State Department of Education [KSDE] 1998) and have even prepared documents that propose exemplary literature-based lessons for achieving the standards (KSDE 2000). In the new millennium, it appears that literature might be subordinated to a secondary role without the continued support of its enthusiastic advocates. The retention of literature-based instruction in its most effective form requires the grassroots support of both teachers and professional organizations. The voice of the profession must speak louder than the voice of state departments of education if the literature-based revolution is to continue.

As teacher educators forge ahead into the twenty-first century, many reading and language arts methods courses in professional programs continue to adopt textbooks that support a response-based, literature-focused philosophy of teaching reading and language arts. Many states continue to require an undergraduate course in children's literature, while others have dropped the requirement to make room for more traditional instructional modes. University professors, literature-based classroom mentoring teachers, and knowledgeable school librarians serve as direct advocates of children's literature in the classroom and ultimately carry the promise of the future through meaningful literature-based instruction to new members of the profession.

This year I have shared Bill Martin Jr. and Steven Kellogg's *A Beasty Story* (1999) with my students as a model of a predictable/pattern book. They have marveled at the poetic and visual effects of Christopher Myers's *Black Cat* (1999). Joan Bransfield Graham's *Flicker Flash* (1999) served as a model of concrete poetry. A chapter read aloud of Avi's *Midnight Magic* (1999) kept them glued to their seats. *My*

Name Is Jorge on Both Sides of the River: Poems in English and Spanish (Medina 1999) brought tears to their eyes. David Wiesner's wordless book *Sector 7* (1999) inspired our class to compose text as imaginative as the award-winning illustrations. Although I have moved from the elementary classroom to the university setting, literature has moved with me as I share with adults what I would share with children. Across genres, across authors, I still remember and model how I want them to teach.

As a liaison between a professional development school (K–5) and my university, I have witnessed and observed hundreds of well-planned, proficiently delivered, and academically challenging literature-based lessons in primary, intermediate, and middle-level classrooms. A first-grade readers theatre script for Archambault and Martin's *A Beautiful Feast for a Big King Cat* (1994), a third-grade choral reading of poetry from Pat Mora's collection *Confetti* (1996), and fourth-grade reader response journals to Jerry Spinelli's *Wringer* (1997) have followed my students from the university to the elementary classroom. The philosophy espoused in university methods courses found its way to the elementary classroom through the professional development school concept. With mentor teachers, knowledgeable librarians and media specialists, and university professors jointly articulating and supporting a literature-based philosophy, the likelihood of carrying that philosophy to a new classroom with a first-year teacher appears likely. The natural appeal of children's literature, the inherent richness of reader response, and the professional satisfaction of quality literature-based teaching still remain in the classroom as the twenty-first century begins.

A Glance toward the Future ... The Wisdom of the Past

As we look to the future of literature in the classroom, optimism and advocacy remain crucial. Those who love literature will be reluctant to put down a read aloud of Christopher Paul Curtis's *Bud, Not Buddy* (1999) in their fifth-grade class and will be unwilling to forsake a novel study of *Sarah, Plain and Tall* (MacLachlan 1985) during a second-grade westward expansion theme. Teachers who are using Doug Florian's *Insectlopedia* (1998) in their science units will continue to infuse poetry across themes. Children who have had a taste of the J. K. Rowling Harry Potter (1998) series will continue to clamor for daily read alouds. With continued high standards for published children's books, introduction of new book awards such as the Pura Belpre Award for Latino literature, and the increased accessibility to higher-quality books through journal reviews and well-informed librarians, teachers will continue to maintain the best books for children in their classrooms. Children who have been educated in literature-based classrooms will continue to read, far beyond their elementary classrooms and beyond their elementary years.

In addition, technology assumes a harmonious, rather than an adversarial, role in a literature-based classroom. Author and illustrator Web sites, children's literature Web sites, online booksellers, children's literature listservs, and other literature-related sites for teachers reveal the interaction of technology and children's books. The survival of the book in a megabyte world (Hancock 2000) appears unquestionable because literature fulfills the human need to belong and be accepted. Literature will always provide a refuge, knowing we are not isolated in our thoughts, actions, and emotions.

Children's literature advocates, including teachers, parents, and children, continue to applaud and savor the best of literature. It took fifty years for literature to gain its rightful place in the classroom, and its advocates will carry it through the next century with enthusiasm and heartfelt support. Those children nurtured under the literature umbrella will continue to read, and those students taught under a literature-based philosophy will continue to flourish. The milestones literature has achieved in the elementary classroom and the personal memories that keep it alive in the lives of teachers, parents, and children move the literature-based revolution forward.

To keep our literature-based dream alive, Charlotte Huck (1989/1979) shares a timeless plea, an enduring philosophy, and a commonsense reason for retaining real literature on the path to real literacy in our lives. Dr. Huck's words ring true for children of any century:

For, through literature, children can begin to develop a sense of their humanness; they can develop new insights into the behavior of others and themselves. Literature can add a new dimension to life and create a new awareness, a greater sensitivity to people and their surroundings. It can educate the heart as well as the head. (262)

The milestones literature has achieved in the classroom and the personal memories of special books that keep literacy alive in our hearts provide the momentum necessary to move children's literature proudly and assuredly onward.

References

Aardema, V. 1975. *Why mosquitoes buzz in people's ears*. Illus. L. Dillon and D. Dillon. New York: Dial.

Anderson, R. C. 1985. *Becoming a nation of readers: The report of the Commission on Reading*. Washington, DC: National Institute of Education.

Arbuthnot, M. H. 1957. *Children and books*. Chicago: Scott Foresman.

Archambault, J., and B. Martin Jr. 1994. *A beautiful feast for a big King Cat*. Illus. B. Degen. New York: HarperCollins.

Atwell, N. 1987. *In the middle*. Portsmouth, NH: Heinemann.

Avi. 1999. *Midnight magic*. New York: Scholastic.

Babbitt, N. 1975. *Tuck everlasting*. New York: Farrar, Straus and Giroux.

Bailey, C. S. 1946. *Miss Hickory*. Illus. R. Gannett. New York: Viking.

Beatty, P. 1987. *Charley Skedaddle*. New York: Morrow.

Brink, C. R. 1935. *Caddie Woodlawn*. New York: Macmillan.

Brown, M. W. 1947. *Goodnight moon*. Illus. C. Hurd. New York: Harper.

Bunting, E. 1994. *Smoky nights*. Illus. D. Diaz. San Diego: Harcourt.

Byars, B. C. 1970. *The summer of the swans*. New York: Viking.

California State Department of Education. 1986. *Recommended readings in literature: Kindergarten through grade eight.* Sacramento, CA: State Department of Education.

Cameron, A. 1988. *The most beautiful place in the world.* Illus. T. B. Allen. New York: Knopf.

Carle, E. 1969. *The very hungry caterpillar.* New York: Philomel.

Chall, J. S. 1967. *Learning to read: The great debate. An inquiry into the science, art, and ideology of old and new methods of teaching children to read, 1910–1965.* New York: McGraw-Hill.

Clay, M. M. 1979. *Reading: The patterning of complex behavior.* 2d ed. Auckland, New Zealand: Heinemann.

Collier, J. L., and C. Collier. 1974. *My brother Sam is dead.* New York: Four Winds.

Cullinan, B. E. 1992. Whole language and children's literature. *Language Arts* 69: 426–430.

Curtis, C. P. 1999. *Bud, not Buddy.* New York: Delacorte.

Cushman, K. 1996. *The ballad of Lucy Whipple.* New York: Clarion.

Daniels, H. 1994. *Literature circles: Voice and choice in the student-centered classroom.* York, ME: Stenhouse.

De Angeli, M. 1949. *The door in the wall.* Garden City, NY: Doubleday.

DiCamillo, K. 2000. *Because of Winn-Dixie.* Cambridge, MA: Candlewick.

Durkin, D. 1966. *Children who read early: Two longitudinal studies.* New York: Teachers College Press.

———. 1974. A six-year study of children who learned to read in school at the age of four. *Reading Research Quarterly* 10: 9–61.

Eeds, M., and D. Wells. 1989. Grand conversations: An exploration of meaning construction in literature study groups. *Research in the Teaching of English* 23: 4–29.

Fish, H. D. 1937. *Animals of the Bible.* Illus. D. Lathrop. Philadelphia: Lippincott.

Fleischman, P. 1988. *Joyful noise: Poems for two voices.* New York: HarperCollins.

Florian, D. 1998. *Insectlopedia: Poems and paintings.* San Diego: Harcourt Brace.

Flournoy, V. 1985. *The patchwork quilt.* Illus. J. Pinkney. New York: Dial.

Forbes, E. 1943. *Johnny Tremain.* Boston: Houghton Mifflin.

Freedman, R. 1987. *Lincoln: A photobiography.* New York: Clarion.

Galda, L., and B. E. Cullinan. 1991. Literature for literacy: What research says about the benefits of using tradebooks in the classroom. In *Handbook of research on teaching the English language arts,* ed. J. Squire, 529–535. New York: Macmillan.

Gardner, M. 1988. An educator's concern about the California initiative. *New Advocate* 1: 250–253.

Gipson, F. 1956. *Old Yeller.* New York: Harper & Row.

Goodman, K. S. 1986. *What's whole in whole language?* Portsmouth, NH: Heinemann.

Graham, J. B. 1999. *Flicker flash.* Illus. N. Davis. Boston: Houghton Mifflin.

Hamilton, V. 1974. *M. C. Higgins, the great.* New York: Macmillan.

———. 1985. *The people could fly: American Black folktales.* Illus. L. Dillon and D. Dillon. New York: Knopf.

Hancock, M. R. 1993. Exploring and extending personal response through literature journals. *The Reading Teacher* 46: 466–474.

———. 2000. *A celebration of literature and response: Children, books, and teachers in K–8 classrooms.* Upper Saddle River, NJ: Merrill.

Heath, S. B. 1982. What no bedtime story means: Narrative skills at home and at school. *Language in Society* 11: 49–76.

Hesse, K. 1997. *Out of the dust.* New York: Scholastic.

Hickman, J., S. I. Hepler, and B. E. Cullinan. 1994. *Children's literature in the classroom: Extending Charlotte's web.* Norwood, MA: Christopher-Gordon.

Hill, B. C., N. J. Johnson, and K. L. Schlick Noe. 1995. *Literature circles and response.* Norwood, MA: Christopher-Gordon.

Holdaway, D. 1979. *The foundations of literacy.* Auckland, New Zealand: Ashton Scholastic.

Holland, K. E., R. A. Hungerford, and S. B. Ernst. 1993. *Journeying: Children responding to literature.* Portsmouth, NH: Heinemann.

Howard, E. F. 1999. *Virgie goes to school with us boys.* Illus. E. B. Lewis. New York: Simon & Schuster.

Huck, C. S. 1989. No wider than the heart is wide. In *Children's literature in the classroom—Weaving Charlotte's web,* ed. J. Hickman and B. E. Cullinan, 251–262. Needham Heights, MA: Christopher-Gordon.

———. 1996. Literature-based reading programs: A retrospective. *New Advocate* 9: 23–33.

Huck, C. S., S. Hepler, J. Hickman, and B. Z. Kiefer. 2001. *Children's literature in the elementary school.* 7th ed. Boston: McGraw-Hill.

Huck, C. S., and D. A. Young. 1961. *Children's literature in the elementary school.* New York: Holt, Rinehart and Winston.

Hunt, I. 1964. *Across five Aprils.* Chicago: Follett.

International Reading Association and National Council of Teachers of English. 1996. *Standards for the English language arts.* Newark, DE/Urbana, IL: International Reading Association/National Council of Teachers of English.

Jacobs, L. B. 1965. *Using literature with young children.* New York: Teachers College Press.

Kansas State Department of Education. 1998. *Kansas curricular standards for reading and writing.* Topeka: Kansas State Department of Education.

————. 2000. *LINKS: Literacy instruction now—Knowledge for teachers implementing state standards*. Topeka: Kansas State Department of Education.

Keats, E. J. 1962. *The snowy day*. New York: Viking.

Kelly, P. R. 1990. Guiding young students' responses to literature. *The Reading Teacher* 43: 464–470.

Konigsburg, E. L. 1967. *From the mixed-up files of Mrs. Basil E. Frankweiler*. New York: Atheneum.

L'Engle, M. 1962. *A wrinkle in time*. New York: Farrar, Straus and Giroux.

Lenski, L. 1945. *Strawberry girl*. Philadelphia: Lippincott.

Lionni, L. 1963. *Swimmy*. New York: Pantheon.

Lowry, L. 1989. *Number the stars*. Boston: Houghton Mifflin.

————. 1993. *The giver*. Boston: Houghton Mifflin.

MacLachlan, P. 1985. *Sarah, plain and tall*. New York: HarperCollins.

Martin, B., and J. Archambault. 1988. *Listen to the rain*. Illus. J. R. Endicott. New York: Henry Holt.

Martin, B., Jr., and S. Kellogg. 1999. *A beasty story*. Illus. S. Kellogg. San Diego: Silver Whistle/Harcourt Brace.

McCloskey, R. 1957. *Time of wonder*. New York: Viking.

McClure, A. A., and J. V. Kristo. 1996. *Books that invite talk, wonder, and play*. Urbana, Ill.: National Council of Teachers of English.

McDermott, G. 1974. *Arrow to the sun: A Pueblo Indian tale*. New York: Viking.

McGee, L. M. 1992. Focus on research: Exploring the literature-based reading revolution. *Language Arts* 69: 529–537.

McKissack, P. 1989. *Mirandy and brother wind*. Illus. J. Pinkney. New York: Knopf.

Medina, J. 1999. *My name is Jorge on both sides of the river: Poems in English and Spanish*. Illus. F. Vandenbroeck. Honesdale, PA: Wordsong/Boyds Mills.

Mora, P. 1996. *Confetti: Poems for children*. Illus. E. O. Sanchez. New York: Lee & Low.

Murphy, J. 1990. *The boys' war: Confederate and Union soldiers talk about the Civil War*. New York: Clarion.

Myers, C. A. 1999. *Black cat*. New York: Scholastic.

Ness, E. 1966. *Sam, Bangs & Moonshine*. New York: Holt, Rinehart and Winston.

Odland, N. 1969. *Teaching literature in the elementary school*. Champaign, IL: National Council of Teachers of English and ERIC Clearinghouse on the Teaching of English.

Paterson, K. 1977. *Bridge to Terabithia*. Illus. D. Diamond. New York: Crowell.

Paulsen, G. 1987. *Hatchet*. New York: Bradbury.

————. 1992. *The haymeadow*. New York: Delacorte.

————. 1996. *Brian's winter*. New York: Delacorte.

Polacco, P. 1990. *Thunder cake*. New York: Philomel.

Raskin, E. 1978. *The Westing game*. New York: E. P. Dutton.

Rathmann, P. 1995. *Officer Buckle and Gloria*. New York: G. P. Putnam's Sons.

Reeder, C. 1989. *Shades of gray*. New York: Macmillan.

Rosenblatt, L. M. 1938. *Literature as exploration*. New York: D. Appleton-Century.

———. 1978. *The reader, the text, the poem: The transactional theory of the literary work*. Carbondale: Southern Illinois University Press.

Routman, R. 1988. *Transitions: From literature to literacy*. Portsmouth, NH: Heinemann.

Rowling, J. K. 1998. *Harry Potter and the sorcerer's stone*. 1st American ed. Illus. M. GrandPré. New York: Scholastic/Arthur A. Levine.

Sendak, M. 1963. *Where the wild things are*. New York: Harper & Row.

Simon, S. 1989. *Storms*. New York: Morrow Junior Books.

Snow, C. E., and A. Ninio. 1986. The contracts of literacy: What children learn from learning to read books. In *Emergent literacy: Writing and reading,* ed. E. Sulzby, 116–138. Norwood, NJ: Ablex.

Speare, E. G. 1958. *The witch of Blackbird Pond*. Boston: Houghton Mifflin.

Spinelli, J. 1990. *Maniac Magee*. Boston: Little, Brown.

———. 1997. *Wringer*. New York: HarperCollins.

Stanley, D. 1996. *Leonardo da Vinci*. New York: Morrow Junior Books.

Stanley, J. 1992. *Children of the Dust Bowl: The true story of the school at Weedpatch Camp*. New York: Crown.

———. 2000. *Hurry freedom: African Americans in Gold Rush California*. New York: Crown.

Steptoe, J. 1987. *Mufaro's beautiful daughters: An African tale*. New York: Lothrop, Lee & Shepard.

Strickland, D. S., and L. M. Morrow. 1989. *Emerging literacy: Young children learn to read and write*. Newark, DE: International Reading Association.

Swanson, D. 1994. *Safari beneath the sea: The wonder world of the North Pacific Coast*. Photographs by the Royal British Columbia Museum. San Francisco: Sierra Club Books for Children.

Taylor, M. D. 1976. *Roll of thunder, hear my cry*. New York: Dial.

———. 1987. *The friendship*. New York: Dial.

Teale, W. H., and E. Sulzby. 1986. *Emergent literacy: Writing and reading*. Norwood, NJ: Ablex.

Tunnell, M. O., and J. S. Jacobs. 1989. Using "real" books: Research findings on literature-based literature instruction. *The Reading Teacher* 42: 470–477.

Van Loon, H. W. 1921. *The story of mankind*. New York: Boni & Liveright.

Walter, M. P. 1986. *Justin and the best biscuits in the world*. Illus. C. Stock. New York: Lothrop, Lee & Shepard.

Warner, G. C. 1942. *The boxcar children*. Morton Grove, IL: Albert Whitman.

White, E. B. 1952. *Charlotte's web*. Illus. G. Williams. New York: Harper & Row.

Wiesner, D. 1999. *Sector 7*. New York: Clarion.

Zelinsky, P. O. 1997. *Rapunzel*. New York: Dutton Children's Books.

20

From the Beginning

A Journey to Learning

Peggy S. Oxley

I have loved children's literature all of my life. I was read to and given books from ear-liest childhood, particularly by my grandmother who said, "Never waste any reading time, because life is short, and there are so many good books to be read!" I still have some of the books she gave me: *A Child's Garden of Verses* (Stevenson 1905), *Just So Stories* (Kipling 1912), *Alice's Adventures in Wonderland* (Carroll 1930a), *Through the Looking Glass and What Alice Found There* (Carroll 1930b), *The Secret Garden* (Burnett 1911), *Sarah's Idea* (Gates 1938), and *Eight Cousins or The Aunt-Hill* (Alcott 1931).

I met Dick and Jane, Sally, Spot and Puff when I attended first grade in a small is-land community school in a cove off San Francisco Bay. But we moved to Berkeley the next year, where I entered second grade at Hillside School, and I never read about that monosyllabic family again until a generation later when my children entered school. At Hillside I saw "readers" on the shelf. But the books we read were introduced by our wonderful teacher, books like *Mary Poppins* (Travers 1934) and *The Little House in the Big Woods* (Wilder 1932). I could hardly wait for her to read to us every day, and I promised myself that if ever I were a teacher, I'd read to my children every day, too. (And I do!)

My grandmother gave me the books that the teacher read and others as I grew, books including *The Silver Pencil* (Dalgliesh 1944), *The Blue Willow* (Gates 1940), and *Toinette's Phillip* (Jamison 1938), a favorite of hers. From friends and relatives I received books such as *Heidi* (Spyri 1925), *The Little Dutch Tulip Girl* (Brandeis 1929), and *Pollyanna, The Glad Book* (Porter 1940). I bought my own copies of the *Nancy Drew Mystery Stories* (Keene 1930), and I haunted both the school library and the Berkeley Public Library, reading widely and voraciously such books as *The Poppy-Seed Cakes* (Clark 1924) and *The Wonderful Wizard of Oz* (Baum 1900). Early influences made me a lifetime reader.

When my children entered school in Ohio in the 1960s, first-grade classrooms had fifty to sixty students. I became reacquainted with Dick and Jane, Sally, Spot and Puff through the books that they brought home. Basal readers, workbooks, and ditto sheets comprised the reading instruction. SRA (Science Research Associates) kits were introduced to their school by the 1970s, and the children in the primary grades worked to reach the silver and gold levels, striving to establish themselves as good readers. Literature was not a part of the school's reading program. But my children had been read to and given books all of their lives, which laid the groundwork for the good readers they became.

When I began teaching second graders twenty-eight years ago, our campus was a traditional parochial school with an average of thirty-five middle-class, primarily white students in each class. I juggled basal readers, workbooks, ditto sheets, criterion tests, and the like, occupations that seemed to fill nearly all the teaching day. When finally I had such things under control, I found that I was bored—and so, I believed, were the children. Although I brought a monthly supply of books from the library for the children and read to them daily, there was little time left for them to read or respond to well-written books, write for real purposes, or become involved in helping to plan class themes and projects. After returning to graduate school, I found that research supported my convictions: children learn best to read by reading real books, and to write by writing for meaningful purposes. Therefore, in 1982 I began to reconstruct my program.

My struggling readers, who always had been given only the most boring and redundant drill work, and who therefore *hated* what they called "reading" and "writing," were the first I switched to authentic literature and purposeful writing—the first steps in my new program. We started with the Little Bear books (Minarik 1957) and the Frog and Toad books (Lobel 1970), and the children thrived. They read eagerly and shared their journal entries about the books when their group met. After reading the Lobel books and engaging in discussion and response activities, they wrote illustrated letters to Arnold Lobel. They received a wonderful reply, written within the green outline he had drawn of Frog's face. Although these students had come to me labeled "at-risk" readers, they did wonderfully well once they were engaged in the language of good books. For the first time, they regarded themselves as real readers.

By 1984, I had switched all the children to a literature-based reading and writing program, then in its embryonic stages. No one else in my school was following such a program, but I had support from past and current principals and from friends in other schools who were teaching in similar ways. Planning and organizing was difficult at first, but has become easier and more fun to arrange as I have gained experience.

In addition to the Little Bear books, other early easy-to-read books for struggling second-grade readers included the Amelia Bedelia series (Parish) and the lovable Frances stories (Hoban). Though these books have remained favorites, other titles have been added annually: Cynthia Rylant's delightful Mr. Putter & Tabby tales and her stories of Poppleton, the neighborly pig, for example. The list for average second-grade readers has included books by Clyde Robert Bulla and Patricia Reilly Giff. Average readers also love more recent books such as Rylant's Henry and Mudge books and James Marshall's Fox series. Advanced second-grade readers continue to relish books including Beverly Cleary's Ramona stories, James Howe's tales of *Howliday Inn* (1982) and *Bunnicula* (Howe and Howe 1979), , Betsy Byars's Blossom Family books, and E. B. White's *Stuart Little* (1945). Readers have volunteered to present plays based on books such as Cleary's *Socks* (1973) and *Ralph S. Mouse* (1982), to prepare Frog and Toad cookie parties, and to participate in many other extensions of the books enjoyed by their literature groups.

The literature reading and writing program in my classroom has evolved to its present flexible schedule. My class of thirty-five second graders starts each day with a whole-class meeting, an idea I acquired from two study tours—one to Great Britain in 1985 and one to New Zealand in 1988—where school days begin in this way. The children gather on the carpet around my chair, and I read to them from poetry, prose, and informational books. I read to share good writing, to introduce new books, and to provide information that ties in with our studies. The children share what they have written in their journals. Some read segments of stories they are writing, and we all look forward to hearing the latest developments and guessing what will happen next. Others read descriptions of events or objects they want to share with the class. After the sharing, we discuss current projects and plans for our day.

Class meeting is followed by reading and writing workshop, during which children engage in independent reading and writing. Those who are ready for final editing—of stories, poems, and articles they wish to publish—schedule conferences with me. It is in these conferences and in class minilessons that I teach the principles of language and the mechanics of writing.

During daily silent reading, I read individually with children from their current books, discuss the books, assess students' strengths, and determine where they need help. In these sessions and in class minilessons, I teach them the reading strategies they need.

Much of our work revolves around whatever content area themes we are currently studying. These themes are arranged under wide umbrellas, which allow the children as much choice as possible in selecting those aspects of the topics they will study. At the unit's end, the disparate parts that small groups studied are presented to the class in whatever form the children wish—through dance, artwork, homemade videos, drama, murals, display boards, and related works of literature. Foods related to the topics are often shared, feasts to delight us all.

Information is gathered from books in the room, trips to the school or public library, interviews with resource people (who are sometimes invited to address the class as well), and other pertinent sources. In the last five years, material also has been gathered from the Internet. (Any information obtained from the Internet, encyclopedias, or other reference materials *must* be reworded by the children in language understandable to themselves and to the class. These translations usually require the help of an adult, either at school—teacher, teacher's aide, or volunteer parent—or at home.) Children often make their presentations in costume, adding an element of excitement. From these presentations on many different aspects of our topics, the class gets a rich, well-rounded composite of information about our themes rather than a one-dimensional collection of facts.

Each year in one form or another, we study westward expansion of the United States, from the landing of the Pilgrims through the trials of the Oregon Trail to the settling of the far West. Along the way we make a study of our own roots as well as of the many cultures that make up the richness of our country. Our studies have fallen under many titles: "Journey West," "Moving On and Settling In," "From Many, One: A Rich Diversity of Cultures," and "Strangers in a Strange New Land." We draw on a wealth of children's books—poetry, prose, and informational—to help with our studies. A few of our recent titles pertaining to immigrant arrivals are *How Many Days to America? A Thanksgiving Story* (Bunting 1988), *When Jesse Came across the Sea* (Hest 1997), *I Was Dreaming to Come to America: Memories from the Ellis Island Oral History Project* (Lawlor 1995), *An Ellis Island Christmas* (Leighton 1992), *Annushka's Voyage* (Tarbescu 1998), *Across the Wide Dark Sea* (Van Leeuwen 1995), *On the* Mayflower: *Voyage of the Ship's Apprentice and a Passenger Girl* (Waters 1996), and *The Memory Coat* (Woodruff 1999). These books, along with older titles, paint vivid pictures of the difficulties faced by our forebears as they traveled to our shores.

We follow the pioneers across the country, continuing to enrich our studies with literature. Examples of recent migration favorites are *Pioneer Girl: The Story of Laura Ingalls Wilder* (Anderson 1998), *Train to Somewhere* (Bunting 1996b), *Dandelions* (Bunting 1995), *I Have Heard of a Land* (Thomas 1998), *Mississippi Mud* (Turner 1997), and *Nothing Here But Trees* (Van Leeuwen 1998). These books have joined earlier favorites such as *The Courage of Sarah Noble* (Dalgliesh 1954) and all the Little House books (Wilder) to help us understand the hardships and the happiness of those who led the way across the land. The books also have provided background for two original historic plays, *Mayflower Crossing* and *Moving West,* written and produced by two of my recent classes.

Last year we followed our study of westward expansion with a careful look at some of the many cultures making up our nation in a unit we called, "America: A Patchwork of Cultures." We focused on six cultures: Native American, African American, Hispanic/Latino, Asian American, Appalachian, and Amish. (Having dealt thoroughly with the Euro-American experience during our roots study, we did not include the many cultures in that category.) The children chose their cultures of study and worked in small groups to produce delightfully informative presentations for us all. For example, three boys made a study of the Adena Indians. They obtained information from many sources, including books and visits to the Ohio Historical Society and to the Adena Mounds. Then they made a video of themselves in the woods in appropriate garb, demonstrating some of the Adena customs. They concluded with a rain dance around the campfire they had built. Six girls who were studying Asian Americans dressed in beautiful kimonos they had made (with help) and staged a Japanese tea party for us. Then each girl rose and read from the back of her handmade fan information she had gathered about the country of her choice—China, Japan, Korea, Cambodia, Laos, or Vietnam. There were many other outstanding reports as well. Some of the children based their information on the direct experiences of their parents or grandparents.

Our classroom collection of books included a sampling from most of the cultures studied. Among recently published Hispanic/Latino books were *A Day's Work* (Bunting 1994), *Going Home* (Bunting 1996a), *Isla* (Dorros 1995), *Cuckoo/Cucu* (Ehlert 1997), *I'm New Here* (Howlett 1993), and *Lights on the River* (Thomas 1994).

Popular books about Native Americans included Joseph Bruchac's *A Boy Called Slow: The True Story of Sitting Bull* (Bruchac 1994) as well as his many other fine books, *The Path of the Quiet Elk: A Native American Alphabet Book* (Stroud 1996)—beautiful alphabet books on nearly every cultural theme are published annually—and *Dream Catcher* (Osofsky 1992).

The *Two Brothers* (Ho and Ros 1995), a Cambodian tale, and *Pedro and the Monkey* (San Souci 1996), a Filipino folktale retold, added background material. From Korea, we shared several books, including *Chi-Hoon: A Korean Girl* (McMahon 1993), *The Princess and the Beggar: A Korean Folktale* (O'Brien 1993), and *Peacebound*

Trains (Balgassi 1996). From Vietnam we had *The Lotus Seed* (Garland 1993) and *The Golden Carp and Other Tales from Vietnam* (Vuong 1993).

Our Japanese collection included *So Far from the Sea* (Bunting 1998); *Little Oh* (Melmed 1997); *Tea with Milk* (Say 1999), Say's sequel to *Grandfather's Journey* (1993); and *A to Zen: A Book of Japanese Culture* (Wells 1992). From China we enjoyed *The Dragon's Robe* (Lattimore 1990), *Our Home Is the Sea* (Levinson 1988), *Eyes of the Dragon* (Leaf 1987), and *Red Thread* (Young 1993).

During our studies, the children became emotionally involved with the horrors of slavery and with the African American struggle for freedom. Harriet Tubman became a class favorite, firing their imaginations with her courage. *Minty: A Story of Young Harriet Tubman* (Schroeder 1996a) was in constant circulation. Other books that were rarely on the shelves were *John Henry* (Lester 1994), whose heroic heart captured theirs, *Molly Bannaky* (McGill 1999), and *Tar Beach* (Ringgold 1991).[1] When I read *The Gold Cadillac* (Taylor 1987) aloud, the class, like classes before theirs, was mesmerized by that gripping book and stunned by the cruelty and intolerance it portrayed. But we all derived great enjoyment from *Night on Neighborhood Street* (Greenfield 1991) and *Wonders: The Best Children's Poems by Effie Lee Newsome* (Bishop 1999), reciting many of the poems chorally, in parts and rounds, or call-and-response fashion as we noted the differences in these poets' styles.

The Amish and the Appalachians, with their distinct lifestyles, provided an intriguing comparison for the class. Although they share quilt making and other hand-crafted goods, as well as an independent spirit, they differ dramatically in cultural heritage. One girl visited the Amish community in Holmes County, Ohio, to research her project, bringing back charming artifacts that enhanced her presentation. In their Appalachian report, two boys painted an enlightening portrait of a culture shaped by its geography as well as its history.

Some of our favorite books about the Amish were *An Amish Christmas* (Ammon 1996), *An Amish Wedding* (Ammon 1998), *Just Plain Fancy* (Polacco 1990), and *Raising Yoder's Barn* (Yolen 1998). All of Cynthia Rylant's age-appropriate books were read and loved as we studied Appalachia, with *Appalachia: The Voices of Sleeping Birds* (Rylant 1991) providing a poetic overview of the area. *Amber on the Mountain* (Johnston 1994) and *My Great-Aunt Arizona* (Houston 1992) also added flavor to our study of Appalachia.

Comparing variations of folktales and fairy tales has long been of interest in my classroom. During our cultural diversity investigation, we read variants of the Cinderella story as retold in several of the cultures in our study. *Yeh-Shen: A Cinderella Story from China* (Louie 1982), one of the oldest versions, is authentically illustrated by Ed Young. *Mufaro's Beautiful Daughter: An African Tale* (Steptoe 1987) is the beautifully retold and illustrated Cinderella tale from Zimbabwe. *The Rough-Face Girl* (Martin 1992) is an Algonquin Cinderella story, while *Sootface: An Ojibwa Cinderella Story* (San Souci 1994) is a slightly different retelling of the story from these Northeast and Great Lakes tribes. Three quite different Appalachian Cinderella stories are *Moss Gown* (Hooks 1987), *Ashpet: An Appalachian Tale* (Compton 1994), and *Smoky Mountain Rose: An Appalachian Cinderella* (Schroeder 1997), though all three are based on the European Cinderella story carried to the southern Appalachian area of the United States. *Cendrillon* (San Souci 1998), a Caribbean contribution, is one of the newest and most colorful Cinderellas. Sharing and comparing these culturally different versions of this ancient tale added a layer of understanding to our study.

Today's rich supply of multicultural books is much larger than it was when I began to teach. The books we use, well written and beautifully illustrated, include genuine information about the cultures they depict, either presented directly in informational books or woven smoothly through the stories in fictional books. Such books as *Crow Boy* (Yashima 1955), which was available for us in earlier days, has been joined by a wealth of fine Asian books, and each of the other cultures we studied has its own expanding literary representation. The current availability and diversity of fine literature and freedom from the restrictions of my first few teaching years in a conservative, traditional school have enabled me to engage in the thematic literary studies described in this chapter.

Whenever possible, I provide multiple copies of books related to the themes we are studying so that groups can read and discuss them, deriving literary benefit and a deeper understanding of our topics. Examples of some titles related to our westward expansion and cultural diversity themes are *The 18 Penny Goose* (Walker 1998), *The Boston Coffee Party* (Rappaport 1990), *Pioneer Cat* (Hooks 1988), *Trouble for Lucy* (Stevens 1979), *The Josefina Story Quilt* (Coerr 1986), *Follow the Drinking Gourd* (Winter 1988), *Wagon Wheels* (Brenner 1978), *The Long Way to a New Land* (Sandin 1981), *The Long Way Westward* (Sandin 1989), *Lili the Brave* (Armstrong 1997), *Molly's Pilgrim* (Cohen 1990), *Make a Wish, Molly* (Cohen 1994), *Daniel's Duck* (Bulla 1979), and *Baseball Saved Us* (Mochizuki 1993).

During our studies, we have used a number of biographies written for young children that have added historical perspective to our studies; for example, *Squanto* (Bulla 1954), *Finding Providence: The Story of Roger Williams* (Avi 1997), *Minty: A Story of Young Harriet Tubman* (Schroeder 1996a), *Emily* (Bédard 1992), and *Eleanor* (Cooney 1996). The children have found these life stories absorbing.

We began a recent science unit that we titled "Sounds Around Us" by reading the lovely poem about the cochlea from *Echoes for the Eye: Poems to Celebrate Patterns in Nature* (Esbensen 1996, 10) and the musically written *Carolina Shout!* (Schroeder 1995). Then we studied what makes sound and how it travels through the ear to the brain. After experimenting with vibrations in various ways, we generated a long list of sounds we hear, including music, bird, insect, and water sounds, and city and country noises. The children again divided into groups to study the various kinds of sounds.

The sharing of poetry played a major role in our study, as did music. During the unit, our principal demonstrated the use of a tuning fork and then accompanied the children's singing on her guitar. Another highlight of the study was taking a backstage tour of the Columbus Symphony Orchestra and watching the musicians practice. At other times, the children wrote and drew to the music of Saint-Saens *The Carnival of the Animals*, Prokofiev's *Peter and the Wolf*, and Britten's *The Young Person's Guide to the Orchestra*. Following their presentations on sound, the children culminated our study by playing musical instruments in their own concert, orchestrated by our music teacher. He concluded our concert by playing a Beethoven selection for us, an unforgettably beautiful performance. Through this concert and the other memorable elements of our study, all of us came to a much deeper appreciation of our ears and of the sounds they allow us to hear.

Many books contributed to our study of sound. *The Magic School Bus Explores the Senses* (Cole 1999) helped us to better understand the function of the ear, while *Eyewitness Books: Music* (Ardley 1989) and *The Philharmonic Gets Dressed* (Kuskin

1982) presented helpful musical background. *Dance with Me: Poems* (Esbensen 1995) and *Song and Dance* (Hopkins 1997) added musical poetry. Background stories about musicians and dancers also enriched the unit. They included *Shake Rag! From the Life of Elvis Presley* (Littlesugar 1998), *Alvin Ailey* (Pinkney 1993), *Duke Ellington: The Piano Prince and His Orchestra* (Pinkney 1998), *Charlie Parker Played Be Bop* (Raschka 1992), *Satchmo's Blues* (Schroeder 1996b), and *Dance* (Jones and Kuklin 1998). City sounds were made explicit through such books as *Street Music: City Poems* (Adoff 1995), *When a City Leans against the Sky: Poems* (De Fina 1997), and *Bam Bam Bam* (Merriam 1995). Reading in pairs from *Joyful Noise: Poems for Two Voices* (Fleischman 1988) provided interesting perspective on insects and an enriching exposure to Fleischman's intricate and original poetry, while sharing humorous poems from *Insectlopedia* (Florian 1998) added insect insight.

Water noises and functions were explored through readings of *Splish Splash! Poems* (Graham 1994) and *Water Music: Poems for Children* (Yolen 1995), while the properties of water were investigated through *A Drop of Water: A Book of Science and Wonder* (Wick 1997).

When I was a child, although we enjoyed fine literature, there were no trade books to support our studies of curriculum subjects. Even a generation later when my children entered school, all of their assigned curricular reading was done in textbooks. Even when I began to teach in 1973, all subjects were being taught from textbooks, occasionally supplemented by trade books. But I have slowly eliminated textbooks from my program, replacing them with poetry, prose, and informational trade books that the children hear me read, read independently, or share with groups as they pursue our integrated curriculum. Their enjoyment of reading, their eagerness for new books, and their enthusiasm for our studies are evidence of the value of a program like mine.

The journey of teaching and learning has carried me from a classroom rigidly following prescribed teaching to a classroom in which literature reading and purposeful writing are integral parts of all curriculum areas. It is exciting to work with children who are eagerly involved in planning and working toward the achievement of our curriculum goals. We are helped tremendously by the increasing number of outstanding fiction and nonfiction books being published in all fields and genres and by the growing number of paperback editions that provide multiple copies for small-group use. It is a good time to be teaching!

Note

1.   It was interesting to compare and contrast the motivational impetus for flying in *Tar Beach* (Ringgold 1991), *Abuela* (Dorros 1991), and *Isla* (Dorros 1995).

References

Adoff, A. 1995. *Street music: City poems.* Illus. K. Barbour. New York: HarperCollins.

Alcott, L. M. 1931. *Eight cousins; or, The aunt hill.* Illus. C. M. Burd. Philadelphia: John C. Winston.

Ammon, R. 1996. *An Amish Christmas.* Illus. P. Patrick. New York: Atheneum.

————. 1998. *An Amish wedding.* Illus. P. Patrick. New York: Atheneum.

Anderson, W. 1998. *Pioneer girl: The story of Laura Ingalls Wilder.* Illus. D. Andreasen. New York: HarperCollins.

Ardley, N. 1989. *Eyewitness books: Music.* New York: Knopf/Dorling Kindersley.

Armstrong, J. 1997. *Lili the brave.* Illus. U. Klavins. New York: Random House.

Avi. 1997. *Finding Providence: The story of Roger Williams.* Illus. J. Watling. New York: HarperTrophy.

Balgassi, H. 1996. *Peacebound trains.* Illus. C. K. Soentpiet. New York: Clarion.

Baum, L. F. 1900. *The wonderful wizard of Oz.* Illus. W. W. Denslow. Chicago: G. M. Hill.

Bédard, M. 1992. *Emily.* Illus. B. Cooney. New York: Doubleday Books for Young Readers.

Bishop, R. S., ed. 1999. *Wonders: The best children's poems of Effie Lee Newsome.* Illus. L. M. Jones. Honesdale, PA: Wordsong/Boyds Mills.

Brandeis, M. 1929. *The little Dutch tulip girl.* New York: Grosset & Dunlap.

Brenner, B. 1978. *Wagon wheels.* Illus. D. Bolognese. New York: Harper & Row.

Bruchac, J. 1994. *A boy called Slow: The true story of Sitting Bull.* Illus. R. Baviera. New York: Philomel.

Bulla, C. R. 1954. *Squanto, friend of the Pilgrims.* Illus. P. Burchard. New York: Scholastic.

————. 1979. *Daniel's duck.* Illus. J. Sandin. New York: Harper & Row.

Bunting, E. 1988. *How many days to America? A Thanksgiving story.* Illus. B. Peck. New York: Clarion.

————. 1994. *A day's work.* Illus. R. Himler. New York: Clarion.

————. 1995. *Dandelions.* Illus. G. Shed. San Diego: Harcourt Brace.

————. 1996a. *Going home.* Illus. D. Diaz. New York: HarperCollins.

————. 1996b. *Train to somewhere.* Illus. R. Himler. New York: Clarion.

————. 1998. *So far from the sea.* Illus. C. K. Soentpiet. New York: Clarion.

Burnett, F. H. 1911. *The secret garden.* New York: Grosset & Dunlap.

Byars, B. C. Blossom Family series. Illus. J. Rogers. New York: Dell.

Carroll, L. 1930a. *Alice's adventures in Wonderland.* Illus. J. Tenniel. New York: Three Sirens.

————. 1930b. *Through the looking-glass and what Alice found there.* Illus. J. Tenniel. New York: Three Sirens.

Clark, M. 1924. *The poppy seed cakes.* Illus. M. F. Petersham and M. Petersham. Garden City, NY: Doubleday.

Cleary, B. Ramona series. Illus. L. Darling and A. Tiegreen. New York: William Morrow.

————. 1973. *Socks.* Illus. B. Darwin. New York: William Morrow.

————. 1982. *Ralph S. Mouse.* Illus. P. O. Zelinsky. New York: William Morrow.

Coerr, E. 1986. *The Josefina story quilt.* Illus. B. Degen. New York: Harper & Row.

Cohen, B. 1990. *Molly's pilgrim.* Illus. M. J. Deraney. New York: Bantam.

———. 1994. *Make a wish, Molly.* Illus. J. N. Jones. New York: Doubleday.

Cole, J. 1999. *The magic school bus explores the senses.* Illus. B. Degen. New York: Scholastic.

Compton, J. 1994. *Ashpet: An Appalachian tale.* Illus. K. Compton. New York: Holiday House.

Cooney, B. 1996. *Eleanor.* New York: Viking.

Dalgliesh, A. 1944. *The silver pencil.* Illus. K. Milhous. New York: Scribner's.

——— 1954. *The courage of Sarah Noble.* Illus. L. Weisgard. New York: Scribner's.

De Fina, A. A. 1997. *When a city leans against the sky: Poems.* Illus. K. Condon. Honesdale, PA: Wordsong/Boyds Mills.

Dorros, A. 1991. *Abuela.* Illus. E. Kleven. New York: Dutton Children's Books.

———. 1995. *Isla.* Illus. E. Kleven. New York: Dutton Children's Books.

Ehlert, L. 1997. *Cuckoo/Cucú: A Mexican folktale.* San Diego: Harcourt Brace.

Esbensen, B. J. 1995. *Dance with me.* Illus. M. Lloyd. New York: HarperCollins.

———. 1996. *Echoes for the eye: Poems to celebrate patterns in nature.* Illus. H. K. Davie. New York: HarperCollins.

Fleischman, P. 1988. *Joyful noise: Poems for two voices.* New York: HarperCollins.

Florian, D. 1998. *Insectlopedia: Poems and paintings.* San Diego: Harcourt Brace.

Garland, S. 1993. *The lotus seed.* Illus. T. Kiuchi. San Diego: Harcourt Brace Jovanovich.

Gates, D. 1938. *Sarah's idea.* Illus. M. Torrey. New York: Viking.

———. 1940. *Blue willow.* Illus. P. Lantz. New York: Viking.

Graham, J. B. 1994. *Splish splash! Poems.* Illus. S. Scott. New York: Ticknor & Fields.

Greenfield, E. 1991. *Night on Neighborhood Street.* Illus. J. S. Gilchrist. New York: Dial.

Hest, A. 1997. *When Jessie came across the sea.* Illus. P. J. Lynch. Cambridge, MA: Candlewick.

Ho, M., and S. Ros. 1995. *The two brothers.* Illus. J. Tseng and M.-s. Tseng. New York: Lothrop, Lee & Shepard.

Hoban, R. Frances series. Illus. L. Hoban and G. Williams. New York: Harper & Row.

Hooks, W. H. 1987. *Moss gown.* Illus. D. Carrick. New York: Clarion.

———. 1988. *Pioneer cat.* Illus. C. Robinson. New York: Random House.

Hopkins, L. B. 1997. *Song and dance: Poems.* Illus. C. M. Taylor. New York: Simon & Schuster.

Houston, G. 1992. *My great-aunt Arizona.* Illus. S. C. Lamb. New York: HarperCollins.

Howe, D., and J. Howe. 1979. *Bunnicula: A rabbit tale of mystery.* Illus. A. Daniel. New York: Atheneum.

Howe, J. 1982. *Howliday Inn.* Illus. L. Munsinger. New York: Atheneum.

Howlett, B. 1993. *I'm new here.* Boston: Houghton Mifflin.

Jamison, C. V. 1938. *Toinette's Philip.* New York: D. Appleton-Century.

Johnston, T. 1994. *Amber on the mountain.* Illus. R. Duncan. New York: Dial.

Jones, B. T., and S. Kuklin. 1998. *Dance.* Illus. S. Kuklin. New York: Hyperion.

Keene, C. 1930. *Nancy Drew mystery stories.* New York: Grosset & Dunlap.

Kipling, R. 1912. *Just so stories.* Illus. J. M. Gleeson and P. Bransom. Garden City, NY: Doubleday/Country Life.

Kuskin, K. 1982. *The Philharmonic gets dressed.* Illus. M. Simont. New York: Harper & Row.

Lattimore, D. N. 1990. *The dragon's robe.* New York: Harper & Row.

Lawlor, V., ed. 1995. *I was dreaming to come to America: Memories from the Ellis Island Oral History Project.* New York: Viking.

Leaf, M. 1987. *Eyes of the dragon.* Illus. E. Young. New York: Lothrop, Lee & Shepard.

Leighton, M. R. 1992. *An Ellis Island Christmas.* Illus. D. Nolan. New York: Viking.

Lester, J. 1994. *John Henry.* Illus. J. Pinkney. New York: Dial.

Levinson, R. 1988. *Our home is the sea.* Illus. D. Luzak. New York: E. P. Dutton.

Littlesugar, A. 1998. *Shake Rag! From the life of Elvis Presley.* Illus. F. Cooper. New York: Philomel.

Lobel, A. 1970. *Frog and Toad are friends.* New York: Harper.

Louie, A.-L. 1982. *Yeh-Shen: A Cinderella story from China.* New York: Philomel.

Marshall, E. Fox series. Illus. J. Marshall. New York: Dial.

Martin, R. 1992. *The rough-face girl.* Illus. D. Shannon. New York: G. P. Putnam's Sons.

McGill, A. 1999. *Molly Bannaky.* Boston: Houghton Mifflin.

McMahon, P. 1993. *Chi-hoon: A Korean girl.* Illus. M. O'Brien. Honesdale, PA: Boyds Mills.

Melmed, L. K. 1997. *Little Oh.* Illus. J. LaMarche. New York: Lothrop, Lee & Shepard.

Merriam, E. 1995. *Bam, bam, bam.* Illus. D. Yaccarino. New York: Henry Holt.

Minarik, E. H. 1957. *Little bear.* Illus. M. Sendak. New York: HarperCollins.

Mochizuki, K. 1993. *Baseball saved us.* Illus. D. Lee. New York: Lee & Low.

O'Brien, A. S. 1993. *The princess and the beggar: A Korean folktale.* New York: Scholastic.

Osofsky, A. 1992. *Dreamcatcher.* Illus. E. Young. New York: Orchard.

Parish, P. Amelia Bedelia series. Illus. F. Siebel. New York: Scholastic.

Pinkney, A. D. 1993. *Alvin Ailey*. Illus. J. B. Pinkney. New York: Hyperion.

———. 1998. *Duke Ellington: The piano prince and his orchestra*. Illus. J. B. Pinkney. New York: Hyperion.

Polacco, P. 1990. *Just plain fancy*. New York: Bantam.

Porter, E. H. 1940. *Pollyanna, the glad book*. New York: Grosset & Dunlap.

Rappaport, D. 1990. *The Boston coffee party*. Illus. E. A. McCully. New York: HarperTrophy.

Raschka, C. 1992. *Charlie Parker played be bop*. New York: Orchard.

Ringgold, F. 1991. *Tar beach*. New York: Crown.

Rylant, C. Henry and Mudge series. Illus. S. Stevenson. New York: Aladdin Paperbacks.

———. Mr. Putter and Tabby series. Illus. A. Howard. San Diego: Harcourt Brace.

———. Poppleton series. Illus. M. Teague. New York: Scholastic.

———. 1991. *Appalachia: The voices of sleeping birds*. Illus. B. Moser. San Diego: Harcourt Brace Jovanovich.

Sandin, J. 1981. *The long way to a new land*. New York: Harper & Row.

———. 1989. *The long way westward*. New York: Harper & Row.

San Souci, R. D. 1994. *Sootface: An Ojibwa Cinderella story*. Illus. D. San Souci. New York: Delacorte.

———. 1996. *Pedro and the monkey*. Illus. M. Hays. New York: Morrow.

———. 1998. *Cendrillon: A Caribbean Cinderella*. Illus. J. B. Pinkney. New York: Simon & Schuster.

Say, A. 1993. *Grandfather's journey*. Boston: Houghton Mifflin.

———. 1999. *Tea with milk*. Boston: Houghton Mifflin.

Schroeder, A. 1995. *Carolina shout!* Illus. B. Fuchs. New York: Dial.

———. 1996a. *Minty: A story of young Harriet Tubman*. Illus. J. Pinkney. New York: Dial.

———. 1996b. *Satchmo's blues*. Illus. F. Cooper. New York: Doubleday.

———. 1997. *Smoky Mountain Rose: An Appalachian Cinderella*. Illus. B. Sneed. New York: Dial.

Spyri, J. 1925. *Heidi*. New York: Grosset & Dunlap.

Steptoe, J. 1987. *Mufaro's beautiful daughters: An African tale*. New York: Lothrop, Lee & Shepard.

Stevens, C. 1979. *Trouble for Lucy*. Illus. R. Himler. New York: Clarion.

Stevenson, R. L. 1905. *A child's garden of verses*. Illus. J. W. Smith. New York: Scribner's.

Stroud, V. A. 1996. *The path of the quiet elk: A Native American alphabet book*. New York: Dial.

Tarbescu, E. 1998. *Annushka's voyage*. Illus. L. Dabcovich. New York: Clarion.

Taylor, M. D. 1987. *The gold Cadillac.* Illus. M. Hays. New York: Dial.

Thomas, J. C. 1998. *I have heard of a land.* Illus. F. Cooper. New York: HarperCollins.

Thomas, J. R. 1994. *Lights on the river.* Illus. M. Dooling. New York: Hyperion.

Travers, P. L. 1934. *Mary Poppins.* Illus. M. Shepard. New York: Harcourt Brace.

Turner, A. W. 1997. *Mississippi mud: Three prairie journals.* Illus. R. J. Blake. New York: HarperCollins.

Van Leeuwen, J. 1995. *Across the wide dark sea: The* Mayflower *journey.* Illus. T. B. Allen. New York: Dial.

———. 1998. *Nothing here but trees.* Illus. P. Boatwright. New York: Dial.

Vuong, L. D. 1993. *The golden carp, and other tales from VietNam.* Illus. M. C. Saito. New York: Lothrop, Lee & Shepard.

Walker, S. M. 1998. *The 18 penny goose.* Illus. E. Beier. New York: HarperCollins.

Waters, K. 1996. *On the* Mayflower: *Voyage of the ship's apprentice and a passenger girl.* Illus. R. Kendall. New York: Scholastic.

Wells, R. 1992. *A to Zen: A book of Japanese culture.* Illus. Yoshi. New York: Simon & Schuster.

White, E. B. 1945. *Stuart Little.* Illus. G. Williams. New York: Harper & Row.

Wick, W. 1997. *A drop of water: A book of science and wonder.* New York: Scholastic.

Wilder, L. I. Little house series. Illus. G. Williams. New York: Harper & Row.

———. 1932. *Little house in the big woods.* Illus. H. Sewell. New York: Harper & Brothers.

Winter, J. 1988. *Follow the drinking gourd.* New York: Scholastic.

Woodruff, E. 1999. *The memory coat.* Illus. M. Dooling. New York: Scholastic.

Yashima, T. 1955. *Crow Boy.* New York: Viking.

Yolen, J. 1995. *Water music: Poems for children.* Illus. J. Stemple. Honesdale, PA: Wordsong/Boyds Mills.

———. 1998. *Raising Yoder's barn.* Illus. B. Fuchs. Boston: Little, Brown.

Young, E. 1993. *Red thread.* New York: Philomel.

Index

About the Editor and Contributors

Michael Cart

Michael Cart holds degrees in journalism from Northwestern University and library science from Columbia University. A nationally respected authority on children's and young adult literature, Cart teaches at Texas Woman's University and UCLA Graduate School of Library and Information Science. In addition to his current *Booklist* column "Carte Blanche," Cart has written more than two hundred articles and reviews for such prestigious publications as the *New York Times*, *School Library Journal,* and *The Lion and the Unicorn*. His books include *From Romance to Realism: 50 Years of Growth and Change in Young Adult Literature* and *What's So Funny? Wit and Humor in American Children's Literature*. His young adult (YA) novel *My Father's Scar* has been selected as an American Library Association (ALA) Best Book for Young Adults 1997. Cart is past president of Young Adult Library Services Association (YALSA) and has served on both the Caldecott and Notable Books committees.

James F. Cipielewski

Jim Cipielewski is an associate professor of reading and language arts at Oakland University. His interests are reading acquisition, what happens to people because they read, and children's literature. He has been fascinated by traditional literature and storytelling since doing his master's thesis in that area, relating Northrop Frye's literary criticism as interpreted by Glenna Sloan to folktales. Prior to his work at the university, Cipielewski taught preschool through eighth grade, spent time as an elementary school principal, and worked as a reading consultant.

Barbara Elleman

Now Distinguished Scholar of Children's Literature at Marquette University, Barbara Elleman served as editor of the Children's Section of *Booklist* magazine and then as editor in chief of *Book Links*. Prior to that, she worked as a school and public librarian. She has been a judge for the American Book Awards, the Golden Kite Awards, the *Boston Globe–Horn Book* Awards, and was a member of the 2000 Caldecott committee. She is editor of *Profiles for Language Arts* and served on the National Council of Teachers of English (NCTE) Notable Books in the Language Arts as well as the Excellence in Poetry committees. She chaired the U.S. Hans Christian Andersen committee and is on the advisory board for *Riverbank Review* and *Parent's Guide to Children's Media*. Her books include *Tomie dePaola: His Art and His Stories* (1999), *Holiday House: The First Sixty-Five Years* (2000), and *Virginia Lee Burton: A Life in Art* (2002).

Evelyn B. Freeman

Freeman is dean and director at The Ohio State University at Mansfield. She is also a professor in the School of Teaching and Learning, where she teaches graduate courses in children's literature and early and middle childhood education. She received her B.A. in sociology from Chatham College, an M.A. in educational psychology from the University of Chicago, and a Ph.D. in early and middle childhood from The Ohio State University. She was a preschool and elementary teacher before joining the university faculty as a teacher educator. Freeman has coauthored *Connecting Informational Children's Books with Content Area Learning* (with Diane Person, Allyn and Bacon, 1998); *Global Perspectives in Children's Literature* (with Barbara Lehman, Allyn and Bacon, 2001); and coedited *Using Nonfiction Trade Books in the Elementary Classroom* (with Diane Person, National Council of Teachers of English, 1992). She currently is coeditor of *Bookbird: A Journal of International Children's Literature*.

James Cross Giblin

James Cross Giblin has written more than twenty informational books for young people, many of which have received awards and honors. His recent titles include *The Life and Death of Adolf Hitler, The Amazing Life of Benjamin Franklin*, and *The Mystery of the Mammoth Bones*. Giblin is also a contributing editor at Clarion Books, where for many years he was editor in chief. He lives in New York City.

Marjorie R. Hancock

Marjorie Hancock is an associate professor in the Department of Elementary Education at Kansas State University, where she has taught undergraduate language arts methods and literature-based graduate courses since 1992. Her research has focused on reader response to literature and has resulted in articles in *Language Arts,* the *Reading Teacher,* the *Journal of Children's Literature,* and *Research in the Teaching of English*. She is the author of a response-based theory-into-practice textbook titled *A Celebration of Literature and Response: Teachers, Readers, and Books in K–8 Classrooms* (Prentice Hall/Merrill, 2000/2004) and an upcoming language arts methods text linking literature, language, and technology. She is past president of the Children's Literature Assembly of the National Council of Teachers of English and has chaired the Notable Children's Books in the Language Arts for that group.

Lee Bennett Hopkins

Lee Bennett Hopkins is an award-winning poet, author, and anthologist of numerous books for children and young adults. Besides teaching elementary school for six years, Hopkins has devoted most of his professional life to the field of poetry. He has founded two major awards: the Lee Bennett Hopkins Poetry Award and the Lee Bennett Hopkins/IRA Promising Poet Award. He has served on the board of directors for the National Council of Teachers of English (NCTE), the Children's Literature Assembly, and has twice chaired the NCTE Poetry Award committee. Hopkins is the recipient of the Southern Mississippi Medallion for "lasting contributions to children's literature." He has published articles in *Horn Book Magazine, Language Arts,* and the *New Advocate.* Five of his books have been named American Library Association (ALA) Notable Books, including *Been to Yesterdays: Poems of a Life* (1995), which was also named one of *School Library Journal*'s Best Books of the Year. His most recent books are *Hoofbeats, Claws and Rippled Fins: Creature Poems* (HarperCollins 2002) and *Home to Me: Poems across America* (Scholastic/Orchard 2002).

Vivian G. Johnson

Vivian Johnson is an assistant professor of education at Marygrove College in Detroit, where she has also taught middle school for sixteen years. Prior to teaching, she was a social worker for ten years. Johnson holds a Ph.D. in reading education, with a minor in children's literature. For the past two years, she has coauthored a column titled "Between the Covers" in *Child Health Talk,* a biannual publication of the National Black Child Development Institute. The column features a bibliography and commentary on African American children's literature. Her focus of interest is urban adolescent literacy. She has published on urban African American adolescent writing and is awaiting publication of a recent symposium contribution, "*Jumping in the Book*": *Urban Adolescents Respond to Literature.*

Teri S. Lesesne

Teri Lesesne is an associate professor in the Department of Library Science at Sam Houston State University, where she teaches classes in children's and young adult literature (YA) at the graduate and undergraduate levels. She coordinates an annual young adult literature conference that draws teachers and librarians from across the state. She is past president of the Assembly on Literature for Adolescents of the National Council of Teachers of English (ALAN). She is the coeditor of the current issue of *Books for You* from the National Council of Teachers of English and the coauthor of the forthcoming *Hit List for Young Adults 2: Frequently Challenged Books* from the American Library Association, and author of the forthcoming *Making the Match: The Right Book for the Right Reader at the Right Time* from Stenhouse. Lesesne writes the YA review column for *Voices from the Middle,* an author interview column for *Teacher Librarian,* and the children's review column for the *Journal of Children's Literature.*

Julius Lester

Julius Lester has published more than thirty books for children and adults. His *To Be a Slave* was a Newbery Honor book, and *John Henry,* illustrated by Jerry Pinkney, was a Caldecott Honor book and a winner of the *Boston Globe–Horn Book* Award. His most recent books are *The Blues Singers* and the novel *When Dad Killed Mom.* Forthcoming is *Why Heaven Is Far Away,* illustrated by Joe Cepeda.

Lois Lowry

Lois Lowry is an author recognized worldwide for her children's classics about the Krupnik children, Anastasia and Sam. *Zooman Sam* (1999) is the fourth in a series about the Krupnik family's youngest child. More significantly, she is a two-time recipient of the Newbery Award for the most distinguished contribution to literature for children: in 1990 for *Number the Stars* and again in 1994 for *The Giver.* Her most recent book, *Gathering Blue* (2000), is a companion volume to the 1994 Newbery Award winner *The Giver.* Lowry's 1998 memoir, *Looking Back,* traces the role of her own past in the creation of her fiction.

Leonard S. Marcus

Leonard Marcus is a historian and critic of children's literature. He has been *Parenting Magazine*'s book reviewer since the magazine's founding in 1987 and has been a frequent contributor to the *New York Times Book Review,* the *Horn Book Magazine,* and other publications. His many books include *Margaret Wise Brown: Awakened by the Moon* (Quill, 1999); *Dear Genius: The Letters of Ursula Nordstrom* (Harper, 1998); *A Caldecott Celebration: Six Artists and their Paths to the Caldecott Medal* (Walker, 1998); *Side by Side* (Walker, 2001); and *Ways of Telling: Conversations on the Art of the Picture Book* (Dutton, 2002). He lives with his wife, illustrator Amy Schwartz, and their son in Brooklyn, New York.

Amy A. McClure

Amy McClure taught in public schools for ten years as a classroom teacher, reading specialist, and coordinator of a program for gifted children. She is currently on the faculty of Ohio Wesleyan University, where she teaches courses in reading and children's literature, supervises student teachers, and directs the Honors Program. She is the winner of the Welch Meritorious Teaching Award and the Robert K. Marshall Award for university service. She is a past president of the Children's Literature Assembly of the National Council of Teachers of English, Children's Literature SIG of the International Reading Association, and the Ohio International Reading Association. She has presented at numerous national conventions and is the author of *Sunrises and Songs: Reading and Writing Poetry in an Elementary Classroom* (Heinemann 1990). She is also the editor of two National Council of Teachers of English (NCTE) publications, *Books That Invite Talk, Wonder and Play* (with Janice Kristo, 1996) and *Inviting Children's Responses to Literature: Guides to 57 Notable Books* (with Janice Kristo, 1994); a co-writer for an edition of Donna Norton's *Through the Eyes of a Child;* and has published numerous book chapters and journal articles. McClure is currently coeditor of the 2002 edition of *Adventuring with Books* (NCTE, 2002). She was named Promising Young Researcher in 1985 by the National Council of Teachers of English and her dissertation was selected as Distinguished Dissertation by Kappa Delta Pi, a national education honorary.

Jonella A. Mongo

Jonella Mongo is assistant superintendent of curriculum and professional development for the school district of Highland Park, Michigan. She is the former coordinator of the Child Development Program and assistant professor of education at Marygrove College in Detroit. She has more than twenty-five years of professional experience in the development and implementation of educational programs for early childhood and elementary schoolchildren, parents, and school personnel. Mongo coauthors a biannual column "Between the Covers: Literature for Children" for a national parent magazine. She has written journal articles on violent play behavior and the early writing of African American boys. She is a frequent contributor to local newspapers, writing on issues related to the care and education of young children. In 1999, Mongo earned her Ph.D. in reading and language arts from Oakland University in Rochester, Michigan.

Peggy S. Oxley

Peggy Oxley is a second-grade teacher at St. Paul School in Westerville, Ohio. She has a B.S. in elementary education and an M.A. in language arts, literature, and reading and has taught for twenty-nine years. A former chair of the National Council of Teachers of English (NCTE) Notable Children's Books committee, she has served on the editorial review boards of *The Reading Teacher* and the *Journal of Children's Literature*. She is a coauthor of *Reading and Writing, Where It All Begins: Helping Your Children at Home* (Literacy Connection, 1991), *Teaching with Children's Books: Path to Literature-Based Instruction* (1995), and *Adventuring with Books* (NCTE, 1999, 2003). She was the 1994 recipient of the Ohio State University Mary Karrer Award for outstanding work in bringing children and books together.

Linda M. Pavonetti

Linda Pavonetti is an associate professor in the Reading and Language Arts Department of Oakland University in Rochester, Michigan, where she teaches graduate and undergraduate courses in children's and young adult literature. From the time she entered the profession as a Head Start teacher's aide, she recognized the value of authentic literature in promoting children's love of reading. Now she works with in-service and preservice teachers, parents, and even grandparents to enhance their understanding of books that motivate and appeal to children and young adults.

Debbie A. Reese

Debbie Reese, Ph.D. (Pueblo Indian), conducts research on the ways Native Americans are represented in children's and young adult literature. She has reviewed for *Horn Book Magazine* and *Multicultural Review;* has published articles in *Horn Book Magazine, School Library Journal,* and *Rethinking Schools;* and has written several chapters in books for teachers and teacher educators. She has served on the National Council of Teachers of English annual convention planning committee for the past three years and is a member of the Racism and Bias in the Teaching of English committee. Reese teaches children's literature at the University of Illinois in the College of Education and the Library School's long-distance education program, and she conducts workshops for teachers and librarians.

Uri Shulevitz

Uri Shulevitz is the author/illustrator of more than forty books. His first book was published in 1963, and in 1969 he received the Caldecott Medal for illustrating Arthur Ransome's *The Fool of the World and the Flying Ship*. Shulevitz's other titles include *The Treasure*, a Caldecott Honor book; *Dawn,* recipient of the Christopher Award; and *Rain, Rain Rivers,* awarded the Bronze Medal, Leipzig International Book Exhibition. His 1998 book *Snow* was named a Caldecott Honor book. Shulevitz was born in Warsaw, Poland, and currently lives in New York City.

Sylvia M. Vardell

Sylvia Vardell is a professor at Texas Woman's University, where she teaches graduate courses in children's literature. Her research has been published in *Language Arts, English Journal, The Reading Teacher, New Advocate,* and the *Horn Book Magazine.* Vardell coauthored *Literature-Based Instruction with English Language Learners K–12* (Allyn & Bacon, 2002) along with Nancy Hadaway and Terrell Young. She served on the National Council of Teachers of English committee that established the Orbis Pictus Award for Outstanding Nonfiction for Children and has received grants from the Middle East Policy Council and the Ezra Jack Keats Foundation. She also taught at the University of Zimbabwe as a Fulbright scholar.

Jane Yolen

Known as the "Hans Christian Andersen of America" (*Newsweek*), Jane Yolen has written more than 250 books for children of all ages, including adults. Many of the books are art folktales or retold stories. Recent collections of interest are *Gray Heroes: Elder Tales from Around the World* (Viking, 1999), *The Fairies' Ring* (Dutton, 1999), the Here There Be . . . series (*Dragons, Unicorns, Ghosts, Angels, Witches*; Harcourt, 1993 forward), *Once upon a Bedtime Story* (with its accompanying CD and tape; Boyds Mill, 1997), *Not One Damsel in Distress: World Folktales for Strong Girls* (Harcourt, 2000), and *Mightier than the Sword: World Folktales for Strong Boys* (Harcourt, 2003).